Deep Learning
in
Modern C++

*End-to-end development and
implementation of deep learning algorithms*

Luiz Carlos d'Oleron

bpb

www.bpbonline.com

First Edition 2025

Copyright © BPB Publications, India

ISBN: 978-93-6589-351-9

To View Complete
BPB Publications Catalogue
Scan the QR Code:

About the Author

Luiz Carlos d'Oleron is an aritificial intelligence engineeer and works at Improvess. With a solid foundation in software architecture and development utilizing Java/JEE/C++ technologies, Luiz possesses significant experience in the practical application of artificial intelligence. His expertise particularly focuses on statistical machine learning, including data mining techniques, as well as Bayesian networks and agent-based systems.

Preface

Chapter 1: Introduction to Deep Learning Programming- This chapter lays the groundwork for understanding deep learning and its application in C++. It outlines the benefits of using deep learning, the challenges developers face without a solid foundation, and the essential architectures. You will discover how deep learning solves complex problems and the specific areas this book will cover.

Chapter 2: Coding Deep Learning with Modern C++- To build effective deep learning models, proficiency in modern C++ is essential. This chapter revisits key C++ features and introduces crucial libraries like Eigen, providing practical examples of how they are utilized in deep learning implementations.

Chapter 3: Testing Deep Learning Code- Robust deep learning models require thorough testing, especially given their stochastic nature. This chapter introduces techniques for testing machine learning code, focusing on controlling randomization and applying statistical tests to ensure reliability.

Chapter 4: Implementing Convolutions- This chapter delves into **convolutional neural networks (CNNs)**, a cornerstone of modern deep learning. You will learn to implement 2D convolutions, understand padding and strides, and apply these concepts in a practical image feature extraction experiment.

Chapter 5: Coding the Fully Connected Layer- Understanding fully connected layers is crucial for building comprehensive neural networks. This chapter covers their implementation, limitations, and practical applications, including flattening 2D data for linear input.

Chapter 6: Learning by Minimizing Cost Functions- Effective model training relies on minimizing cost functions. This chapter introduces various cost functions for regression and classification, demonstrating how they are used to optimize model performance.

Chapter 7: Defining Activation Functions- Activation functions introduce non-linearity into neural networks, enabling them to learn complex patterns. This chapter covers essential activation functions like sigmoid, ReLU, and softmax, and their practical implementation.

Chapter 8: Using Pooling Layers- Pooling layers are vital for reducing dimensionality and extracting key features. This chapter explores MaxPooling and AveragePooling, explaining their role in building efficient deep learning models.

Chapter 9: Coding the Gradient Descent Algorithm- The gradient descent algorithm is the foundation of model optimization. This chapter details its implementation, including gradient calculation and stop conditions, using kernel training as a practical example.

Chapter 10: Coding the Backpropagation Algorithm- Backpropagation enables efficient training of deep neural networks. This chapter explains its implementation, demonstrating its use with the MNIST dataset for handwritten digit recognition.

Chapter 11: Underfitting, Overfitting, and Regularization- Improve your training pipeline by implementing cross-validation, mini-batching, and using performance metrics. This chapter explains the training loop and how to properly evaluate your model.

Chapter 12: Implementing Cross-validation, Mini Batching, and Model Performance Metrics- Achieving optimal model performance requires addressing underfitting and overfitting. This chapter introduces regularization techniques to improve generalization.

Chapter 13: Implementing Optimizers- Advanced optimizers like SGD, Momentum, RMSProp, and Adam enhance training efficiency. This chapter details their implementation and application in deep learning.

Chapter 14: Introducing Computer Vision Models- This chapter introduces the field of computer vision and its applications in deep learning. You will learn about data augmentation, and how to implement it within your data set and model.

Chapter 15: Developing an Image Classifier- This chapter provides a practical guide to building an image classifier using the CIFAR dataset, covering model definition, training, and evaluation.

Chapter 16: Leveraging Training Performance with Transfer Learning- This chapter will explain transfer learning, and model freezing. You will learn how to leverage pre-trained networks, and greatly speed up the learning process.

Chapter 17: Developing an Object Localization System- The final chapter demonstrates the implementation of an object localization system, applying the learned concepts to a real-world computer vision task, and using IoU to evaluate model performance.

Code Bundle and Coloured Images

Please follow the link to download the
Code Bundle and the *Coloured Images* of the book:

https://rebrand.ly/ooggvft

The code bundle for the book is also hosted on GitHub at
https://github.com/bpbpublications/Deep-Learning-in-Modern-C-Plus-Plus.
In case there's an update to the code, it will be updated on the existing GitHub repository.

We have code bundles from our rich catalogue of books and videos available at
https://github.com/bpbpublications. Check them out!

Errata

We take immense pride in our work at BPB Publications and follow best practices to
ensure the accuracy of our content to provide with an indulging reading experience to our
subscribers. Our readers are our mirrors, and we use their inputs to reflect and improve
upon human errors, if any, that may have occurred during the publishing processes
involved. To let us maintain the quality and help us reach out to any readers who might be
having difficulties due to any unforeseen errors, please write to us at :

errata@bpbonline.com

Your support, suggestions and feedbacks are highly appreciated by the BPB Publications'
Family.

Piracy

If you come across any illegal copies of our works in any form on the internet, we would be grateful if you would provide us with the location address or website name. Please contact us at **business@bpbonline.com** with a link to the material.

If you are interested in becoming an author

If there is a topic that you have expertise in, and you are interested in either writing or contributing to a book, please visit **www.bpbonline.com**. We have worked with thousands of developers and tech professionals, just like you, to help them share their insights with the global tech community. You can make a general application, apply for a specific hot topic that we are recruiting an author for, or submit your own idea.

Reviews

Please leave a review. Once you have read and used this book, why not leave a review on the site that you purchased it from? Potential readers can then see and use your unbiased opinion to make purchase decisions. We at BPB can understand what you think about our products, and our authors can see your feedback on their book. Thank you!

For more information about BPB, please visit **www.bpbonline.com**.

Join our book's Discord space

Join the book's Discord Workspace for Latest updates, Offers, Tech happenings around the world, New Release and Sessions with the Authors:

https://discord.bpbonline.com

Table of Contents

CHAPTER 1

Introduction to Deep Learning Programming

Introduction

As engineers, one of the first questions we think of whenever we have a new problem at hand is: which technology should we use to solve it? For the last 15 years, deep learning has been the more common answer to this question.

Projects involving physical simulation, medical diagnosis, fraud detection, art generation, autonomous driving, surveillance, entertainment, autonomous investment, molecular dynamics, text translation, bot attendance systems, and an endless list of applications proved the power of deep learning algorithms to execute high complex tasks with a human (and sometimes over-human) performance level.

Structure

This first chapter is the more conceptual one, covering the following definitions:

- Understanding deep learning
- Understanding fully connected layers
- Limitations of fully connected layers
- Convolutional neural networks
- Recurrent neural networks

- Generative adversarial networks
- Reinforcement learning

Objectives

In this book, we will introduce the relevant details of the most important deep learning algorithms from an implementing-drive perspective.

Although the algorithms are friendly described, we will illustrate their implementation using C++ as the programming language. In particular, we will use modern C++ features which provide a streamlined, concise, fast, and reliable way to implement the models.

In addition to the proper algorithms, we will also talk about real-world implementation concerns, like vectorization and GPU programming.

Since deep learning is also programmed as any other kind of code, it must be tested before being deployed in production. Thus, we will cover how to test deep learning code from a software engineering point of view, considering its intrinsic stochastic nature and concerns regarding reproducibility.

Understanding deep learning

Deep learning is a field of machine learning, and **machine learning** (**ML**) is a field of **artificial intelligence** (**AI**). Indeed, most of the concepts approached in deep learning were already known many years before this technology emerged. Optimization, error propagation, under/overfitting and neural networks were known years before deep learning researchers started considering convolutional layers. Most of the time, talking about deep learning is as simple or complex as talking about ML. The following figure illustrates this relationship:

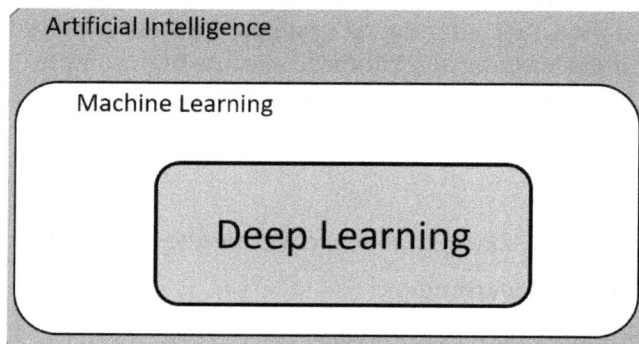

Figure 1.1: The relationship between AI, ML, and deep learning

So, what makes deep learning more special or relevant than ML? Let us understand how models worked before deep learning to answer this question.

Understanding fully connected layers

Consider the following representation of a classic multi-layer neural network:

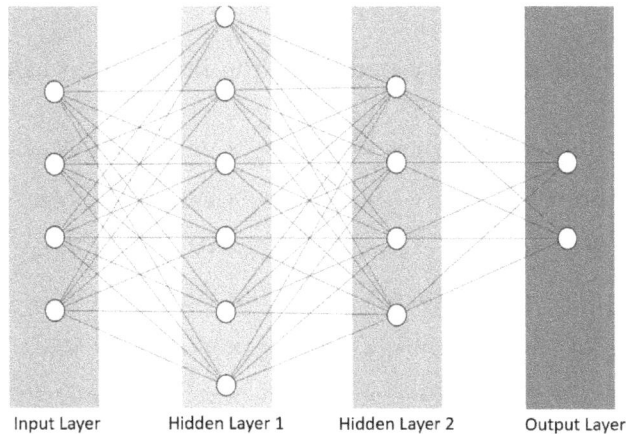

Figure 1.2: *4-layer neural network with fully connected layers*

For many years, models like this were the only type of neural network architecture available. In such networks, each neuron is fully connected to the next layer's neurons in such networks. That is why layers like this are called **fully connected layers**. In fully connected layers, each connection is represented by a float number, also called weight or synapsis.

How can we perform computation in fully connected layers? It is a simple process. The value of each neuron is a linear combination of the neuron values from the previous layers and the respective weights. For example, the value of the neuron N_0:

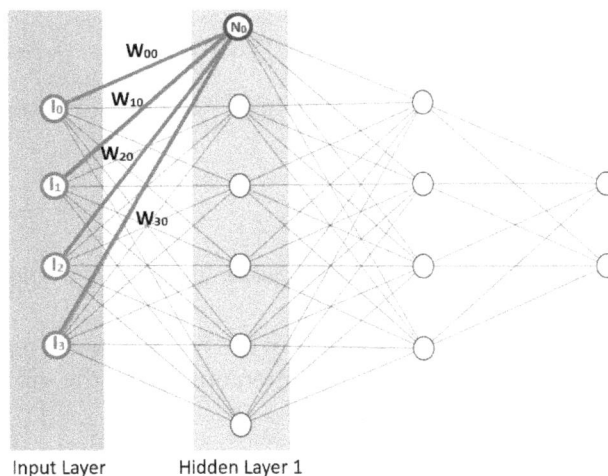

Figure 1.3: *Evaluation of neuron N_0*

The value of N_0 is given by:

$$N_0 = I_0 \times W_{00} + I_1 \times W_{10} + I_2 \times W_{20} + I_3 \times W_{30}$$

Figure 1.4: Obtaining the value of neuron N_0

We can calculate the value of every neuron in the first hidden layer, as shown in the following figure:

$$N_0 = I_0 \times W_{00} + I_1 \times W_{10} + I_2 \times W_{20} + I_3 \times W_{30}$$

$$N_1 = I_0 \times W_{01} + I_1 \times W_{11} + I_2 \times W_{21} + I_3 \times W_{31}$$

$$N_2 = I_0 \times W_{02} + I_1 \times W_{12} + I_2 \times W_{22} + I_3 \times W_{32}$$

$$N_3 = I_0 \times W_{03} + I_1 \times W_{13} + I_2 \times W_{23} + I_3 \times W_{33}$$

$$N_4 = I_0 \times W_{04} + I_1 \times W_{14} + I_2 \times W_{24} + I_3 \times W_{34}$$

$$N_5 = I_0 \times W_{05} + I_1 \times W_{15} + I_2 \times W_{25} + I_3 \times W_{35}$$

Figure 1.5: Obtaining the value of remaining neurons

Reducing these equations to a single matrix computation, we get:

$$
\begin{bmatrix} N_0 \\ N_1 \\ N_2 \\ N_3 \\ N_4 \\ N_5 \end{bmatrix}
=
\begin{bmatrix}
W_{00} & W_{10} & W_{20} & W_{30} \\
W_{01} & W_{11} & W_{21} & W_{31} \\
W_{02} & W_{12} & W_{22} & W_{32} \\
W_{03} & W_{13} & W_{23} & W_{33} \\
W_{04} & W_{14} & W_{24} & W_{34} \\
W_{05} & W_{15} & W_{25} & W_{35}
\end{bmatrix}
\times
\begin{bmatrix} I_0 \\ I_1 \\ I_2 \\ I_3 \end{bmatrix}
$$

Figure 1.6: Matrix formula to obtaining the value of the first hidden layer neurons

Or, in short:

$$N = W^{01} \times I$$

Figure 1.7: Matrix formula for first hidden layer in short notation

Where **N** is the vector representing the neurons of the first hidden layer, **I** is the vector with the input values, and **W**^{01} is the weight matrix interconnecting the input layer and the first hidden layer. In the same way, we can find:

$$M = W^{12} \times N$$

Figure 1.8: Finding the values of the second hidden layer

Where **M** is the second hidden layer, and:

$$O = \mathbf{W}^{23} \times M$$

Figure 1.9: *Finding the output values*

Where **O** is the output layer:

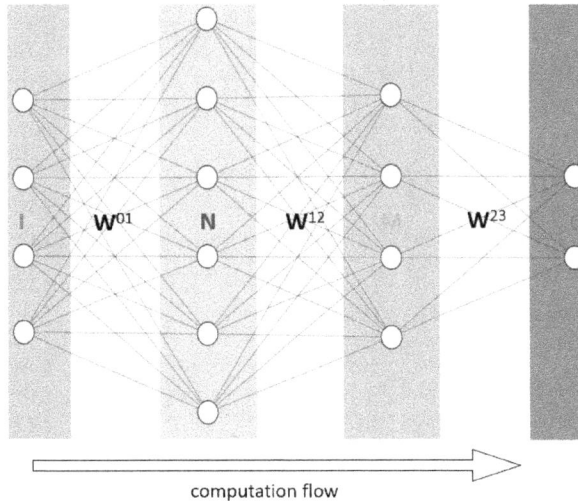

computation flow

Figure 1.10: *Full forward computation*

Another way to see a neural network is as a **function composition**:

$$F = O(M(N(I())))$$

Figure 1.11: *Modelling neural network as function compositions*

In this approach, each layer is taken as a function that uses the values from the previous layer as input to produce some computation. Indeed, this is the formal definition of neural networks, which is more useful to applied mathematicians proving theorems and mathematical properties of neural networks.

Besides neurons and weights, neural networks have other elements to cite, such as activation functions and bias. We will cover them and other relevant topics of neural networks in *Chapters 5, 6*, and *7*. For a while, let us understand why this classical model does not work well for complex, real-world scenarios.

Limitations of fully connected layers

For decades, multi-layer networks with fully connected layers were the unique neural network model available. However, since the early times, it was clear that this model had severe practical limitations. Understanding the main problem with fully connected layers is not so hard. Let us revisit our previous example:

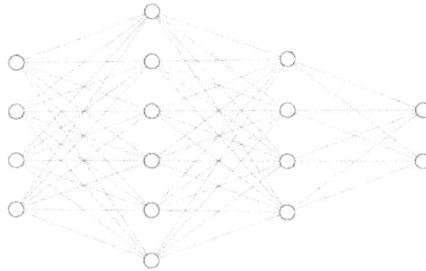

Figure 1.12: The previous network having 6 neurons in the first hidden layer

If you try to count them, you will find out that this model has 16 neurons and 56 connections. Now, let us duplicate the number of neurons in each layer:

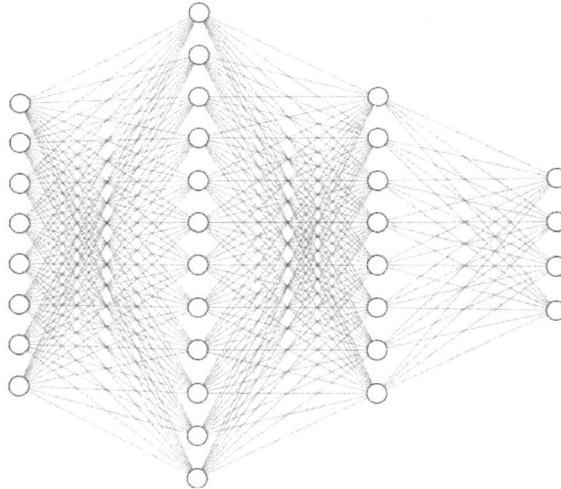

Figure 1.13: New network having a double of neurons

We now have 32 neurons but 224 connections, which is four times more than the previous model.

It is noticeable that the number of connections increased drastically by merely doubling the number of neurons. If we use layers having 1,000 or 4,000 neurons, the fully connected layers will result in huge weight matrices with millions of coefficients. Working with such large weight matrices is a real problem because, even with computers with large memories to hold such data, performing the matrix multiplications will be slow and not feasible for real-time applications.

Note: Fully connected layers are extremely costly in terms of memory and processing.

In conclusion, because of the massive growth of connections, old-style neural networks using only fully connected layers, and a high number of neurons are often dauntingly slow and mostly impractical for real-world scenarios. As a result, vanilla neural networks tend to be **shallow networks**, typically consisting of (at most) four internal layers.

In addition to this scalability problem, fully connected layers have another critical drawback: they are not **invariant** to translation, scale, or rotation. This issue means that if, for example, you train a network to recognize images of apples, the position of the apples in the training data will matter. If they are positioned more to the right, to the center, to the left, or if the apples are far or close to the camera, all these factors will severely influence the capacity of the model to detect apples in different positions, angles, and sizes:

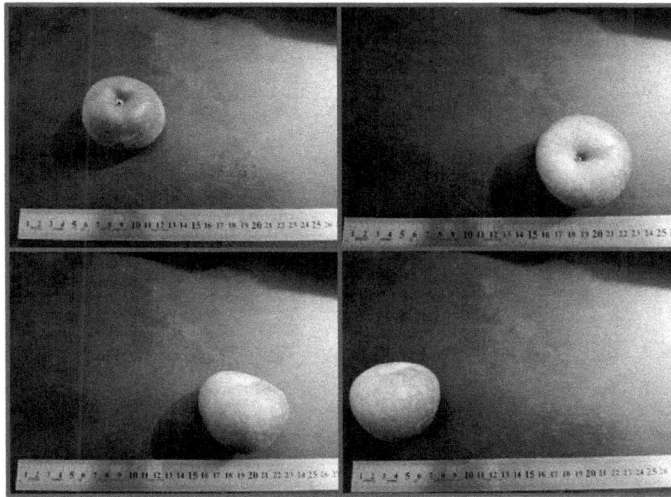

Figure 1.14: *Translation and pose variance*

This matter of invariance haunted the machine learning community for years since the fully connected models—almost the unique neural network model available since then, do not generalize well when objects are in a different pose than the ones found in training data.

Luckily, the approaches developed in deep learning help us to overcome these limitations, allowing us to design networks with dozens or hundreds of layers, the so-called **deep models**. But how did the deep learning scientists manage to create such deep models? Using **convolutional layers**, as explained ahead.

Convolutional neural networks

The convolutional neural network [1], or simply **CNN**, was the first noticeable improvement introduced by deep learning. As its name suggests, CNNs use convolutional layers. Convolutional layers use convolution, a fancy matrix operation:

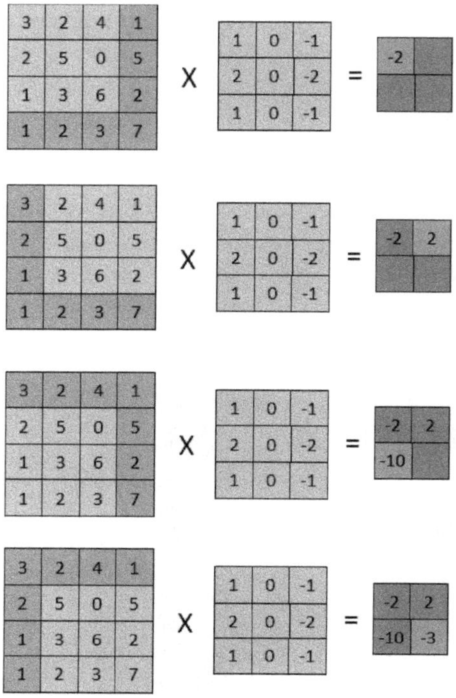

Figure 1.15: Example of convolution

The example above shows the convolution of a 4x4 input matrix by a 3x3 kernel. This operation results in a 2x2 output matrix. Note that the kernel slides over the input matrix, making this operation more addressable to grid-like inputs (images, for example).

We will cover convolutions in detail in *Chapter 4, Implementing Convolutions*. For now, we can briefly describe this operation by examining the example above.

In this convolution, the 2x2 output matrix is computed in the following way:

1. Multiplying each coefficient of the first 3x3 slice by the respective kernel coefficients and summing them up: *3x1 + 2x0 + 4x-1 + 2x2 + 5x0 + 0x-2 + 1x1 + 3x0 + 6x-1 = -2*, storing the resulting value in position (0,0) of the output matrix.

2. Multiplying each coefficient of the second 3x3 slice by the kernel coefficients: *2x1 + 4x0 + 1x-1 + 5x2 + 0x0 + 5x-2 + 3x1 + 6x0 + 2x-1 = 2*, storing the result in position (0,1) of the output matrix.

3. Repeating the product to the third slice: *2x1 + 5x0 + 0x-1 + 1x2 + 3x0 + 6x-2 + 1x1 + 2x0 + 3x-1 = -10* and storing the result in position (1,0) of the output matrix.

4. Finally, calculate the product of the last slice by the kernel: *5x1 + 0x0 + 5x-1 + 3x2 + 6x0 + 2x-2 + 2x1 + 3x0 + 7x-1 = -3* and assign the value to position (1,1) of the output matrix.

Convolutions are important because they solve several important problems for neural networks:

- Kernels are very small compared to fully connected weight matrices, drastically reducing the computational time and memory cost per layer. As a result, we can use larger models in terms of the number of neurons and layers.

- Since the kernel slides over the input data, there is no fixed connection as the ones seen in fully connected layers. Thus, kernels are more prone to capture the regularities in the data even if there are variances in terms of translation, rotation, or scale. In other words, due to a phenomenon known as **parameter sharing** [2], convolutional neural networks are more robust to variance than fully connected models.

Convolutional neural networks significantly impacted the machine learning field, in particular to computer vision tasks. After CNNs, using neural networks to process regular-size images became feasible and practical in a world first. Image classifiers, object detectors, face recognition systems, and many other complex applications were finally developed with CNNs at the core.

In this context, AlexNet [3] was one of the first notable convolutional networks, winning the **ImageNet Large Scale Visual Recognition Challenge** (**ILSVRC**) in 2012 [4]. AlexNet architecture is represented as follows:

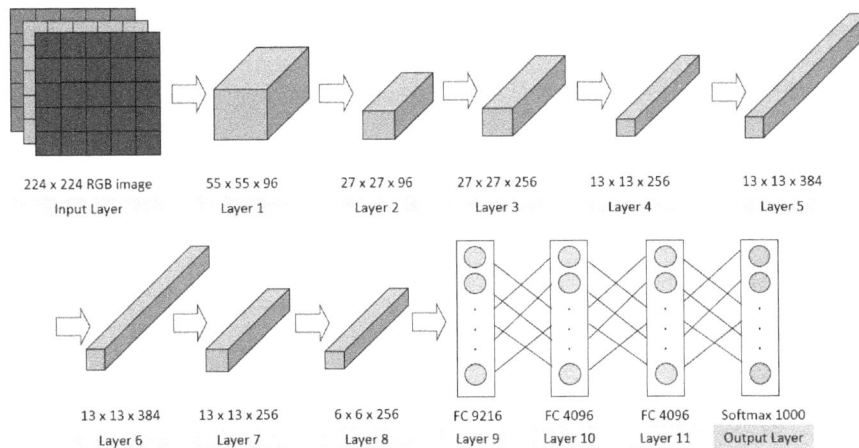

| 224 x 224 RGB image | 55 x 55 x 96 | 27 x 27 x 96 | 27 x 27 x 256 | 13 x 13 x 256 | 13 x 13 x 384 |
| Input Layer | Layer 1 | Layer 2 | Layer 3 | Layer 4 | Layer 5 |

| 13 x 13 x 384 | 13 x 13 x 256 | 6 x 6 x 256 | FC 9216 | FC 4096 | FC 4096 | Softmax 1000 |
| Layer 6 | Layer 7 | Layer 8 | Layer 9 | Layer 10 | Layer 11 | Output Layer |

Figure 1.16: *The AlexNet architecture*

Not considering the input and output layers, AlexNet has eleven internal layers, which makes it a genuine example of a deep learning model. Five out of the eleven hidden layers are convolutional layers, and three are max-pooling layers. The last three hidden layers are fully connected layers. Indeed, we will find this same structural pattern in several other CNN architectures: a sequence of convolutional layers intercalated by max-pooling layers at the beginning of the network followed by a small group of fully connected layers in the tail. In networks like this, the first set containing convolutional and max-pooling layers is often called **feature extractor**, whereas the last sequence of fully connected layers is usually called **head** or **top**. Refer to the following figure:

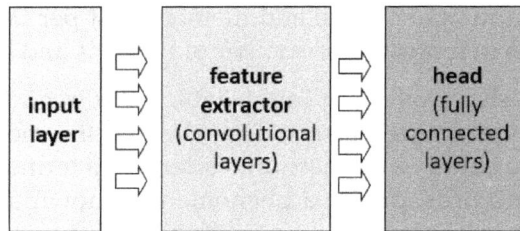

Figure 1.17: *General CNN architecture*

Note: Max-pooling layers are covered in Chapter 8, Using Pooling Layers

Dividing networks into feature extractors and heads is an opportunity to reuse pre-trained models to solve new problems, a technique traditionally called **transfer learning**. Transfer learning and other advanced techniques are discussed in the last part of this book.

The following table [5] summarizes the architecture of AlexNet:

Layer	Tensor size	Weights	Bias	Parameters
Input Image	227x227x3	0	0	0
Conv-1	55x55x96	34,848	96	34,944
MaxPool-1	27x27x96	0	0	0
Conv-2	27x27x256	614,400	256	614,656
MaxPool-2	13x13x256	0	0	0
Conv-3	13x13x384	884,736	384	885,120
Conv-4	13x13x384	1,327,104	384	1,327,488
Conv-5	13x13x256	884,736	256	884,992
MaxPool-3	6x6x256	0		0
FC-1	4096×1	37,748,736	4,096	37,752,832
FC-2	4096×1	16,777,216	4,096	16,781,312
FC-3	1000×1	4,096,000	1000	4,097,000
Output	1000×1	0	0	0
Total				62,378,344

Table 1.1: *Metrics*

Note that the majority of parameters are stored in the fully connected layers, which significantly affects the overall training cost of this network.

The last layer in AlexNet uses a special type of activation function called **softmax**. An important aspect of softmax activations is that their outputs simulate discrete random distributions. In simple words, the output of AlexNet can be taken as a probability for each one of the 1000 possible classes. The majority of these values are nearly zero, but the predicted class is the one with the higher output value.

Check the following representation of how softmax activation works in AlexNet:

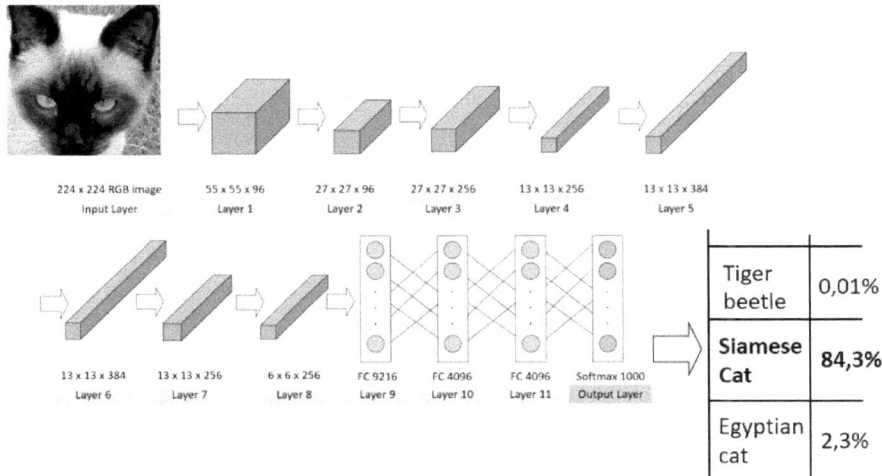

Figure 1.18: Softmax output in AlexNet

In this example, softmax scores the **Siamese Cat** class with the max value. All the other 999 classes are scored with a positive small value. Since the softmax output works like a random discrete distribution, the sum of all scores is always 100%.

Note: Softmax and other relevant activation functions are discussed in Chapter 7, Defining Activation Functions.

In addition to AlexNet, many other different network architectures were proposed, always using convolution as the core component. The following table [6] resumes some of the most popular of them:

Model	Size (MB)	Top-1 Accuracy	Top-5 Accuracy	Parameters	Depth
VGG16	528	71.3%	90.1%	138.4M	16
VGG19	549	71.3%	90.0%	143.7M	19
ResNet50	98	74.9%	92.1%	25.6M	107
InceptionV3	92	77.9%	93.7%	23.9M	189
MobileNet	16	70.4%	89.5%	4.3M	55
EfficientNetB0	29	77.1%	93.3%	5.3M	132

EfficientNetB1	31	79.1%	94.4%	7.9M	186
EfficientNetB2	36	80.1%	94.9%	9.2M	186
EfficientNetB3	48	81.6%	95.7%	12.3M	210
EfficientNetB4	75	82.9%	96.4%	19.5M	258
EfficientNetB5	118	83.6%	96.7%	30.6M	312
EfficientNetB6	166	84.0%	96.8%	43.3M	360
EfficientNetB7	256	84.3%	97.0%	66.7M	438

Table 1.2: Popular CNN architectures

There are several important details in the design and training of convolutional networks, such as pooling layers, activation functions, strides, padding, and others. These aspects will be discussed throughout this book.

Recurrent neural networks

Convolutional neural networks significantly improved the performance of models to make inferences on grid-like data, such as images. However, a different type of data, often called sequence data, kept challenging even the new models.

Sequence data is usually found in application domains involving natural language processing. Consider the following examples:

- Given a text written in a language X, automatically translate it to another language Y.

- Given a clip of someone's speech, make a transcript of the message in textual form.

- Given a text, determine the meaning of the message.

Sentimental analysis is a well-known example of extracting the meaning of a text [7]. The problem of classifying the sentiment of a movie review as positive, negative, or neutral was a popular benchmark for several sequence models proposed in the early stages of deep learning.

However, why do conventional or CNN models not work for this data? Let us take two fictitious reviews:

Review	Sentiment
This movie is awesome.	Positive
Personally, I did not like the movie that much.	Negative

Table 1.3: Fictitious review examples

The first problem here is that this data is not originally numeric. To multiply the inputs by weight matrixes, they must be numeric. Thus, the first question is: how to encode the text data into a numeric representation? For the sake of simplicity, let us use a dictionary:

Word	Index		Word	Index		Word	Index
a	0		...	...		personally	9576
...	...		is	4805		...	...
awesome	104		it	4806		That	9601
...	...		...	...		...	...
be	408		like	7028		The	9699
...	...		...	...		...	...
didn't	1504		movie	8123		This	9875
...	...		...	...		...	...
i	4001		much	9148		Zulu	9999
			...	...			

Table 1.4: Example of a dictionary

The dictionary is an index where words are lexicographically sorted in ascending order. Now, we can encode the sentences:

Sentence	Representation
This movie is awesome.	9875 8123 4805 104
Personally, I did not like the movie that much.	9576 4001 1504 7028 9699 8123 9601 9148

Table 1.5: Example of encoding

The main challenge here is obvious: the two representations have different lengths. Any attempt to use a fixed length input here will force to trunk a sequence (leading to information loss) or use a huge padding input to hold sentences of any length (also costly and problematic). **Recurrent neural networks** (**RNNs**) came to play to solve this issue.

The most common type of recurrent neural network is defined by a loop where the same structure is fed several times [1], sequentially, by each token in the input.

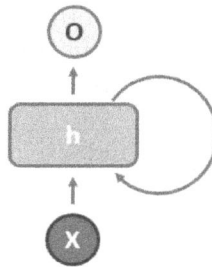

Figure 1.19: *Representation of a recurrent neural network*

In our sentimental analysis problem, we can feed the network with the list of words, whether the sequence is short or long. The resulting output is the network output after the last iteration. This behavior is illustrated as follows:

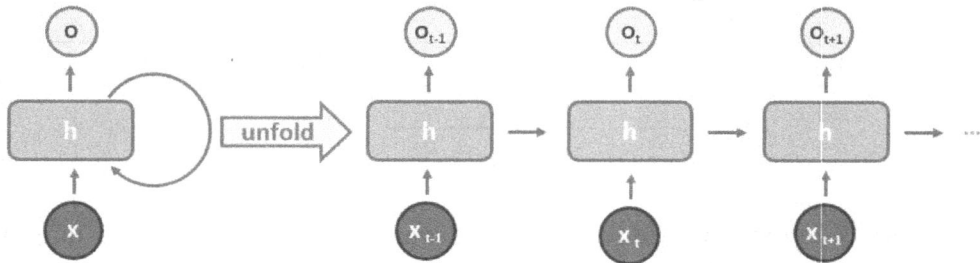

Figure 1.20: *Performing inference on an RNN*

This particular RNN architecture solves two important issues:

- Inputs have different lengths
- There is a dependence on each word and the words that come before it.

However, this network cannot capture the relationship between a word and the subsequent words. Various RNN architectural designs have been proposed to solve this bi-directional dependence and other relevant issues found in sequence data.

Generative adversarial networks

The networks discussed so far in this chapter are examples of **discriminative models**. In discriminative models, the network performs classification or regression tasks using input data from the feature space. Today, another common usage is **generative models**. In generative models, the network outputs realistic examples of the feature space. Let us see some examples of discriminative and generative tasks in the following table:

Discriminative models	Generative models
Given an image, detect whether there is a cat or a dog.	Given an input X = cat or X = dog generate a realistic image of a cat or a dog.
Given a clip of speech, extract the message.	Given a text, generate a realistic audio clip of someone reciting the given text.
Find human faces in an image.	Generate realistic images of human faces.
Identify if a movie review is positive or negative.	Generate a positive or negative movie review.
Given a text within a question, extract what the text is asking.	Given a question, generate an answer.

Table 1.6: Comparison between discriminative and generative models

Generative models are all the hype today, causing much controversy regarding intellectual property, ethics, and the future of jobs. You can see some examples of realistic fake faces on this website: **https://www.thispersondoesnotexist.com/**.

From the engineering point of view, there are several approaches to creating generative models. Generative adversarial networks [2] are one of the most well-succeded networks nowadays. A **generative adversarial network (GAN)** model consists of two networks: the discriminator and the generator.

To make it easier to understand, let us suppose we are building a GAN to generate realistic fake images of cats. In such GANs, the generator is the model that generates fake images, and the discriminator is the model that identifies if an image is real or fake. Refer to the following figure:

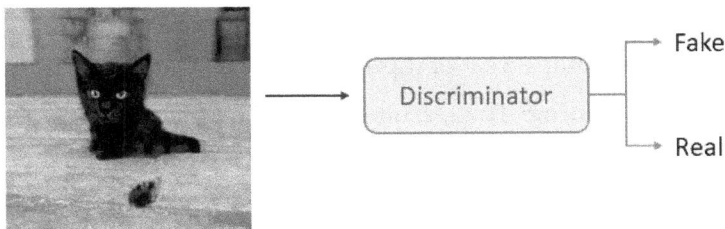

Figure 1.21: Discriminator inferring if an image is fake or real

Why do we need the discriminator? The discriminator is used during the generator training. Before being trained, the generator could not yet generate realistic images of cats. In the same way, before the train, the discriminator also does not know how to determine if an image is real or fake. During the training, the discriminator will learn how to classify an image as fake or real, and the generator will learn how to generate realistic fake images. For this purpose, the training uses real images of cats.

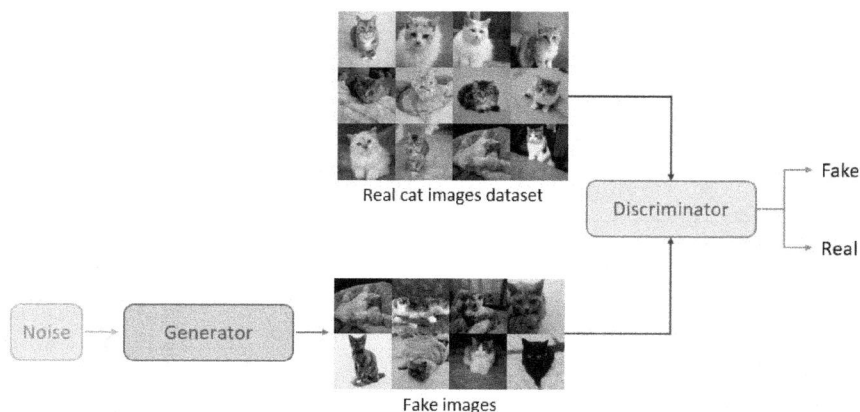

***Figure 1.22**: Training a generative adversarial network with images of cats*

Therefore, the training of GANs consists of a game where the generator tries to fool the discriminator, generating realistic outputs, while the discriminator tries to learn how to detect if an image is fake or real. If the training is good, in the end, the generator can generate highly realistic outputs to fool the discriminator. In this stage, we can discard the discriminator and use the generator to output fake realistic images. You can see some examples of fake realistic images of cats here: **http://thesecatsdonotexist.com/**

Reinforcement learning

In ML, usually, systems are modeled as one of three following categories: supervised learning, unsupervised learning, and reinforcement learning. These categories are described as follows:

- **Supervised learning**: The learning process consists of discovering an approximation for a function that maps a set of inputs X in the respective outputs Y. [8]

- **Unsupervised learning**: The learning process consists of discovering underlying patterns and regularities in the data without explicit feedback.

- **Reinforcement learning**: The learning process involves creating the training data through interactions with the environment. The model learns from the feedback after the interactions. [9]

In reinforcement learning, instead of using the term model, we use the term **agent** in the meaning of an actual agent that performs actions on the environment around it. These actions result in feedback that can be seen from the agent's point of view as a numeric representation of a positive, negative, or neutral response signal. In systems like that, the model (the agent) learns from this process of **choosing actions to take**, performing the actions, and getting and understanding the feedback, known as the **reward signal**.

In its essence, the main objective of a reinforcement learning agent is to maximize the global reward signal. Since the agent only knows the reward signal after performing an action, the agent chooses the action that maximizes the **reward estimative**. Several aspects, however, make this decision-making process intrinsically hard, such as:

- Non-stationary environments
- Delayed rewards
- Perception noise
- Actuator noise
- Diversity of perceptions
- Unobservability

At this point, deep learning comes into play in reinforcement learning systems.

The most common application of deep learning in reinforcement learning systems is performing action selection, which very often is called **deep reinforcement learning** [10]. One of the most successful approaches of deep learning with reinforcement learning is using CNN networks to define Q-functions: functions to estimate the reward of taking actions given a state, surpassing human performance in some tasks such as playing video games. Refer to the following figure:

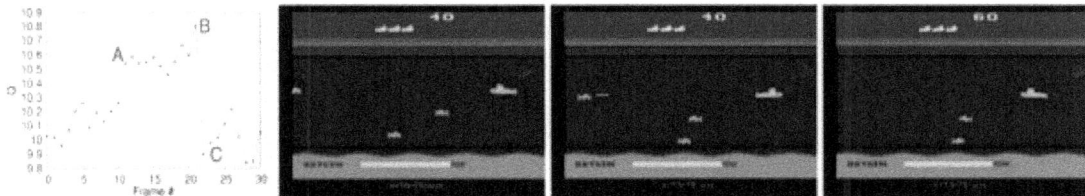

Figure 1.23: *Playing an old videogame with deep reinforcement learning* [9]

A more detailed discussion of deep learning applied to reinforcement and unsupervised learning is beyond the scope of this book. Thus, the next chapters will cover deep learning applied specifically to supervised learning problems.

Conclusion

This chapter introduced the concept of deep learning to the readers. We discussed the origins of deep learning, significant developments in the field, and the most advanced architectural designs and paradigms.

In the next chapter, we will approach the aspects of using modern C++ as the programming language for implementing deep learning algorithms.

Exercises

1. Provide real-world examples of supervised learning, unsupervised, and reinforcement learning systems.

2. Write a function std::vector<std::vector<double>> product(const std::vector<std::vector<double>> &A, const std::vector<std::vector<double>> &B) to calculate the matrix product of A and B. In this exercise, consider that A and B are always rectangular 2D vectors. Check this reference [11] to learn how to calculate matrix multiplications.

3. Write a function std::vector<std::vector<double>> convolution(const std::vector<std::vector<double>> &A, const std::vector<std::vector<double>> &K) to calculate the matrix convolution of A by the kernel K. In this exercise, consider that A is always a rectangular 2D vector, and K is always a 3x3 matrix.

4. Rewrite product(...) and convolution(...) to return the total count of algebraic multiplications and sums performed internally. Compare the computational cost of the two functions.

References

[1] Aggarwal, Neural Networks and Deep Learning, Chapter 8, Convolutional Neural Network, Springer, 2018.

[2] Goodfellow, Bengio & Courville, Deep Learning, MIT Press, 2016.

[3] Krizhevsky, Sutskever & Hinton: ImageNet Classification with Deep Convolutional Neural Networks.

[4] ImageNet Large Scale Visual Recognition Challenge (ILSVRC) 2012, URL: **https://www.image-net.org/challenges/LSVRC/2012/index.php**

[5] Satya Mallick and Sunita Nayak, Number of Parameters and Tensor Sizes in a Convolutional Neural Network (CNN), available at https://learnopencv.com/number-of-parameters-and-tensor-sizes-in-convolutional-neural-network/

[6] Keras applications, URL: **https://keras.io/api/applications**

[7] Maas et al., Learning Word Vectors for Sentiment Analysis, 2011.

[8] Russell & Norvig, Artificial Intelligence, a Modern Approach, Prentice Hall, 2010.

[9] Richard Sutton and Andrew G. Barto, Reinforcement Learning: An Introduction, MIT Press, 2018.

[10] Volodymyr Mnih et al., Playing Atari with Deep Reinforcement Learning.

[11] Matrix multiplication, available at: **https://www.ucl.ac.uk/~ucahmto/0005_2021/Ch3.S2.html**

CHAPTER 2
Coding Deep Learning with Modern C++

Introduction

This chapter introduces some relevant C++ features and APIs to program deep learning models. In addition, this chapter also introduces Eigen, an open-source C++ library for linear algebra and matrix programming required to implement the algorithms. Finally, this chapter discusses vectorization in C++ programs.

Structure

This is the general roadmap for the chapter:

- Coding and compiling a C++ program
- Building C++ projects
- Coding modern C++ programs
- Using functional programming
- Matrix programming in C++
- Generating random numbers
- Vectorization

Objectives

This chapter will teach you how to write C++ programs using modern features such as functional programming. You will also know how to use the Eigen API to perform matrix computations and understand the guidelines for writing vectorizable code.

Coding and compiling a C++ program

Let us start with a very simple C++ **hello_world.cpp** example:

```
1.  #include <iostream>
2.
3.  int main(int, char**)
4.  {
5.      std::cout << "Hello World\n";
6.      return 0;
7.  }
```

To run this program, it is necessary to compile it first using a C++ compiler. There are several alternatives to C++ compilers, GNU Compiler Collection, in short GCC [1], being one of the most popular compilers nowadays.

Assuming that the code above was saved as a **hello_world.cpp** file, we can use GCC to compile it by the following command:

g++ hello_world.cpp -o my_program

This command results in an executable file called **my_program**, which can be executed as follows:

./my_program

Running the program on Linux looks like the following figure:

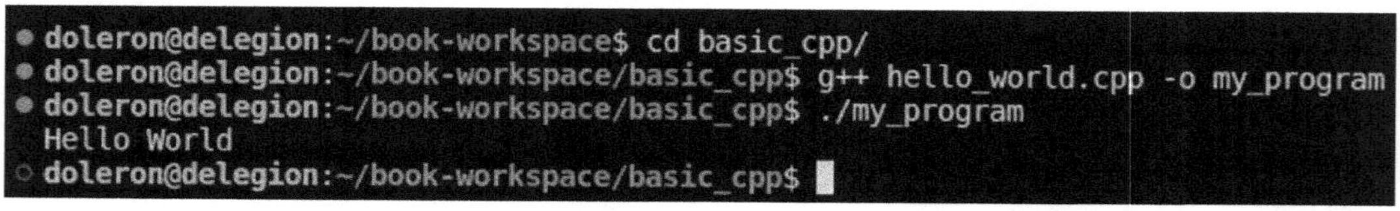

Figure 2.1: Compiling and running the Hello World program on Linux

GCC is available for Linux and Windows systems. How GCC is installed on Linux machines depends on the exact Linux distribution. On Windows, you can install GCC using Mingw-w64 via MSYS2 [2]. Running the program on Windows looks like the following figure:

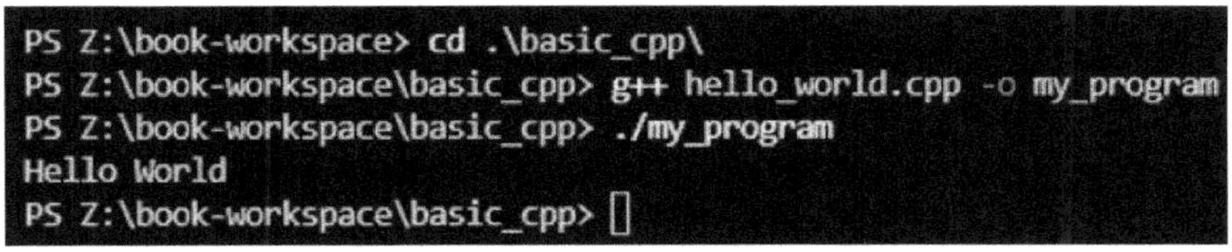

```
PS Z:\book-workspace> cd .\basic_cpp\
PS Z:\book-workspace\basic_cpp> g++ hello_world.cpp -o my_program
PS Z:\book-workspace\basic_cpp> ./my_program
Hello World
PS Z:\book-workspace\basic_cpp> []
```

Figure 2.2: Compiling and running the Hello World program on Windows

The choice of the exact C++ compiler or operating system is personal. You can use any C++17 [3] compliant compiler of your preference to run the examples in this book. Check this link for a C++17 compilers list: **https://en.cppreference.com/w/cpp/compiler_support/17**

Building C++ projects

Building modern real-world programs requires the compilation of multiple source files, third-party libraries, and auxiliary resources. In practice, building automation tools help us keep things easier and tidy. In particular, we use CMake [4], the most popular building tool for C++ combined with GNU Make [5].

Building a project with CMake and Make is very simple. Consider the following **CMakeLists.txt** file:

```
1.  cmake_minimum_required(VERSION 3.8)
2.
3.  set(PROJECT_NAME hello_world)
4.  project(${PROJECT_NAME} CXX)
5.
6.  # Default to Release build type
7.  if(NOT CMAKE_BUILD_TYPE)
8.    set(CMAKE_BUILD_TYPE Release CACHE STRING "Build type" FORCE)
9.  endif()
10.
11. message(STATUS "Build type: ${CMAKE_BUILD_TYPE}")
12.
13. # C++17 is mandatory
14. set(CMAKE_CXX_STANDARD 17)
15. set(CMAKE_CXX_STANDARD_REQUIRED ON)
16. set(CMAKE_CXX_EXTENSIONS OFF)
17.
18. add_executable(${PROJECT_NAME} ${PROJECT_SOURCE_DIR}/hello_world.
    cpp)
19. target_compile_options(${PROJECT_
```

```
       NAME} PRIVATE -Wall -Wextra -pedantic)
20.
21. # defining an output folder
22. set_target_properties(${PROJECT_NAME} PROPERTIES RUNTIME_OUTPUT_
    DIRECTORY "bin")
```

We can use this file to build our simple example as follows:

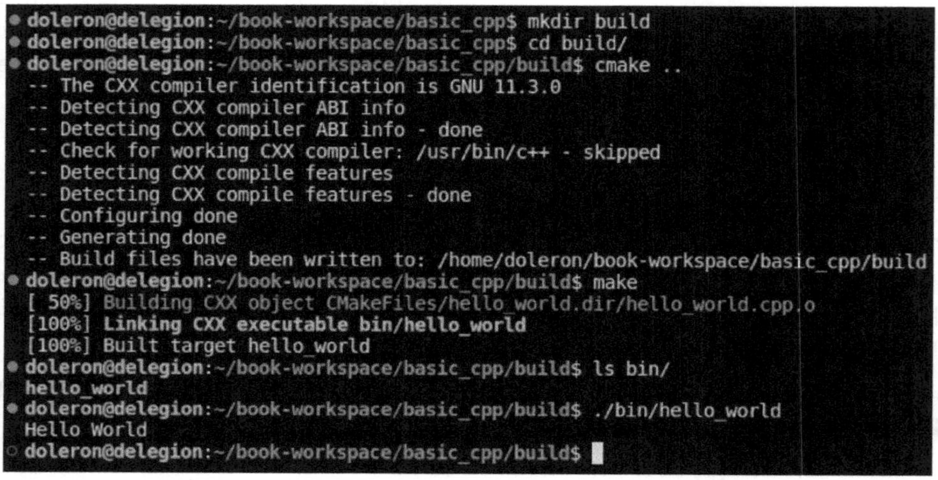

```
● doleron@delegion:~/book-workspace/basic_cpp$ mkdir build
● doleron@delegion:~/book-workspace/basic_cpp$ cd build/
● doleron@delegion:~/book-workspace/basic_cpp/build$ cmake ..
-- The CXX compiler identification is GNU 11.3.0
-- Detecting CXX compiler ABI info
-- Detecting CXX compiler ABI info - done
-- Check for working CXX compiler: /usr/bin/c++ - skipped
-- Detecting CXX compile features
-- Detecting CXX compile features - done
-- Configuring done
-- Generating done
-- Build files have been written to: /home/doleron/book-workspace/basic_cpp/build
● doleron@delegion:~/book-workspace/basic_cpp/build$ make
[ 50%] Building CXX object CMakeFiles/hello_world.dir/hello_world.cpp.o
[100%] Linking CXX executable bin/hello_world
[100%] Built target hello_world
● doleron@delegion:~/book-workspace/basic_cpp/build$ ls bin/
hello_world
● doleron@delegion:~/book-workspace/basic_cpp/build$ ./bin/hello_world
Hello World
○ doleron@delegion:~/book-workspace/basic_cpp/build$ █
```

Figure 2.3: Building our project with cmake and make on Linux

We can use CMake and Make on Windows too:

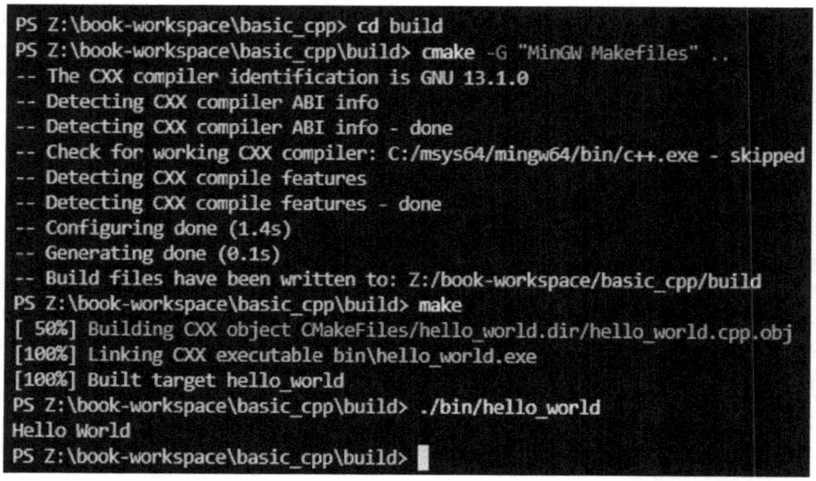

```
PS Z:\book-workspace\basic_cpp> cd build
PS Z:\book-workspace\basic_cpp\build> cmake -G "MinGW Makefiles" ..
-- The CXX compiler identification is GNU 13.1.0
-- Detecting CXX compiler ABI info
-- Detecting CXX compiler ABI info - done
-- Check for working CXX compiler: C:/msys64/mingw64/bin/c++.exe - skipped
-- Detecting CXX compile features
-- Detecting CXX compile features - done
-- Configuring done (1.4s)
-- Generating done (0.1s)
-- Build files have been written to: Z:/book-workspace/basic_cpp/build
PS Z:\book-workspace\basic_cpp\build> make
[ 50%] Building CXX object CMakeFiles/hello_world.dir/hello_world.cpp.obj
[100%] Linking CXX executable bin\hello_world.exe
[100%] Built target hello_world
PS Z:\book-workspace\basic_cpp\build> ./bin/hello_world
Hello World
PS Z:\book-workspace\basic_cpp\build> █
```

Figure 2.4: Building our project with cmake and make on Windows

It is a good practice to build the project in a different folder than the one where the source files are stored. We can do that by simply:

```
mkdir build
cd build
cmake ..
```

It turns out that building the project in a different folder makes it easy to clean up the build without the risk of mistakenly deleting a source file or project resource.

Coding modern C++ programs

Since the standard C++11[6], C++ language has introduced several important features which aim the development of more complex programs in a faster and more reliable way. These features are informally known as **modern C++**. In this book, we will make intense use of some of these features, in particular:

- Functional features
- The **<algorithm>**, **<functional>**, and **<numeric>** headers
- Statistical headers

Using functional programming

C++ is a versatile programming language that supports multiple paradigms. This means that it can be used to create programs using different styles, including OOP, procedural, and functional. Check the example as follows:

```
1.  #include <algorithm> // std::for_each
2.  #include <functional> // std::less, std::less_
    equal, std::greater, std::greater_equal
3.  #include <iostream> // std::cout
4.
5.  int main()
6.  {
7.
8.      std::vector<std::function<bool(double, double)>> comparators
9.      {
10.         std::less<double>(),
11.         std::less_equal<double>(),
12.         std::greater<double>(),
13.         std::greater_equal<double>()
14.     };
15.
16.     double x = 10.;
17.     double y = 10.;
```

```
18.     auto compare = [&x, &y]
      (const std::function<bool(double, double)> &comparator)
19.     {
20.             bool b = comparator(x, y);
21.             std::cout << (b?"TRUE": "FALSE") << "\n";
22.     };
23.
24.     std::for_each(comparators.begin(), comparators.end(), compare);
25.
26.     return 0;
27. }
```

This example uses some features which we want to dedicate time to understanding. Let us start by introducing the **<functional>** header. **std::function**, **std::less**, **std::less_equal**, **std::greater**, and **std::greater_equal** are examples of performing polymorphic calls without using pointers.

One key point in this code is the usage of lambdas:

```
1. auto compare = [&x, &y]
      (const std::function<bool(double, double)> &comparator)
2. {
3.     bool b = comparator(x, y);
4.     std::cout << (b?"TRUE": "FALSE") << "\n";
5. };
```

A lambda consists of three parts:

- The capture list. In this example, it is **[&x, &y]**.
- A parameter list **(const std::function<bool(double, double)> &comparator)**.
- The body (the statements between the curly braces {...}).

Things to take in mind when using lambdas are:

- The parameter list and body clauses work in the same way as in any regular function.
- The capture clause defines which external variables are addressable in the lambda's body.
- Different from regular functions, in C++, lambdas have no name.
- Since lambdas are essentially objects, we can assign them to variables as with any other object.
- In the last example, **compare** is only the name of a variable we assigned our lambda.

Lambdas are extremely useful. We will play with them during this book to simplify our example as much as possible.

Understanding mutable lambdas

By default, lambdas are immutable objects, which means that the lambda itself does not change after any call. Very often, this behavior is just enough. For example, consider the following L2 regularizer:

```
1.  auto L2 = [](const std::vector<double> &V)
2.  {
3.      double p = 0.01;
4.      return std::inner_product(V.begin(), V.end(), V.
    begin(), 0.0) * p;
5.  };
```

Do not worry if you do not know yet what a regularizer is. We will talk more about them in *Chapter 12, Implementing Cross-validation, Mini Batching, and Model Performance Metrics*. So far, we are concerned only with understanding how to use lambdas. This lambda computes the inner product of the vector V by itself, multiplying the result by **0.01**. No change needs to be done on V or any other position in memory.

Now, consider this another example:

```
1.  #include <algorithm>
2.  #include <iostream>
3.
4.  using vector = std::vector<double>;
5.
6.  int main()
7.  {
8.
9.      auto momentum_optimizer = [V = vector()]
    (const vector &gradient) mutable
10.     {
11.         if (V.empty()) V.resize(gradient.size(), 0.);
12.         std::transform(V.begin(), V.end(), gradient.begin(), V.
    begin(), [](double v, double dx)
13.         {
14.             double beta = 0.7;
15.             return v = beta * v + dx;
16.         });
```

```
17.          return V;
18.      };
19.
20.      auto print = [](double d) { std::cout << d << " "; };
21.
22.      const vector current_grads {1., 0., 1., 1., 0., 1.};
23.      for (int i = 0; i < 3; ++i)
24.      {
25.          vector weight_update = momentum_optimizer(current_grads);
26.          std::for_each(weight_update.begin(), weight_update.
    end(), print);
27.          std::cout << "\n";
28.      }
29.
30.      return 0;
31. }
```

The key point here is that the lambda was defined using the keyword **mutable**:

```
1.  auto momentum_optimizer = [V = vector()]
    (const vector &gradient) mutable
2.  {
3.      //. . .
4.  };
```

A mutable lambda can perform **write operations** on any variable captured by value. In the example, the only variable in the capture list is the vector **V**. As a result, every lambda call will generate a different output:

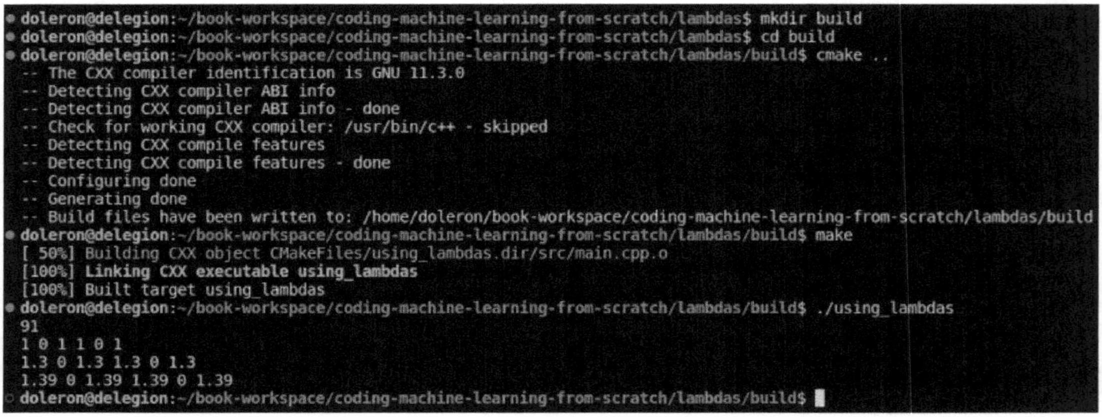

Figure 2.5: *A side-effect lambda using mutable*

In *Chapter 13, Implementing Optimizers*, we will see that memorization is a very important approach to make the algorithm search faster, for example, by implementing optimizers. Mutable lambdas allow us to implement memorization more easily.

Matrix programming in C++

Matrices are grid-like data structures broadly used in machine learning, statistical programming, image processing, games, and scientific computing. Despite its broad usage, C++ does not have a native matrix data structure implementation.

As we will see in the forthcoming chapters, matrices (and their sibling tensors) play a central role in deep learning algorithms. Although we can (try) to use the STL containers (such as vector, list, deque, etc.) to mimic matrices, the best approach here is to use a reliable third-party matrix implementation. In this book, we will use Eigen [6] for this purpose.

There are several advantages to using Eigen. One of them is that Eigen is composed only of headers. Thus, you do not need to build or install Eigen on your machine. Instead, you can only download Eigen from its GitLab repository at **https://gitlab.com/libeigen/eigen** and copy it to a folder. Tell your compiler where it can find the headers, and you are all set.

Although simple, manually downloading Eigen is not the best alternative. You can save time by automatizing this process with CMake as follows:

```
1. cmake_minimum_required(VERSION 3.8)
2.
3. set(PROJECT_NAME eigen_premier)
4. project(${PROJECT_NAME} CXX)
5.
6. # Default to Release build type
7. if(NOT CMAKE_BUILD_TYPE)
8.   set(CMAKE_BUILD_TYPE Release CACHE STRING "Build type" FORCE)
9. endif()
10.
11. message(STATUS "Build type: ${CMAKE_BUILD_TYPE}")
12.
13. set(CMAKE_CXX_STANDARD 17)
14. set(CMAKE_CXX_STANDARD_REQUIRED ON)
15.
16. # downloading and setting up Eigen
17. include(FetchContent)
18.
19. FetchContent_Declare(
```

```
20.    Eigen3
21.    GIT_REPOSITORY https://gitlab.com/libeigen/eigen.git
22.    GIT_TAG        6e4d5d4832a1736ba2f6faa7087b61227dba8e7b
23. )
24. FetchContent_MakeAvailable(Eigen3)
25.
26. add_executable(${PROJECT_NAME} "${PROJECT_SOURCE_DIR}/src/main.cpp")
27.
28. target_compile_options(${PROJECT_
    NAME} PRIVATE -Wall -Wextra -pedantic)
29. target_link_libraries(${PROJECT_NAME} Eigen3::Eigen)
```

Then you can build the project as usual:

```
$ mkdir build
$ cd build
$ cmake ..
$ make
```

This simple Eigen project can be found in the book's GitHub repository. We are using the **GIT_TAG 6e4d5d4832a1736ba2f6faa7087b61227dba8e7b**, a recent commit for the Eigen 3.4.90 version. You can change it to *master* if you want to use the latest library improvements.

If you have Eigen already installed on your machine and want to use it, everything you need to do is ask CMake to find the library:

```
1.  cmake_minimum_required (VERSION 3.0)
2.  project (eigen_premier)
3.
4.  find_package (Eigen3 3.4 REQUIRED NO_MODULE)
5.
6.  add_executable (${PROJECT_NAME} main.cpp)
7.  target_link_libraries (${PROJECT_NAME}  Eigen3::Eigen)
```

Depending on how you have installed Eigen on your system, CMake can be unable to find it. In this case, check the Eigen online documentation to know how to proceed.

Common matrix operations

Once we have Eigen on the path, let us learn how to use it to perform matrix operations in C++. The most notorious matrix operation is the matrix-by-matrix multiplication, often called matrix product or **mulmat**:

```cpp
1.  #include <iostream>
2.  #include <Eigen/Dense>
3.
4.  int main(int, char **)
5.  {
6.      Eigen::MatrixXd A(2, 2);
7.      A(0, 0) = 2.;
8.      A(1, 0) = -2.;
9.      A(0, 1) = 3.;
10.     A(1, 1) = 1.;
11.
12.     Eigen::MatrixXd B(2, 3);
13.     B(0, 0) = 1.;
14.     B(1, 0) = 1.;
15.     B(0, 1) = 2.;
16.     B(1, 1) = 2.;
17.     B(0, 2) = -1.;
18.     B(1, 2) = 1.;
19.
20.     auto C = A * B;
21.
22.     std::cout << "A:\n" << A << std::endl;
23.     std::cout << "B:\n" << B << std::endl;
24.     std::cout << "C:\n" << C << std::endl;
25.
26.     return 0;
27. }
```

Note that we are including the Eigen header:

```cpp
1.  #include <Eigen/Dense>
```

Once executed, this code outputs:

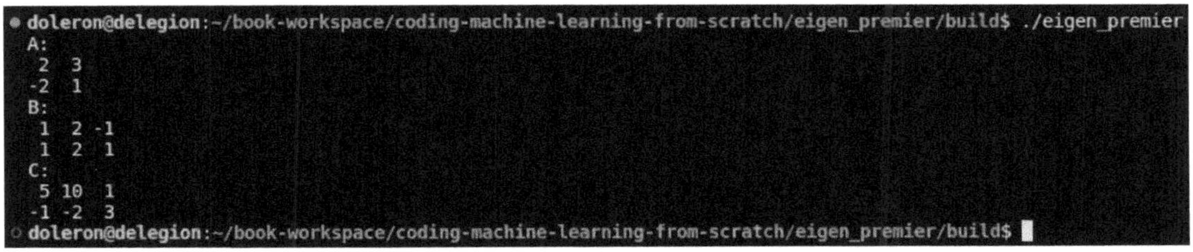

Figure 2.6: *Matrix product with Eigen*

If you are familiar with matrix multiplication, you probably know this operation is only defined for two matrices with **compatible sizes**. The restriction is that the number of columns of the first matrix must be exactly equal to the number of rows of the second matrix. Take a look at the following figure as an example:

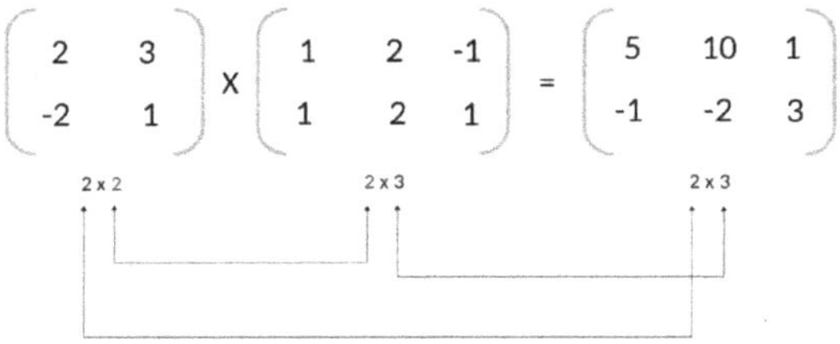

Figure 2.7: Example matrix multiplication

The resulting matrix has the same number of rows as the first matrix and the same number of columns as the second matrix.

There exists another way to multiply two matrices. We can perform **coefficient-wise** multiplication, as illustrated:

```
1.  auto D = B.cwiseProduct(C);
2.  std::cout << "coefficient-
    wise multiplication of B & C is:\n" << D << std::endl;
```

In coefficient-wise multiplication, either the number of columns or the number of rows of the two matrices must perfectly match:

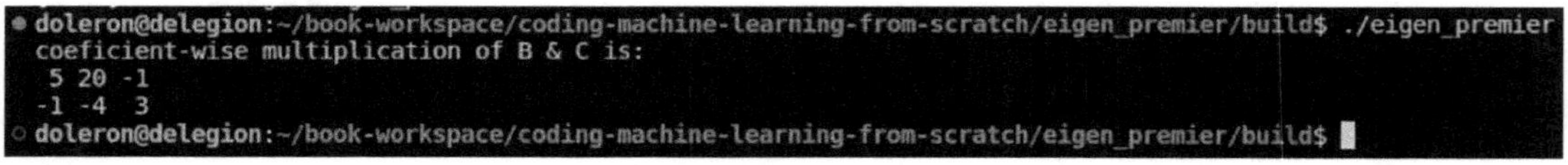

Figure 2.8: Coefficient-wise matrix multiplication

Note that both **B** and **C** have the same number of columns and rows. Besides coefficient-wise multiplication, you can perform several other arithmetic operations such as sum, subtraction, division, and so on.

Computing the transpose, inverse, and determinant of a matrix

With Eigen, we can easily obtain the **matrix determinant** an **inverse** of a **squared matrix**:

```
1.  std::cout << "The inverse of A is:\n" << A.inverse() << std::endl;
2.  std::cout << "The determinant of A is:\n" << A.
    determinant() << std::endl;
```

In the same way, we can transpose any arbitrary matrix:

```
1. std::cout << "The transpose of B is:\n" << B.
   transpose() << std::endl;
```

Unary and binary coefficient-wise operations

Eigen allows us to perform any unary or binary element-wise operation with ease:

```
1.    std::cout << "Example of unary operation:\n\n";
2.    auto func_X_X = [](double x){return x * x;};
3.    std::cout << A.unaryExpr(func_X_X) << std::endl;
4.
5.    std::cout << "\nExample of binary operation:\n\n»;
6.    auto func_X_Y = [](double x, double y){return x * y;};
7.    std::cout << B.binaryExpr(C, func_X_Y) << std::endl;
```

Eigen has a list of built-in coefficient-wise math functions [13] ready to be used in our programs.

Generating random numbers

Some deep learning algorithms have an intrinsic stochastic behavior. For example, we often use randomly generated numbers to initialize the model parameters. Another important example is during the training when the training instances are randomized in order to reduce the effect of any bias in the order of registers.

C++11 introduced built-in random number generators, providing an easier way to generate random numbers that obey a specific statistic distribution. These features are available in the **<random>** header. Let us start with an illustrative example of plotting a normal distribution:

```
1.  #include <cmath>
2.  #include <iomanip>
3.  #include <iostream>
4.  #include <map>
5.  #include <random>
6.  #include <string>
7.
8.  std::random_device rd {};
9.
10. int main(int, char**)
11. {
```

```
12.     std::mt19937 random_generator {rd()};
13.
14.     std::normal_distribution<> distro {2, 3};
15.
16.     std::map<int, int> histogram;
17.
18.     for (int n = 0; n < 10'000; ++n) {
19.         int val = std::round(distro(random_generator));
20.         histogram[val]++;
21.     }
22.
23.     for (auto [x, y] : histogram) {
24.         std::cout << std::setw(2) << x << ' ' << st-
    d::string(y / 20, '*') << '\n';
25.     }
26.
27.     return 0;
28. }
```

This code draws a rudimentary plot of a normal distribution with mean 2 and standard deviation 3:

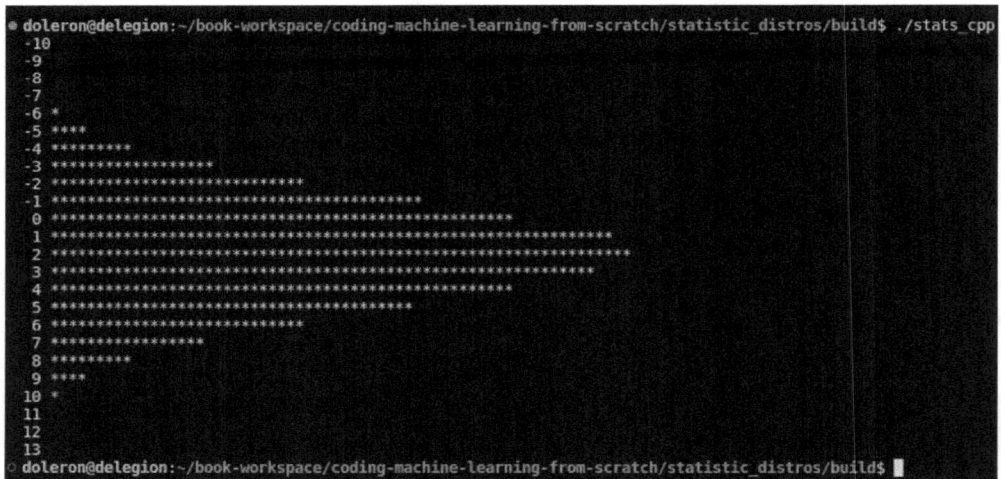

Figure 2.9: The bell shape of normal distributions

As expected, the normal distribution chart has this characteristic bell shape. If we replace the normal distribution:

```
1.      std::normal_distribution<> distro {2, 3};
```

By a uniform distribution:

```
1.     std::uniform_real_distribution<> distro {-10, 13};
```

We obtain a (similar) result as the following:

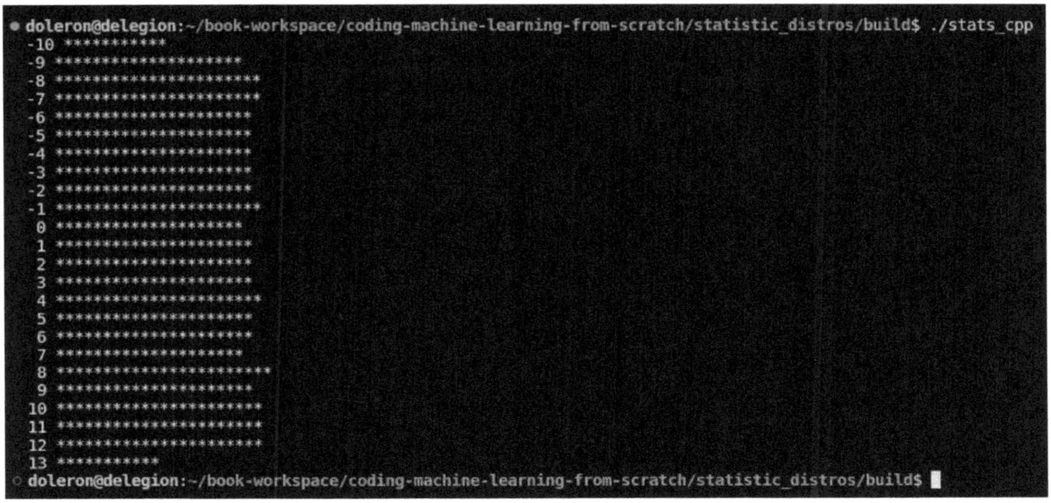

Figure 2.10: The rectangular shape of uniform distributions

Unlike the normal distribution, the uniform distribution has this rectangular shape, as shown above.

We can use the **central limit theorem** [8] to check if things are really working as expected:

```
1.  #include <cmath>
2.  #include <iomanip>
3.  #include <iostream>
4.  #include <map>
5.  #include <random>
6.  #include <string>
7.
8.  std::random_device rd {};
9.
10. int main(int, char**)
11. {
12.     const unsigned int seed = rd();
13.     std::mt19937 random_generator {seed};
14.
15.     std::uniform_real_distribution<> distro {-10, 13};
16.     std::uniform_real_distribution<> distro2 {-5, 8};
17.     std::uniform_real_distribution<> distro3 {3, 9};
```

```
18.      std::uniform_real_distribution<> distro4 {-8, -1};
19.      std::uniform_real_distribution<> distro5 {-10, 10};
20.
21.      std::map<int, int> histogram;
22.
23.      for (int n = 0; n < 10'000; ++n) {
24.          double val = distro(random_generator);
25.          val += distro2(random_generator);
26.          val += distro3(random_generator);
27.          val += distro4(random_generator);
28.          val += distro5(random_generator);
29.          val /= 5.;
30.          histogram[std::round(val)]++;
31.      }
32.
33.      for (auto [x, y] : histogram) {
34.          std::cout << std::setw(2) << x << ' ' << st-
    d::string(y / 20, '*') << '\n';
35.      }
36.
37.      std::cout << distro(random_generator) << "\n";
38.
39.      return 0;
40. }
```

How can this code help us to check if the random package is doing its job? According to *Rényi* [9]:

> "...*the distribution of the sum of a large number of independent random variables approaches, under very general conditions, the normal distribution*".

This finding is known as the **central limit theorem** (CLT). CLT justifies why the normal distribution is so often encountered in practical settings, natural phenomena, and ML models as well. By the CLT, the sum up of random variables of any kind has a shape of the normal distribution. This is what the code is intended to do:

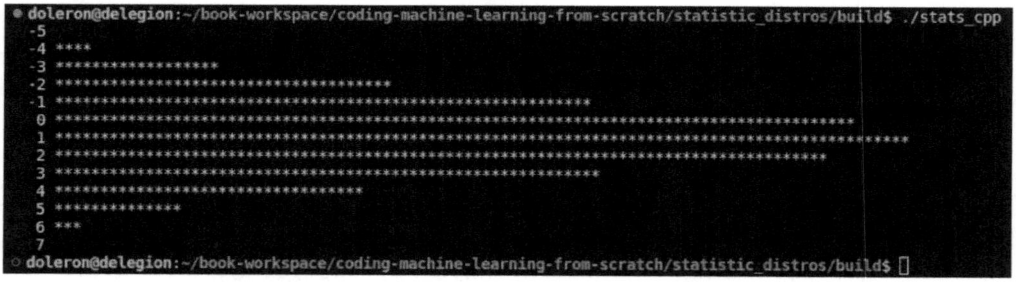

Figure 2.11: Bell-shape of a sum of uniform distributions

This simple experiment indicates that, indeed, the random package is doing what it should do, at least in terms of the central limit trend.

Due to the (pseudo) built-in random generation feature, every time we run this program, the result is slightly different. What if we need to control the randomness to get some reproducible results? In this case, we can statically set the seed:

```
1. int main(int, char**)
2. {
3.     const unsigned int seed = 1234;
4.     std::mt19937 random_generator {seed};
5.     ...
6. }
```

Now, the program outputs the same result for every execution.

It is noteworthy that the built-in statistic distributions available in the **<random>** header are designed only for random number generation. In the next chapter, we will introduce the Boost statistical package, where we can find more complete statistic distribution implementations.

Vectorization

There are two main concerns in coding anything:

- The code must provide the right output
- The code must execute fast.

Of course, it is not always possible to achieve both goals. Here we will discuss vectorization, a modern approach that allows us to get the most of the CPU resources to achieve faster algorithm executions without affecting the quality of the algorithm output.

Vectorization is a generic term referring to the capacity of some process units [10][11] to perform independent arithmetic operations in parallel, reducing the overall computation time by the number of execution units.

Note that vectorization does not provide the same type of parallelism as the one provided by threads, where different sequences of code perform in a concurrent way.

The key idea in vectorization is to execute sequential independent operations in parallel. Consider the following example:

```
1. for (int i = 0; i < 1024; i++)
2. {
3.     A[i] = A[i] + B[i];
4. }
```

A vectorization-support compiler will replace this code with something like:

```
1. for(i=0; i < 512; i += 2)
2. {
3.     A[i] = A[i] + B[i];
4.     A[i + 1] = A[i + 1] + B[i + 1];
5. }
```

If the underlying hardware (CPU) also supports vectorization, the two operations inside the loop will be executed in parallel, reducing the overall processing time by a theoretical factor of two. This is only possible because the CPU has duplicated resources, such as duplicated registers, which work like two independent execution units.

Note: In practice, there is some overhead in copying the data to parallel registers. As a result, the gain in performance when using vectorization is not always straight linear.

On hardware with four execution units, the loop will be unrolled as follows:

```
1. for(i=0; i < 256; i += 4)
2. {
3.     A[i] = A[i] + B[i];
4.     A[i + 1] = A[i + 1] + B[i + 1];
5.     A[i + 2] = A[i + 2] + B[i + 2];
6.     A[i + 3] = A[i + 3] + B[i + 3];
7. }
```

This new set of instructions results in (nearly) 4 times faster execution. Vectorization is really handy firstly because it increases the execution performance without affecting the program's output. Second, it is implemented by the compiler, operating system, and hardware without the programmer's direct interference. Thus, in general, the original source need not be modified to use vectorization. But the programmer must pay attention to some points [12]:

- It is important to make sure that the compiler has support for vectorization. Some compilers have vectorization flags that must be set to activate vectorization

- The loop boundaries must be known before the loop starts, usually by static literals, constants, or variables not affected by the loop body.

- The instructions in the loop's body should not reference a previous state. Performing things like **A[i] = A[i − 1] + B[i]** can prevent vectorization if the compiler cannot safely determine whether A[i-1] is valid during the current instruction call.

- The instructions in the body must be simple and straight-line code. Inline function calls and previously vectorized functions are also allowed. Complex logic, subroutines, nested loops, and function calls, in general, prevent vectorization from working.

Following these rules can be tricky. It is always hard to determine if the code is running in a vectorized way. One alternative is to inspect the machine code generated by the compiler, looking for the specific vectorization instructions. This is, of course, time costly and not exactly a simple task.

As a rule of thumb, a streamlined code using routines from the `<algorithm>`, `<functional>`, and `<numeric>` headers, in addition to the STL containers, is more likely to be vectorized.

Vectorization in deep learning

In real-world deep learning projects, vectorization plays an important role by reducing the overall training time or inference time. For example, during the training, subsets of the train dataset called batches are processed in a vectorized way.

Eigen, the linear algebra library used in the examples in this book, performs its matrix operations in a vectorized way. Because of this, we usually aggregate the row data into batches to achieve faster operation executions. Consider the following example:

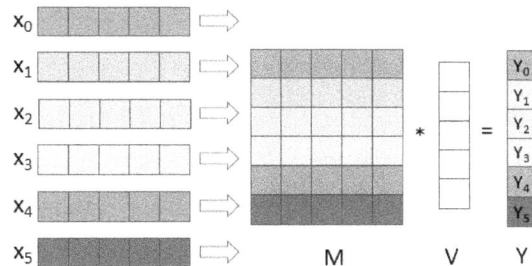

Figure 2.12: Vectorizing operations

In this example, instead of performing six individual inner products using each of the six input vectors (X_0, X_1, X_2, X_3, X_4, and X_5), we will prefer to stack them to mount a single matrix. Then, we can run a single **mulmat** multiplication to achieve the same result but in a way faster execution.

Vectorization in Eigen

Eigen has its own built-in vectorization system which is enabled by default if the compiler and the underlying hardware support vectorization. Please, check the documentation [14] to know the details of how to set up vectorization in Eigen.

Conclusion

In this chapter, we introduced some of the more relevant programming techniques and APIs to code deep learning algorithms. We discussed modern C++ features, in particular functional programming, which allow us to develop more reliable and faster code in a friendly way. Eigen, the linear algebra library for C++ used in the book examples, was introduced, and some of its features were briefly discussed. We finished the chapter talking about vectorization, listing some guidelines to code vectorizable programs to achieve faster executions.

Exercises

1. Using Eigen, write a program to flip a matrix vertically or horizontally.

2. Using Eigen, write a program to rotate a matrix by 90 degrees clockwise or counterclockwise.

3. Using lambdas, write a function to find the k-smallest numbers of an arbitrary vector of integers.

References

[1] GNU GCC, available at **https://gcc.gnu.org/**

[2] MSYS2, available at **https://www.msys2.org/**

[3] C++17, available at **https://en.cppreference.com/w/cpp/17**

[4] CMake, available at **https://cmake.org/**

[5] GNU Make, available at **https://www.gnu.org/software/make/**

[6] C++11, available at **https://en.cppreference.com/w/cpp/11**

[7] Eigen, available at **https://eigen.tuxfamily.org/**

[8] Yuval Filmus, Two Proofs of the Central Limit Theorem, available at **https://www.cs.toronto.edu/~yuvalf/CLT.pdf**

[9] A. Rényi, Probability Theory, Dover, 1970

[10] Intel Single Instruction Multiple Data, available at **https://www.intel.com/content/www/us/en/developer/articles/technical/simd-made-easy-with-intel-ispc.html**

[11] AMD Optimizing CPU Libraries, available at **https://www.amd.com/en/developer/aocl.html**

[12] Intel, Vectorization of Loops , available at **https://www.intel.com/content/www/us/en/developer/articles/technical/requirements-for-vectorizable-loops.html**

[13] Eigen coefficient-wise math functions, available at **https://eigen.tuxfamily.org/dox-3.3/group__CoeffwiseMathFunctions.html**

[14] Vectorization in Eigen, available at **https://eigen.tuxfamily.org/index.php?title=FAQ#Vectorization**

CHAPTER 3
Testing Deep Learning Code

Introduction

As with any general-purpose code, deep learning algorithms must be tested before being deployed in production. However, two main concerns make testing deep learning code more critical, namely: **high adaptability** and the **stochastic nature** commonly found in deep learning models. In this chapter, we will understand these concerns and learn how to use GoogleTest Framework and Boost statistical package to build reliable test suites for our models.

Structure

This is the chapter roadmap:

- Importance of testing deep learning code
- Stochastic nature of deep learning models
- Introducing GoogleTest Framework
- Dealing with the stochastic nature of deep learning codes
- Understanding hypothesis tests
- Test-Driven Development

Objectives

By the end of this chapter, you will understand how to test your deep learning code using the GoogleTest Framework and statistical tests. You will also know about the most important aspects that differentiate deep learning code from other traditional code from a test engineering point of view.

Importance of testing deep learning code

As pointed out in the literature[1], debugging deep learning models is not a simple task. In general, when implementing new algorithms, it is hard to determine if a poor performance was achieved due to the algorithm's inefficiency or an implementation mistake. Now, let us understand the two main sources of challenges in assessing deep learning code correctness.

High adaptability of deep learning components

One of the more noticeable challenges in developing deep learning models is that they consist of multiple small parts that are often highly adaptive. It turns out that if one component is not performing well because it has a bug, the other components can adapt to make the whole model achieve a suboptimal, but not catastrophic, performance.

Although this adaptability makes the model more robust, on the other hand, finding bugs becomes a challenging task for us, the algorithm developers. Using the proper terminology, the high adaptability of deep learning models makes their **testability**[2] harder.

The recommended approach for this issue is very straightforward and absolutely not new for software developers: we will test every single part independently or using smaller arrangements. By testing model units individually, we will be able to assess the correctness of each part without being affected by the external influence of other parts. This approach will be covered later on in this chapter.

Stochastic nature of deep learning models

One of the main concerns in deep learning is finding a suitable model to perform a specified task. This search is known as **model training**. Models are trained using a special procedure called **training algorithm**. In a nutshell, the training algorithm performs an **algorithm search**, something like walking through different paths over a multidimensional space. During this walking, the algorithm uses the information collected from the data to decide which path is more promising to follow.

In the initial stage, the training algorithm has not collected any information yet. Thus, there is no way to know a priori which path is more or less promising to go. To make the first step, the training algorithm uses a technique called **random initialization** to decide which path to go.

Random initialization is one of the randomness sources in deep learning models. In fact, randomness is broadly used as an alternative to exploring different paths during the search.

In addition to the random initialization, we can also cite:

- The shuffle of registers before the training start
- The shuffle of registers during each epoch
- The random node drops in dropout

Although randomness is useful for dealing with the spatial complexity of search spaces, it turns out that it also injects a stochastic behavior into the models, making them output values that are not a priori exactly **predictable**. This **non-deterministic behavior** makes achieving **reproducible** outputs not easy. Since **reproducibility** is a key aspect of testing [2], randomness becomes an important concern in assessing the deep learning algorithms' correctness.

Therefore, when evaluating the implementation of algorithms, we must take in mind that some features are not eligible to be tested using the traditional way, where you have an expected exact value to check against the feature's actual output. For cases like this, we will assess the code's correctness in a statistical way instead. This approach will be illustrated in this chapter.

Introducing GoogleTest Framework

At the beginning of this chapter, we talked about the importance of testing the individual model's components to reduce the drawback influence of high adaptability on testability. In software engineering, we use **unit tests** for this purpose. GoogleTest Framework [3] is a popular and mature engine for creating unit tests for C++ code. Now, we will introduce it.

We can follow the GoogleTest documentation to know how to wire up our **cmake** build:

```
1.  cmake_minimum_required(VERSION 3.8)
2.
3.  set(PROJECT_NAME googletest_example)
4.  project(${PROJECT_NAME} CXX)
5.
6.  set(CMAKE_CXX_STANDARD 17)
7.  set(CMAKE_CXX_STANDARD_REQUIRED ON)
8.  set(CMAKE_CXX_EXTENSIONS OFF)
9.
10. include_directories(include)
11.
12. option(BUILD_TESTS "Build the tests" OFF)
```

```
13.
14. if(BUILD_TESTS)
15.
16.    # using google test. See https://github.com/google/googletest/
       blob/main/docs/quickstart-cmake.md
17.
18.    include(FetchContent)
19.    FetchContent_Declare(
20.      googletest
21.      URL https://github.com/google/googletest/
       archive/03597a01ee50ed33e9dfd640b249b4be3799d395.zip
22.    )
23.    set(gtest_force_shared_crt ON CACHE BOOL "" FORCE)
24.    FetchContent_MakeAvailable(googletest)
25.
26.    enable_testing()
27.
28.    set(PROJECT_TEST_NAME test_${PROJECT_NAME})
29.
30.    file(GLOB_RECURSE TEST_SRC_FILES "${PROJECT_SOURCE_DIR}/tests/*.
       cpp" "${PROJECT_SOURCE_DIR}/src/*.cpp")
31.    add_executable(${PROJECT_TEST_NAME} ${TEST_SRC_FILES})
32.    target_compile_options(${PROJECT_TEST_
       NAME} PRIVATE -Wall -Wextra -pedantic -Wno-enum-compare -Wno-maybe-
       uninitialized -Wno-uninitialized -Wno-unused-parameter)
33.    target_link_libraries(${PROJECT_TEST_NAME} GTest::gtest_main)
34.
35.    include(GoogleTest)
36.    gtest_discover_tests(${PROJECT_TEST_NAME})
37.
38. endif()
```

The CMake configuration file above is very similar to the **CMakeList.txt** file that we used in *Chapter 2, Coding Deep Learning with Modern C++*. The difference here is only the **BUILD_TESTS** section:

```
1. option(BUILD_TESTS "Build the tests" OFF)
2.
3. if(BUILD_TESTS)
4.    ...
5. endif()
```

By default, the **BUILD_TESTS** flag is set to **OFF**. To enable tests, we must set **BUILD_TESTS** to **ON**. This can be done at runtime when calling **cmake**:

```
cmake -DBUILD_TESTS=ON ..
```

CMake will then download GoogleTest and set it up for our project. Now, let us create some tests for our models.

Coding the first unit test

Suppose that we developed the following function:

```
1. float sigmoid(float z) {
2.     float result;
3.     if (z >= 45.f)
4.         result = 1.f;
5.     else if (z <= -45.f)
6.         result = 0.f;
7.     else
8.         result = 1.f / (1.f + exp(-z));
9.     return result;
10. }
```

This function is one of the most well-known activation functions in machine learning, called the **sigmoid function**. We will introduce sigmoid and other **activation functions** later on in *Chapter 7, Defining Activation Functions*. For a while, we will consider this function just as a feature that must be tested.

Before writing the first test, let us get a better understanding of the feature to be tested. A neat way to do that is by observing the function plot:

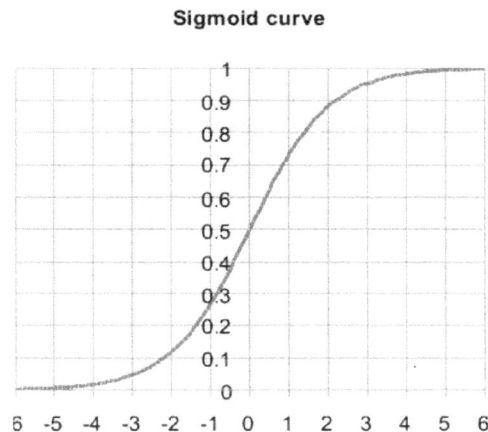

Figure 3.1: Plot of the sigmoid function

By analyzing this plot, we can realize that this function has two important limits: when $z \longrightarrow + \infty$ and when $z \longrightarrow - \infty$, which are respectively 1 and 0. Checking out the plot again, we can also figure out that **sigmoid(0) = 0.5**. We will use this information to write our first unit test:

```
1.  #include <gtest/gtest.h>
2.
3.  #include "my_functions.hpp"
4.
5.  TEST(SigmoidTest, BaseCases)
6.  {
7.    float actual = sigmoid(-100.);
8.    float expected = 0;
9.
10.  EXPECT_NEAR(actual, expected, 1e-
       7f) << "Sigmoid lower bound test failed";
11.
12.  EXPECT_NEAR(sigmoid(100.), 1., 1e-
       7f) << "Sigmoid upper bound test failed";
13.
14.  EXPECT_NEAR(sigmoid(.0), .5, 1e-
       7f) << "Sigmoid center position test failed";
15. }
```

This is a very simple test. We are using **sigmoid(z)** to calculate the value of the sigmoid function for the value **z**, and then we compare this actual output against our theoretical values. We are using the GoogleTest macro **EXPECT_NEAR** to perform this comparison. **EXPECT_NEAR** has three parameters:

- The actual value
- The expected value
- The tolerance threshold to compare float points

Due to float point precision issues present in any system, we should never directly compare float point numbers using the equality operator like in **x == 0.3018705302f**. Instead, we should use some tolerance interval such as **(x <= 0.3018705302f + epsilon) && (x >= 0.3018705302f – epsilon)**. This is what **EXPECT_NEAR** does, being **epsilon = 1e-7f** in the last example.

We can prepare our test project as follows:

```
PS Z:\book-workspace\pbp-deep-learning-in-modern-cpp> cd .\googletest_setup\
PS Z:\book-workspace\pbp-deep-learning-in-modern-cpp\googletest_setup> mkdir build


    Directory: Z:\book-workspace\pbp-deep-learning-in-modern-cpp\googletest_setup


Mode                 LastWriteTime         Length Name
----                 -------------         ------ ----
d-----        7/15/2023  10:22 AM                 build


PS Z:\book-workspace\pbp-deep-learning-in-modern-cpp\googletest_setup> cd .\build\
PS Z:\book-workspace\pbp-deep-learning-in-modern-cpp\googletest_setup\build> cmake -G "MinGW Makefiles" -DBUILD_TESTS=ON ..
-- The CXX compiler identification is GNU 13.1.0
-- Detecting CXX compiler ABI info
-- Detecting CXX compiler ABI info - done
-- Check for working CXX compiler: C:/msys64/mingw64/bin/c++.exe - skipped
-- Detecting CXX compile features
-- Detecting CXX compile features - done
CMake Warning (dev) at C:/CMake/share/cmake-3.27/Modules/FetchContent.cmake:1316 (message):
  The DOWNLOAD_EXTRACT_TIMESTAMP option was not given and policy CMP0135 is
  not set.  The policy's OLD behavior will be used.  When using a URL
  download, the timestamps of extracted files should preferably be that of
  the time of extraction, otherwise code that depends on the extracted
  contents might not be rebuilt if the URL changes.  The OLD behavior
  preserves the timestamps from the archive instead, but this is usually not
  what you want.  Update your project to the NEW behavior or specify the
  DOWNLOAD_EXTRACT_TIMESTAMP option with a value of true to avoid this
  robustness issue.
Call Stack (most recent call first):
  CMakeLists.txt:19 (FetchContent_Declare)
This warning is for project developers.  Use -Wno-dev to suppress it.


-- The C compiler identification is GNU 13.1.0
-- Detecting C compiler ABI info
-- Detecting C compiler ABI info - done
-- Check for working C compiler: C:/msys64/mingw64/bin/cc.exe - skipped
-- Detecting C compile features
-- Detecting C compile features - done
-- Found Python: C:/msys64/mingw64/bin/python3.10.exe (found version "3.10.11") found components: Interpreter
-- Configuring done (13.5s)
-- Generating done (0.2s)
-- Build files have been written to: Z:/book-workspace/pbp-deep-learning-in-modern-cpp/googletest_setup/build
PS Z:\book-workspace\pbp-deep-learning-in-modern-cpp\googletest_setup\build>
```

Figure 3.2: Using CMake to generate the project make files on Windows

Then, calling **make**:

```
PS Z:\book-workspace\pbp-deep-learning-in-modern-cpp\googletest_setup\build> make
[  9%] Building CXX object _deps/googletest-build/googletest/CMakeFiles/gtest.dir/src/gtest-all.cc.obj
[ 18%] Linking CXX static library ..\..\..\lib\libgtest.a
[ 18%] Built target gtest
[ 27%] Building CXX object _deps/googletest-build/googletest/CMakeFiles/gtest_main.dir/src/gtest_main.cc.obj
[ 36%] Linking CXX static library ..\..\..\lib\libgtest_main.a
[ 36%] Built target gtest_main
[ 45%] Building CXX object CMakeFiles/test_googletest_example.dir/src/my_functions.cpp.obj
[ 54%] Building CXX object CMakeFiles/test_googletest_example.dir/tests/test_my_functions.cpp.obj
[ 63%] Linking CXX executable test_googletest_example.exe
[ 63%] Built target test_googletest_example
[ 72%] Building CXX object _deps/googletest-build/googlemock/CMakeFiles/gmock.dir/src/gmock-all.cc.obj
[ 81%] Linking CXX static library ..\..\..\lib\libgmock.a
[ 81%] Built target gmock
[ 90%] Building CXX object _deps/googletest-build/googlemock/CMakeFiles/gmock_main.dir/src/gmock_main.cc.obj
[100%] Linking CXX static library ..\..\..\lib\libgmock_main.a
[100%] Built target gmock_main
PS Z:\book-workspace\pbp-deep-learning-in-modern-cpp\googletest_setup\build>
```

Figure 3.3: Building our tests with make

Tip: On a Windows system, we should invoke CMake as follows:

```
cmake -G "MinGW Makefiles" -DBUILD_TESTS=ON ..
```

On a Linux machine, we can invoke just by:

```
cmake -DBUILD_TESTS=ON ..
```

```
without the -G "MinGW Makefiles" flag
```

Once the project is built, we can finally run it to see the results:

```
PS Z:\book-workspace\pbp-deep-learning-in-modern-cpp\googletest_setup\build> .\test_googletest_example.exe
Running main() from Z:\book-workspace\pbp-deep-learning-in-modern-cpp\googletest_setup\build\_deps\googletest-src\googletest\src\gtest_main.cc
[==========] Running 1 test from 1 test suite.
[----------] Global test environment set-up.
[----------] 1 test from SigmoidTest
[ RUN      ] SigmoidTest.BaseCases
[       OK ] SigmoidTest.BaseCases (0 ms)
[----------] 1 test from SigmoidTest (52 ms total)

[----------] Global test environment tear-down
[==========] 1 test from 1 test suite ran. (161 ms total)
[  PASSED  ] 1 test.
PS Z:\book-workspace\pbp-deep-learning-in-modern-cpp\googletest_setup\build>
```

Figure 3.4: Running the tests

The test has been passed, which is a good thing. We can change the line:

```
1. float actual = sigmoid(-100.);
```

to:

```
1. float actual = sigmoid(-10.);
```

Run **make** again:

```
PS Z:\book-workspace\pbp-deep-learning-in-modern-cpp\googletest_setup\build> make
[ 18%] Built target gtest
[ 36%] Built target gtest_main
[ 45%] Building CXX object CMakeFiles/test_googletest_example.dir/tests/test_my_functions.cpp.obj
[ 54%] Linking CXX executable test_googletest_example.exe
[ 63%] Built target test_googletest_example
[ 81%] Built target gmock
[100%] Built target gmock_main
PS Z:\book-workspace\pbp-deep-learning-in-modern-cpp\googletest_setup\build>
```

Figure 3.5: Building our tests twice

Now, when we run the test, it results in a failure:

```
PS Z:\book-workspace\pbp-deep-learning-in-modern-cpp\googletest_setup\build> .\test_googletest_example.exe
Running main() from Z:\book-workspace\pbp-deep-learning-in-modern-cpp\googletest_setup\build\_deps\googletest-src\googletest\src\gtest_main.cc
[==========] Running 1 test from 1 test suite.
[----------] Global test environment set-up.
[----------] 1 test from SigmoidTest
[ RUN      ] SigmoidTest.BaseCases
Z:\book-workspace\pbp-deep-learning-in-modern-cpp\googletest_setup\tests\test_my_functions.cpp:11: Failure
The difference between actual and expected is 4.5397868234431371e-05, which exceeds 1e-7f, where
actual evaluates to 4.5397868234431371e-05,
expected evaluates to 0, and
1e-7f evaluates to 1.0000000116860974e-07.
Sigmoid lower bound test failed
[  FAILED  ] SigmoidTest.BaseCases (300 ms)
[----------] 1 test from SigmoidTest (364 ms total)

[----------] Global test environment tear-down
[==========] 1 test from 1 test suite ran. (424 ms total)
[  PASSED  ] 0 tests.
[  FAILED  ] 1 test, listed below:
[  FAILED  ] SigmoidTest.BaseCases

 1 FAILED TEST
PS Z:\book-workspace\pbp-deep-learning-in-modern-cpp\googletest_setup\build> ▮
```

Figure 3.6: Getting a test failure

Note: In real life, getting a test failure is not a bad thing, absolutely. It only means that the effort to write the test was rewarded by a bug identification. The real problem is when we have code without a test to check.

A test failure is always cast whether an assertive like **EXPECT_NEAR** or **EXPECT_EQ** is not met. We will learn more about them ahead.

Using EXPECT_EQ and EXPECT_THROW

Consider the following no-optimized function, which is intended to find the middle value of an unsorted array:

```cpp
1.  int find_middle(const std::vector<int> & arr) {
2.
3.      const size_t N = arr.size();
4.
5.      if (N == 0) {
6.          throw std::invalid_
    argument("cannot find the middle of an empty vector");
7.      }
8.
9.      std::vector<int> copy = arr;
10.
11.     std::sort(copy.begin(), copy.end());
12.
13.     int result = copy[N/2];
```

```
14.
15.     return result;
16.
17. }
```

This code performs basically two main operations:

- *Line 9*, making a full copy of the array and
- *Line 11*, sorting the copied array.

Indeed, the way how **find_middle()** function was implemented makes this code not very suitable for production settings. With a little bit of effort, we might figure out a leaner alternative. However, optimizing this implementation is not our concern now. At this moment, we are only interested in testing **find_middle()** as is. Let us think of two scenarios to test this function. The first case is when the array's length is odd:

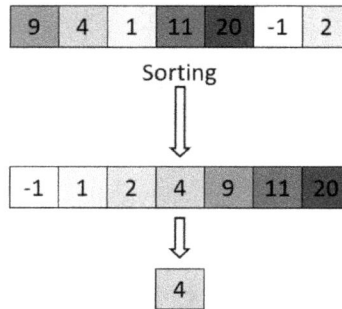

Figure 3.7: Getting the middle value of an odd-size array

Now, let us consider the case when the array length is even:

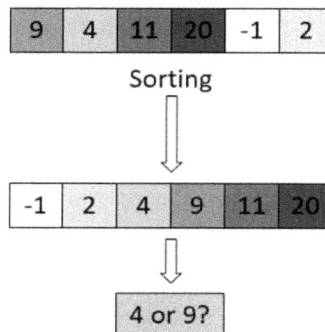

Figure 3.8: Getting the middle value of an even-size array

If the length of the array is even, we have two options to return, that is, one of the two numbers in the center of the sorted array. Our implementation of **find_middle()** uses the rightmost one. Now, it is time to write down some tests for these scenarios:

```
1.  TEST(OddCase, BaseCases)
2.  {
3.      std::vector<int> vec {9, 4, 1, 11, 20, -1, 2};
4.      int actual = find_middle(vec);
5.
6.      EXPECT_EQ(4, actual);
7.  }
8.
9.  TEST(EvenCase, BaseCases)
10. {
11.     std::vector<int> vec {9, 4, 11, 20, -1, 2};
12.     int actual = find_middle(vec);
13.
14.     EXPECT_EQ(9, actual);
15. }
16.
17. TEST(CheckEmptyVector, BaseCases)
18. {
19.
20.     EXPECT_THROW({
21.         std::vector<int> vec; // an empty vector
22.         find_middle(vec);
23.     }, std::invalid_argument);
24.
25. }
```

How does this example differ from the previous example, where we tested the sigmoid function? This example uses two assertions: **EXPECT_EQ** and **EXPECT_THROW**. The first one checks if the function provides the expected output. Note that **EXPECT_EQ** does not need a third parameter to control the float-point tolerance. Since we are comparing integer values, we do not need to worry about float-point precision issues.

The second assertion checks if the function actually throws an exception of type **invalid_argument** when an empty array is passed as a parameter. Similarly, we can use **EXPECT_NO_THROW** and **EXPECT_ANY_THROW** to check for the absence or presence of any type of exception, respectively.

Tip: The book repository on GitHub contains the example shown so far.

More examples of using GoogleTest assertions can be found in the GoogleTest repository [3] on GitHub.

Refactoring and regression test suites

Tests are particularly useful to help us check out if and how a change affects code behavior. For example, taking the **find_middle()** function from the previous section again, we can think of several ways to improve its performance in either use of memory or processing time. Improving the performance of a feature without changing its behavior is called **refactoring**.

The only way to be sure if a refactoring actually did not change the feature behavior is by running a considerable battery of tests before and after carrying out the refactoring, checking if the output was not affected. In this context, the test battery is called a **regression test suite**.

The development of deep learning algorithms is always an iterative process. In industrial development settings, regression test suites are essential to make the development team sure about code evolution or devolution. We will explore this concept later on in the exercise section.

Dealing with the stochastic nature of deep learning code

As we discussed earlier in this chapter, some of the model parameters are randomly initialized. In practice, this is implemented using some sort of random generator. There are several different approaches to performing this, but, in general, they lay down in one of two categories:

- Generating random values from a small uniform distribution
- Generating random values from a small normal distribution

Just as a refresher, this is an example of a uniform distribution:

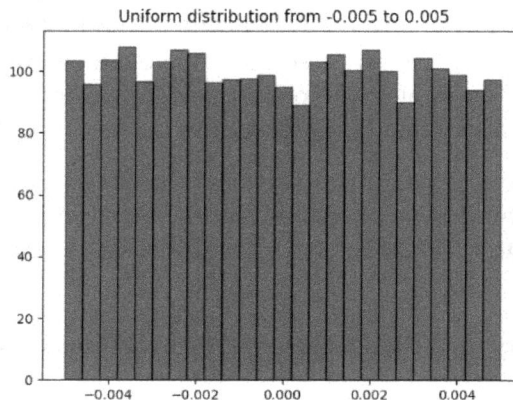

Figure 3.9: *Example of uniform distribution*

This one is an example of a normal distribution:

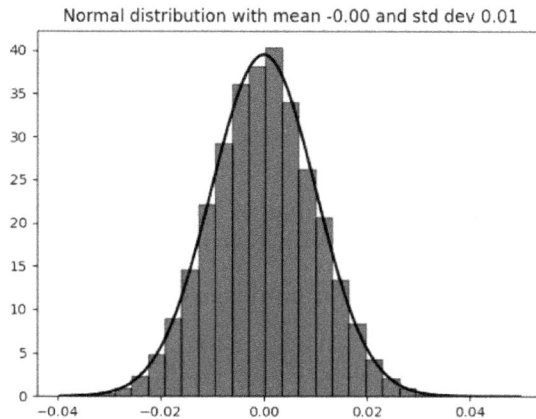

Figure 3.10: *Example of normal distribution*

The normal distribution has this well-known bell shape, whereas the uniform distribution is almost a rectangle shape.

Although the literature describes several different distributions, in practice, when coding deep learning algorithms, are uniform and normal distributions the most often found. For example, consider the **glorot_initializer** [4] as shown:

```
1.  std::vector<float> glorot_initializer(int fan_in, int fan_out) {
2.
3.      int size = fan_in * fan_out;
4.
5.      float std_dev = sqrt(2. / (fan_in + fan_out));
6.
7.      unsigned seed = std::chrono::system_clock::now().time_since_
    epoch().count();
8.      std::default_random_engine generator (seed);
9.      std::normal_distribution<float> distribution(.0, std_dev);
10.
11.     std::vector<float> result(size);
12.     std::generate(result.begin(), result.
    end(), [&generator, &distribution]
    () { return distribution(generator); });
13.
14.     return result;
15. }
```

This function generates a vector filled with random numbers. These numbers are drawn from a normal distribution with mean zero and standard deviation given by:

$$\text{std\_dev} = \frac{2}{\text{fan\_in} + \text{fan\_out}}$$

Figure 3.11: Glorot standard deviation

Looking at **glorot_initializer()**, we may wonder: since, for every call, we end up with a different vector, how can we test a function like this?

One (bad) alternative is to control the randomness **seed** like shown:

```
1.      unsigned seed = 1234;
```

This will make the random generation reproducible. Although this approach is sometimes valid for a spot evaluation, applying this to the whole test suite is a methodological mistake, violating the principle of independence between tests. In practical terms, using this approach makes our suite flawed.

The right approach for testing stochastic features is using hypothesis tests, as described in the next section.

Understanding hypothesis tests

A hypothesis test is a common and simple statistical procedure to help us identify if some data at hand supports an assumption about one or more statistical parameters. The most popular hypothesis test is the **t-test**, or **student test** [5], which is used to verify the sample mean.

In hypothesis tests, we define two mutually exclusive hypotheses:

- The NULL hypothesis: a statement about a population parameter assumed to be true.
- The alternative hypothesis, which is basically the negation of the null hypothesis

The hypothesis test establishes a routine to reject or not the null hypothesis. Note that *not reject* hypothesis differs from saying *the hypothesis is true*.

Note: The core idea in hypothesis tests is to figure out if the data carries enough evidence to reject the null hypothesis. If not, we cannot exactly say that the null hypothesis is true, only that there is no evidence that it is false.

Thus, the output of a hypothesis test is one of the following alternatives:

- The NULL hypothesis was rejected
- The NULL hypothesis was not rejected

A non-rejected NULL hypothesis does not mean a true NULL hypothesis. In practice, we can use enough data and fair confidence intervals to make the test as reliable as possible. Let us see how to use it to validate the **glorot_initializer()** function.

Using hypothesis tests to check the Glorot initializer

We will proceed with two hypothesis tests to check **glorot_initializer()**. The first one will propose the following NULL hypothesis:

- The standard deviation of the resulting weights is **std_dev = sqrt(2 / (fan_in + fan_out))**

Once we find that this hypothesis was not rejected, we can carry out a second hypothesis test, checking the following hypothesis:

- The resulting weights' mean is zero

The idea is to automate these hypothesis tests using GoogleTest unit tests, as shown ahead.

Checking the data standard deviation and mean

The most popular statistical test to examine standard deviations is the **chi-square test** [5]. One of the requirements for running a test like this is to know how to calculate **Probability Density Functions** (**PDFs**). As discussed before, C++ has no built-in implementation of these PDFs (and should not have one). Thus, we end up with two options: implementing these PDFs ourselves or using a third-party library. Let us take the latter approach, using Boost statistical headers [6]:

```
1.  #include <boost/math/distributions/chi_squared.hpp>
2.  #include <boost/math/distributions/students_t.hpp>
3.
4.  using namespace boost::math;
5.
6.  /**
7.   * The NULL hypothesis states sample_std eq population_std
8.   *
9.   * This function returns true if the NULL hypothesis was rejected
10. */
11. bool chi_squared_test(float population_std, float sample_
    std, int sample_size, float confidence)
12. {
13.     float variance_rate = sample_std / population_std;
```

```
14.     variance_rate = variance_rate * variance_rate;
15.     float t_stat = (sample_size - 1) * variance_rate;
16.
17.     chi_squared distro(sample_size - 1);
18.
19.     float upper_limit = quantile(complement(distro, confidence / 2));
20.     float lower_limit = quantile(distro, confidence / 2);
21.
22.     return t_stat > upper_limit && t_stat < lower_limit;
23.
24. }
```

The function above implements the chi-squared test. The inputs are:

- The population standard deviation
- The sample standard deviation
- The sample size
- A threshold coefficient, usually set to 0.05

This function checks if the sample standard deviation and the population standard deviation are equivalent in a statistical way, taking the provided confidence level. This function results **true** when the NULL hypothesis was **REJECTED**.

Similarly, we can check the sample mean and population mean using the t-test:

```
1.  /**
2.   * The NULL hypothesis states sample_mean eq population_mean
3.   *
4.   * This function returns true if the NULL hypothesis was rejected
5.   */
6.  bool t_test(float population_mean, float sample_mean, float sample_std_
    dev, int sample_size, float confidence)
7.  {
8.      float diff = sample_mean - population_mean;
9.
10.     float t_stat = diff * sqrt(double(sample_size)) / sample_std_dev;
11.
12.     unsigned degree_of_freedom = sample_size - 1;
13.     students_t distro(degree_of_freedom);
14.     float q = cdf(complement(distro, fabs(t_stat)));
15.
```

```
16.     float confidence _2 = confidence / 2.;
17.
18.     return q < confidence _2;
19.
20. }
```

Once we have the two tests at hand, we can define a unit test with GoogleTest to check both the standard deviation and mean given by our **glorot_initializer()** implementation:

```
1.  TEST(CheckGlorot, StatCases)
2.  {
3.      int fan_in = 6;
4.      int fan_out = 5;
5.
6.      auto weigths = glorot_initializer(fan_in, fan_out);
7.
8.      const int N = weigths.size();
9.
10.     EXPECT_EQ(N, fan_in * fan_out);
11.
12.     float sum = std::accumulate(weigths.begin(), weigths.end(), 0.0);
13.     float weight_mean =  sum / N;
14.
15.     float acc = 0.0;
16.
17.     auto differ = [&acc, &weight_mean](const float val) {
18.         const float diff = val - weight_mean;
19.         acc += diff * diff;
20.     };
21.
22.     std::for_each(weigths.begin(), weigths.end(), differ);
23.
24.     float actual_stdev = sqrt(acc / (N - 1));
25.
26.     float expected_stddev = sqrt(2. / (fan_in + fan_out));
27.
28.     bool std_dev_rejected = chi_squared_test(expected_
    stddev, actual_stdev, N, 0.05);
29.
```

```
30.    if (std_dev_rejected) {
31.        FAIL() << "The weights standard devia-
   tion do not look like expected by the Glorot initializer";
32.    }
33.
34.    bool mean_rejected = t_test(0., weight_mean, actual_
   stdev, N, 0.05);
35.
36.    if (mean_rejected) {
37.        FAIL() << "The weights mean do not look like expect-
   ed by the Glorot initializer";
38.    }
39.
40. }
```

After building and running, we get the following output:

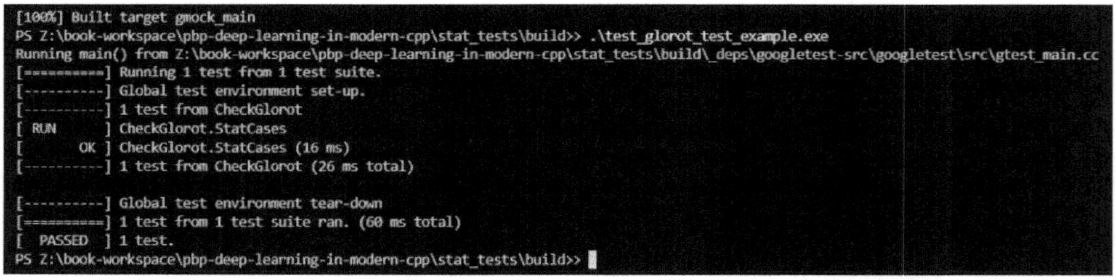

Figure 3.12: *Running the Glorot initializer tests*

Different statistical distributions require different statistical tests. In general, the same hypothesis test framework is used. The two differences are the way how the **t_test** statistic and the critical limits are calculated.

Test-Driven Development

At this point, it is clear that tests play a very critical aspect in deep learning development. Some people take tests so seriously that they put them at the top of the development process. **TDD**, an acronym for **Test-Driven Development** [7], is a set of practices to implement this concept.

In a nutshell, using TDD to develop deep learning algorithms consists of four stages:

1. **Conceptual understanding**: The team learns the theoretical basis, literature, and benchmarks.

2. **Unit test implementation**: Developers code the unit tests to validate what and how the algorithm must behave. Since the algorithm itself is not implemented yet, the tests will fail at the beginning. This step consists basically in converting the theoretical requirements into software.

3. **Algorithm implementation**: The algorithm is implemented by having the tests as a reference. The objective is to develop a mass of code that meet the established precise requirements in the tests.

4. **Refactoring**: Once the algorithm implementation passes all the tests, the development team can concentrate the efforts on making improvements and optimizations.

The process is depicted pictorially in the following figure:

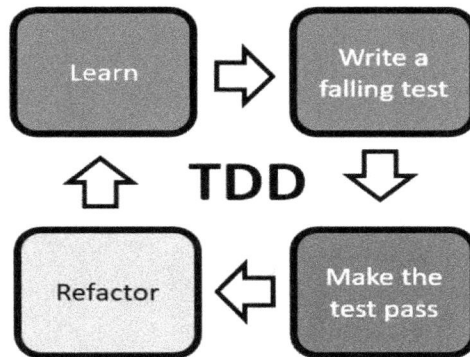

Figure 3.13: TDD cycle

Every day it is more common to find ML development teams using TDD as a methodology, regardless of the maturity or incipience of the business on top of them.

Conclusion

In this chapter, we discussed the importance of tests in the development of deep learning algorithms. We discussed that evaluating deep learning code is strongly affected by the high adaptability of its components, an aspect that makes identifying bugs a challenge. We learned how to use GoogleTest Framework to build unit tests to approach this issue.

In addition, we talked about the influence of randomness in deep learning code and how this aspect makes writing reproducible tests hard. We introduced the technique of hypothesis testing to overcome this issue, writing robust, reproducible test batteries.

In the next chapter, we will begin the second part of this book, where we learn how to implement deep learning components, such as convolutions and activation functions.

Exercises

1. Consider the following example of a popular activation function called ReLU:

$$\text{ReLU}(z) = \begin{cases} z, \text{ if } z > 0 \\ 0, \text{ otherwise} \end{cases}$$

Figure 3.14: ReLU activation function

Now, consider the following implementation:

```
1. float ReLU(float z)
2. {
3.     return (z > 0.f) ? z : 0.f;
4. }
```

Draw a plot of ReLU and write a test to check if the implementation above is actually correct.

2. Consider the function **find_middle()** as follows:

```
1.  int find_middle(const std::vector<int> & arr) {
2.
3.      const size_t N = arr.size();
4.
5.      if (N == 0) {
6.          throw std::invalid_
    argument("cannot find the median of an empty vector");
7.      }
8.
9.      std::vector<int> copy = arr;
10.
11.     std::sort(copy.begin(), copy.end());
12.
13.     int result = copy[N/2];
14.
15.     if (N % 2 == 0) {
16.         result += copy[(N - 1)/2];
17.         result /= 2;
18.     }
19.
20.     return result;
21.
22. }
```

Since we are making a full copy of the vector at *line 9*, the implementation above has a space complexity of O(N). The sorting step at *line 11* makes this function cost at least O(N log N) in terms of time.

Is it possible to improve these computational costs? If so, refactor **find_middle()** to achieve it. Think of the necessary tests to guarantee the correctness of the new version, applying the same tests for both implementations.

3. Consider the following weight initializer:

```
1.  std::vector<float> uniform_
    initializer(int size, float from, float to) {
2.
3.      unsigned seed = std::chrono::system_clock::now().time_since_
    epoch().count();
4.      std::default_random_engine generator (seed);
5.      std::uniform_real_
    distribution<double><float> distribution(from, to);
6.
7.      std::vector<float> result(size);
8.      std::generate(result.begin(), result.
    end(), [&generator, &distribution]
    () { return distribution(generator); });
9.
10.     return result;
11. }
```

Using Boost, write a statistical test to check this implementation.

References

[1] Goodfellow, Bengio & Courville, Deep Learning, MIT Press, 2016.

[2] Pezzè & Young, Software Testing and Analysis, Wiley, 2007.

[3] GoogleTest Framework, available at **https://github.com/google/googletest**

[4] Glorot & Bengio, Understanding the difficulty of training deep feedforward neural networks, Proceedings of Machine Learning Research, 2010.

[5] John Mandel, The statistical Analysis of Experimental Data, John Wiley & Sons, 1964

[6] Boost statistical distributions, available at **https://www.boost.org/doc/libs/1_79_0/libs/math/doc/html/dist.html**

[7] Kent Beck, Test-Driven Development by Example, Addison Wesley, 2002.

Join our book's Discord space

Join the book's Discord Workspace for Latest updates, Offers, Tech happenings around the world, New Release and Sessions with the Authors:

https://discord.bpbonline.com

CHAPTER 4

Implementing Convolutions

Introduction

Convolutions are the most iconic operation of deep learning. They are the core component of every high-performing modern ML system, allowing us to build massive pattern recognition systems that exceed human performance in a variety of complex tasks. In this chapter, we will introduce this operation, implementing the algorithm from scratch or using the Eigen Tensor API.

Structure

The roadmap of this chapter is as follows:

- Introduction to convolutions
- Implementing 2D convolutions
- Using padding
- Detecting edges in an image
- Implementing convolutions using tensors
- Using tensors in C++
- Tensor convolutions

- Strides
- Padding using Eigen Tensor API

Objectives

By the end of this chapter, you will be able to implement 2D convolutions by coding them from scratch or using the Eigen Tensor API. You will understand must-to-know concepts such as padding and strides. Finally, you will also know how convolutions are used to perform complex pattern recognition tasks.

Introduction to convolutions

In the deep learning domain, convolutions [1] are binary operations computed using two grid-like operands called **tensors**. The result of a convolution is a tensor as well. A good way to start with convolutions is by using matrices. Check out the following example (*Figure 4.1* and *Figure 4.2*), where we perform the convolution of a 6x6 input matrix by a 3x3 kernel to generate a 4x4 output matrix:

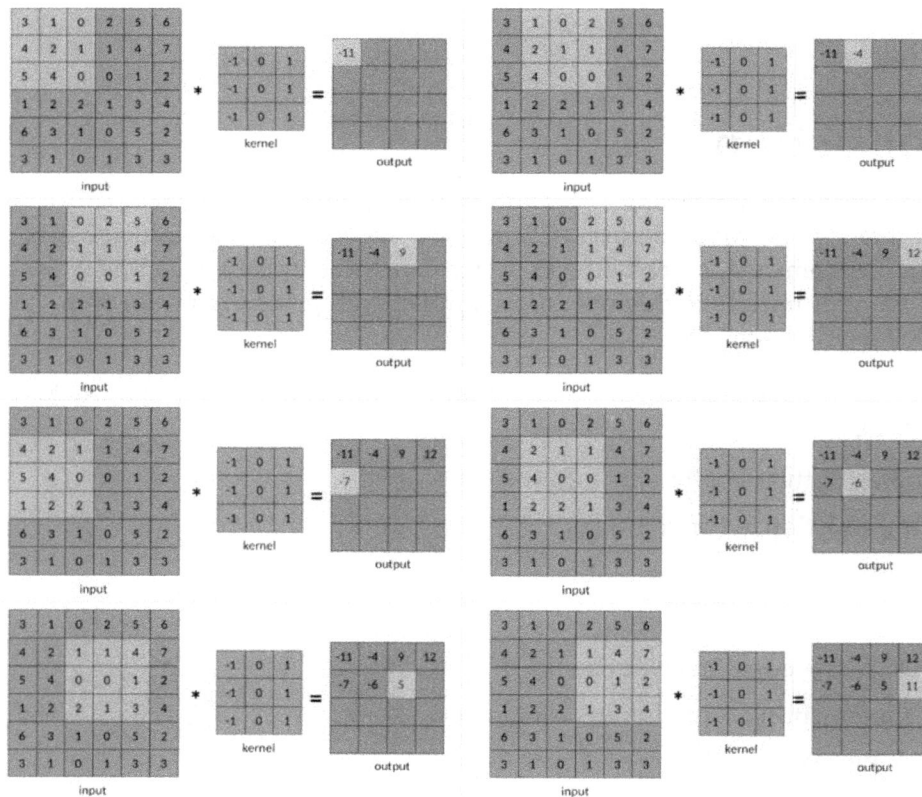

Figure 4.1: Computing the convolution (part 1)

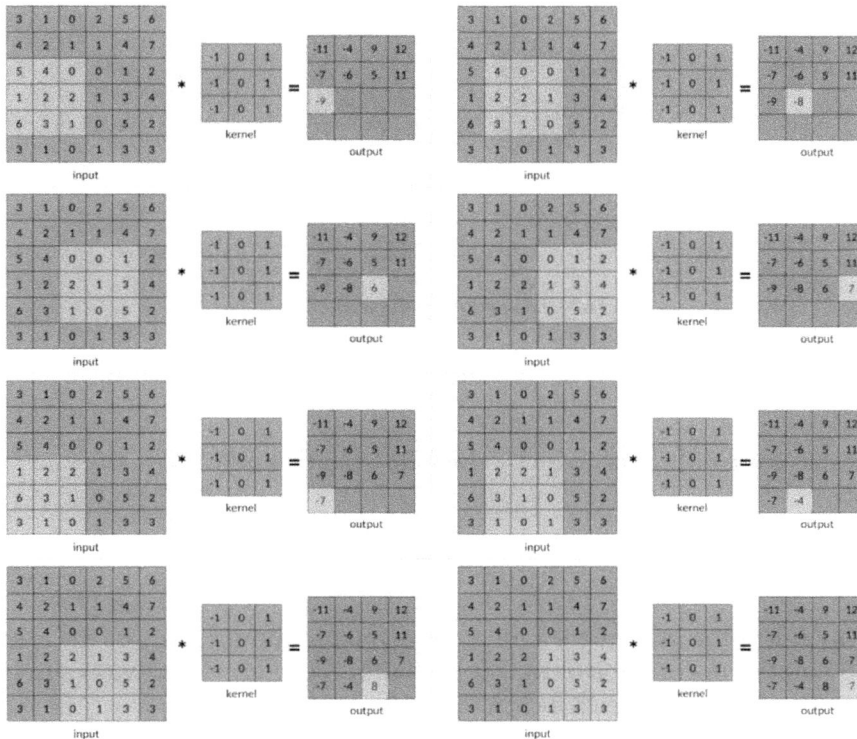

Figure 4.2: Computing the convolution (part 2)

Since matrices are 2D grids, this type of convolution is usually called **2D convolution**. In this mode, the **kernel** slides over the **input** matrix to generate the **output** matrix [3].

The example illustrates the mechanics of convolution. In each step, we calculate the **dot product** between the kernel and the respective region of the input matrix to obtain one coefficient of the output matrix.

In simple words, each coefficient of the output matrix is given by the sum of the coefficient-wise multiplication between the kernel and the respective sub-region from the input matrix [2]. In the example, the coefficient (0,0) of the output matrix is found as follows:

```
3x-1 + 1x0 + 0x1 + 4x-1 + 2x0 + 1x1 + 5x-1 + 4x0 + 0x1 = -11
```

Figure 4.3: Computing the coefficient (0,0)

The coefficient (1,1) is given by:

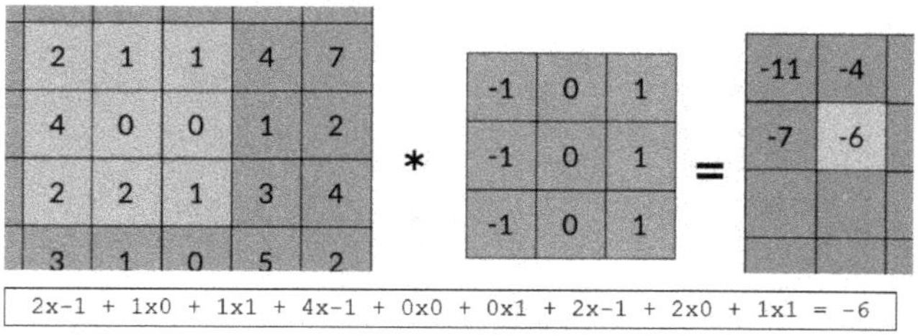

2x−1 + 1x0 + 1x1 + 4x−1 + 0x0 + 0x1 + 2x−1 + 2x0 + 1x1 = −6

Figure 4.4: Computing the coefficient (1,1)

The convolution finishes when all output matrix coefficients have been computed as described above.

The dimension of the output is given by the following formula:

$$\text{dim(Output)} = (m - k + 1, n - k + 1)$$

Figure 4.5: Calculating the output dimensions

In this formula, **k** is the side of the kernel, **m** is the number of rows of the input matrix, and **n** is the number of columns of the input matrix. The kernel is always squared, and **k** is often a small, odd number such as 3, 5, 7, or 11.

Note: As pointed out in [3], there is some controversy around the usage of the term convolution in ML. In fact, in mathematics and signal processing terminology, convolution is a little bit different operation, being the operation used in CNNs more appropriately identified as cross-correlation. In spite of this, the machine learning community uses the term convolution to represent the operation described in this chapter.

Implementing 2D convolutions

There are different ways to implement convolutions, each one with its pros and cons in terms of computational cost and numeric stability. Let us start with a straightforward approach using regular for loops:

```
1.  auto Conv_2D = [](const Eigen::MatrixXd& X, const Eigen::MatrixXd&
    K)
2.  {
3.      const int k_rows = K.rows();
4.      const int k_cols = K.cols();
5.      const int rows = (X.rows() - k_rows) + 1;
6.      const int cols = (X.cols() - k_cols) + 1;
7.
```

```
8.      Eigen::MatrixXd res = Eigen::MatrixXd::Zero(rows, cols);
9.
10.     for (int i = 0; i < rows; ++i)
11.     {
12.         for (int j = 0; j < cols; ++j)
13.         {
14.             double sum = X.block(i, j, k_rows, k_cols).
    cwiseProduct(K).sum();
15.             res(i, j) = sum;
16.         }
17.     }
18.
19.     return res;
20. };
```

This is our very first version of convolutions. As described earlier, we slide the kernel over the input matrix, performing the **dot product** between the kernel coefficients and the respective region from the input matrix.

Let us invoke our **Conv_2D** function to analyze the results:

```
1.  auto Conv_2D = ...;
2.
3.  int main(int, char **)
4.  {
5.      Eigen::MatrixXd K(3, 3);
6.      K <<
7.          -1, 0, 1,
8.          -1, 0, 1,
9.          -1, 0, 1;
10.
11.     Eigen::MatrixXd X(6, 6);
12.     X << 3, 1, 0, 2, 5, 6,
13.          4, 2, 1, 1, 4, 7,
14.          5, 4, 0, 0, 1, 2,
15.          1, 2, 2, 1, 3, 4,
16.          6, 3, 1, 0, 5, 2,
17.          3, 1, 0, 1, 3, 3;
18.
19.     auto out = Conv_2D(X, K);
20.
21.     std::cout << "Kernel:\n" << K << "\n\n";
```

```
22.     std::cout << "Input:\n" << X << "\n\n";
23.     std::cout << "Convolution:\n" << out << "\n";
24.
25.     return 0;
26. }
```

The above-mentioned code outputs the following result:

Figure 4.6: *Invoking Conv_2D*

At least so far, the code outputs the expected result. An important detail to point out in the examples so far in this book is that the output matrix is always smaller than the input. This reduction is sometimes not ideal. **Padding** can be used to avoid this behavior.

Using padding

We can avoid the output matrix reduction by using blank artificial coefficients around the input matrix:

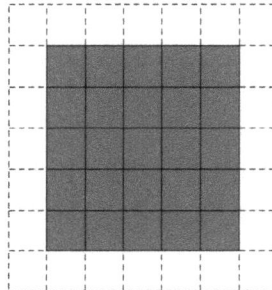

Figure 4.7: *Using padding*

This approach is called **padding**. Convolutions like this are called **padded convolutions**. When the convolution uses padding in a way that results in a matrix with exactly the same dimensions as the input matrix, we call it **SAME padding**. The original zero padding convolution, that is, a convolution in which the output is smaller than the input, is called a **VALID convolution**.

The following figure is an example of SAME padding convolution:

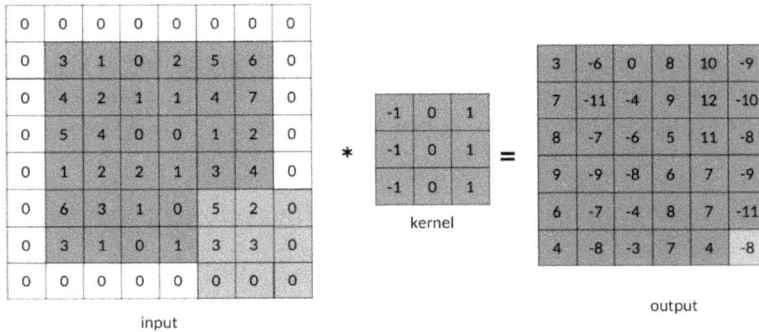

Figure 4.8: SAME padding

Implementing padding requires a little bit of work. Consider the following very first and naive version of padded convolutions:

```
1.  auto naive_Padded_Conv_2D = [](const Eigen::MatrixXd&
    X, const Eigen::MatrixXd& K, int padding)
2.  {
3.      int K_rows = K.rows();
4.      int K_cols = K.cols();
5.      int rows = X.rows() - K_rows + 2*padding + 1;
6.      int cols = X.cols() - K_cols + 2*padding + 1;
7.
8.      Eigen::MatrixXd pad = Eigen::MatrixXd::Zero(X.
    rows() + 2*padding, X.cols() + 2*padding);
9.      pad.block(padding, padding, X.rows(), X.cols()) = X;
10.
11.     Eigen::MatrixXd res = Eigen::MatrixXd::Zero(rows, cols);
12.
13.     for(int i = 0; i < rows; ++i)
14.     {
15.         for(int j = 0; j < cols; ++j)
16.         {
17.             double sum = pad.block(i, j, K_rows, K_cols).
```

```
            cwiseProduct(K).sum();
18.              res(i, j) = sum;
19.          }
20.      }
21.
22.      return res;
23. };
```

Although this code actually does the job, there are some memory concerns that must be approached before we can move ahead. The main issue here is in *lines 8* and *9*, where we have spent a lot of memory to make a larger blank matrix to hold the data in the padded area.

A better implementation can use indices to control the padding behavior:

```
1.  auto Padded_Conv2D = [](const Eigen::MatrixXd&
    X, const Eigen::MatrixXd& K, int padding)
2.  {
3.      const int X_rows = X.rows();
4.      const int X_cols = X.cols();
5.      const int K_rows = K.rows();
6.      const int K_cols = K.cols();
7.
8.      if (X_rows < K_rows) throw std::invalid_
    argument("The input has less rows than the kernel");
9.      if (X_cols < K_cols) throw std::invalid_
    argument("The input has less columns than the kernel");
10.
11.     const int rows = X_rows - K_rows + 2*padding + 1;
12.     const int cols = X_cols - K_cols + 2*padding + 1;
13.
14.     auto fitting_dims = [&padding](int pos, int k, int length)
15.     {
16.         int input = pos - padding;
17.         int kernel = 0;
18.         int size = k;
19.         if (input < 0)
20.         {
21.             kernel = -input;
22.             size += input;
23.             input = 0;
```

```
24.          }
25.          if (input + size > length)
26.          {
27.              size = length - input;
28.          }
29.          return std::make_tuple(input, kernel, size);
30.      };
31.
32.      Eigen::MatrixXd res = Eigen::MatrixXd::Zero(rows, cols);
33.
34.      for(int i = 0; i < rows; ++i)
35.      {
36.          const auto [input_i, kernel_i, size_i] = fitting _dims(i, K_
    rows, X_rows);
37.          for(int j = 0; size_i > 0 && j < cols; ++j)
38.          {
39.              const auto [input_j, kernel_j, size_j] = fitting _
    dims(j, K_cols, X_cols);
40.              if (size_j > 0)
41.              {
42.                  auto input_roi = X.
    block(input_i, input_j, size_i, size_j);
43.                  auto in_kernel = K.
    block(kernel_i, kernel_j, size_i, size_j);
44.                  result(i, j) = input_roi.cwiseProduct(in_kernel).
    sum();
45.              }
46.          }
47.      }
48.      return res;
49. };
```

This new (in-place) version of the padded 2D convolution is way better since we are not allocating another matrix to control the padding. Let us see it working in action:

```
1.  auto Padded_Conv_2D = ...;
2.
3.  int main(int, char **)
4.  {
5.      Eigen::MatrixXd K(3, 3);
```

```
6.      K <<
7.          -1, 0, 1,
8.          -1, 0, 1,
9.          -1, 0, 1;
10.
11.     Eigen::MatrixXd X(6, 6);
12.     X <<
13.         3, 1, 0, 2, 5, 6,
14.         4, 2, 1, 1, 4, 7,
15.         5, 4, 0, 0, 1, 2,
16.         1, 2, 2, 1, 3, 4,
17.         6, 3, 1, 0, 5, 2,
18.         3, 1, 0, 1, 3, 3;
19.
20.         auto out = Padded_Conv_2D(X, K, 1);
21.
22.         std::cout << "Kernel:\n" << K << "\n\n";
23.         std::cout << "Input:\n" << X << "\n\n";
24.         std::cout << "Convolution:\n" << out << "\n";
25.
26.         return 0;
27. }
```

This code outputs the following result:

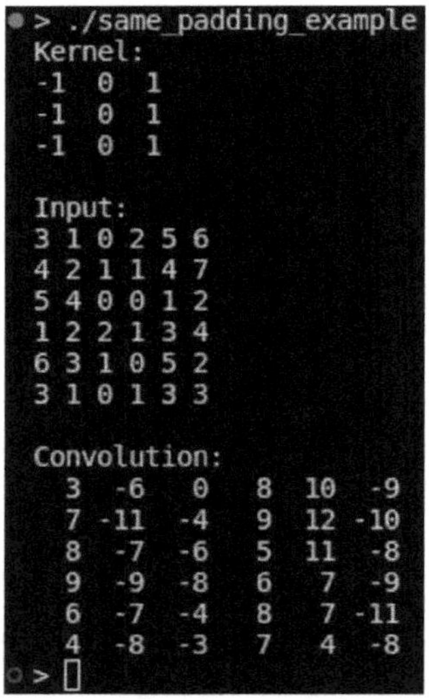

Figure 4.9: Running the SAME padding example

Now, using the SAME padding, we can note that both input and output matrices have the same size.

At this point, one can wonder how convolutions can solve so many complex problems. Indeed, despite being a very simple operation, convolutions are extremely powerful. Let us use them to detect features in an image automatically.

Using OpenCV in deep learning

Many of the examples discussed in this book use images to feed deep learning models. The use of images as data sources plays a central role in ML, having its own field called **computer vision**.

OpenCV [6] is an open-source library that provides a vast and powerful set of computer vision algorithms. However, in this book, we use OpenCV only to perform simple tasks such as loading images, writing images, rotations, blur, and color transformations.

The following example shows how to use OpenCV to load a colored image and then rotate, convert it to grayscale, and store it locally:

```
1.  #include <opencv2/opencv.hpp>
2.
3.  int main(int, char **) {
4.
5.      cv::Mat source = cv::imread("../leds.jpg", cv::IMREAD_COLOR);
6.
7.      cv::Mat rotated, gray;
8.      cv::rotate(source, rotated, cv::ROTATE_90_CLOCKWISE);
9.      cv::cvtColor(rotated, gray, cv::COLOR_BGR2GRAY);
10.
11.     cv::imshow("source", source);
12.     cv::imshow("rotated", rotated);
13.     cv::imshow("gray", gray);
14.
15.     cv::imwrite("leds_rot.jpg", gray);
16.
17.     cv::waitKey();
18.
19.     return 0;
20.
21. }
```

Once executed, this program outputs the following result:

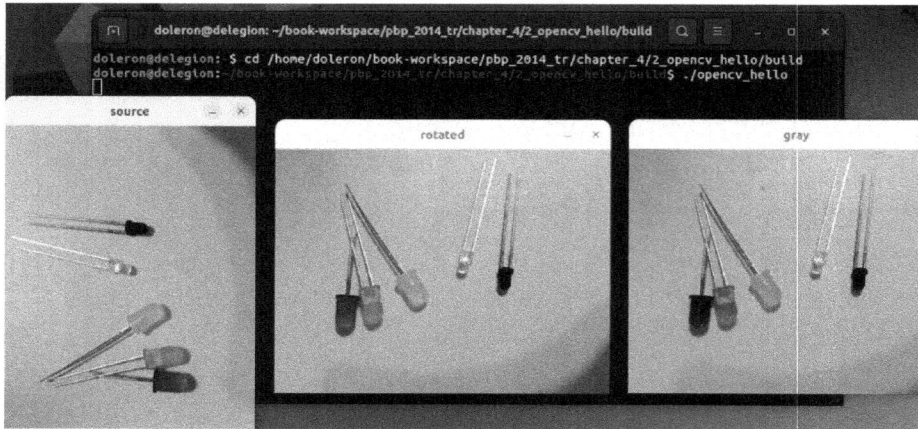

Figure 4.10: *Simple OpenCV example*

Unlike Eigen, OpenCV must be installed in the host operating system. The way to install OpenCV varies by operation systems, compilers, and language support. We recommend checking the OpenCV documentation to know how to install OpenCV in your system properly.

Detecting edges in an image

Consider the following example of applying convolutions to an image:

```
1.  #include <opencv2/opencv.hpp>

2.  #include <opencv2/core/eigen.hpp>

3.

4.  int main(int, char **) {

5.

6.      auto Padded_Conv2D = [](const Eigen::MatrixXd&
    X, const Eigen::MatrixXd& K, int padding){

7.          // ...

8.      };

9.

10.     Eigen::MatrixXd G_x(3, 3), Gy(3, 3);

11.

12.     G_x <<

13.         1., 0., -1.,

14.         2., 0., -2.,

15.         1., 0., -1.;
```

```
16.
17.     G_y <<
18.         1., 2., 1.,
19.         0., 0., 0.,
20.         -1., -2., -1.;
21.
22.     cv::Mat src = cv::imread("../chess.jpg", cv::IMREAD_COLOR);
23.     cv::Mat img;
24.     cv::cvtColor(src, img, cv::COLOR_BGR2GRAY);
25.     Eigen::MatrixXd X;
26.     cv::cv2eigen(img, X);
27.
28.     const int padding = (G_x.rows() - 1) / 2;
29.     auto G_x_conv = Padded_Conv2D(X, G_x, padding);
30.     auto G_y_conv = Padded_Conv2D(X, G_y, padding);
31.
32.     cv::Mat temp, G_x_res, G_y_res;
33.
34.     cv::eigen2cv(G_x_conv, temp);
35.     temp.convertTo(G_x_res, CV_8UC1);
36.
37.     cv::eigen2cv(G_y_conv, temp);
38.     temp.convertTo(G_y_res, CV_8UC1);
39.
40.     cv::imshow("source", src);
41.     cv::imshow("gray scale", img);
42.     cv::imshow("applying Gx", G_x_res);
43.     cv::imshow("applying Gy", G_y_res);
44.
45.     cv::waitKey();
46.
47.     return 0;
48.
49. }
```

This code uses two famous kernels called Sobel Gx and Gy [4]:

1	0	-1
2	0	-2
1	0	-1

1	2	1
0	0	0
-1	-2	-1

Figure 4.11: Sobel's kernels

The Sobel's kernels are able to capture the vertical and horizontal edges in a grayscale image, as shown in the following figures:

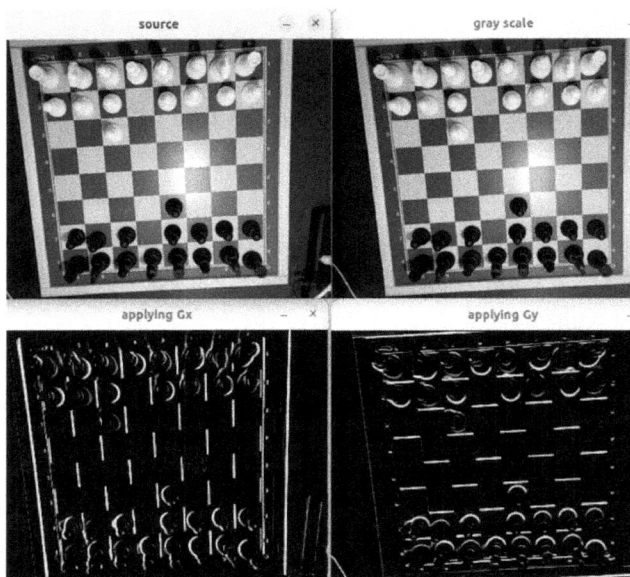

Figure 4.12: Vertical and horizontal edge detection

Verticals or horizontals, edges are **features** representing the object boundaries. In fact, images have several different types of features, such as **textures** and **shapes**. These features are intuitively captured by our eyes and brain, generating the semantic objects that we deal with in daily life.

What Sobel's kernel example suggests is that, in addition to living beings, convolutions can also detect features from images. This finding raises two important questions:

- Which kernel should we use to detect a feature?
- Which feature is relevant to detect a pattern, for example, a human face?

The motivation behind ML is to answer questions like this by using an autonomous procedure called **model training**. As discussed in forthcoming chapters, we will develop reliable training routines to identify the kernels given a training dataset automatically.

Implementing convolutions using tensors

So far, we have run convolutions using matrices. In this section, we will introduce a very important concept for deep learning programming: tensors.

Tensors [3] are grid-like data structures that generalize the concept of vectors and matrices for an arbitrary number of axes. The following figure shows different examples of tensors with different ranks:

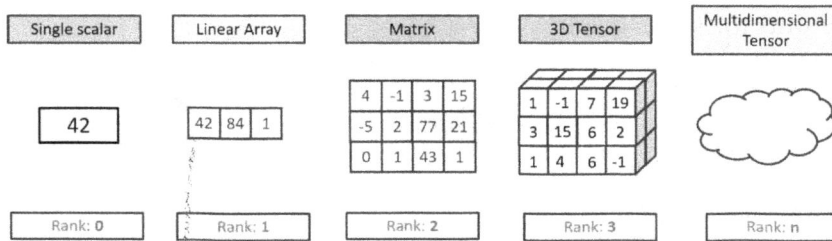

Figure 4.13: *Examples of tensors with different ranks*

In real life, tensors are the primary way to represent data in deep learning algorithms. From this point on, we will be using tensors whenever possible in our deep learning code.

Using tensors in C++

In the same way as with matrices, C++ does not have a built-in tensor implementation. Luckily, Eigen, the matrix library that we are using so far, has a tensor module [5]. Check the following example of how to use it:

```
1.  #include <unsupported/Eigen/CXX11/Tensor>
2.
3.  int main(int, char **)
4.  {
5.
6.      // allocating a 3-Rank tensor
7.      Eigen::Tensor<int, 3> my_tensor(2, 3, 4);
8.
9.      // setting up all coefficients to 42
10.     my_tensor.setConstant(42);
11.
12.     std::cout <<
13.         "my_tensor:\n\n" << my_tensor
14.         << "\n\n";
```

```
15.
16.     std::cout <<
17.         "tensor size is " << my_tensor.size()
18.         << "\n\n";
19.
20.     return 0;
21. }
```

This code outputs the given result:

Figure 4.14: Running the tensor example

The line:

```
1.     Eigen::Tensor<int, 3> my_tensor(2, 3, 4);
```

Defines and allocates the required memory to hold a three-dimensional tensor object:

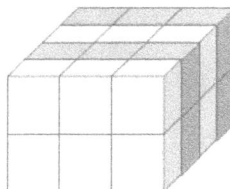

```
my_tensor
```

Figure 4.15: A 3-rank tensor object with 24 coefficients

Since the dimensions are 2, 3, and 4, the tensor holds **2 x 3 x 4 = 24** memory positions. Each position is called a **coefficient**.

Tip: We recommend you read the tensor module documentation [5] to learn more about how to initialize and use tensors in Eigen.

The Eigen Tensor Module is one of the most widely adopted <unsupported/Eigen> features. According to the Eigen Gitlab repository logs, the maintainers' team is continuously working to fix and improve this module used in the core part of Google's TensorFlow framework and several other libraries and systems.

Tensor convolutions

So far, we have implemented our own version of convolution. However, the Eigen Tensor module has a handy built-in implementation ready for usage. Check out the following example:

```
1.  Eigen::Tensor<float, 4> X(1, 6, 6, 3);
2.  X.setRandom();
3.
4.  std::cout << "input dims:\n\n" << X << "\n\n";
5.
6.  Eigen::Tensor<float, 2> K(3, 3);
7.  K.setRandom();
8.
9.  std::cout << "kernel dims:\n\n" << K << "\n\n";
10.
11. Eigen::Tensor<float, 4> out(1, 4, 4, 3);
12.
13. Eigen::array<int, 2> dim({1, 2});
14. out = X.convolve(K, dim);
15.
16. std::cout << "output dims:\n\n" << out << "\n\n";
```

This code generates the following output:

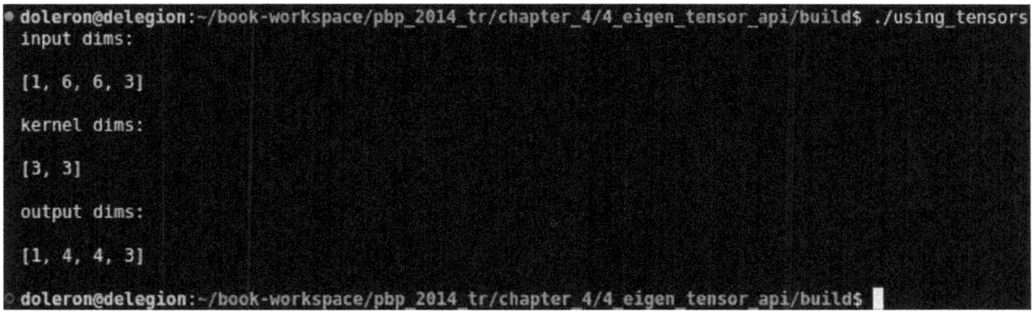

Figure 4.16: Using tensor convolutions in Eigen

The Eigen Tensor API allows us to use more complex convolutions, such as stride, padding, dilatations, etc. The following section introduces some of these features.

Strides

Strides are a common feature found in tensor code, providing a reduced view of the original tensor. Strides work by **skipping** some elements by a preset number, which is called a **stride**. Check out the following example:

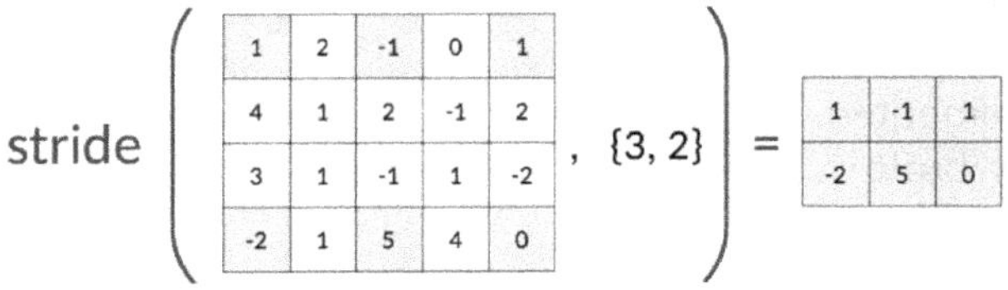

$$
\text{stride}\left(\begin{array}{|c|c|c|c|c|}
\hline 1 & 2 & -1 & 0 & 1 \\
\hline 4 & 1 & 2 & -1 & 2 \\
\hline 3 & 1 & -1 & 1 & -2 \\
\hline -2 & 1 & 5 & 4 & 0 \\
\hline
\end{array}, \{3, 2\}\right) = \begin{array}{|c|c|c|}
\hline 1 & -1 & 1 \\
\hline -2 & 5 & 0 \\
\hline
\end{array}
$$

Figure 4.17: *Using strides*

We can use strides with Eigen as follows:

```
1.  int main() {
2.      Eigen::Tensor<int, 2> A(4, 5);
3.      A.setValues({
4.          {1, 2, -1, 0, 1},
5.          {4, 1, 2, -1, 2},
6.          {3, 1, -1, 1, -2},
7.          {-2, 1, 5, 4, 0}
8.      });
9.
10.     Eigen::array<Eigen::DenseIndex, 2> strides({3, 2});
11.     Eigen::Tensor<int, 2> B = A.stride(strides);
12.
13.     std::cout << "A is\n\n" << A.
    dimensions() << "\n\n" << A << "\n\n";
14.     std::cout << "B is\n\n" << B.
    dimensions() << "\n\n" << B << "\n\n";
15.     return 0;
16. }
```

This code outputs:

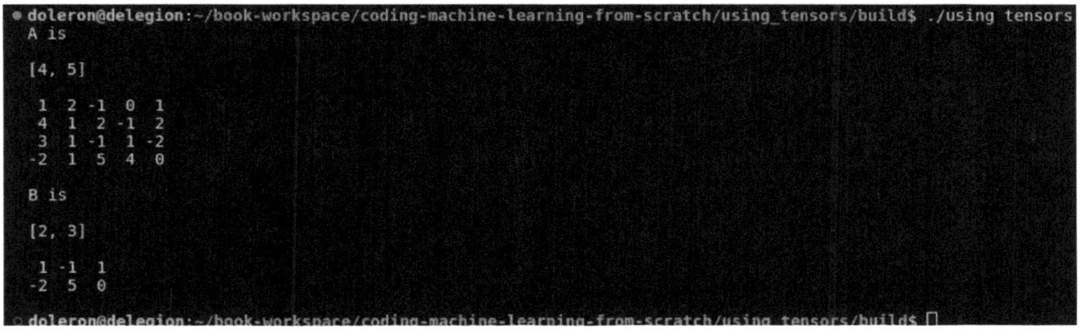

Figure 4.18: Running the strides example

It is noteworthy that the **stride()** operation does not actually create another smaller tensor. Indeed, the operation provides only a view of the original tensor.

Note: The majority of Eigen Tensor functions work in an eager fashion. This means that, instead of returning an actual tensor, the function returns an object that knows how to compute the resulting tensor. Working this way allows Eigen to optimize the overall performance by reducing redundant executions. As a drawback, this approach makes the code harder to debug and a little bit more complex to implement. Please check this link for more details:

https://eigen.tuxfamily.org/dox-devel/unsupported/eigen_tensors.html#title6

Padding using Eigen Tensor API

Similar to strides, we can create a padded view of a tensor using Eigen, as shown:

```
1.  Eigen::Tensor<int, 2> A(2, 3);
2.  A.setValues({{0, 100, 200}, {300, 400, 500}});
3.
4.  Eigen::array<std::pair<int, int>, 2> padding;
5.  padding[0] = std::make_pair(0, 1);
6.  padding[1] = std::make_pair(2, 3);
7.
8.  Eigen::Tensor<int, 2> B = A.pad(padding);
9.
10. std::cout << "A is\n\n"
11.            << A.dimensions() << "\n\n" << A << "\n\n";
12. std::cout << "B is\n\n"
13.            << B.dimensions() << "\n\n" << B << "\n\n";
```

Which outputs the following result:

Figure 4.19: Running the padding example

The Eigen Tensor API supports a variety of different operations, such as reductions, contractions, broadcasting, reshaping, and so on.

Tip: Check this link for a complete list and examples of tensor built-in operations: https://eigen.tuxfamily.org/dox-devel/unsupported/eigen_tensors.html

Conclusion

This chapter introduced convolutions, one of the most important operations in deep learning. We learned how to implement a padded version of the 2D convolution using matrices and finally learned how to use the Tensor Eigen API to compute the same operation but using high-ranked tensor objects.

Furthermore, we discussed the example of detecting features from an image using Sobel kernels. This example provided valuable insights into the applicability of convolutions in solving complex pattern recognition tasks.

In the next chapter we will continue our journey to implement deep learning models. In particular, we will introduce the fully connected layers, implementing them using Eigen Tensors.

Exercises

1. Write a formula to calculate the output dimensions of a 2D convolution given (m, n) as the shape of the input matrix, k as the side of the squared kernel, p as the padding set, and s as the stride.

2. Write a program to compute the 2D convolution given a 3-rank input matrix with dimensions (a, b, 3) and a 2D kernel with side k. Consider that a and b are always greater than k.

3. We have seen that padding is helpful to avoid the reduction of the output matrix size. Is there any other motivation to use padding? If so, explain it in simple words.

4. Consider the example of using Sobel's kernels to detect edges again. List the pros and cons of using strides in a problem like this.

References

[1] Aggarwal, Neural Networks and Deep Learning, Chapter 8, Convolutional Neural Network, Springer, 2018.

[2] Dumoulin & Visin, A guide to convolution arithmetic for deep learning, 2018.

[3] Goodfellow, Bengio & Courville, Deep Learning, MIT Press, 2016.

[4] Szeliski., Computer Vision: Algorithms and Applications, 2010.

[5] Eigen Tensor API, available at **https://eigen.tuxfamily.org/dox/unsupported/group__CXX11__Tensor__Module.html**

[6] Introduction to OpenCV, available at **https://docs.opencv.org/4.x/df/d65/tutorial_table_of_content_introduction.html**

Join our book's Discord space

Join the book's Discord Workspace for Latest updates, Offers, Tech happenings around the world, New Release and Sessions with the Authors:

https://discord.bpbonline.com

CHAPTER 5
Coding the Fully Connected Layer

Introduction

This chapter introduces **fully connected** (**FC**) layers, a core component of any artificial neural network. FC layers were the first approach to building ANNs and are still essential to any modern deep learning model, particularly in defining the last network elements. In this chapter, we will describe FC layers and learn how to use them to build one of the first types of neural networks, the multilayer perceptron model.

Structure

The roadmap of this chapter is as follows:

- Significance of using artificial neural networks
- Implementing our very first neural network
- Calculating the layer values
- Invoking the activation function
- Forward propagation using batches
- Using multi-dimensional arrays as input
- Calculating the model size
- Flattening tensors

Objectives

After reading this chapter, you will be able to implement fully connected layers using tensors. You will also understand how to perform the computation over neural networks using the forward propagation algorithm, implementing this operation using C++ lambdas.

Significance of using artificial neural networks

Before we start, we should wonder: why neural networks? Indeed, machine learning has many different model types [1], such as decision trees, Bayesian networks, random forests, support vector machines, genetic algorithms, ..., and artificial neural networks, of course. Why should we talk about the latter only?

The answer to this question was partially given in *Chapter 1, Introduction to Deep Learning Programming*. There, we discussed how deep learning is somehow a subset of machine learning. Indeed, although the machine learning field studies a wide range of different models, the deep learning community focused on using mostly artificial neural networks as a base. This means that many of the cutting-edge technologies developed in the last 15 years were variations—better saying, deeper extensions—of the traditional neural network model called **multilayer perceptron** (**MLP**).

MLPs are basically neural networks having only fully connected layers. Let us learn more about them now.

Implementing our very first neural network

Consider again the network example that we draw in *Chapter 1, Introduction to Deep Learning Programming*:

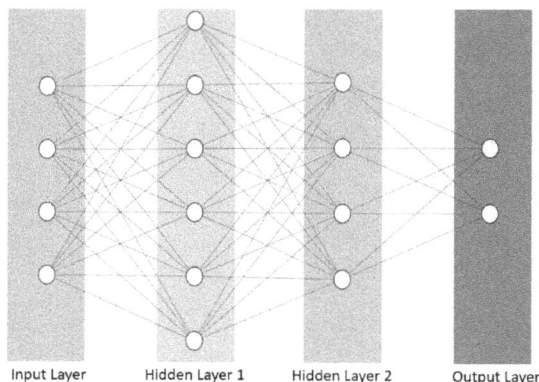

Input Layer   Hidden Layer 1   Hidden Layer 2   Output Layer

Figure 5.1: *4-layer neural network with fully connected layers*

This network consists only of FC layers, also called **Dense** layers. How can we use a network like this to find the output for a given input X? We use **forward propagation**, as shown: [2]

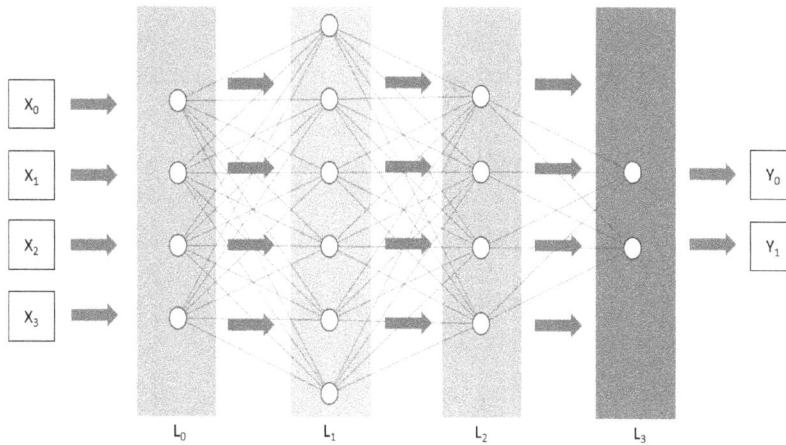

Figure 5.2: Forward propagation computation

In forward propagation, we first calculate the values of the input layer. Then, we use the values from the input layer to obtain the values of the second layer. We repeat this process until we have found the values of the last layer, which is called the **output layer**. In the end, the output layer values are the output of the network for a given input X. This routine is described in the following pseudo-code:

```
forward_propagation(X) {

    L_0 = X
    m = size(layers)
    for (i = 1; i<m; ++i)
    {
        L_i = act(L_{i-1} * W_i + b_i)
    }
    return L_{m-1}

}
```

Figure 5.3: Forward propagation pseudo-code

This pseudo-code introduces new elements, such as the bias **b** and the activation function **act**. We will talk about these terms ahead.

Calculating the layer values

In order to calculate the network output for an input X, the first step is to compute the valuation of the first layer. The value of the input layer L_0 is given by:

$$L_0 = X$$

Figure 5.4: *Evaluating the input layer*

This formula basically assigns each coefficient of X to a neuron in the input layer. Of course, to make this work, the number of coefficients in X must be equal to the number of neurons in the input layer.

Once we have filled the input layer with X, we can find the values of the next layers. Let us call one of these next layers by L_i. The valuation of the neurons in L_i is given by:

$$L_i = act(L_{i-1} \times W_i + b)$$

Figure 5.5: *Evaluating layer L_i*

Where:

- L_{i-1} is the valuation of the neurons from the previous layer;
- W_i is the weight matrix representing the connections between the layer L_i and L_{i-1}, and
- **b** is the bias array.

The operation × is the traditional matrix product, and **act()** is an **activation function**.

Invoking the activation function

So far in this book, we have seen the following example [3] of an activation function:

```
1.  float sigmoid(float z) {
2.      float result;
3.      if (z >= 45.f)
4.          result = 1.f;
5.      else if (z <= -45.f)
6.          result = 0.f;
7.      else
8.          result = 1.f / (1.f + exp(-z));
9.      return result;
10. }
```

This implementation works for a scalar value **z** only. Since we are using tensors, we must wrap it as follows:

```
1.  template <typename T, int _RANK >
2.  auto sigmoid_activation(Eigen::Tensor<T, _RANK>& Z)
3.  {
```

```
    auto result = Z.unaryExpr(std::ref(sigmoid));
    return result;
}
```

Call it:

```
int main(int, char **)
{

    Eigen::Tensor<float, 2> A(2, 3);
    A.setRandom();

    std::cout << "A:\n\n"
              << A << "\n\n";

    Eigen::Tensor<float, 2> B = sigmoid_activation(A);

    std::cout << "B:\n\n"
              << B << "\n\n";

    return 0;
}
```

Note: We used a template function to define the sigmoid activation. In C++, templates are molds to define a family of functions. The actual function will be defined by the compiler only at compile time.

This code outputs something like this:

```
PS Z:\book-workspace\pbp-deep-learning-in-modern-cpp\fc_layers\build> .\activation_example.exe
A:

0.896227 0.872269 0.605188
0.290171  0.24641 0.251816

B:

0.710173 0.705218 0.646842
0.572038 0.561293 0.562623

PS Z:\book-workspace\pbp-deep-learning-in-modern-cpp\fc_layers\build>
```

***Figure 5.6**: Invoking the activation function*

Once we have the activation function ready, we can compute the layer output as follows:

```
1. Eigen::Tensor<float, 1> calc_layer
   (const Eigen::Tensor<float, 1> &input, const Eigen::Tensor<float, 2>
   &weights, const Eigen::Tensor<float, 1> &bias) {
2.
3.     Eigen::array<Eigen::IndexPair<int>, 1> op_dims =
   {Eigen::IndexPair<int>(0, 0)};
4.     auto prod = input.contract(weights, op_dims);
5.     Eigen::Tensor<float, 1> Z = prod + bias;
6.
7.     auto result = sigmoid_activation(Z);
8.     return result;
9. }
```

Note that, instead of **Eigen::Matrix**, we are using objects of type **Eigen::Tensor**. According to the documentation, the **Eigen::Tensor.contract()** method is a generalization of the matrix product to the multidimensional case. **bias** is a vector of scalars that are added to compute the neuron's output.

We can see our **calc_layer()** function in the following action:

```
1. int main(int, char **)
2. {
3.
4.     Eigen::Tensor<float, 1> X(2);
5.     X.setValues({-1.5, 0.4});
6.
7.     Eigen::Tensor<float, 2> W(2, 3);
8.     W.setValues({{1, 2, 3}, {4, 5, 6}});
9.
10.    Eigen::Tensor<float, 1> B(3);
11.    B.setValues({-1, 1, 2});
12.
13.    std::cout << "X:\n\n"
14.            << X << "\n\n";
15.
16.    std::cout << "W:\n\n"
17.            << W << "\n\n";
18.
19.    std::cout << "B:\n\n"
20.            << B << "\n\n";
```

```
21.
22.     auto R = calc_layer(X, W, B);
23.
24.     std::cout << "R:\n\n"
25.               << R << "\n\n";
26.
27.     return 0;
28. }
```

This program results in the following output:

Figure 5.7: Fully connected layer example output

This implementation is our very first attempt to code a fully connected layer. It is limited to 1-rank inputs. That is, **calc_layer()** only works with vectors as input. In our real programs, we need to calculate the output of several instances at once, a technique called **batching**, as described ahead.

Forward propagation using batches

In the last example, we performed the evaluation of a single instance. What happens if we have five different instances to calculate? Of course, one alternative is to perform five **calc_layer()** calls:

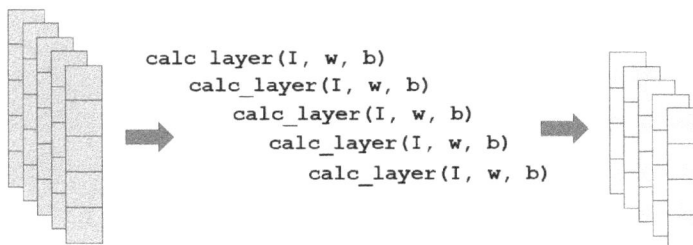

Figure 5.8: Sequential forward calls

The problem with this approach is that we are not using most of the underlying computational resources. It turns out that the hardware nowadays has additional registers which allow us to run parallel computation on sequential data, a technique usually known as **vectorization**.

Tip: Vectorization was briefly introduced in Chapter 1, Introduction to Deep Learning Programming.

Thus, instead of making multiple calls sequentially, we can use **batch multiplication** to achieve better results, as shown:

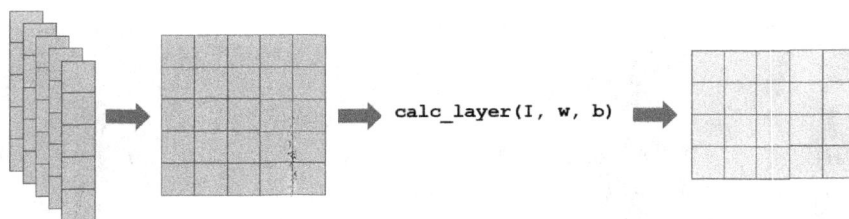

Figure 5.9: Batched forward call

In this case, we aggregated the five individual vectors to form a single matrix. Note that the output is also a matrix. As a result, instead of performing five individual matrix products between five individual vectors and one weight matrix, we end up having only one single matrix product between two matrices. Our last implementation can be slightly modified to support this case.

It is noteworthy that since **bias** is a 1D vector, we need to **broadcast** it in order to add it to each instance in the batch:

Figure 5.10: Broadcasting the bias

This is not our last attempt to code the fully connected layer. Before finishing, we need to cover the case when the input is a multidimensional tensor. This is covered in the next section.

Using multi-dimensional arrays as input

Consider the case where we have a 3-rank tensor as the input of our fully connected layer:

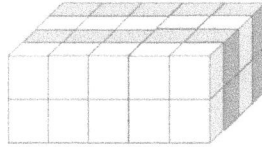

Figure 5.11: *A multidimensional input*

Since it is not a 2D grid, we cannot directly use the traditional matrix product in the same way that we did in the last case. The solution here is using **reshape** to transform the multidimensional batch in a 2D grid, keeping the input tensor's last dimension unchanged:

Figure 5.12: *Converting a n-rank input into a 2-rank tensor*

Now, the input is a 2D tensor and, finally, we can again use the traditional matrix product with it. This algorithm is implemented in the following template:

```
1.  template <typename T, int _RANK>
2.  class Dense
3.  {
4.  public:
5.
6.      Dense(Eigen::Tensor<T, 2> _weights,
7.            Eigen::Tensor<T, 1> _bias,
8.            std::function<Eigen::Ten-
    sor<T, 2>(const Eigen::Tensor<T, 2> &)> _activation):
9.            weights(std::move(_weights)),
10.           bias(std::move(_bias)),
11.           activation(_activation) {}
12.     virtual ~Dense() {}
13.
14.     virtual Eigen::Tensor<T, _RANK>
15.     evaluate(const Eigen::Tensor<T, _RANK> &input)
16.     {
17.
18.         const auto input_dims = input.dimensions();
19.         const auto weight_dims = this->weights.dimensions();
```

```
20.
21.          const int instance_size = input_dims[_RANK - 1];
22.          const int output_size = weight_dims[1];
23.
24.          // performing some runtime checks
25.
26.          if (instance_size != weight_dims[0])
27.              throw std::invalid_argument("in-
    put size does not match the shape of the weight matrix");
28.
29.          if (this->bias.dimension(0) != output_size)
30.              throw std::invalid_argu-
    ment("bias size does not match the shape of the weight matrix");
31.
32.          int instances = input.size() / instance_size;
33.
34.          // fitting the input tensor rank to two
35.          Eigen::array<long long int, 2> new_dim({instances, instance_
    size});
36.          Eigen::Tensor<T, 2> reshaped = input.reshape(new_dim);
37.
38.          Eigen::array<Eigen::IndexPair<int>, 1> contract_
    dims = {Eigen::IndexPair<int>(1, 0)};
39.          Eigen::Tensor<T, 2> prod = reshaped.
    contract(weights, contract_dims);
40.
41.          // broadcasting the bias to match the output dimensions
42.          Eigen::array<long long int, 2> bias_new_dim({1, output_size});
43.          auto bias_reshaped = this->bias.reshape(bias_new_dim);
44.          Eigen::array<long long int, 2> bias_bcast({instances, 1});
45.          Eigen::Tensor<T, 2> bias_broadcast = bias_reshaped.
    broadcast(bias_bcast);
46.
47.          // adding the bias
48.          auto Z = prod + bias_broadcast;
49.
50.          // applying activation function
51.          auto output = this->activation(Z);
52.
53.          // reshaping the output to the proper RANK
```

```
54.            auto result_dims = input_dims;
55.            result_dims[_RANK - 1] = output_size;
56.            auto result = output.reshape(result_dims);
57.
58.            return result;
59.        }
60.
61.        virtual Eigen::Tensor<T, _RANK>
62.        operator()(const Eigen::Tensor<T, _RANK> &input)
63.        {
64.            return this->evaluate(input);
65.        }
66.
67. private:
68.        Eigen::Tensor<T, 2> weights;
69.        Eigen::Tensor<T, 1> bias;
70.        std::function<Eigen::Ten-
    sor<T, 2>(const Eigen::Tensor<T, 2> &)> activation;
71. };
```

Let us highlight some parts of this code. Here, we reshape the original input to fit a 2D tensor:

```
1.  const int instance_size = input_dims[_RANK - 1];
2.  int instances = input.size() / instance_size;
3.  Eigen::array<long long int, 2> new_dim({instances, instance_size});
4.  Eigen::Tensor<T, 2> reshaped = input.reshape(new_dim);
```

This is the code to reshape the output tensor to fit the original tensor rank:

```
1.  auto result_dims = input_dims;
2.  result_dims[_RANK - 1] = output_size;
3.  auto result = output.reshape(result_dims);
```

Note that we have again broadcasted the bias to fit it to the 2D-grid layout:

```
1.  Eigen::array<long long int, 2> bias_new_dim({1, output_size});
2.  auto bias_reshaped = this->bias.reshape(bias_new_dim);
3.  Eigen::array<long long int, 2> bias_bcast({instances, 1});
4.  Eigen::Tensor<T, 2> bias_broadcast = bias_reshaped.broadcast(bias_
    bcast);
5.  auto Z = prod + bias_broadcast;
```

Note that the matrix product using the reshaped 2D input tensor results in a 2D tensor, either. Due to this, we need to reshape the output to the proper rank before returning it:

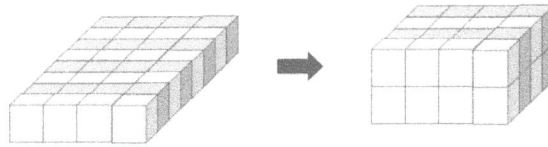

Figure 5.13: *Reshaping the output*

Finally, we have our FC layer working. Let us see how to use it to build our first neural network.

Building a multilayer perceptron

Multiplayer perceptrons are neural networks having only fully connected layers [2]. We can build the same MLP shown in *Figure 5.1* using our **Dense** class:

```
1.  #include <iostream>
2.  #include <random>
3.
4.  #include "fully_connected_layers.hpp"
5.
6.  int main(int, char**)
7.  {
8.      srand((unsigned int) time(0));
9.
10.     auto bias_initializer = [](const int size) {
11.         Eigen::Tensor<float, 1> result(size);
12.         result.setZero();
13.         return result;
14.     };
15.
16.     auto weight_initializer = []
    (const int rows, const int cols, float range = 0.05f) {
17.         Eigen::Tensor<float, 2> _random(rows, cols);
18.         _random.setRandom();
19.         Eigen::Tensor<float, 2> result = (_random - _random.
    constant(.5f)) * _random.constant(range);
20.         return result;
21.     };
22.
23.     Dense<float, 2> layer1(weight_initializer(4, 6), bias_
```

```
         initializer(6), sigmoid_activation<float, 2>);
24.      Dense<float, 2> layer2(weight_initializer(6, 4), bias_
         initializer(4), sigmoid_activation<float, 2>);
25.      Dense<float, 2> output_layer(weight_initializer(4, 2), bias_
         initializer(2), sigmoid_activation<float, 2>);
26.
27.      auto model = [&](const Eigen::Tensor<float, 2>& X) {
28.          auto l_1 = layer1(X);
29.          auto l_2 = layer2(l_1);
30.          auto result = output_layer(l_2);
31.          return result;
32.      };
33.
34.      Eigen::Tensor<float, 2> input(1, 4);
35.      input.setValues({{-1.5, 0.4, 2.1, -1.2}});
36.
37.      auto output = model(input);
38.
39.      std::cout << "The output is\n\n" << output << "\n\n";
40.
41.      return 0;
42.
43. }
```

Building and running this code generates an output like this:

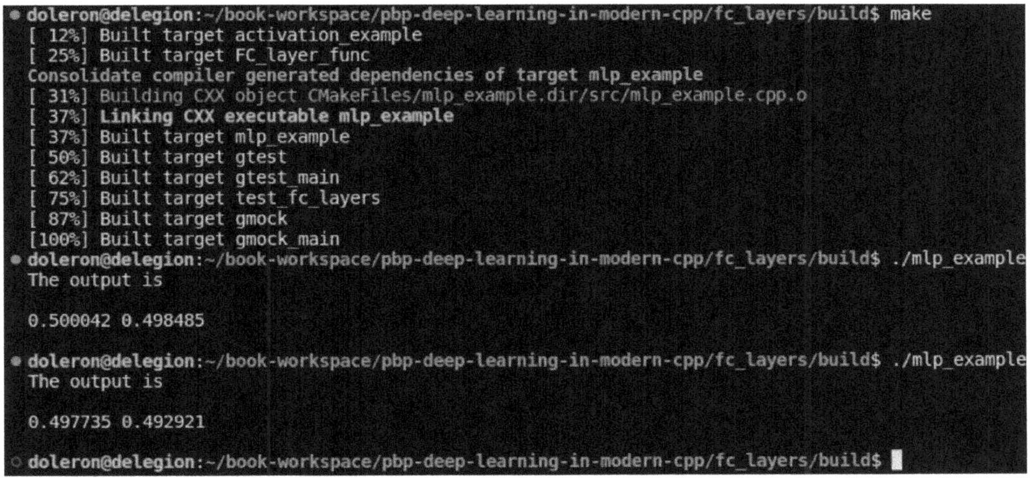

Figure 5.14: Network output

Of course, because of the following line, in each execution, the output is slightly different.:

```
1. srand((unsigned int) time(0));
```

It turns out that we are randomly initializing the weights:

```
1. auto weight_initializer = []
   (const int rows, const int cols, float range = 0.05f) {
2.     Eigen::Tensor<float, 2> _random(rows, cols);
3.     _random.setRandom();
4.     Eigen::Tensor<float, 2> result = (_random - _random.
   constant(.5f)) * _random.constant(range);
5.     return result;
6. };
```

As we discussed in *Chapter 3, Testing Deep Learning Code*, this initial randomization is a key aspect to make the algorithms work properly on high dimensional spaces. This concept will be explored in more detail in the next chapter as well.

Calculating the model size

When building models, an important metric is the actual number of coefficients. In the case of the network in the previous example, we have 68 coefficients:

- **Layer 1**: 30 coefficients (24 for the weight matrix and 6 for the bias)
- **Layer 2**: 28 coefficients (24 for the weight matrix and 4 for the bias)
- **Output layer**: 10 coefficients (8 for the weight matrix and 2 for the bias)

For **Dense** layers, obtaining the size is very straightforward:

```
1. int size()
2. {
3.     return this->bias.size() + this->weights.size();
4. }
```

In practice, we use this size to compare different models and estimate their performance.

Flattening tensors

Fully connected layers are always found in modern neural network architectures, usually after convolution layers. Since convolutions outputs grids, it is necessary to do some conversion. This conversion is usually called **flatten** [4], as illustrated:

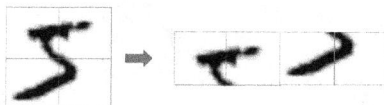

Figure 5.15: Flattening a 2D tensor

Flatten basically reshapes the input:

```
1.  template <typename T, int _RANK>
2.  auto flatten(const Eigen::Tensor<T, _RANK> &input) {
3.
4.      const auto input_dims = input.dimensions();
5.
6.      const int batch_size = input_dims[0];
7.      int instance_size = input.size() / batch_size;
8.
9.      Eigen::array<long long int, 2> new_dim({batch_size, instance_size});
10.     Eigen::Tensor<T, 2> result = input.reshape(new_dim);
11.
12.     return result;
13. }
```

flatten() transform multidimensional grids into linear grids. Note that this operation takes the first dimension as the batch size, not changing it. Check out the following example of usage:

```
1.  int main(int, char**)
2.  {
3.      Eigen::Tensor<float, 3> input(10, 3, 3);
4.      input.setRandom();
5.
6.      std::cout << "Intput dimensions are: " << input.
    dimensions() << "\n\n";
7.
8.      auto output = flatten(input);
9.
10.     std::cout << "Output dimensions are: " << output.
    dimensions() << "\n\n";
11.
12.     return 0;
13.
14. }
```

This code outputs the following result:

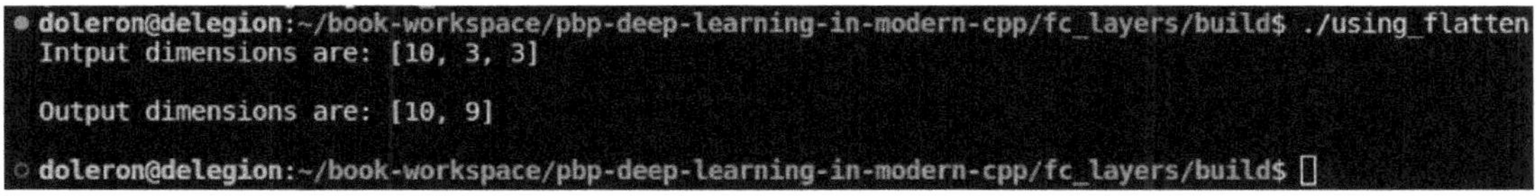

```
● doleron@delegion:~/book-workspace/pbp-deep-learning-in-modern-cpp/fc_layers/build$ ./using_flatten
  Intput dimensions are: [10, 3, 3]

  Output dimensions are: [10, 9]

○ doleron@delegion:~/book-workspace/pbp-deep-learning-in-modern-cpp/fc_layers/build$ []
```

Figure 5.16: Example of using the flatten function

Conclusion

In this chapter, we introduced the fully connected layers, using them to build our first neural network. We have seen that neural networks are a core concept in deep learning. In models like this, the computation occurs from the initial layer, called the input layer, up to the last layer, called the output layer.

We also learned how to set the inputs using batches, helping to achieve better processing usage by using vectorization.

In the next chapter, we will learn the basis of network training algorithms, implementing different cost functions and learning how to use them to fit models from data.

Exercises

1. Consider the following representation of an MLP network:

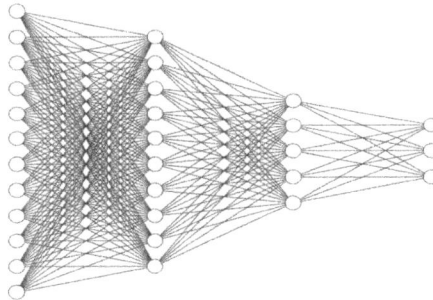

Figure 5.17: Exercise 1 network

   Determine the total number of coefficients in this network (make sure to include the bias). Hint: Do not count the links. Calculate it by counting the number of neurons instead.

2. Consider the last network again. But this time, instead of 12 neurons in the input layer, the network has 10x more neurons, that is, 120 neurons. Also consider that the first hidden layer now has 100 neurons. Calculate the total number of coefficients and compare it with the number found in the previous question.

3. Consider the following MLP network:

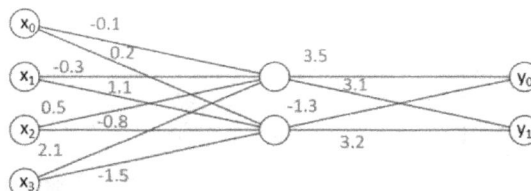

Figure 5.18: Exercise 3 network

where, each weight value was drawn in red. Assuming that the layers use sigmoid as activation function, compute the network output $Y = [y_0, y_1]$ for the input $X = [x_0, x_1, x_2, x_3] = [5.1, 3.5, 1.4, 0.2]$. Consider that all bias values are zero.

References

[1] Mitchell, Machine Learning, McGraw-Hill, 1997.

[2] Haykin, Neural Networks: A Comprehensive Foundation, Prentice Hall, 1999.

[3] Bishop, Pattern Recognition and Machine Learning, Springer, 2006.

[4] Flatten layer, Keras API, available at **https://keras.io/api/layers/reshaping_layers/flatten/**

Join our book's Discord space

Join the book's Discord Workspace for Latest updates, Offers, Tech happenings around the world, New Release and Sessions with the Authors:

https://discord.bpbonline.com

CHAPTER 6
Learning by Minimizing Cost Functions

Introduction

The faculty of using experience to improve performance is a key aspect of any artificial intelligence system, which has been studied for decades in a specific field called **machine learning**. In this chapter, we will define what learning is in the context of machines and use this definition to establish an algorithm to implement this definition.

Structure

This is the chapter roadmap:

- Understanding what learning is
- Finding good function approximations
- Introducing other cost functions

Objectives

By reading this chapter, you will be able to implement cost functions and understand their role in training computer programs to perform complex tasks.

Understanding what learning is

It always amazes us how some of the concepts in artificial intelligence are similar to their relatives in other areas of social, biological, and physical phenomena. In particular, in the last century [1], we have figured out that machines are also able to learn by experience in a very close way as biological beings learn. In 1997, Tom Mitchell wrote his famous definition of machine learning [2]:

> *A computer program is said to learn from experience E with respect to some class of tasks T and performance measure P, if its performance at tasks in T, as measured by P, improves with experience E.*

This definition drove the human efforts to make computer programs learn for decades, culminating in what we now call deep learning. Three elements are core in this definition:

- The task
- The experience
- The performance measure

Let us start talking about which classes of tasks the computer programs are intended to execute and how to represent them.

Defining tasks as functions

Following is a short list [3] of popular tasks performed by computers:

- **Classification**: In classification problems, the system assigns one or more discrete values (usually referred to as a class, label, or category) to a given input. This action of assigning a value to an input is often named **prediction**. The simpler type of classifier is called a **binary classifier**. A binary classifier can predict only one of two possible classes.

- **Regression**: Regression is similar to classification, only differing in the output type. Whereas classifiers predict discrete values, in regression problems, the output is one or more continuous numeric values.

- **Transcription**: Transcription tasks are also called sequence-to-sequence problems. The most popular example of transcription is language translation, where a sentence written in language X is rewritten in language Y.

- **Content generation**: Today, artificial intelligence hype is focused on generating content with human-like (or sometimes superhuman) performance. Some examples are the autonomous generation of photography, music, poetry, analytical reports, and so on.

Of course, this list is not even half complete. Every day, we realize a new way to apply computers to execute tasks before only performed by humans. Luckily, we have figured out a general way to represent any task executed by computers: a **function**.

A function is a mathematical concept that represents a special type of relationship (called **mapping**) between two sets: the inputs and the outputs. We can think about functions as black boxes in which we can feed inputs to obtain outputs. For example, suppose a system to recognize a person by their face:

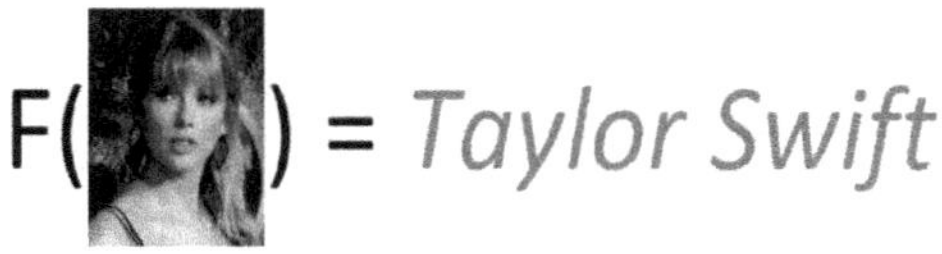

F(⬛) = *Taylor Swift*

Figure 6.1: Representing a face recognition system with a function

We can model a system like that as a function that has an image as input and outputs an identifier. Now, consider another system that is designed to estimate the shipping cost to deliver a packet from location A to location B. We can also model this task as a function F(*A*, *B*):

$$F(A, B) = \$14.30$$

Figure 6.2: Representing a shipping cost estimator using a function

Finally, consider a language translator. We can model it as a function that gets a sentence written in language X as input and returns the same sentence written in language Y:

$$F(\text{'Hello World'}, EN, FR) = \text{'Bonjour le monde'}$$

Figure 6.3: A function representing a translator

Modeling tasks as functions makes them easier to be handled by machine learning algorithms. The hardest part of this approach is that we often have no idea of how functions actually consist of internally. That is, we often have no idea of the function's formula (**theoretical ignorance**). Even if we know how to calculate the function, sometimes there are practical concerns like unknown parameters (**practical ignorance**) or unfeasible computational cost (**practical laziness**). Finally, sometimes the function domain is so complex that it is not possible to define a function deterministically (**theoretical laziness**). These are the more common sources of uncertainty [1] in modeling systems.

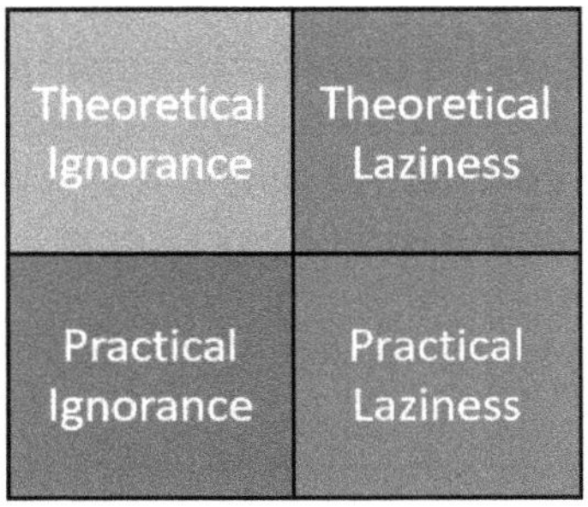

Figure 6.4: Sources of uncertain when modeling functions

Machine learning has a strong alternative to overcome our ignorance and laziness about functions: we can use a **function approximation** instead of using the (possibly unknown) original function's formula. In fact, finding ways to obtain good function approximations is the most active concern of ML engineers and researchers.

Finding good function approximations

Suppose we have a task T, and we represent this task by an **unknown** function F:

$$F(X) = Y$$

Figure 6.5: *A function mapping X to Y*

This function defines a relationship between two sets, the inputs X and outputs Y. Let us assume that we have some evidence (i.e. data) of the relationship between X and Y:

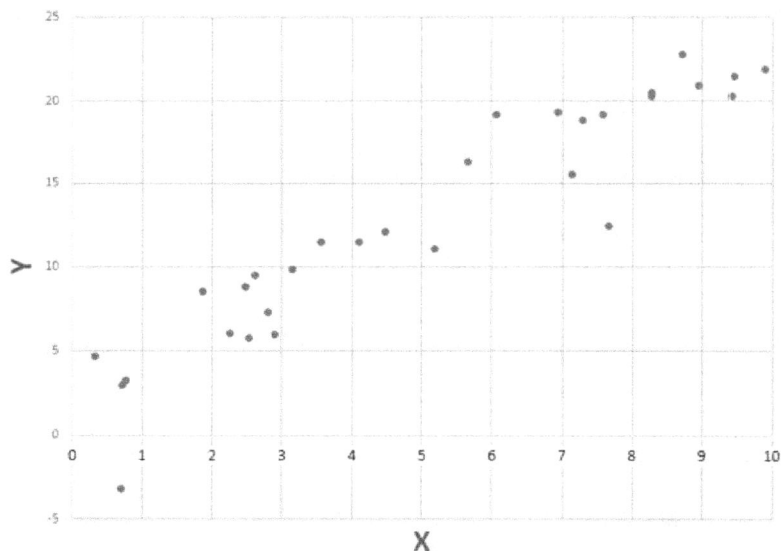

Figure 6.6: *Dataset consisting of pairs X, Y*

The **scatter plot** chart above suggests a **linear relationship** between X and Y. In 2D spaces like this, linear relations are well represented by straight lines. In other words, we can approximate this data using a **hypothetical** function H(X) like this:

$$H(X) = aX + b$$

Figure 6.7: *A hypothetical function to represent our dataset*

So far, H(X) is unknown. However, we can represent it by the following red line in the following figure:

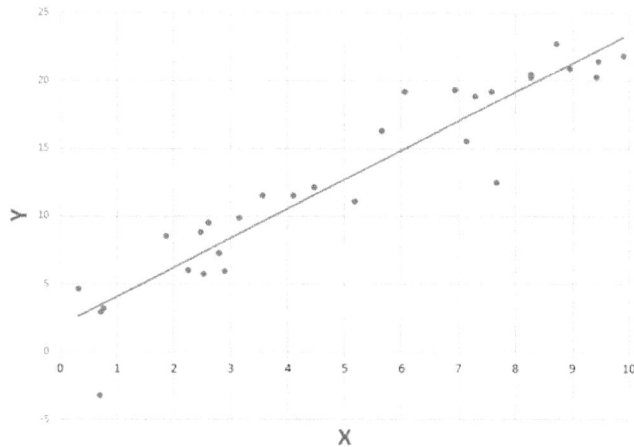

Figure 6.8: *Approximating our data by a straight line*

How to find H(X)? Of course, a priori, we do not know the values of **a** and **b**. What if we make some guesses, for example:

$$H_0(X) = -1X + 4$$

$$H_1(X) = 1.5X + 1$$

Figure 6.9: *Trying to guess H(X)*

H_0 and H_1 are two different guesses about H(X). The question is, how good is H_0 or H_1 at approximating H(X)? In machine learning, we can use **cost functions** to solve problems like this. For example:

$$mse(PRED, REAL) = \frac{1}{Size} \sum_{d \in D} (REAL_d - PRED_d)^2$$

Figure 6.10: *Mean square error cost function*

This function is called **mean squared error** (**MSE**)[5]. It uses the quadratic error to provide a numeric value representing how much the predicted values differ from the real ones. One way to implement MSE using tensors of any rank is as follows:

```
1. template <typename T, int _RANK>
2. T mse(const Eigen::Tensor<T, _RANK> &PRED, const Eigen::Tensor<T, _
   RANK> &TRUE) {
3.     auto diff = TRUE - PRED;
4.     auto pow = diff.pow(2);
5.     T sum = ((Eigen::Tensor<T, 0>)(pow.sum()))(0);
6.     T result = sum / PRED.size();
7.     return result;
8. }
```

Let us apply it to H_0 or H_1 to find which one is a better approximation to H(X):

```cpp
1.  int main(int, char**)
2.  {
3.      int seed = 1234;
4.      std::mt19937 rng(seed);
5.
6.      auto synthetic_generator = [&rng]
    (int size, float range, float a, float b, float noise) {
7.          Eigen::Tensor<float, 2> X(1, size);
8.          X = X.random() * range;
9.          Eigen::Tensor<float, 2> Y(1, size);
10.         Y.setConstant(b);
11.
12.         std::normal_distribution<float> normal_distro(0, noise);
13.         auto random_gen = [&rng, &normal_distro, a]
    (float interceptor, float x) {
14.             return interceptor + normal_distro(rng) + x*a;
15.         };
16.         Y = Y.binaryExpr(X, random_gen);
17.         return std::make_pair(X, Y);
18.     };
19.
20.     // generating 30 instanc-
    es, in a range of 0 <= X < 10, with a = 2, b = 3 and noise devia-
    tion = 2
21.     auto [X, Y] = synthetic_generator(30, 10.f, 2.f, 3.f, 2.f);
22.
23.     Eigen::Tensor<float, 2> H0 = X.unaryExpr([]
    (float x) {return -1.f*x + 4.f;});
24.     Eigen::Tensor<float, 2> H1 = X.unaryExpr([]
    (float x) {return 1.5f*x + 1.f;});
25.
26.     float cost_h0 = mse(H0, Y);
27.     float cost_h1 = mse(H1, Y);
28.
29.     std::cout << "Cost(Y, H0): " << cost_h0 << std::endl;
30.     std::cout << "Cost(Y, H1): " << cost_h1 << std::endl;
31.
```

```
32.     return 0;
33. }
```

Once executed, this code outputs:

```
PS Z:\book-workspace\pbp-deep-learning-in-modern-cpp\cost_functions\build> .\cost_functions.exe
Cost(Y, H0): 287.866
Cost(Y, H1): 27.1451
PS Z:\book-workspace\pbp-deep-learning-in-modern-cpp\cost_functions\build>
```

Figure 6.11: *Calculating the cost of H_0 and H_1*

MSE is only one type of cost function. More generally speaking, a cost function measures the cost of using a function approximation given some data [3]. In the example above, the cost of using H_0 is greater than the cost of using H_1. Therefore, if we need to decide between one or the other, the most rational approach is choosing H_1. This is the basic idea behind the machine learning algorithms that we will see here in this book. Most of the time, we will try to figure out **how to find function approximations that minimize cost functions**.

A motivating example

Let us check again the previous example. So far, by using MSE, we have found that H_1 is a better approximation than H_0. What if we plot H_0 and H_1?

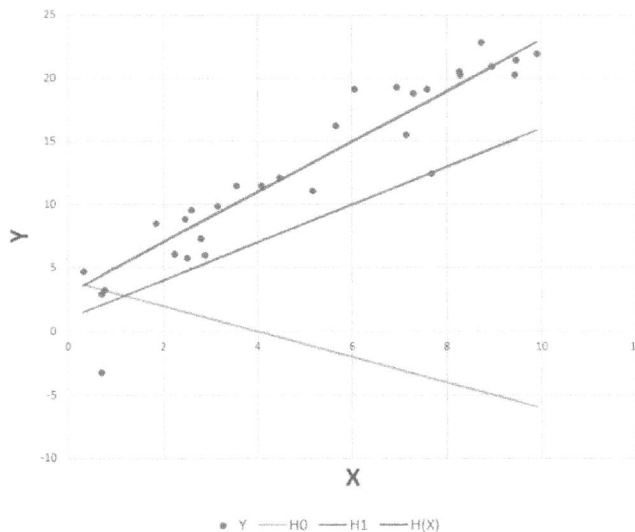

Figure 6.12: *Plotting H_0, H_1, and $H(X)$*

Indeed, H_1 looks like a better alternative to fit the data than H_0. However, if we compare it to $H(X)$, we may realize that H_1 probably is not the best approximation for our data. Indeed, the best approximation for our data is $H(X)$, but $H(X)$ is still unknown. The question persists: how can we find $H(X)$?

The algorithm to actually solve questions like this, which is used to fit neural networks to data, is called **backpropagation** (**BP**). BP will be introduced in *Chapter 10, Coding the Backpropagation Algorithm*. For a while, aiming to get some insight, let us use a simple but efficient approach to fit linear 2D data [4]:

1. First, let us *find the center C = (Cx, Cy)* of the data:

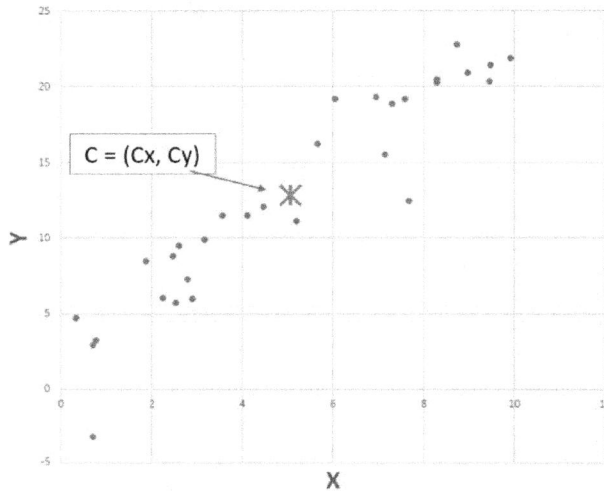

Figure 6.13: Finding the center of the data

2. Second, put a random straight-line S(X) passing by C:

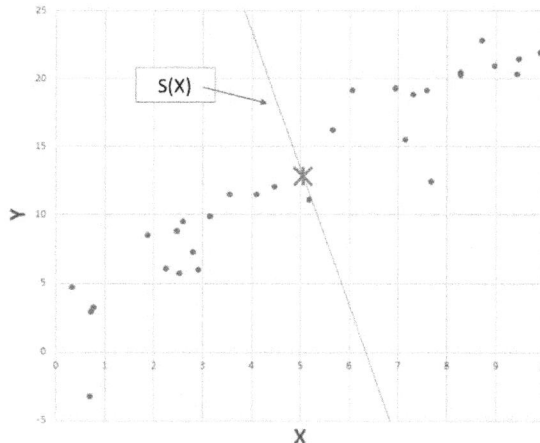

Figure 6.14: Our initial guess of S(X)

3. Finally, turn the line, increasing the slope by small steps, for example, 0.01. For each step, we memorize (a, b) for the best result:

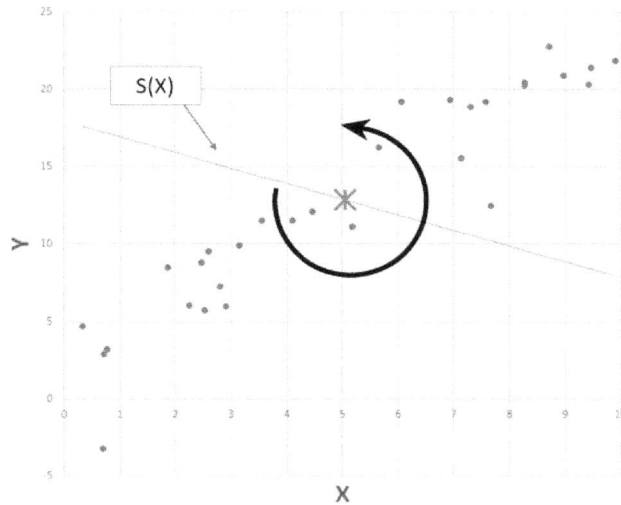

Figure 6.15: *Step 3 — Turning S(X)*

4. Finally, return the best configuration (a, b):

How can we decide if a configuration is better than a previous one? We can do it by simply choosing the one with the smallest cost. Check out the following code:

```
1.  int main(int, char**)
2.  {
3.      auto [X, Y] = synthetic_generator(30, 10.f, 2.f, 3.f, 2.f);
4.
5.      float Cx = ((Eigen::Tensor<float, 0>)(X.mean()))(0);
6.      float Cy = ((Eigen::Tensor<float, 0>)(Y.mean()))(0);
7.      float best_cost = std::numeric_limits<float>::max();
8.      const float step = 0.01;
9.      float a = -4;
10.     float best_a = a;
11.
12.     auto S = [&a, &Cx, &Cy](float x) {
13.         return a * (x - Cx) + Cy;
14.     };
15.
16.     int epochs = 0;
17.
18.     for (; a < 4; a += step) {
19.         Eigen::Tensor<float, 2> pred = X.unaryExpr(S);
20.         float cost = mse(pred, Y);
```

```
21.          if (cost < best_cost) {
22.              best_cost = cost;
23.              best_a = a;
24.          }
25.          epochs++;
26.      }
27.
28.      const float best_b = Cy - best_a*Cx;
29.
30.      std::cout << "Best configura-
     tion is (a, b) = (" << best_a << ", " << best_b << ")"
     << " with cost " << best_cost << "\n";
31.
32.      std::cout << "Took " << epochs << " epochs.\n";
33.
34.      return 0;
35. }
```

In this example, the pairs (X,Y) are synthetically generated by the following function:

```
1.  auto synthetic_generator = [&rng]
    (int size, float range, float a, float b, float noise) {
2.
3.      Eigen::Tensor<float, 2> X(1, size);
4.      X = X.random() * range;
5.
6.      Eigen::Tensor<float, 2> Y(1, size);
7.      Y.setConstant(b);
8.
9.      std::normal_distribution<float> normal_distro(0, noise);
10.
11.     auto random_gen = [&rng, &normal_distro, a]
    (float interceptor, float x) {
12.         return interceptor + normal_distro(rng) + x*a;
13.     };
14.
15.     Y = Y.binaryExpr(X, random_gen);
16.
17.     return std::make_pair(X, Y);
18.
19. };
```

Running this code, we can find that the best configuration for this data is:

```
● doleron@delegion:~/book-workspace/bpb-2014-deep-learning-in-modern-cpp/chapters_src_code/chapter_6/build$ make
 [ 50%] Built target h0_h1_example
 Consolidate compiler generated dependencies of target fitting_example
 [ 75%] Building CXX object CMakeFiles/fitting_example.dir/src/fitting_example.cpp.o
 [100%] Linking CXX executable fitting_example
 [100%] Built target fitting_example
● doleron@delegion:~/book-workspace/bpb-2014-deep-learning-in-modern-cpp/chapters_src_code/chapter_6/build$ ./fitting_example
 Best configuration is (a, b) = (1.96999, 2.86147) with cost 5.56664
 Took 1300 epochs.
● doleron@delegion:~/book-workspace/bpb-2014-deep-learning-in-modern-cpp/chapters_src_code/chapter_6/build$
```

Figure 6.16: Cost function output

Now we can plot the data, the unknown function H(X), and the found approximation S(X):

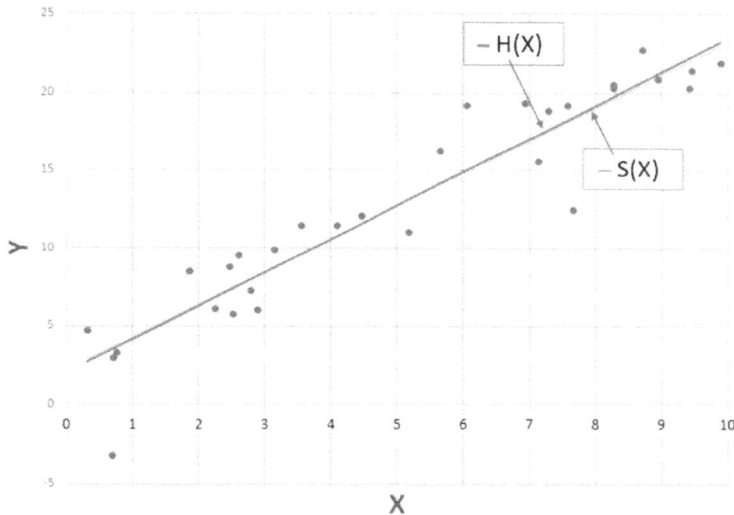

Figure 6.17: Finding the best approximation for H(X)

The plot shows that the final solution S(X) actually approximates the unknown function H(X) at some level. This simple algorithm [6] illustrates the key points of any deep learning algorithm:

1. The process of finding the best function approximation usually is an **iterative, try-and-error** approach.

2. The search for a good approximation can be reduced to a process of **cost function minimization** (in our example, we used the MSE cost function).

3. The quality of the search depends on the choice of a **discrete step** (in our example, 0.01).

It is noteworthy that this simple procedure used a very greedy approach, visiting every state out of the 800 possible in the search space. For more complex scenarios, it turns out that this greedy approach is not computationally feasible. Hopefully, we can use a more convenient strategy based on the **gradient heuristic**, as explained ahead.

Using gradient to minimize the cost function

In order to get more insight, let us plot the MSE cost found in the previous example:

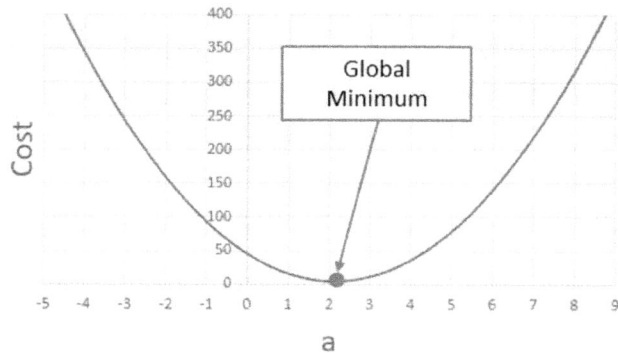

Figure 6.18: Plotting cost curve

Since we are looking for the minimum cost, we are interested in finding the smallest point of this chart. What our previous (naïve and greedy) algorithm did was basically calculate every value of this plot, returning the smaller. Although this approach worked for our simple example, it is too expensive to be broadly applied to any real multidimensional problem. In other words, we need to find a better alternative.

Looking again at the chart, it is pretty clear that we can use the slope of the curve to decide in which direction the algorithm should go toward the cost minimum. For example, in the first step, a is -4. We can calculate the slope between the two points: at -4 and a at (-4 + 0.01):

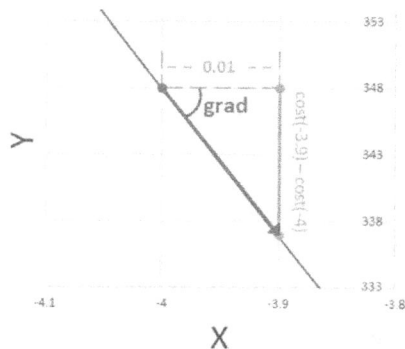

Figure 6.19: Finding the gradient at a = -4

The slope of this curve is given by:

$$grad = \frac{cost(-3.9) - cost(-4)}{0.01}$$

Figure 6.20: Calculating the gradient at a = -4

Now that we know how to calculate the gradient, we can use it to make a decision: if the *grad* is positive, in order to move towards the minimum point, we must move the parameter *a* to the left. If the slope is negative, we must move the parameter a to the right. In other words, if the slope is negative, we should increase *a*. But increase by what? The better choice is to use the slope itself to make this **parameter update**:

$$a_{n+1} := a_n - \text{step} * \text{grad}$$

Figure 6.21: Parameter update rule

If we repeat this process again and again, at some point, one or more of the following scenarios will occur:

- The cost will be zero or too small

- The slope will be zero or too small

- The number of steps will be too high

We can then stop the algorithm if we detect at least one of these **stop conditions**. The following code illustrates this algorithm:

```
1.  int main(int, char**)
2.  {
3.
4.      auto [X, Y] = synthetic_generator(30, 10.f, 2.f, 3.f, 2.f);
5.      float Cx = ((Eigen::Tensor<float, 0>)(X.mean()))(0);
6.      float Cy = ((Eigen::Tensor<float, 0>)(Y.mean()))(0);
7.
8.      auto cost_calc = [&Cx, &Cy](float a, auto X, auto Y) {
9.          auto S = [&a, &Cx, &Cy](float x) {
10.             return a * (x - Cx) + Cy;
11.         };
12.         Eigen::Tensor<float, 2> pred = X.unaryExpr(S);
13.         return mse(pred, Y);
14.     };
15.
16.     float a = -4.f;
17.     const float step = 0.01f;
18.
19.     float best_a = a;
20.     float best_cost = std::numeric_limits<float>::max();
21.
```

```
22.      const int MAX_EPOCHS = 20;
23.      int epoch = 0;
24.
25.      while (epoch++ < MAX_EPOCHS) {
26.
27.          float cost_init = cost_calc(a, X, Y);
28.
29.          if (cost_init < best_cost) {
30.              best_cost = cost_init;
31.              best_a = a;
32.          }
33.
34.          // stopping if cost is too small
35.          if (cost_init < 5.f) break;
36.
37.          a += step;
38.          float cost_end = cost_calc(a + step, X, Y);
39.
40.          float grad = (cost_end - cost_init) / step;
41.          std::cout << "epoch:\t" << epoch << "\ta:\t" << a << "\
    tMSE:\t" << cost_init << "\tgrad:\t" << grad << "\n";
42.
43.          // stopping if grad is too small
44.          if (abs(grad) < 10e-5) break;
45.
46.          a = a - step * grad;
47.
48.      }
49.
50.      const float b = Cy - best_a*Cx;
51.
52.      std::cout << "Best configura-
    tion is (a, b) = (" << best_a << ", " << b << ")"
    << " with cost " << best_cost << "\n";
53.
54.      return 0;
55. }
```

The expected output is:

```
doleron@delegion:~/book-workspace/bpb-2014-deep-learning-in-modern-cpp/chapters_src_code/chapter_6/build$ ./using_gradient
epoch:  1    a:    -3.99      MSE:    326.732 grad:    -214.847
epoch:  2    a:    -1.83153          MSE:    136.468 grad:    -137.029
epoch:  3    a:    -0.451247         MSE:    58.8202 grad:    -87.2704
epoch:  4    a:    0.431457          MSE:    27.1665 grad:    -55.4482
epoch:  5    a:    0.995938          MSE:    14.2866 grad:    -35.0996
epoch:  6    a:    1.35693 MSE:    9.06061 grad:    -22.0856
epoch:  7    a:    1.58779 MSE:    6.95002 grad:    -13.7634
epoch:  8    a:    1.73542 MSE:    6.10388 grad:    -8.44121
epoch:  9    a:    1.82984 MSE:    5.76872 grad:    -5.03769
epoch:  10   a:    1.89021 MSE:    5.63861 grad:    -2.86098
epoch:  11   a:    1.92882 MSE:    5.58986 grad:    -1.46928
epoch:  12   a:    1.95352 MSE:    5.57276 grad:    -0.579023
epoch:  13   a:    1.96931 MSE:    5.56759 grad:    -0.00967979
epoch:  14   a:    1.9794  MSE:    5.56664 grad:    0.354099
epoch:  15   a:    1.98586 MSE:    5.567   grad:    0.58713
epoch:  16   a:    1.98999 MSE:    5.56762 grad:    0.735712
epoch:  17   a:    1.99263 MSE:    5.56818 grad:    0.831318
epoch:  18   a:    1.99432 MSE:    5.5686  grad:    0.891876
epoch:  19   a:    1.9954  MSE:    5.5689  grad:    0.930834
epoch:  20   a:    1.99609 MSE:    5.5691  grad:    0.955963
Best configuration is (a, b) = (1.9694, 2.86445) with cost 5.56664
doleron@delegion:~/book-workspace/bpb-2014-deep-learning-in-modern-cpp/chapters_src_code/chapter_6/build$ █
```

Figure 6.22: Using gradients to find the approximation

Checking this log, we can note that the cost (MSE) is consistently decreasing over the first epochs. We can check this behavior with a plot:

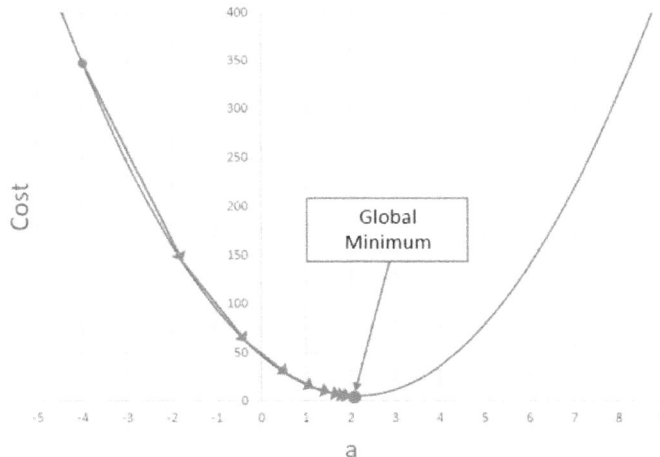

Figure 6.23: Algorithm convergence

The red arrows indicate how the algorithm converged in the first 8 epochs. It is easy to see that, in fact, the algorithm walked toward the global minimum, as suggested by our notion of gradients. Also note that, instead of performing the 800 iterations to scan all the search space like done by the previous naive algorithm, this **gradient-based algorithm** [3] found the solution in less than a few dozen epochs.

This example was really insightful. It illustrated the more significant aspects of the training algorithms that we will cover later on in this book. Now, let us check other useful cost functions.

Introducing other cost functions

So far, we have used MSE to calculate the cost of our functions. Indeed, MSE is one of the most used cost functions in deep learning, in particular for regression problems. However, there are other cost functions that are, sometimes, more addressable to the data at hand. Some examples are [7]:

- Regression problems:
  - Mean absolute error
  - Cosine similarity
  - Hyperbolic log cosine
  - Huber loss
- Classification:
  - Binary cross entropy
  - Categorical cross entropy
  - Sparse categorical cross entropy

We will talk about some of these functions in the following sections.

Mean absolute error

Although **mean absolute error** (**MSE**) works very well for a wide range of problems, it has two main issues:

- The penalization for differences between the predicted and real values is not linear but quadratic. As a result, outliers and noisy input cause a huge impact on the final value.

- The value provided by MSE is not easily interpretable. For example, if the PRED unit is measured in meters, the value provided by MSE is given in meters^2.

MAE [8] is a cost function that addresses these issues:

$$mae(PRED,\ REAL) = \frac{1}{Size} \sum_{d\ \in\ D} \ |\ (REAL_d\ -\ PRED_d)\ |$$

Figure 6.24: MAE formula

The MAE formula is very similar to the MSE formula. The basic difference is that we use the absolute value instead of a square to calculate the loss. As a result, MAE is not formally differentiable when PRED is equal to REAL, which makes this cost function not well suitable to be used in differentiation-based algorithms. However, wildly predictions or outliers will not strongly affect the final result like in MSE.

We can write MAE as follows:

```
1. template <typename T, int _RANK>
2. auto mae(const Eigen::Tensor<T, _
   RANK> &PRED, const Eigen::Tensor<T, _RANK> &TRUE) {
3.     auto diff = TRUE - PRED;
4.     auto loss = diff.abs();
5.     T sum = ((Eigen::Tensor<T, 0>)(loss.sum()))(0);
6.     T result = sum / PRED.size();
7.     return result;
8. }
```

A good point of MAE is its **interpretability**: it provides a value in the same unit of the predictions. For example, if MAE is 50 and the predictions are in meters, we can deduce that the model error is ± 50 meters.

Hyperbolic log cosine

The hyperbolic log cosine cost function [9], or simply LOGCOSH, is similar to MAE and MSE. Like MAE, it provides a value in the same unit as the prediction (providing good interpretability), penalizing wrong predictions linearly. However, like MSE, LOGCOSH is differentiable in the neighborhood of *PRED = REAL*.

Check the LOGCOSH formula:

$$logcosh(PRED, REAL) = \frac{1}{Size} \sum_{d \in D} log(cosh(REAL_d - PRED_d))$$

Figure 6.25: Algorithm convergence

We can implement LOGCOSH as follows:

```
1. template <typename T, int _RANK>
2. auto logcosh(const Eigen::Tensor<T, _
   RANK> &PRED, const Eigen::Tensor<T, _RANK> &TRUE) {
3.     auto diff = TRUE - PRED;
4.     auto cosh = diff.unaryExpr([](T val){return std::cosh(val);});
5.     auto loss = cosh.log();
6.     T sum = ((Eigen::Tensor<T, 0>)(loss.sum()))(0);
7.     T result = sum / PRED.size();
8.     return result;
9. }
```

Check the following LOGCOSH plot:

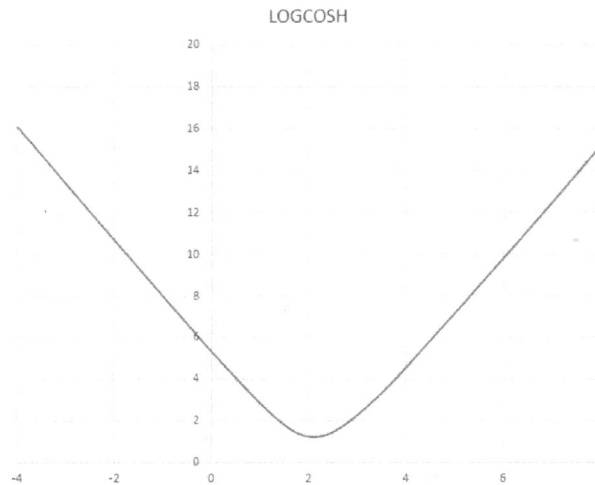

Figure 6.26: LOGCOSH function plot

Cost functions for classification problems

Cost functions such as MSE, MAE, and LOGCOSH are useful when the model's outcome is a **real number**. In our example, the line slope, a, can assume any real number. In cases like this, we name the task a **regression problem**.

As discussed in the beginning of this chapter, in ML there exist other types of tasks. A **classification problems** is a very common type of task where a system must to decide which label (or labels) should be assigned to a specific input. For example, consider the following **classifier**:

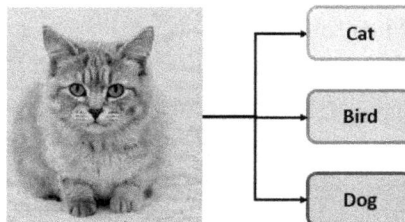

Figure 6.27: Algorithm convergence

In this example, the classifier must decide the species of the animal in the picture between 3 alternatives: Bird, Cat, and Dog.

The point here is that, differently from regression problems, the classifier outputs are a discrete, usually not ordered, finite set of labels. Thus, in general, we cannot use one of the previous cost functions, such as MSE or LOGCOSH, to evaluate a classifier directly. To calculate the cost of classifiers, we use functions designed for the mission. Two of them, **binary cross entropy** and **categorical cross entropy**, are discussed ahead.

Binary cross entropy

A **binary classifier** is a particular case of a classifier that decides between only one of two labels. For example:

Is there a cat in the image?

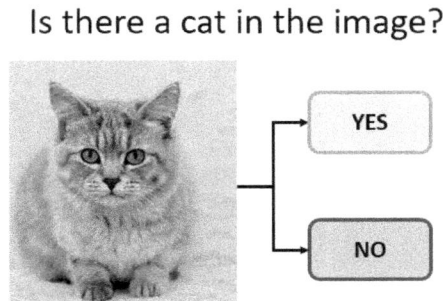

Figure 6.28: A classifier to detect a cat

One way to model the output of a classifier is by assigning 0 (zero) to one label and 1 (one) to the other label. If we follow this standard, we can use the following cost function known as **binary cross entropy** (**BCE**):

$$BCE(PRED, REAL) = \frac{1}{Size} \sum_{d \in D} REAL_d \times log(PRED_d) + \left(1 - REAL_d\right) \times log(1 - PRED_d)$$

Figure 6.29: Binary Cross Entropy formula

This function has two parts. If $REAL_d$ is 1, the sum term is basically:

$$1 \times log(PRED_d) = log(PRED_d)$$

Figure 6.30: BCE formula when REAL is 1

On the other hand, if $REAL_d$ is 0, this part is zero, the sum term is basically:

$$(1 - 0) \times log(1 - PRED_d) = log(1 - PRED_d)$$

Figure 6.31: BCE formula when REAL is 0

Something to pay attention to with BCE is that log(x) is only defined for x > 0. Thus, very often, we add a small factor like:

$$log(PRED_d + \epsilon)$$

Figure 6.32: Fixing numeric stability issues when using log()

Where ε is a small number like **1e-7**. The following program the usage of BCE:

```
1.  template <typename T, int _RANK>
2.  T bce(const Eigen::Tensor<T, _RANK> &PRED, const Eigen::Tensor<T, _
    RANK> &TRUE) {
3.      auto COMP_TRUE = TRUE.constant(1.) - TRUE;
4.      auto COMP_PRED = PRED.constant(1.) - PRED;
5.      auto part1 = TRUE * (PRED + PRED.constant(1e-7)).log();
6.      auto part2 = COMP_TRUE * (COMP_PRED + COMP_PRED.constant(1e-7)).
    log();
7.      auto parts = part1 + part2;
8.      float sum = ((Eigen::Tensor<T, 0>)(parts.sum()))(0);
9.      float result = -sum / PRED.size();
10.     return result;
11. }
12.
13. int main(int, char**)
14. {
15.
16.     Eigen::Tensor<float, 2> TRUE(1, 10);
17.     TRUE.setValues({
18.         {1.f, 0.f, 1.f, 1.f, 0.f, 1.f, 1.f, 0.f, 1.f, 0.f}
19.     });
20.     Eigen::Tensor<float, 2> PRED(1, 10);
21.     PRED.setValues({
22.         {.59f, 0.12f, .9f, .77f, 0.f, .95f, 1.f, 0.22f, .55f, 0.123f}
23.     });
24.
25.     std::cout << "TRUE: \n\n" << TRUE << "\n\n";
26.     std::cout << "PRED: \n\n" << PRED << "\n\n";
27.
28.     std::cout << "BCE: \n\n" << bce(PRED, TRUE) << "\n\n";
29.
30.     return 0;
31. }
```

This program outputs the following:

```
[100%] Built target bce_example
PS Z:\book-workspace\pbp-deep-learning-in-modern-cpp\cost_functions\build> .\bce_example.exe
TRUE:

1 0 1 1 0 1 1 0 1 0

PRED:

 0.59  0.12   0.9  0.77     0  0.95     1  0.22  0.55 0.123

BCE:

0.205103

PS Z:\book-workspace\pbp-deep-learning-in-modern-cpp\cost_functions\build> []
```

Figure 6.33: BCE example output

BCE works for problems where the outcome can be one out of two possibilities. For multiclass problems, BCE is no longer suitable. In this case, we should use the cost function introduced in the next section.

Categorical cross entropy

Previously, when we introduced binary cross entropy, we represented each class using the numbers 0 or 1. For the multilabel case, perhaps one thinks of using the same strategy, for example, representing the labels by 0, 1, 2, 3. However, this is not a good idea since indexing the labels this way will imply some order among them, which is seldom true.

For multiclass classification problems, we usually represent the output with the **one-hot encoding**. Check out the following example:

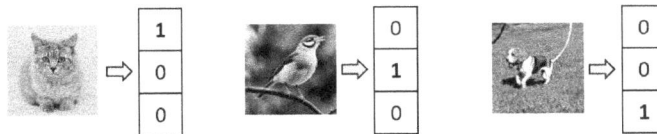

Figure 6.34: Using one-hot encoding

In other works, our predicitons are arrays of size C where C is the number of possible classes. If we use one-hot encoding, we can define the **categorical cross entropy** (**CCE**) cost loss as follows:

$$CCE(PRED, REAL) = -\frac{1}{Size}\sum_{d \in D}\sum_{c \in K} REAL_d \times log(PRED_d)$$

Figure 6.35: Categorical cross entropy formula

To make this formula work out, $PRED_d$ must follow two rules:

- Each coefficient $PRED_d[i]$ is such $0 \leq PRED_d[i] \leq 1$
- All coefficients of $PRED_d$ must sum up 1

These rules mean that $PRED_d$ must behave like a **discrete probability distribution**. In the next chapter, we will learn how to use the **softmax activation function** to guarantee that $PRED_d$ actually has all of these properties.

Conclusion

In this chapter, we introduced the most common cost functions used in deep learning. We have seen that cost functions play a central role in ML by allowing us to fit models to data. We have also discussed the foundation ideas applied to the design of the algorithms used to train models, such as gradient heuristics, minimization, update rule, and stop conditions.

In the next chapter, we will learn what are and how to implement activation functions such as ReLU and softmax.

Exercises

1. In the example in the section *Using gradient to minimize the cost function* we used a step of 0.01 to calculate the smallest cost. What happens if we change this step? Run the code with different steps such as 0.1, 1.0, 0.001, 0.00001, etc., and check the results in terms of convergence and number of epochs.

2. In the example in the section *Using gradient to minimize the cost function* the data was syntetically generated using a gaussian error with standard deviation of 2:

    ```
    1.  // generating 30 instances, in a range of 0 <= X < 10,
        with a = 2, b = 3 and noise deviation = 2
    2.  auto [X, Y] = synthetic_generator(30, 10.f, 2.f, 3.f, 2.f);
    ```

    What happens if there is no noise in the data? What happens if the noise is too high such a standard deviation of 5 or 10?

3. Run the example *Using gradient to minimize the cost function,* but instead of using MSE, use MAE and LOGCOSH cost functions. Determine which cost function converges faster in terms of number of epochs. Explain why?

References

[1] Russell & Norvig, Artificial Intelligence, a Modern Approach, Prentice Hall, 2010.

[2] Mitchell, Machine Learning, McGraw-Hill, 1997.

[3] Goodfellow, Bengio & Courville, Deep Learning, MIT Press, 2016.

[4] Duda at all, Pattern Classification, Wiley, 2000.

[5] Mean Squared Error (MSE), available at **https://www.britannica.com/science/mean-squared-error**

[6] Lemaréchal, Cauchy and the Gradient Method, 2012.

[7] Losses, available at **https://keras.io/api/losses/**

[8] Mean absolute error (MAE), available at **https://www.statisticshowto.com/absolute-error/**

[9] Saleh & Saleh, Statistical Properties of the log-cosh Loss Function

Used in Machine Learning, 2022.

[10] Binary Cross Entropy, available at **https://arize.com/blog-course/binary-cross-entropy-log-loss/**

[11] Understanding Categorical Cross-Entropy Loss, available at **https://gombru.github.io/2018/05/23/cross_entropy_loss/**

Join our book's Discord space

Join the book's Discord Workspace for Latest updates, Offers, Tech happenings around the world, New Release and Sessions with the Authors:

https://discord.bpbonline.com

CHAPTER 7
Defining Activation Functions

Introduction

Activation functions are fundamental building blocks of deep learning models being used to control the output of the layers. So far, we have seen only one example of activation, namely, the sigmoid activation function. However, many other types are available. In this chapter, we will cover the relevant aspects of activation functions, introducing some of the more popular types, such as ReLU and softmax. The chapter also introduces an example of using softmax and categorical cross entropy to train a classifier using the Iris dataset.

Structure

This is the chapter roadmap:

- Sigmoid activation
- Tanh activation
- ReLU activation
- Softmax activation
- Calculating gradients with the chain rule
- Example: Classification Iris dataset

Objectives

By reading this chapter, you will be able to implement, design, and properly use the same activation functions used in modern cutting-edge deep learning models. You will learn how to use softmax to make your network output a discrete probabilistic distribution, a very desired property for classifiers.

Sigmoid activation

Sigmoid is the activation function we have used so far in this book. Indeed, this model is one of the first activation models found in literature being used in the oldest examples [1] of artificial neural networks.

The principal features of sigmoid are:

- **Differentiable**: this function is differentiable for any input. This is important because it allows us to use this function in gradient-based algorithms such as backpropagation.

- **Bounded**: Sigmoid is high-bounded at 1 and low-bounded at 0. This makes this function almost perfect to be used in binary classification problems.

- **S-shape**: Sigmoid plot has its characteristic shape of an S. This shape makes the gradient-based algorithms often converge fast. Of course, this happens only when the input is far from the high or bottom saturation zones.

A simple way to check whether a function is differentiable is by checking its plot. A differentiable function has a smooth one, which is the case of sigmoid:

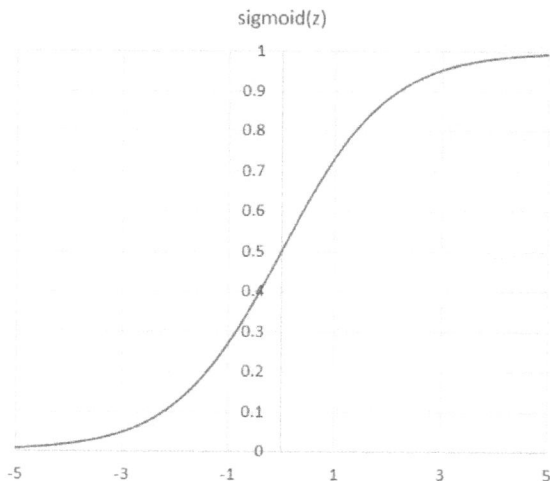

Figure 7.1: Plot of the sigmoid activation function

There are several ways to formulate this function. For example:

$$sigmoid(z) = \frac{e^z}{1 + e^z}$$

Or, often used:

$$sigmoid(z) = \frac{1}{1 + e^{-z}}$$

Due to numeric stability, we will prefer to use this last formula to implement sigmoid:

```
1.  #define SIGMOID_THRESHOLD 45
2.
3.  Template <typename T>
4.  T sigmoid(T z)
5.  {
6.      T result;
7.      if (z >= T(SIGMOID_THRESHOLD)) result = 1.;
8.      else if (z <= - T(SIGMOID_THRESHOLD)) result = 0.;
9.      else result = T(1.) / (T(1.) + std::exp(-z));
10.     return result;
11. }
```

Now, let us check its derivative.

Sigmoid derivative

In *Chapter 9, Coding the Gradient Descent Algorithm*, we will see that derivatives play a central role in training deep learning models. For now, we may think of them as a (derivate) function to calculate gradients, similar to what we did in the previous chapter.

The sigmoid derivative is defined as:

$$\frac{d\ sigmoid(z)}{dz} = sigmoid(z) \times (1 - sigmoid(z))$$

A curious detail of sigmoid is that its derivative is defined using the function itself.

Check the plot of the sigmoid and its derivative as shown:

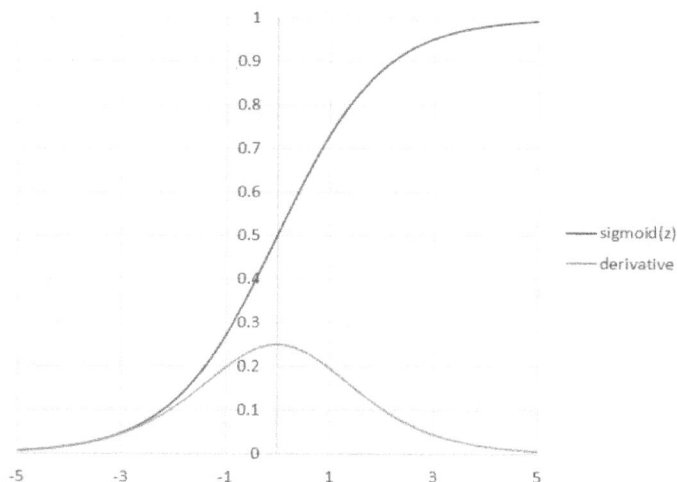

Figure 7.2: Plotting sigmoid and its derivative

Either sigmoid and its derivative are continuous and smooth, two important properties for interactive algorithms. One drawback is the cost to compute because of the calls to **exp()**. The other drawback is the saturation zones $z > 5$ and $z < -5$, which can cause the algorithms to converge slowly.

Tanh activation

Tanh is based on the homonymy trigonometric function tanh [2]. Looking at the tanh plot, it is clear that this activation function is very similar to the sigmoid function:

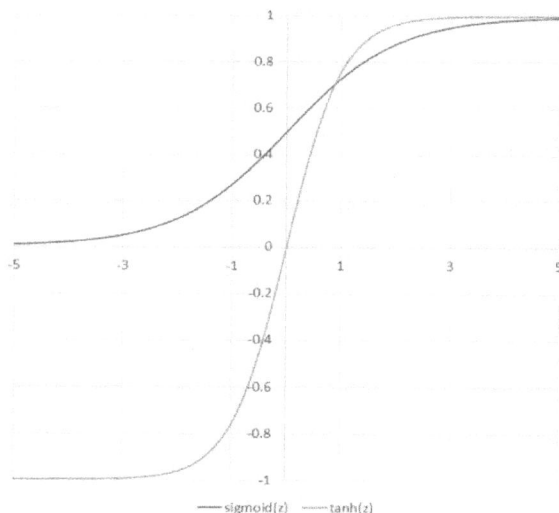

Figure 7.3: Plotting tanh and sigmoid

Indeed, there is a relationship between the two functions:

$$tanh(z) = 2 \times sigmoid(z) - 1$$

The most important difference between sigmoid and tanh is that tanh is bounded in the interval [-1, 1], whereas sigmoid is bounded in the interval [0, 1].

Tanh derivative

The derivative of tanh is given by the following formula:

$$\frac{d\ tanh(z)}{dz} = 1 - (tanh(z))^2$$

Similarly to sigmoid, the derivative of tanh is also defined using *tanh(z)*.

Both tanh and sigmoid are very useful and still used in modern deep learning models. However, the computation cost of these functions was always a recurring issue. In addition, these functions have long saturation zones, which often make the training of models slow. Indeed, the issues in sigmoid and tanh are the motivations behind the introduction of ReLU, the activation function discussed in the next section.

ReLU activation

ReLU [3] is a simple but powerful activation function. It is given by the following formula:

$$ReLU(z) = max\ (0, z)$$

ReLU is a very low-cost function to evaluate in terms of computational processing. In addition, it does not have a saturation zone on its positive side, which changes linearly. In fact, ReLU gained so much popularity during the early stages of deep learning. Nevertheless, this function has two important drawbacks:

- **Non-differentiable**: formally, this function is not differentiable when the input is zero. We often workaround this by defining the derivative equal to 0 in the origin.
- **No-upper-bounded**: this function is not high-bounded. Thus, this is not suitable for being used as an activation of output layers, at least in classification problems.

In practice, unless we are talking about some specific application, ReLU is used in internal layers only. However, when used in this way, ReLU provides faster convergence than sigmoid or tanh activations.

ReLU derivative

For our practical purposes, the derivative of ReLU is defined as follows:

$$\frac{d\ ReLU(z)}{dz} = \begin{cases} 1, if\ z \geq 0 \\ 0, otherwise \end{cases}$$

Plotting this derivative makes it clear that it is not continuous at the origin:

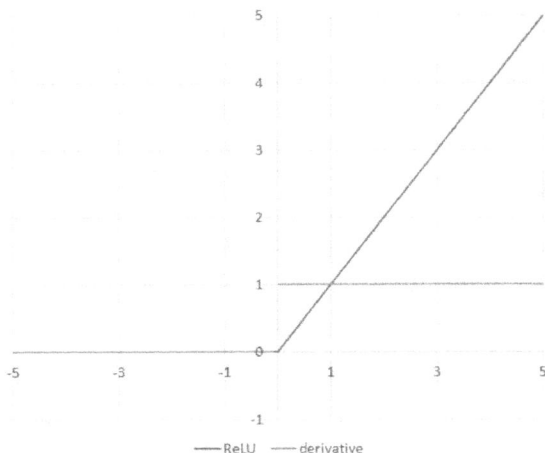

Figure 7.4: Plotting ReLU and its derivative

ReLU overcomes the limitations of sigmoid and tanh regarding saturation, being the most used activation function of internal layers. A problem in ReLU is the flat zone for negative inputs. For every value $x < 0$, ReLU(x) results in zero. The gradient of a flat curve is zero, resulting in a dead neuron. Aiming this problem, several variations of ReLU were proposed [4], such as Leaky ReLU, ELU, and SELU.

Softmax activation

In *Chapter 6, Learning by Minimizing Cost Functions*, we discussed the task of classifying an image into one of three types: Cat, Dog, or Bird:

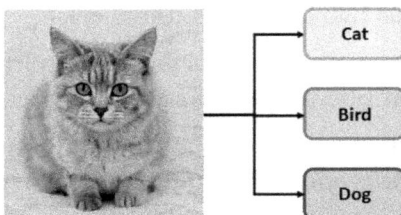

Figure 7.5: Classifying an image into Cat, Bird, or Dog

We can design this system as a function:

probability of being a cat	probability of being a dog	probability of being a bird

Figure 7.6: Modeling the classifier as a discrete probability function.

Taking a **close world assumption**, the sum of probabilities above must be 1. Of course, each probability p must be such as $0 \leq p \leq 1$. This means that `f(image)` works as a discrete probability function. The question is: How do we control the layer's output in a way that the two mentioned conditions are satisfied? In deep learning, we can use softmax to do that.

This is the softmax [5] formula:

$$softmax(Z)_i = \frac{e^{Z_i}}{\sum_{j=1}^{k} e^{Z_j}}$$

Note that Z is an array of k values. Each i-th coefficient of softmax is obtained by the division of the exponentiation of Z_i and the sum of exponentiation of all k coefficients Z_j.

To make things clear, let us try an example:

$$\textbf{Softmax}([1, 4, 5]) = [\ \frac{e^1}{e^1 + e^4 + e^5}, \frac{e^4}{e^1 + e^4 + e^5}, \frac{e^5}{e^1 + e^4 + e^5}\ ]$$

$$\textbf{Softmax}([1, 4, 5]) = [0.0132, 0.2654, 0.7214]$$

Figure 7.7: Softmax example

Indeed, the sum of 0.0132 + 0.2654 + 0.7214 is 1, which holds one of the previous requirements. The other requirement states that each value must be greater or equal to zero and less or equal to 1, which obviously is met by the provided values.

Although this formula is correct, softmax is rarely calculated using it. Instead, we use the following formula:

$$softmax(Z)_i = \frac{e^{Z_i - m}}{\sum_{j=1}^{k} e^{Z_j - m}}$$

$$m = \max (Z_0, Z_1, Z_2, \dots, Z_{k-1})$$

Note that this last softmax formula is achieved by multiplying both the numerator and denominator by e^{-m}:

$$\frac{e^{Z_i}}{\sum_{j=1}^{k} e^{Z_j}} = \frac{e^{Z_i}}{\sum_{j=1}^{k} e^{Z_j}} \times \frac{e^{-m}}{e^{-m}} = \frac{e^{Z_i - m}}{\sum_{j=1}^{k} e^{Z_j - m}}$$

The reason to use the latter is that the former is not numerically unstable. Since $exp(x)$ overflows even for small values of x, it is necessary to normalize the values of Z before applying the exponentiation. Check the following implementation:

```
1.  Eigen::Tensor<float, 1> softmax(const Eigen::Tensor<float, 1> &z)
2.  {
3.      const Eigen::Tensor<float, 0> m = z.maximum();
4.      auto normalized = z - z.constant(m(0));
5.      auto expo = normalized.exp();
6.      const Eigen::Tensor<float, 0> expo_sums = expo.sum();
7.      Eigen::Tensor<float, 1> result = expo / expo.constant(expo_
    sums(0));
8.
9.      return result;
10. }
```

We can check this function as follows:

```
1.  int main(int, char **)
2.  {
3.      Eigen::Tensor<float, 2> input(8, 3);
4.      input.setValues({
5.          {0.1, 1., -2.},{10., 2., 5.},{5., -5., 0.},{2., 3., 2.},
6.          {100., 1000., -500.},{3., 3., 3.},{-1, 1., -1.},{-
    11., -0.2, -.1}
7.      });
8.
9.      const int batch_size = input.dimension(0);
10.     const int output_size = input.dimension(1);
11.
12.     Eigen::array<Eigen::Index, 2> extent = {1, output_size};
13.     Eigen::array<int, 1> reshape_dim({output_size});
14.     for (int i = 0; i < batch_size; i++) {
15.         Eigen::array<Eigen::Index, 2> offset = {i, 0};
16.         Eigen::Tensor<float, 1> row = input.slice(offset, extent).
    reshape(reshape_dim);
17.
18.         Eigen::Tensor<float, 1> output = softmax(row);
19.         std::cout << "soft-
    max([" << row << "]): [" << output << "]\n";
20.     }
21.
22.     return 0;
23. }
```

This code outputs:

```
PS Z:\book-workspace\pbp-deep-learning-in-modern-cpp\activation_functions\build> .\using_softmax.exe
softmax([0.1   1  -2]): [0.279169 0.686645 0.034186]
softmax([10  2  5]): [   0.992976 0.000333106  0.00669062]
softmax([ 5 -5  0]): [   0.993262 4.5094e-05 0.00669255]
softmax([2 3 2]): [0.211942 0.576117 0.211942]
softmax([ 100 1000 -500]): [0 1 0]
softmax([3 3 3]): [0.333333 0.333333 0.333333]
softmax([-1  1 -1]): [0.106507 0.786986 0.106507]
softmax([ -11 -0.2 -0.1]): [9.6901e-06   0.475016   0.524974]
PS Z:\book-workspace\pbp-deep-learning-in-modern-cpp\activation_functions\build> ▌
```

Figure 7.8: Running the softmax example

Implementing softmax for one-dimensional tensors is quite simple. In general, we have a function that deals with multidimensional inputs representing batches of one-dimensional inputs. For example, consider the following input:

-2	1	0.1
5	2	10
0	-5	5
2	3	2
-500	1000	100
3	3	3
-1	1	-1
-0.1	-0.2	-11

Figure 7.9: The tensor input from the example

This single 2-rank tensor 8x3 is the same tensor we used in the previous example. As we discussed in *Chapter 1, Introduction to Deep Learning Programming*, aiming to use most of the underlying computational resources, we will prefer to process a tensor like this at once instead of using a loop.

To do that, some manipulation is required, however. First, it is necessary to calculate the maximum for each input:

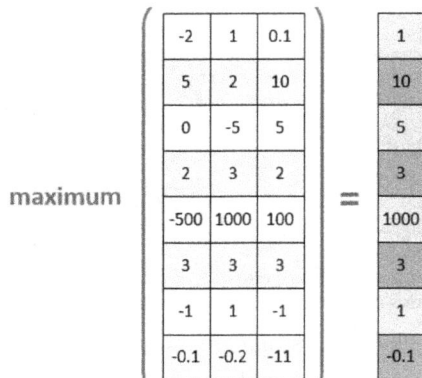

Figure 7.10: Finding the max for each row

Note that this maximum operation must roll over the first axes. Now, we can broadcast the array of maximums to fit the same dimension as the input tensor:

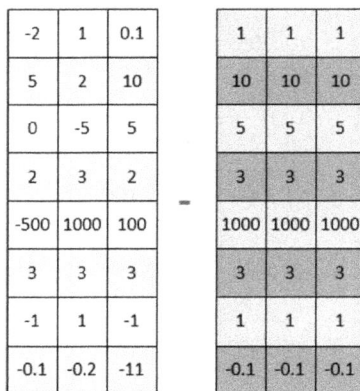

Figure 7.11: Broadcasting the array of maximums

Once the two tensors have the same dimensions, we can calculate the difference between them to normalize each coefficient accordingly. We can see these ideas in action in the following code:

```
1.  Eigen::Tensor<float, 2> softmax_2D(const Eigen::Tensor<float, 2> &z)
2.  {
3.
4.      auto dimensions = z.dimensions();
5.
6.      int batch_size = dimensions.at(0);
7.      int instances_size = dimensions.at(1);
8.
9.      // Getting the maximum for each instance.
```

```
10.     // Note that this operation reduces 1 dimension
11.     Eigen::array<int, 1> depth_dim({1});
12.     auto z_max = z.maximum(depth_dim);
13.
14.     // Getting the max array as an 2-rank tensor
15.     Eigen::array<int, 2> reshape_dim({batch_size, 1});
16.     auto max_reshaped = z_max.reshape(reshape_dim);
17.
18.     // Broadcasting max
19.     Eigen::array<int, 2> bcast({1, instances_size});
20.     auto max_values = max_reshaped.broadcast(bcast);
21.
22.     // Normalizing the input
23.     auto normalized = z - max_values;
24.
25.     // calculating softmax
26.     auto expo = normalized.exp();
27.     auto expo_sums = expo.sum(depth_dim);
28.     auto sums_reshaped = expo_sums.reshape(reshape_dim);
29.     auto sums = sums_reshaped.broadcast(bcast);
30.     Eigen::Tensor<float, 2> result = expo / sums;
31.
32.     return result;
33. }
```

Finally, we can compare the two versions:

```
1. auto output_2D = softmax_2D(input);
2. std::cout << "\noutput_2D:\n" << output_2D << "\n\n";
```

To obtain:

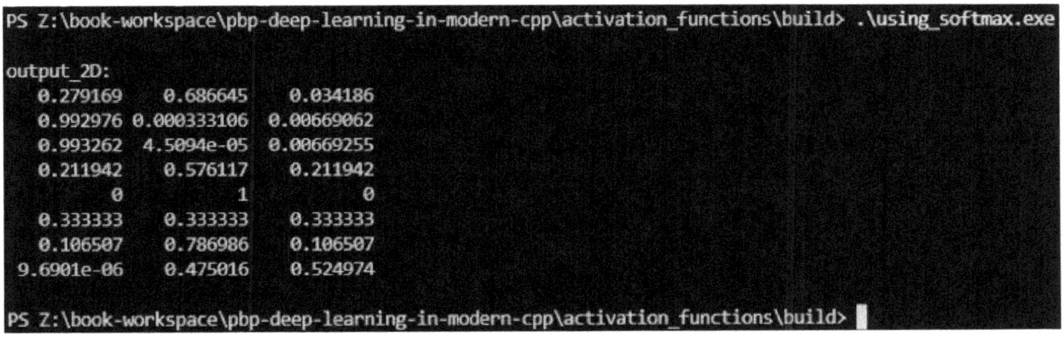

Figure 7.12: *Running the vectorized version of softmax*

The most important thing to note here is that softmax actually works like a discrete probabilistic distribution:

- Each coefficient value is inside the interval $[0, 1]$

- The sum of coefficients is 1

Particularly, this property is relevant to use in combination with the categorical cross-entropy cost function when we are solving classification problems. The usage of softmax and categorical cross entropy is exactly the scenario of the example at the end of this chapter.

Softmax derivative

In general, activation functions are coefficient-wise operations. In coefficient-wise activation functions, the output of each output coefficient depends only on the respective input coefficient. This is the case of the sigmoid, ReLU, tanh, and several other activations functions. As we have seen so far, this is not the case with softmax.

In softmax, each coefficient is dependent on all input value coefficients. As a result, each coefficient has a non-zero derivative for each index, which can be found by the following formula:

$$\frac{d\, S(Z)_i}{dZ_j} = S(Z)_i(\delta(i,j) - S(Z)_j)$$

Where $S(Z)_i$ is the softmax value for Z_i and $\delta(i, j)$ is the **Kronecker delta function**:

$$\delta(i,j) = \begin{cases} 1, if\ i = j \\ 0, otherwise \end{cases}$$

If we apply this function to each pair (i, j), we end up with the following non-diagonal **Jacobian matrix**:

$$J(Z)$$
$$= \begin{bmatrix} S(Z)_0(1 - S(Z)_0) & -S(Z)_0\,S(Z)_1 & -S(Z)_0\,S(Z)_2 & \cdots & -S(Z)_0\,S(Z)_{k-1} \\ -S(Z)_1\,S(Z)_0 & S(Z)_1(1 - S(Z)_1) & -S(Z)_1\,S(Z)_2 & \cdots & -S(Z)_1\,S(Z)_{k-1} \\ -S(Z)_2\,S(Z)_0 & -S(Z)_2\,S(Z)_1 & S(Z)_2(1 - S(Z)_2) & \cdots & -S(Z)_2\,S(Z)_{k-1} \\ \vdots & \vdots & \vdots & \ddots & \vdots \\ -S(Z)_{k-1}\,S(Z)_0 & -S(Z)_{k-1}\,S(Z)_1 & -S(Z)_{k-1}\,S(Z)_2 & \cdots & S(Z)_{k-1}(1 - S(Z)_{k-1}) \end{bmatrix}$$

Implementing this derivative is relatively simple in the one-dimensional case. First, one can use the matrix product to obtain a squared $S_i S_j$ matrix:

$$\begin{bmatrix} S_0 \\ S_1 \\ S_2 \\ S_3 \\ S_4 \end{bmatrix} \times \begin{bmatrix} S_0 & S_1 & S_2 & S_3 & S_4 \end{bmatrix} = \begin{bmatrix} S_0S_0 & S_0S_1 & S_0S_2 & S_0S_3 & S_0S_4 \\ S_1S_0 & S_1S_1 & S_1S_2 & S_1S_3 & S_1S_4 \\ S_2S_0 & S_2S_1 & S_2S_2 & S_2S_3 & S_2S_4 \\ S_3S_0 & S_3S_1 & S_3S_2 & S_3S_3 & S_3S_4 \\ S_4S_0 & S_4S_1 & S_4S_2 & S_4S_3 & S_4S_4 \end{bmatrix}$$

***Figure 7.13**: Calculating the Jacobian matrix of softmax—part 1*

Then, we can define a **diagonal matrix** using the *S* coefficients, subtracting the previous tensor from this matrix:

$$\begin{bmatrix} S_0 & 0 & 0 & 0 & 0 \\ 0 & S_1 & 0 & 0 & 0 \\ 0 & 0 & S_2 & 0 & 0 \\ 0 & 0 & 0 & S_3 & 0 \\ 0 & 0 & 0 & 0 & S_4 \end{bmatrix} - \begin{bmatrix} S_0S_0 & S_0S_1 & S_0S_2 & S_0S_3 & S_0S_4 \\ S_1S_0 & S_1S_1 & S_1S_2 & S_1S_3 & S_1S_4 \\ S_2S_0 & S_2S_1 & S_2S_2 & S_2S_3 & S_2S_4 \\ S_3S_0 & S_3S_1 & S_3S_2 & S_3S_3 & S_3S_4 \\ S_4S_0 & S_4S_1 & S_4S_2 & S_4S_3 & S_4S_4 \end{bmatrix} = \begin{bmatrix} S_0-S_0S_0 & -S_0S_1 & -S_0S_2 & -S_0S_3 & -S_0S_4 \\ -S_1S_0 & S_1-S_1S_1 & -S_1S_2 & -S_1S_3 & -S_1S_4 \\ -S_2S_0 & -S_2S_1 & S_2-S_2S_2 & -S_2S_3 & -S_2S_4 \\ -S_3S_0 & -S_3S_1 & -S_3S_2 & S_3-S_3S_3 & -S_3S_4 \\ -S_4S_0 & -S_4S_1 & -S_4S_2 & -S_4S_3 & S_4-S_4S_4 \end{bmatrix}$$

***Figure 7.14**: Calculating the Jacobian matrix of softmax—part 2*

This last matrix is the Jacobian of softmax with respect to its input. In practice, we calculate this Jacobian in batches in the same way we did to calculate the softmax output. This approach will be discussed later at the end of this chapter.

Calculating gradients with the chain rule

Before we can see softmax working in a more interesting example, there is something quite important to talk about: how to calculate the gradient of composite functions.

As you already know, derivatives like the softmax derivative introduced in the previous section are used by gradient-based algorithms to train models from data. These algorithms use the update rule to iteratively update the model weights:

$$W := W - \eta \times grad$$

Where *grad* is given by the gradient of the **output cost** with respect to the weights:

$$grad = \frac{\partial Cost}{\partial W}$$

A central question since the early days of machine learning has been: how can we calculate gradients for complex models? This can be solved by the chain rule, as explained ahead.

Finding the gradient of weights

Let us start with the softmax's derivative. Each coefficient of the Jacobian matrix represents the slopes of the softmax function with respect to each coefficient of Z. However, we know that Z is a result of another function. For example, the output *Out* of a dense layer using softmax is given by:

$$Z = X \times W$$

$$Out = softmax(Z)$$

What the Jacobian matrix from the previous section provides are the partial derivatives regarding Z:

$$\frac{\partial\ Out}{\partial Z} = \frac{\partial\ softmax(Z)}{\partial Z}$$

However, since our objective is to update the coefficients of W, we are interested in finding the gradients with respect to the weight matrix W. In other words, we are interested in finding:

$$\frac{\partial\ Out}{\partial W} = \frac{\partial\ softmax(X \times W)}{\partial W}$$

To solve this problem, there is a procedure called **chain rule** [6] which allows us to find **derivatives of composite functions**. For example, supposing a composite function $A(x) = B(C(x))$, we can find the derivative of A with respect to x using the following rule:

$$\frac{\partial A}{\partial x} = \frac{\partial B}{\partial C} \times \frac{\partial C}{\partial x}$$

By applying this rule to our problem, we end up with:

$$\frac{\partial\ Out}{\partial W} = \frac{\partial\ softmax(X \times W)}{\partial Z} \times \frac{\partial Z}{\partial W}$$

Since we know that:

$$\frac{\partial Z}{\partial W} = X$$

The formula then becomes:

$$\frac{\partial\ Out}{\partial W} = \frac{\partial\ softmax(X \times W)}{\partial Z} \times X$$

Finally, we can find the gradient of the cost function with respect to the weights as follows:

$$grad = \frac{\partial Cost}{\partial W} = \frac{\partial Cost}{\partial\ Out} \times \frac{\partial\ Out}{\partial W} = \frac{\partial Cost}{\partial\ Out} \times \frac{\partial\ softmax(X \times W)}{\partial Z} \times X$$

If you look carefully, you may note that we have everything we need to obtain the gradient:

$$\frac{\partial \, Cost}{\partial \, W} \; = \; \underbrace{\frac{\partial \, Cost}{\partial \, Out}}_{\substack{\text{Derivative} \\ \text{of the cost} \\ \text{function}}} \; \times \; \underbrace{\frac{\partial \, softmax(X \times W)}{\partial \, Z}}_{\substack{\text{Derivative of the} \\ \text{activation function}}} \; \times \; \underbrace{X}_{\text{Input}}$$

Figure 7.15: *The components of the output cost gradient*

In other words, to calculate the gradient of weights, we need only to know:

- The cost function gradient
- The activation function gradient
- The input

We will see this calculation in action in the following example.

Example: Classification Iris dataset

We will finish this chapter with an example of using all the concepts introduced so far in the book: layers, cost functions, activation functions, and gradients. We will train a model using the famous **Iris dataset** [7] to classify an instance into one of three classes: setosa, versicolor, or virginica.

The Iris dataset

Iris is a very popular dataset used in machine learning for long. This dataset contains only a small sequence of 150 registers, being each register composed of five fields:

- **Sepal length**: a numeric value representing the flower sepal length in cm
- **Sepal width**: a numeric value representing the flower sepal width in cm
- **Petal length**: a numeric value representing the flower petal length in cm
- **Petal width**: a numeric value representing the flower petal width in cm
- **Class**: one of the following values: setosa, versicolor, or virginica

In classification tasks like this, usually, the first fields are called **features**, and the last one is called the **class label**.

The data is available in a **comma-separated-values** format. In the book GitHub repository, you can find the code used in this example. There, you can find a utility lambda function:

```
1. auto load_iris_dataset = [](std::string file_
   path, bool shuffle = true, float split_percentage = .8)
```

This lambda loads the dataset given the local file path (you need to download the file by yourself):

```
1. auto [training_X_ds, training_Y_ds, test_X_ds, test_Y_ds] = load_
   iris_dataset("data/iris.csv", false);
```

Once called, the function results in four tensors:

- training_X_ds: A tensor of size (120, 4) containing the features of 120 registers.
- training_Y_ds: A tensor of size (120, 3) containing the one-hot encoded label of the same 120 registers in **training_X_ds/**
- test_X_ds: Similar format as **training_X_ds**, containing the features remaining 30 registers.
- test_Y_ds: Similar format as **training_Y_ds**, containing the one-hot encoded labels of the remaining 30 registers.

The labels are encoded as follows:

- Setosa => [1, 0, 0]
- Versicolor => [0, 1, 0]
- Virginica => [0, 0, 1]

The tensors will be used in the next steps. In particular, **training_X_ds** and **training_Y_ds** will be used to train our model.

Defining the model

The model consists of a single dense layer using softmax activation. We will use the categorical cross entropy for the train:

```
1. Softmax<2> activation;
2. Dense layer(initial_weights, &activation);
3. CategoricalCrossEntropy<2> loss_function;
```

In this example, we will perform a very simple model training. In a nutshell, the process consists of a loop with only 3 steps: the forward step, the backward step, and the model update. These 3 steps will be continuously performed until the algorithm reach one of the stop conditions.

The forward pass

The forward pass is very simple, consisting only in calculating the output (the predictions) of the **given training_X_ds**:

```
1. // Obtaining the output for the training dataset
2. auto output = layer.forward(training_X_ds);
```

Since the **layer** is dense, what this line is actually performing is:

$$Z = X \times W$$

$$Out = softmax(Z)$$

Calculating the gradient

The cost gradient with respect to the output is given by the derivative of the cost function:

```
1. // Calculating the derivative of the cost with respect to the output
2. auto dcost_doutput = loss_function.derivative(training_Y_ds, output);
```

What this line is actually doing is calculating:

$$\frac{\partial Cost}{\partial\ Out}$$

Once we have found the cost gradient, we can feed it to the layer in order to perform the weight gradient calculation:

```
1. // calculating layer gradients
2. layer.backward(dcost_doutput);
```

This line performs the following calculation:

$$\frac{\partial Cost}{\partial W} = \frac{\partial Cost}{\partial\ Out} \times \frac{\partial\ softmax(X \times W)}{\partial Z} \times X$$

The weight gradients are stored internally in the layer. They will be used by the layer in the next step.

> **Note: Here the decision to use classes is a software engineering decision only, it is not a model requirement at all. We usually prefer to work with classes and stateful objects to keep things tidy. It is up to you to perform your calculations using only functions if you prefer.**

Updating the model

Once the layer has calculated the weight gradient, it is time for an update. The update is performed using the previously known update rule. In this rule, there is a learning rate adjusting the intensity of the update:

```
1. // In this step, the internal
2. layer.update_state(learning_rate);
```

This step performs the update rule:

$$W := W - \eta \times grad$$

Where *grad* was obtained in the previous step.

Here we are using $\eta = 0.1$ as the learning rate. There is some controversy about how to set up a good hyperparameter, such as the learning rate. The most common (and probably the best) approach is running the model training several times with different learning rates, choosing the one with the best results.

Finding when to stop

In this example, we run the training loop one thousand times:

```
1. const int MAX_EPOCHS = 1000;
2. int epoch = 0;
3. while (epoch++ < MAX_EPOCHS)
4. {
5.     //...
6. }
```

Note: We can improve the code to include more complex stop conditions. For example, we can stop the loop when the cost or the cost gradient is too low.

Evaluating the results

At the end of each loop, we evaluate the model performance using the training data and the validation data:

```
1. auto val_output = layer.predict(test_X_ds);
2. float val_loss = loss_function.evaluate(test_Y_ds, val_output);
3.
4. float training_acc = accuracy(training_Y_ds, output);
5. float validation_acc = accuracy(test_Y_ds, val_output);
```

Here, we are measuring the model performance using two metrics: the same cost function used to train the model, and a metric called **accuracy**. Accuracy is a very simple and well-known metric that provides the percentage of correct predictions.

The model performance on validation data works like an estimator of the actual model performance when used in production. Indeed, evaluating the model performance only on training data is a methodological mistake.

Note: Evaluation metrics and the guidelines for training models (including common pitfalls) will be discussed in the next part of this book.

Putting it all together

Joining all the pieces, the loop looks like that:

```cpp
1.  int main(int, char **)
2.  {
3.
4.      srand((unsigned int) time(0));
5.
6.      auto [training_X_ds, training_Y_ds, test_X_ds, test_Y_
    ds] = load_iris_dataset("data/iris.csv", true);
7.
8.      auto init_weights = [](int rows, int cols, float range) {
9.          Eigen::Tensor<float, 2> result(rows, cols);
10.         result = result.random() * result.constant(range) - result.
    constant(range / 2.);
11.         return result;
12.     };
13.
14.     auto initial_weights = init_weights(4, 3, 0.1);
15.
16.     Softmax<2> activation;
17.     Dense layer(initial_weights, &activation);
18.
19.     CategoricalCrossEntropy<2> loss_function;
20.
21.     const int MAX_EPOCHS = 1000;
22.     const float learning_rate = 0.1;
23.     int epoch = 0;
24.     while (epoch++ < MAX_EPOCHS)
25.     {
26.
27.         // obtaining the output for the training dataset
28.         auto output = layer.forward(training_X_ds);
29.
30.         // calculating the derivative of the cost with respect to the output
31.         auto dcost_doutput = loss_function.derivative(training_Y_ds, output);
32.
33.         // calculating layer gradients
34.         layer.backward(dcost_doutput);
35.
```

```
36.              // in this step, the internal
37.              layer.update_state(learning_rate);
38.
39.              // evaluating training loss
40.              float loss = loss_function.evaluate(training_Y_ds, output);
41.
42.              if (epoch == 1 || epoch % 50 == 0) {
43.
44.                  // evaluating validation loss
45.                  auto val_output = layer.predict(test_X_ds);
46.                  float val_loss = loss_function.evaluate(test_Y_ds, val_output);
47.
48.                  float training_acc = accuracy(training_Y_ds, output);
49.                  float validation_acc = accuracy(test_Y_ds, val_output);
50.
51.                  std::cout << "epoch:\t" <<   epoch
52.                      << "\tloss:\t" << loss << "\tacc:\t" << training_acc
53.                      << "\tval_loss:\t" << val_loss << "\tval_
    acc:\t" << validation_acc << "\n";
54.              }
55.
56.          }
57.
58.      return 0;
59. }
```

Running this training results in the following output:

```
Z:\book-workspace\pbp-deep-learning-in-modern-cpp\activation_functions\build>iris_example.exe
epoch:  1       loss:   1.13493 acc:    35      val_loss:       1.02262 val_acc:        40
epoch:  50      loss:   0.673918        acc:    65      val_loss:       0.675356        val_acc:        60
epoch:  100     loss:   0.530265        acc:    65      val_loss:       0.514088        val_acc:        63.3333
epoch:  150     loss:   0.398573        acc:    73.3333 val_loss:       0.375341        val_acc:        86.6667
epoch:  200     loss:   0.292656        acc:    93.3333 val_loss:       0.256562        val_acc:        93.3333
epoch:  250     loss:   0.255584        acc:    95.8333 val_loss:       0.205326        val_acc:        100
epoch:  300     loss:   0.236654        acc:    96.6667 val_loss:       0.186048        val_acc:        100
epoch:  350     loss:   0.221411        acc:    96.6667 val_loss:       0.171103        val_acc:        100
epoch:  400     loss:   0.208852        acc:    96.6667 val_loss:       0.159058        val_acc:        100
epoch:  450     loss:   0.198317        acc:    96.6667 val_loss:       0.149162        val_acc:        100
epoch:  500     loss:   0.189347        acc:    95.8333 val_loss:       0.140897        val_acc:        100
epoch:  550     loss:   0.181612        acc:    95.8333 val_loss:       0.1339   val_acc:        100
epoch:  600     loss:   0.174872        acc:    95.8333 val_loss:       0.127906        val_acc:        100
epoch:  650     loss:   0.168941        acc:    95.8333 val_loss:       0.122717        val_acc:        100
epoch:  700     loss:   0.163681        acc:    95.8333 val_loss:       0.118185        val_acc:        100
epoch:  750     loss:   0.158982        acc:    95.8333 val_loss:       0.114196        val_acc:        100
epoch:  800     loss:   0.154758        acc:    95.8333 val_loss:       0.110659        val_acc:        100
epoch:  850     loss:   0.150937        acc:    95      val_loss:       0.107505        val_acc:        100
epoch:  900     loss:   0.147465        acc:    95.8333 val_loss:       0.104675        val_acc:        100
epoch:  950     loss:   0.144294        acc:    95.8333 val_loss:       0.102124        val_acc:        96.6667
epoch:  1000    loss:   0.141387        acc:    95.8333 val_loss:       0.099813        val_acc:        96.6667
Z:\book-workspace\pbp-deep-learning-in-modern-cpp\activation_functions\build>
```

Figure 7.16: Running the example

Note: Due to randomization, each time, the training provides a slightly different output.

If we plot the metrics, we will find a chart like this:

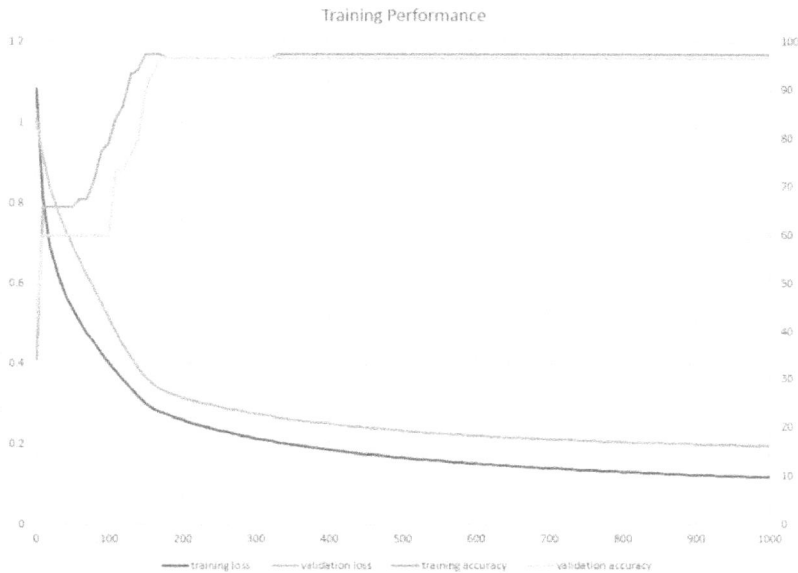

Figure 7.17: *Plotting the training performance*

The shape of this chart is very common in the training of models. Usually, the cost starts at the top, decreasing the most in the first epochs. At some point, the cost starts to decrease asymptotically. Accuracy often has the opposite behavior, starting low and increasing until it saturates at some level.

The practical concerns of training models, including using the backpropagation algorithm, will be discussed in the forthcoming chapters. The most important point here is to understand how to use the components seen so far to mount a simple but insightful training routine.

Conclusion

In this chapter, we learned the most popular activation functions. We learned their derivatives, understanding how to use them to calculate the weight gradients. We also learned how to use softmax to make a layer works like discrete probabilistic distribution. To understand exactly why this property is so important, we introduced an example where a model is trained using the Iris dataset.

In the next chapter, we will finish our journey on deep learning components by discussing the pooling layers, an essential component in modern CNN architectures.

Exercises

1. Consider the following max-min normalization:

$$X_n = \frac{X - X_{min}}{X_{max} - X_{min}}$$

Figure 7.18: Max-min normalization

Apply this normalization to the Iris dataset before inputting the data into the training loop. How does this normalization affect the training in terms of quality and time convergence?

2. In our example, we used softmax as the activation function and categorical cross entropy as the cost function:

    1. `Softmax<2> activation;`
    2. `Dense layer(initial_weights, &activation);`
    3. `CategoricalCrossEntropy<2> loss_function;`

    Replace these two functions by sigmoid and MSE, as follows:

    1. `Sigmoid<2> activation;`
    2. `Dense layer(initial_weights, &activation);`
    3. `MSE<2> loss_function;`

Run the training using these new functions and check the results, comparing them with the results using softmax and categorical cross entropy.

References

[1] Haykin, Neural Networks: A Comprehensive Foundation, Prentice Hall, 1999.

[2] Goodfellow, Bengio & Courville, Deep Learning, MIT Press, 2016.

[3] Aggarwal, Neural Networks and Deep Learning, Springer, 2018.

[4] Dabal Pedamonti, Comparison of non-linear activation functions for deep neural networks on

MNIST classification task, 2018.

[5] Bishop, Pattern Recognition and Machine Learning, Springer, 2006.

[6] The chain rule, available at **https://web.mit.edu/wwmath/calculus/differentiation/ chain.html**

[7] Iris dataset, avaialble at **https://archive.ics.uci.edu/dataset/53/iris**

CHAPTER 8
Using Pooling Layers

Introduction

This chapter introduces **pooling layers**, an essential component of convolutional neural network architectures. Pooling layers reduce the size of the input tensor by applying a summarization statistic such as max or mean. This chapter will describe and implement them, covering the most popular types: 2D max pooling and 2D average pooling.

Structure

This is the chapter roadmap:

- Introducing pooling layers
- Implementing pooling layers
- Pros and cons of using pooling layers

Objectives

After reading this chapter, you will be able to understand how to implement and use 2D pooling layers. In addition, you will understand the pros and cons of using this component in convolutional neural networks.

Introducing pooling layers

In a typical scenario, a convolutional neural network consists of one or more convolutional layers followed by a special type of layer called a pooling layer. Consider the following example:

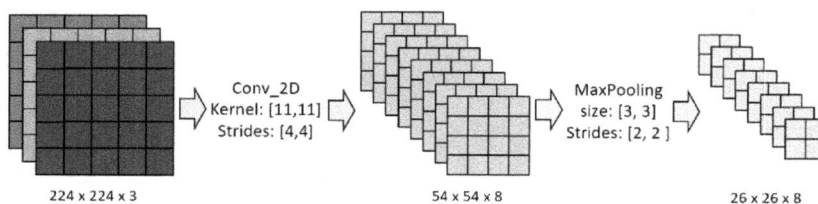

224 x 224 x 3   54 x 54 x 8   26 x 26 x 8

Figure 8.1: A fragment of a CNN network

This sequence consisting of input-convolution-pooling is a sort of very common strategy [1], particularly useful when we are defining more complex networks with huge inputs. In some way, pooling layers work like convolutions by sliding over the input layer. But, unlike convolutions, pooling layers do not have **trainable coefficients**.

Consider the following example, where a 3x3 max-pooling layer is applied to a *7x7* input grid using strides of 2 to generate a *3x3* output:

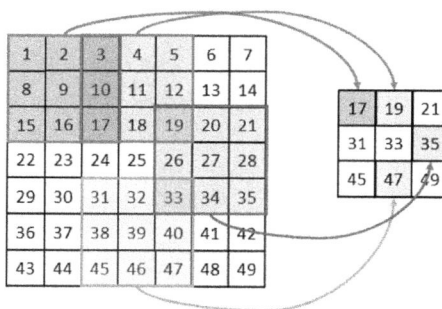

Figure 8.2: Example of 2D max pooling

As its name suggests, max pooling calculates the output using the maximum value. The following formulas give the size of the pooling layer:

$$output\_rows = floor((X\_rows - pool\_rows)/strides) + 1$$
$$output\_cols = floor((X\_cols - pool\_cols)/strides) + 1$$

Figure 8.3: Computing the output dimensions of a pooling layer

In general, **pool_rows** is equal to **pool_cols**. Let us see how to use these formulas in the example discussed in the next section.

Implementing pooling layers

Pooling layers can be implemented in the same way as convolutions. However, here, we can use the **Eigen** utility function **extract_image_patches**, which will make our job easier. Check the following example:

```
1.  template <typename T>
2.  const Eigen::Tensor<T, 2> pooling(-
    const Eigen::Tensor<T, 2> &X, int pool_size, int strides = 1) {
3.
4.      // reshaping the input to the 4-Rank shape (depth, rows, columns, batch)
5.      Eigen::array<Eigen::DenseIndex, 4> reshaped_dims{{1, X.
    dimension(0), X.dimension(1), 1}};
6.      auto reshaped = X.reshape(reshaped_dims);
7.
8.      // getting the patches
9.      Eigen::Tensor<T, 5> patches = reshaped.extract_image_
    patches(pool_size, pool_size, strides, strides, Eigen::PADDING_
    VALID);
10.
11.     // getting the max of each patch
12.     Eigen::array<Eigen::DenseIndex, 2> dims({1, 2});
13.     auto max_patches = patches.maximum(dims);
14.
15.     // reshaping back to fit 2-RANK dimensions. Note that extract_
    image_patches visit each row/col
16.     // Thus, there is an automatic padding in the left & bottom ends
17.     int pre_rows = X.dimension(0) / strides;
18.     int pre_cols = X.dimension(1) / strides;
19.     Eigen::array<Eigen::DenseIndex, 2> pre_dims{{pre_rows, pre_cols}};
20.     auto pre = max_patches.reshape(pre_dims);
21.
22.     int rows = (X.dimension(0) - pool_size) / strides + 1;
23.     int cols = (X.dimension(1) - pool_size) / strides + 1;
24.
25.     Eigen::array<Eigen::DenseIndex, 2> offsets = {0, 0};
26.     Eigen::array<Eigen::DenseIndex, 2> extents = {rows, cols};
27.     Eigen::Tensor<T, 2> result = pre.slice(offsets, extents);
28.
29.     return result;
30. }
```

```
31.
32. int main(int, char**)
33. {
34.
35.     Eigen::Tensor<float, 2> input(6, 8);
36.     input.setValues({
37.                 { 0.f,  1.f,  2.f,  3.f,  4.f,  5.f,  6.f,  7.f},
38.                 { 8.f,  9.f, 10.f, 11.f, 12.f, 13.f, 14.f, 15.f},
39.                 {16.f, 17.f, 18.f, 19.f, 20.f, 21.f, 22.f, 23.f},
40.                 {24.f, 25.f, 26.f, 27.f, 28.f, 29.f, 30.f, 31.f},
41.                 {32.f, 33.f, 34.f, 35.f, 36.f, 37.f, 38.f, 39.f},
42.                 {40.f, 41.f, 42.f, 43.f, 44.f, 45.f, 46.f, 47.f}
43.             });
44.
45.     auto res_strides_1 = pooling(input, 2);
46.     std::cout << "res_strides_1: \n\n" << res_strides_1 << "\n\n";
47.
48.     auto res_strides_2 = pooling(input, 2, 2);
49.     std::cout << "res_strides_2: \n\n" << res_strides_2 << "\n\n";
50.
51.     return 0;
52. }
```

This code uses **maximum()**, which is one of the built-in reducers from the Eigen Tensor API. This reducer calculates the maximum value along the specified axes:

```
1. Eigen::array<Eigen::DenseIndex, 2> dims({1, 2});
2. auto max_patches = patches.maximum(dims);
```

Once executed, this code generates the following output:

```
PS Z:\book-workspace\pbp-deep-learning-in-modern-cpp\pooling\build> .\pooling_example.exe
res_strides_1:

 9 10 11 12 13 14 15
17 18 19 20 21 22 23
25 26 27 28 29 30 31
33 34 35 36 37 38 39
41 42 43 44 45 46 47

res_strides_2:

 9 11 13 15
25 27 29 31
41 43 45 47

PS Z:\book-workspace\pbp-deep-learning-in-modern-cpp\pooling\build> []
```

Figure 8.4: Using 2D max pooling

Another common example of pooling is 2D average pooling [3]. We can modify the previous example to calculate 2D average pooling simply by changing the line:

```
1. auto max_patches = patches.maximum(dims);
```

To:

```
1. auto max_patches = patches.mean(dims);
```

After making this change, building and running the code again results in the following output:

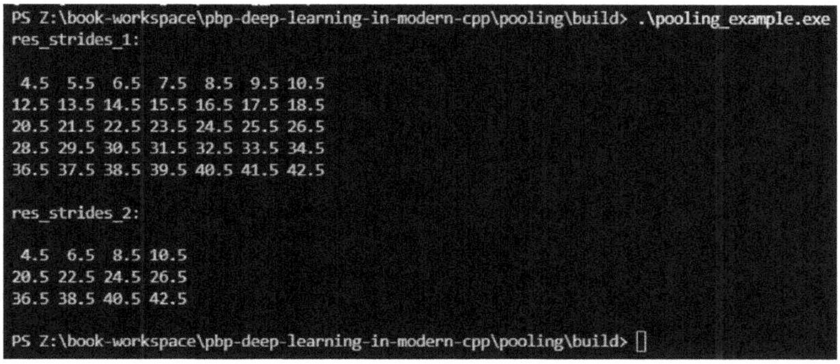

Figure 8.5: Using 2D average pooling

2D average pooling works in a very similar way to 2D max pooling:

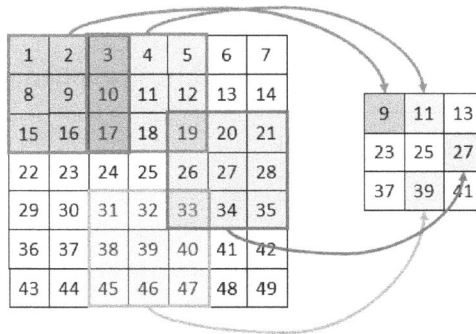

Figure 8.6: Example of using 2D average pooling

Although pooling layers are often found in modern deep learning architectures, using this component is not always beneficial. The following section covers the pros and cons of using pooling layers in our models.

Pros and cons of using pooling layers

Pooling layers play an important role in CNNs. The two main reasons why we use pooling layers are [1][2]:

- **Local translation invariance**: When we use pooling, small local translation will not affect (or the effect will be reduced) the output. This makes networks more robust to noise and local variability.

- **Computational efficiency**: Pooling often reduces the size of its outputs. This makes the next layer perform less computation.

However, sometimes pooling can imply some disadvantages, for example [1]:

- **Loss of pixel-perfect accuracy**: Since pooling summarizes the neighborhood using some statistical operation, some loss of information is inevitable. To a system that requires pixel-scale precision, pooling can make things harder to achieve.

- **Sequence-to-sequence encoders**: Pooling can bring additional difficulties to top-down architectures such as Boltzmann machines and autoencoders.

It is also important to note that pooling layers include at least two more **hyperparameters** to set: the pool size and the strides. The values of these parameters are usually found by an experimental study.

A recurrent setup found in many deep learning architectures is the use of a pool size equal to strides. In a setup like this, the pool size is 2 or 3, resulting in an output that is 2 or 3 times smaller than the input.

Although there is some theoretical and practical guidance [4], finding the best settings for these parameters often requires some intuition throughout a try-and-error process.

Backward in max-pooling layers

Consider the following example where max-pooling is applied to a *6x5* input matrix:

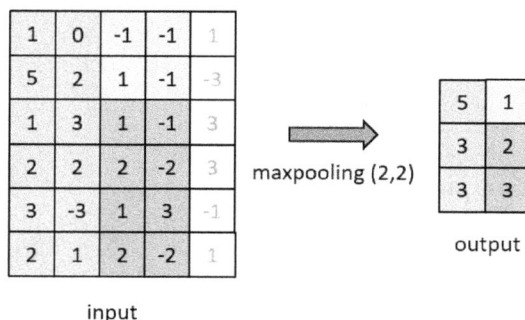

Figure 8.7: Applying max-pooling to a 6x5 input matrix

In this example, both the pool size and strides are 2. Thus, the operation results in a *3x2* output matrix. Note that, because of the strides, the leading column is totally skipped. In a scenario like this, how can we find the derivative ?

The max-pooling derivative of the output with respect to the input consists of a sparse matrix with the same dimension as the input matrix. This matrix is practically fully filled by zeroes, having 1s in each position coincident with the local max value. For example, this derivative in the case of the previous example is represented as follows:

$$\frac{\partial\ output}{\partial\ input} = \begin{array}{|c|c|c|c|c|} \hline 0 & 0 & 0 & 0 & 0 \\ \hline 1 & 0 & 1 & 0 & 0 \\ \hline 0 & 1 & 0 & 0 & 0 \\ \hline 0 & 0 & 1 & 0 & 0 \\ \hline 1 & 0 & 0 & 1 & 0 \\ \hline 0 & 0 & 0 & 0 & 0 \\ \hline \end{array}$$

Figure 8.8: The max-pooling derivative of the output with respect to the input

The usage of this derivative will be clear in the forthcoming chapters.

Conclusion

In this chapter, we introduced the pooling layers. In particular, we covered the 2D max pooling and 2D average pooling layers, discussing their applicability in the context of convolutional neural networks.

This chapter concludes the second part of this book. In the next chapter, we will start the third part, where we cover the details of training deep learning models using the components implemented so far.

Exercises

1. Consider the template function introduced in this chapter:

```
1  template <typename T>
2  const Eigen::Tensor<T, 2> pooling(-
   const Eigen::Tensor<T, 2> &X, int pool_size, int strides = 1)
```

Redesign this function to support different vertical and horizontal strides/pooling sizes. In other words, allow the use of different row strides and col strides, row pool size, and col pool size.

References

[1] Goodfellow, Bengio & Courville, Deep Learning, MIT Press, 2016.

[2] Aggarwal, Neural Networks and Deep Learning, Springer, 2018.

[3] Jason Brownlee, A Gentle Introduction to Pooling Layers for Convolutional Neural Networks, 2019, available at **https://machinelearningmastery.com/pooling-layers-for-convolutional-neural-networks/**

[4] Boureau, A theoretical analysis of feature pooling in visual recognition, 2010, ACM.

Join our book's Discord space

Join the book's Discord Workspace for Latest updates, Offers, Tech happenings around the world, New Release and Sessions with the Authors:

https://discord.bpbonline.com

CHAPTER 9

Coding the Gradient Descent Algorithm

Introduction

This chapter opens the book's third part, *Training Deep Learning Models*. Here, we will introduce the gradient descent algorithm, one of the most important, or maybe the most important, deep learning algorithms. In this chapter, we will revisit the subject of gradients, introducing automatic differentiation, a technique to calculate gradients automatically. The chapter finishes with a practical experiment to train a small network using gradient descent and convolutions.

Structure

This is the chapter roadmap:

- Introducing gradient descent
- Revisiting gradients
- Implementing the gradient descent algorithm
- Gradient of convolutions
- Using automatic differentiation

Objectives

This chapter is the basis for understanding the more complex algorithms introduced later in this book. By reading this chapter, you will be able to implement the gradient descent algorithm, training single-layer networks from data using the concepts seen so far in this book. You will understand how to compute the gradient of a convolutional layer and how to use it to update the kernel. Finally, you will know how to implement automatic differentiation using Eigen.

Introducing gradient descent

Suppose that you are on vacation, spending some time hiking over a hill. Everything is good when suddenly a dense fog covers the place. You get concerned with the fog, deciding to meet with your friends at the bottom of the hill. You do not know their exact localization, only knowing that they are at the bottom most point of the hill. Refer to the following figure for reference:

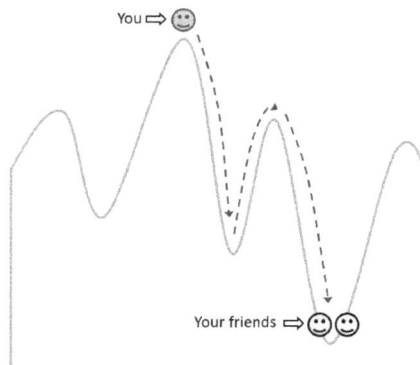

Figure 9.1: Metaphor of searching for friends downhill

Due to the fog, you cannot see very far. You decide to check for the descendant sharpest slope nearby, hoping to find your friends. Keeping this strategy, after some time and luck, you finally reach the bottom of the hill, seeing your friends.

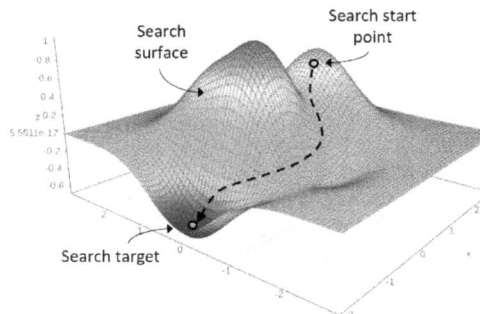

Figure 9.2: Searching over a cost function surface

This hypothetical scenario is very similar to the task of training machine learning models. Searching on a cost surface is like looking for friends downhill. Instead of a hill, the training algorithm navigates over a multidimensional cost surface like the one shown in *Figure 9.2*. The slopes are equivalent to gradients, and the decision process is the same: moving toward the bigger descendant slope and searching for the minimum point of the surface. The algorithm to implement this search is called gradient descent.

Revisiting gradients

Gradients are slopes of functions. The operation to calculate the gradient of a function at a given point is called partial derivative. We use a special notation to denote partial derivatives. For example:

$$\frac{\partial F}{\partial x}$$

This notation does not mean a division or a fraction. In this case, $\frac{\partial F}{\partial x}$ means the **partial derivative** of function F **with respect to** variable x. Functions can have multiple partial derivatives. For example, the following function:

$$F(x,y) = x^2 + 3xy + 4y^3$$

It has two partial derivatives, namely $\frac{\partial F}{\partial x}$ and $\frac{\partial F}{\partial y}$.

Only using the notation does not hint at how to evaluate the derivatives. Checking a book of calculus [1], we can find some rules to calculate derivatives, such as:

Derivative of constant	$\frac{\partial a}{\partial x} = 0$
Derivative of linear	$\frac{\partial ax}{\partial x} = a$
Derivative of quadratic	$\frac{\partial x^2}{\partial x} = 2x$
Derivative of cubic	$\frac{\partial x^3}{\partial x} = 3x^2$
Derivative of sum	$\frac{\partial(F+G)}{\partial x} = \frac{\partial F}{\partial x} + \frac{\partial G}{\partial x}$
Chain rule	$\frac{\partial F}{\partial x} = \frac{\partial F}{\partial y} \times \frac{\partial y}{\partial x}$

Table 9.1: Popular derivative rules

Using these rules, we can find $\frac{\partial F(x,y)}{\partial x}$ as follows:

$$\frac{\partial F(x,y)}{\partial x} = \frac{\partial(x^2 + 3xy + 4y^3)}{\partial x} = 2x + 3y$$

Similarly, we can find $\frac{\partial F(x,y)}{\partial y}$:

$$\frac{\partial F(x,y)}{\partial y} = \frac{\partial(x^2 + 3xy + 4y^3)}{\partial y} = 3x + 12y^2$$

Note: Derivatives of functions are themselves functions as well.

It is always worth remembering what gradients really mean: slopes of surfaces. The following figure depicts it:

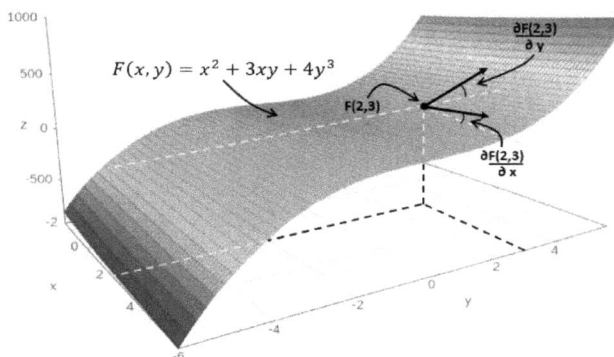

Figure 9.3: Surface and gradients at x = 2, y = 3

The last plot illustrates that $F(x,y)$ represents a surface in the three-dimensional space. Every point (a, b) of the surface $F(a, b)$ has two slopes $\frac{\partial F(a,b)}{\partial x}$ and $\frac{\partial F(a,b)}{\partial y}$. The image illustrates that and represent respectively the surface **slope** in the direction of axes x and y at point (a, b).

For us working with machine learning, these slopes are relevant because the gradient descent uses them to update the parameters during the training loop. A detailed discussion of how to calculate derivatives is beyond the scope of this book.

Note: We recommend reading Practical Mathematics for AI and Deep Learning— Tamoghna and Shravan, BPB, 2022—for readers looking to review or learn more about this subject.

In real-world problems, instead of only two variables x and y, F is usually defined over 100, 1000, or more variables. Of course, it is impossible to plot the function surface in a multi-dimensional case like this. However, although we can no longer visualize the surface, the gradient approach works similarly.

Implementing the gradient descent algorithm

Despite the challenges of using differentiation rules to calculate partial derivatives, the gradient descent algorithm is very straightforward. We can describe its behavior by the following pseudocode [2]:

```
Gradient-Descent (W, X, T, η, C, EPOCHS) :
BEGIN:
    for each epoch in EPOCHS:
        Y = forward(X)
        ∇W = backward(Y, T, C)
        W = W - η ∇W
END
```

Where:

- **W** is the trainable parameter
- **∇W** is the gradient of **W**
- **X** is the set of inputs
- **T** is the set of expected outputs
- **EPOCHS** is the maximum number of times the algorithm runs
- **η** is the learning rate
- **C** is the cost function

The objective of gradient descent is to find the parameters W that **minimize** the value given by a cost function C. In other words, the algorithm searches for the values of W that make $C(X; W)$ the minimum. In this context, the parameters W are usually called **trainable parameters**. To find the optimal value of W, gradient descent uses the strategy of continuously updating W by the **gradient** *using the following rule*:

$$W = W - \eta \nabla W$$

In this equation, is a numeric scalar called **learning rate,** which controls the parameter update.

> Note that the learning rate η is not a model parameter. Indeed, η is a parameter of the training algorithm. Parameters such as η are called hyperparameters.

Usually, the forward and update steps are the simplest and the lowest computational consumption part of the algorithm. Thus, the majority of processing time is used in the computation of .

The following section illustrates the implementation of gradient descent by an insightful, practical experiment using convolutions.

Fitting a convolution kernel to data

In *Chapter 4, Implementing Convolutions,* we learned how to use Sobel kernels to detect edges in an image, as shown:

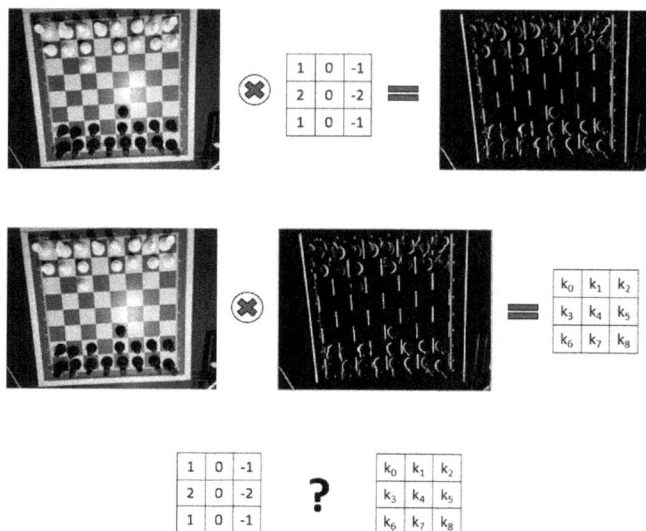

Figure 9.4: Detecting edges using convolutions

What if we use gradient descent to perform the reverse operation? That is, given an image and its edges, how can we estimate the kernel? The following section shows how to do it.

Loading the image dataset

This experiment consists of generating a synthetic dataset by applying a known kernel to a set of images. Next, we use the original and synthetic datasets to train a new kernel. Our objective is to evaluate the capacity of the training to recreate the original kernel. Thus, in the end, we compare the two kernels to evaluate whether they are or not similar.

The following code loads the images from a specified folder, generating a pair (X, T) where T is the result of the convolution of a Sobel filter on X:

```
1. #include <filesystem>
2. namespace fs = std::filesystem;
3.
4. #include <opencv2/opencv.hpp>
5. #include <opencv2/core/eigen.hpp>
6.
7. cv::Mat resize_image(const cv::Mat &image, int target_
   rows, int target_cols)
```

```
8.  {
9.      const int image_rows = image.rows;
10.     const int image_cols = image.cols;
11.
12.     int new_rows = 0;
13.     int new_cols = 0;
14.
15.     if (image_rows > image_cols) {
16.         new_rows = target_rows;
17.         new_cols = image_cols * target_rows / image_rows;
18.     } else {
19.         new_cols = target_cols;
20.         new_rows = image_rows * target_cols / image_cols;
21.     }
22.     cv::Mat resized;
23.     resize(image, resized, cv::Size(new_cols, new_rows), cv::INTER_
    LINEAR);
24.
25.     cv::Mat result = cv::Mat::zeros(cv::Size(target_cols, target_
    rows), CV_8UC1);
26.
27.     resized.copyTo(result(cv::Rect((target_cols - new_
    cols)/2, (target_rows - new_rows)/2, resized.cols, resized.rows)));
28.
29.     return result;
30. }
31.
32. auto load_dataset(const std::string data_
    folder, const Eigen::Tensor<float, 2> &Gen, const Eigen::Index image_
    size) {
33.
34.     std::vector<std::string> files;
35.
36.     for (const auto & entry : fs::directory_iterator(data_folder)) {
37.         files.push_back(data_folder + entry.path().c_str());
38.     }
39.
40.     Eigen::Tensor<float, 3> X(files.size(), image_size, image_size);
```

```
41.      Eigen::Tensor<float, 3> T(files.size(), image_size, image_size);
42.
43.      const Eigen::array<Eigen::Index, 3> extent = {1, image_
   size, image_size};
44.
45.      Eigen::array<std::pair<int, int>, 3> padding;
46.      padding[0] = std::make_pair(1, 1);
47.      padding[1] = std::make_pair(1, 1);
48.      padding[2] = std::make_pair(0, 0);
49.
50.      for (unsigned int i = 0; i < files.size(); ++i) {
51.          const auto & file = files[i];
52.          cv::Mat image = cv::imread(file, cv::IMREAD_GRAYSCALE);
53.          cv::Mat formatted_image = resize_image(image, image_
   size, image_size);
54.          cv::Mat frame32f;
55.          formatted_image.convertTo(frame32f, CV_32F);
56.          frame32f /= 255.f;
57.
58.          Eigen::Tensor<float, 3> eigen_frame(image_size, image_
   size, 1);
59.          cv::cv2eigen(frame32f, eigen_frame);
60.
61.          Eigen::Tensor<float, 3> convolved(image_size, image_size, 1);
62.          Eigen::array<int, 2> dims({0, 1});
63.          convolved = eigen_frame.pad(padding).convolve(Gen, dims);
64.
65.          Eigen::array<Eigen::Index, 3> offset = {i, 0, 0};
66.          Eigen::array<Eigen::Index, 3> new_dim({image_size, image_
   size, 1});
67.          X.slice(offset, extent) = eigen_frame.reshape(extent);
68.          T.slice(offset, extent) = convolved.reshape(extent);
69.
70.      }
71.
72.      return std::make_tuple(X, T);
73.
74. };
```

Note: We are using OpenCV to load and show the images only. OpenCV is a free and open-source library containing computer vision algorithms and IO routines for image processing. You can download and install OpenCV from sources or using binary distributions such as dev packages.

Each element of T is the result of the convolution of an image and the Sobel kernel, as shown in *Figure 9.5*:

```
1. Eigen::Tensor<float, 3> convolved(image_size, image_size, 1);
2. Eigen::array<int, 2> dims({0, 1});
3. convolved = eigen_frame.pad(padding).convolve(Gen, dims);
```

1	0	-1
2	0	-2
1	0	-1

Figure 9.5: *Gx Sobel kernel used to generate the example dataset*

Note that we are using a SAME convolution to obtain a tensor *T* with the same dimensions of tensor *X*, as shown in *Figure 9.6*:

```
1. Eigen::array<std::pair<int, int>, 3> padding;
2. padding[0] = std::make_pair(1, 1);
3. padding[1] = std::make_pair(1, 1);
4. padding[2] = std::make_pair(0, 0);
```

Figure 9.6: *Source image from tensor X and convoluted image from tensor T*

Once we have the data, it is time to train the model.

Training a kernel

Our objective is to use gradient descent to fit a kernel to the dataset consisting of (*X*, *T*) instances. The forward pass consists of only a convolution of the input by the training kernel:

```
1. auto convolution2D = [](const Eigen::Tensor<float, 3> &in-
   put, const Eigen::Tensor<float, 2> &kernel)
2. {
3.     Eigen::array<std::pair<int, int>, 3> padding;
4.     padding[0] = std::make_pair(0, 0);
5.     padding[1] = std::make_pair(1, 1);
6.     padding[2] = std::make_pair(1, 1);
7.
8.     auto padded = input.pad(padding);
9.     Eigen::array<int, 2> dims({1, 2});
10.    Eigen::Tensor<float, 3> result  = padded.convolve(kernel, dims);
11.    return result;
12. };
13.
14. auto forward = []
    (const Eigen::Tensor<float, 3> &X, const Eigen::Tensor<float, 2> &ker-
    nel)
15. {
16.    return convolution2D(X, kernel);
17. };
```

Now, we can calculate the output cost using a suitable cost function. In this experiment, we opted to use the mean squared error cost:

```
1. auto MSE = []
   (const Eigen::Tensor<float, 3> &T, const Eigen::Tensor<float, 3> &Y)
2. {
3.     auto diff = T - Y;
4.     auto quadratic = diff * diff;
5.     Eigen::Tensor<float, 0> sum = quadratic.sum();
6.
7.     float result = sum(0) / Y.size();
8.     return result;
9. };
```

After we have obtained the cost, we can calculate the kernel's gradient in the backward pass:

```
1. auto BatchedConvolution = [](const Eigen::Tensor<float, 3> &A, const
   Eigen::Tensor<float, 3> &B)
2. {
3.
```

```
4.      // to get a resulting 3x3 output, we need to set the padding to 1
5.      // 3 = 2*pad_set + 320 - 320 + 1
6.      const int pad_set = 1;
7.      Eigen::array<std::pair<int, int>, 3> padding;
8.      padding[0] = std::make_pair(0, 0);
9.      padding[1] = std::make_pair(pad_set, pad_set);
10.     padding[2] = std::make_pair(pad_set, pad_set);
11.
12.     const int batch_size = A.dimension(0);
13.     const int dim1 = A.dimension(1);
14.     const int dim2 = A.dimension(2);
15.     Eigen::Tensor<float, 3> output(batch_size, dim1, dim2);
16.
17.     auto padded = A.pad(padding);
18.     Eigen::array<int, 3> conv_dims({0, 1, 2});
19.     output = padded.convolve(B, conv_dims);
20.
21.     return output;
22. };
23.
24. auto backward = [](const Eigen::Tensor<float, 3> &X, Eigen::Tensor<-
    float, 3> &T, Eigen::Tensor<float, 3> &Y)
25. {
26.     auto DIFF = Y - T;
27.     Eigen::Tensor<float, 3> batch = BatchedConvolution(X, DIFF);
28.
29.     Eigen::array<Eigen::Index, 2> two_dims{{batch.
    dimension(1), batch.dimension(2)}};
30.     Eigen::Tensor<float, 2> result = batch.reshape(two_dims);
31.     result = result * result.constant(2.f / X.size());
32.
33.     return result;
34. };
```

The difference **Y - T** comes from the derivative of MSE. We use a batched convolution because we need to convolve **batch_size** elements from tensor **X** by **batch_size** elements in tensor **DIFF**. Note that both **X** and **DIFF** are 3-rank tensors.

After computing the gradient, we can finally update the kernel as shown:

```
1. auto update = grad * grad.constant(learning_rate);
2. kernel -= update;
```

We can call these three routines to implement gradient descent in a loop, as follows:

```
1. Eigen::Tensor<float, 2> kernel(3, 3);
2. kernel = kernel.random();
3.
4. const int MAX_EPOCHS = 5'000;
5. const double learning_rate = .1;
6. int epoch = 0;
7. while (epoch < MAX_EPOCHS)
8. {
9.   auto output = forward(X, kernel);
10.
11.   auto grad = backward(X, T, output);
12.
13.   auto update = grad * grad.constant(learning_rate);
14.   kernel -= update;
15.
16.   double loss = MSE(T, output);
17.   std::cout << "epoch:\t" << epoch << "\tloss:\t" << loss << "\n";
18.   epoch++;
19. }
20.
21. std::cout << "\nGenerative kernel is:\
    n\n" << std::fixed << std::setprecision(2) << Sobel_Gx << "\n\n";
22. std::cout << "\nTrained kernel is:\
    n\n" << std::fixed << std::setprecision(2) << kernel << "\n\n";
```

Running this code results in the following output:

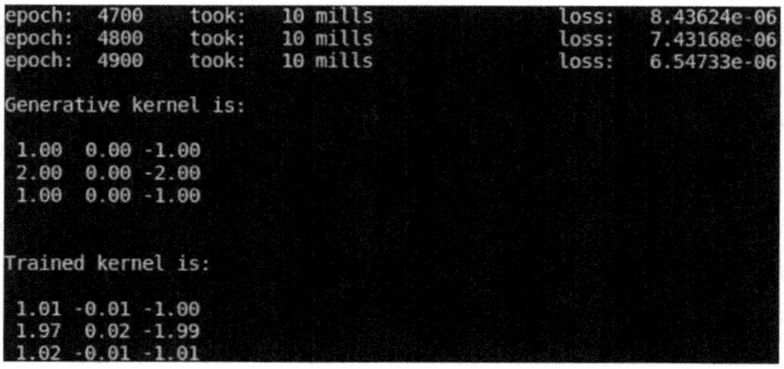

Figure 9.7: Reconstructing the Sobel kernel from data

As expected, the achieved kernel is similar to the original Sobel kernel. We can plot the loss over the epochs to confirm that the algorithm is actually working:

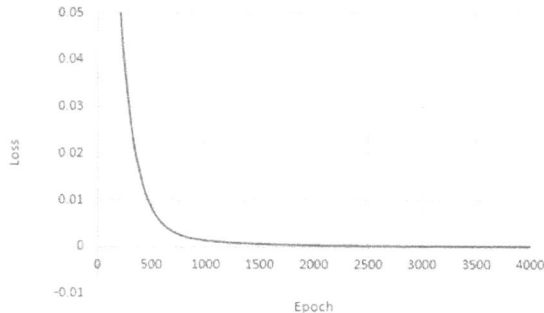

Figure 9.8: Training loss curve

This familiar shape is a good indication that the algorithm is consistently fitting the kernel towards the minimum cost. However, ten thousand epochs is a significant amount of time to train. We can think of how to reduce this time by improving gradient descent in several ways. This is discussed in the following section.

Extending gradient descent

We can see gradient descent as a platform to explore and extend approaches aiming to get better results and faster. For example:

- Instead of passing a single batch of images, we can use a list of **mini-batches** with a small number of images;

- We can try different ways to update the trainable parameters. For example, we can memorize the last update and combine it with the current update to get a smooth and faster search. The components to implement this kind of logic are called **optimizers** such as Momentum and RMSProp.

- We can include **callbacks** to perform asynchronous tasks, such as saving intermediary copies of the trainable parameters in a file.

- We can use parallel computing, such as multithreading or GPU programming, to reduce the computation time.

- We can implement more complex logic to **stop the training earlier**. For example, we can check if the loss is no longer decreasing after successive epochs.

- We can check the model performance using an alternative **validation dataset** filled with data not used to fit the kernel. This helps us to distinguish an **overfitted** model from a good one.

Many of these improvements will be tackled in the forthcoming chapters. For a while, let us understand how the kernel gradient was calculated.

Gradient of convolutions

Remember how to calculate simple convolutions, as illustrated in the following figure:

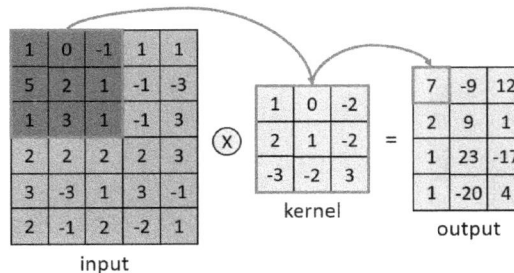

Figure 9.9: Calculating a convolution

We can define convolution as follows:

$$Y = convolution(X, K)$$

In convolutions, each output coefficient is the result of the **dot product** between the kernel and the respective region from the input. The kernel is a trainable parameter. Therefore, during the gradient descent execution, we need to calculate the kernel gradient $\frac{\partial C}{\partial K}$.

Using the chain rule, one can find that the following equation gives the gradient of the cost C with respect to kernel K [5]:

$$\frac{\partial C}{\partial K} = convolution(X, \frac{\partial C}{\partial Y})$$

Where X is the input and $\frac{\partial C}{\partial Y}$ is the gradient of cost with respect to output Y (sometimes called **upstream gradient**).

> **Note: It is curious (and also makes a lot of sense) that the gradient of a convolution is another convolution.**

Suppose that $\frac{\partial C}{\partial Y}$ is:

$$\frac{\partial C}{\partial Y}$$

Figure 9.10: Upstream gradient

The kernel gradient $\frac{\partial C}{\partial K}$ is found by:

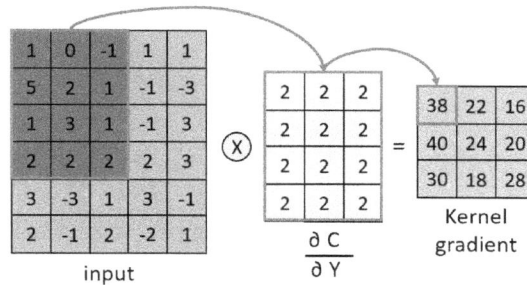

Figure 9.11: Calculating the kernel gradient

Downstream gradient

So far in this book, we have used the chain rule to find the gradient of trainable parameters, such as the convolution kernel K or the weight W from fully connected layers. In some circumstances, however, it is necessary to calculate the gradient with respect to the input X, denoted by:

$$\frac{\partial C}{\partial X}$$

Where X is the layer input. In this context, this gradient is called the **downstream gradient**. In the case of a convolution, the downstream gradient $\frac{\partial C}{\partial X}$ is given by [3]:

$$\frac{\partial C}{\partial X} = convolution\left(\frac{\partial C}{\partial Y}, K_{rot180}, pad\right)$$

Where is the rotation clockwise of kernel *K* by *180* degrees [4]:

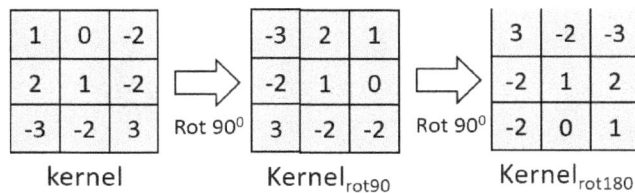

Figure 9.12: Rotating the kernel by 180-degree

In addition to rotating the kernel, the gradient calculation uses a padding value to fit the final size of the X:

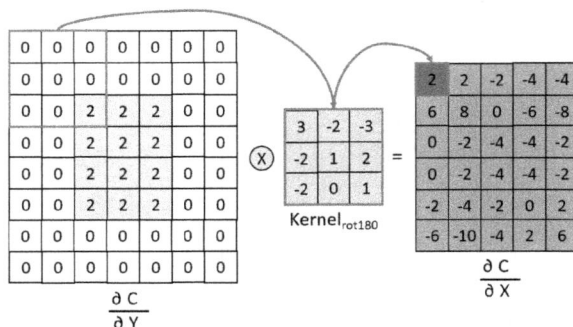

Figure 9.13: *Calculating the downstream gradient*

The following code exemplifies the calculation of $\frac{\partial C}{\partial K}$ and $\frac{\partial C}{\partial X}$:

```
1.  #include <iostream>
2.
3.  #include <unsupported/Eigen/CXX11/Tensor>
4.
5.  auto convolution2D = [](const Eigen::Tensor<float, 2> &in-
    put, const Eigen::Tensor<float, 2> &kernel, int pad = 0)
6.  {
7.
8.      if (pad > 0) {
9.
10.         Eigen::array<std::pair<int, int>, 2> padding;
11.         padding[0] = std::make_pair(pad, pad);
12.         padding[1] = std::make_pair(pad, pad);
13.         auto padded = input.pad(padding);
14.
15.         Eigen::array<int, 2> dims({0, 1});
16.         Eigen::Tensor<float, 2> result  = padded.
    convolve(kernel, dims);
17.         return result;
18.
19.     } else {
20.
21.         Eigen::array<int, 2> dims({0, 1});
22.         Eigen::Tensor<float, 2> result  = input.
    convolve(kernel, dims);
23.         return result;
```

```
24.      }
25.
26. };
27.
28. auto rotate180 = [](const Eigen::Tensor<float, 2> &tensor){
29.      Eigen::array<bool, 2> reverse({true, true});
30.      Eigen::Tensor<float, 2> result = tensor.reverse(reverse);
31.      return result;
32. };
33.
34. int main(int, char**) {
35.
36.      Eigen::Tensor<float, 2> X(6, 5);
37.      X.setValues({
38.          {1, 0, -1, 1, 1},
39.          {5, 2, 1, -1, -3},
40.          {1, 3, 1, -1, 3},
41.          {2, 2, 2, 2, 3},
42.          {3, -3, 1, 3, -1},
43.          {2, -1, 2, -2, 1}
44.      });
45.
46.      Eigen::Tensor<float, 2> dC_dO(4, 3);
47.      dC_dO.setValues({
48.          {2., 2., 2.},
49.          {2., 2., 2.},
50.          {2., 2., 2.},
51.          {2., 2., 2.}
52.      });
53.
54.      auto dC_dK = convolution2D(X, dC_dO);
55.
56.      std::cout << "dC_dK:\n" << dC_dK << "\n";
57.
58.      Eigen::Tensor<float, 2> kernel(3, 3);
59.      kernel.setValues({
60.          {1, 0, -2 },
```

```
61.            {2, 1, -2},
62.            {-3, -2, 3}
63.        });
64.
65.        auto kernel_180 = rotate180(kernel);
66.
67.        std::cout << "\nkernel_180:\n" << kernel_180 << "\n";
68.
69.        auto dC_dX = convolution2D(dC_dO, kernel_180, 2);
70.
71.        std::cout << "\ndC_dX:\n" << dC_dX << "\n";
72.
73.        return 0;
74. }
```

This program generates the following output:

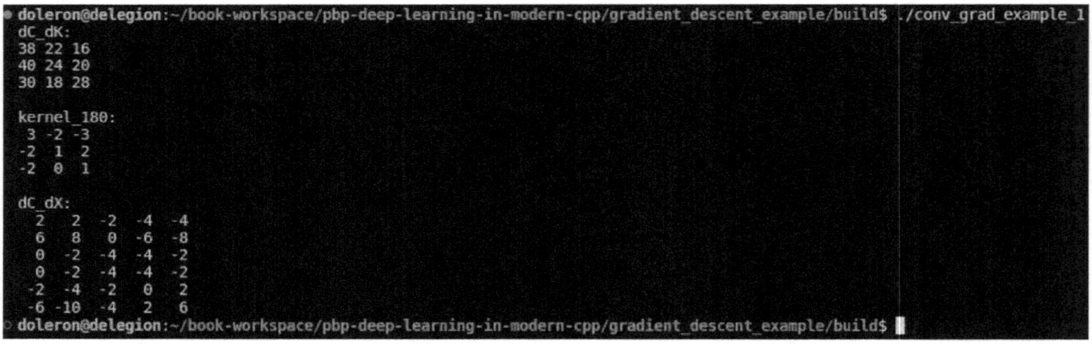

Figure 9.14: Running the convolution gradient example

In the next chapter, when covering the backpropagation algorithm, we will use the downstream gradient to propagate the error throughout the network layers.

Using automatic differentiation

In the previous section, we learned how to calculate the gradient of convolutions using a formula derived from the chain rule. Indeed, differentiating functions is not always easy and intuitive. Luckily, modern libraries such as Eigen have an **automatic differentiation** (**AD**) feature to help us implement any code that needs a derivative.

Let us start by implementing the derivative of the function introduced at the beginning of this chapter:

$$F(x, y) = x^2 + 3xy + 4y^3$$

Applying the already known calculus rules, one can find the following derivatives:

$$\frac{\partial F(x, y)}{\partial x} = 2x + 3y$$

And,

$$\frac{\partial F(x, y)}{\partial y} = 3x + 12y^2$$

Using these two formulae, we can find the value of $\frac{\partial F(x,y)}{\partial x}$ and $\frac{\partial F(x,y)}{\partial y}$ for a given point. For example, if $x = 2$ and $y = 3$, we can find the following values:

$$\frac{\partial F(2, 3)}{\partial x} = 2 \times 2 + 3 \times 3 = 13$$

$$\frac{\partial F(2, 3)}{\partial y} = 3 \times 2 + 12 \times 3^2 = 114$$

Calculating $\frac{\partial F(2,3)}{\partial x}$ and $\frac{\partial F(2,3)}{\partial y}$ values was not so hard. However, it is not always simple to previously obtain the $\frac{\partial F(x,y)}{\partial x}$ and $\frac{\partial F(x,y)}{\partial y}$ formulae. Indeed, many of the bugs found in deep learning systems come from an error in the calculation of gradients. That is the motivation behind automatic differentiation, a feature available in modern algebra libraries such as Eigen.

Automatic differentiation in Eigen

Using the **Eigen::AutoDiff** [6] header, we can calculate derivatives such as and even if we do not know the formulas of and . To make this work, the first step is to define $F(x, y)$ as a **template function**:

```
1. template<typename T>
2. T F(const T& x, const T& y)
3. {
4.     T result = x*x + 3*x*y + 4*y*y*y;
5.     return result;
6. }
```

Now, instead of calling **F(x, y)** passing float values as usual, we need to pass **X** and **Y** using a special Eigen type **Eigen::AutoDiffScalar**:

```
1. int main(int, char **)
2. {
3.
4.     Eigen::AutoDiffScalar<Eigen::Vector2f> X;
```

```
5.      Eigen::AutoDiffScalar<Eigen::Vector2f> Y;

6.

7.      X.derivatives() = Eigen::Vector2f::Unit(2, 0);

8.      X.value() = 2;

9.

10.     Y.derivatives() = Eigen::Vector2f::Unit(2, 1);

11.     Y.value() = 3.;

12.

13.     auto Z = F(X, Y);

14.

15.     std::cout << "Z: " << Z << "\n\n";

16.     std::cout << "derivatives:\n" << Z.derivatives() << "\n";

17.

18.     return 0;

19. }
```

Z is also an **Eigen::AutoDiffScalar** containing the output of **F(X,Y)** and the derivative values of **F** with respect to **X** and **Y**:

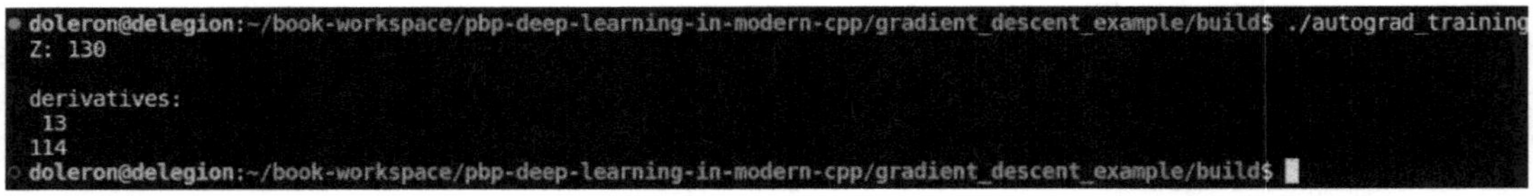

Figure 9.15: Simple autograd example

This simple example showed that we do not need to calculate the derivatives of **F(x,y)** by ourselves. Eigen can find them automatically using AD under the wood. Let us check how AD works in a more complex case.

Using automatic differentiation on convolutions

Assume that we have the following function:

```
1.  template <typename T>

2.  T custom_function(-
    const Eigen::Tensor<T, 2> &X, const Eigen::Tensor<T, 2> &K)

3.  {

4.      Eigen::array<int, 2> dims({0, 1});

5.      auto conv = X.convolve(K, dims);

6.      Eigen::Tensor<T, 2> output = conv * conv;

7.      auto loss = output.sum();
```

```
8.      T result = ((Eigen::Tensor<T, 0>)loss)(0);
9.      return result;
10. };
```

Note that we have defined the function as a template again. By the previous example, we know that we have to pass the values as **Eigen::AutoDiffScalar**. Since **X** and **K** are tensors, the first thing to do is converting regular float Eigen tensors:

```
1.  auto convert = []
    (const Eigen::Tensor<float, 2> &tensor, int offset, int size)
2.  {
3.      const int rows = tensor.dimension(0);
4.      const int cols = tensor.dimension(1);
5.
6.      Eigen::Tensor<AutoDiff_T, 2> result(rows, cols);
7.
8.      for (int i = 0; i < rows; ++i)
9.      {
10.         for (int j = 0; j < cols; ++j)
11.         {
12.             int index = i * cols + j;
13.             result(i, j).
    derivatives() = Eigen::VectorXf::Unit(size, offset + index);
14.             result(i, j).value() = tensor(i, j);
15.         }
16.     }
17.
18.     return result;
19. };
```

As its name suggests, **convert** produces a copy of the original tensor using the type **Eigen::AutoDiffScalar<Eigen::VectorXf>**. We can call the function **custom_function** as follows:

```
1.  #include <unsupported/Eigen/CXX11/Tensor>
2.  #include <unsupported/Eigen/AutoDiff>
3.
4.  typedef typename Eigen::AutoDiffScalar<Eigen::VectorXf> AutoDiff_T;
5.
6.  int main(int, char **)
7.  {
```

```
8.     Eigen::Tensor<float, 2> x_in(6, 5);
9.     x_in.setValues({{1, 0, -1, 1, 1},
10.                     {5, 2, 1, -1, -3},
11.                     {1, 3, 1, -1, 3},
12.                     {2, 2, 2, 2, 3},
13.                     {3, -3, 1, 3, -1},
14.                     {2, -1, 2, -2, 1}});
15.
16.    Eigen::Tensor<float, 2> k_in(3, 3);
17.    k_in.setValues({{1, 0, -2},
18.                    {2, 1, -2},
19.                    {-3, -2, 3}});
20.
21.    Eigen::Tensor<AutoDiff_T, 2> X = convert(x_in, 0, x_
   in.size() + k_in.size());
22.    Eigen::Tensor<AutoDiff_T, 2> K = convert(k_in, x_in.size(), x_
   in.size() + k_in.size());
23.
24.    auto LOSS = custom_function(X, K);
25.
26.    auto [dY_dX, dY_dK] = gradients(LOSS, X, K);
27.
28.    std::cout << "X:\n"
29.              << X << "\n\n";
30.    std::cout << "K:\n"
31.              << K << "\n\n";
32.    std::cout << "LOSS:\n"
33.              << LOSS << "\n\n";
34.    std::cout << "dY_dX:\n"
35.              << dY_dX << "\n\n";
36.    std::cout << "dY_dK:\n"
37.              << dY_dK << "\n\n";
38.
39.    return 0;
40. }
```

Once the **custom_function** returns the output value, we can unpack the gradients using the following function:

```
1.  auto gradients(-
    const AutoDiff_T &Y, const Eigen::Tensor<AutoDiff_T, 2>
    &X, const Eigen::Tensor<AutoDiff_T, 2> &K)
2.  {
3.
4.      auto derivatives = Y.derivatives();
5.
6.      int index = 0;
7.      Eigen::Tensor<float, 2> dY_dX(X.dimension(0), X.dimension(1));
8.      for (int i = 0; i < X.dimension(0); ++i)
9.      {
10.         for (int j = 0; j < X.dimension(1); ++j)
11.         {
12.             float val = derivatives[index];
13.             dY_dX(i, j) = val;
14.             index++;
15.         }
16.     }
17.
18.     Eigen::Tensor<float, 2> dY_dK(K.dimension(0), K.dimension(1));
19.     for (int i = 0; i < K.dimension(0); ++i)
20.     {
21.         for (int j = 0; j < K.dimension(1); ++j)
22.         {
23.             float val = derivatives[index];
24.             dY_dK(i, j) = val;
25.             index++;
26.         }
27.     }
28.
29.     return std::make_pair(dY_dX, dY_dK);
30. }
```

In this example, we obtained both the kernel gradient and the downstream gradient . Note that, depending on the need, one can calculate only one of them. Running the program results in the following output:

```
doleron@delegion:~/book-workspace/pbp-deep-learning-in-modern-cpp/gradient_descent_example/build$ ./conv_autograd
X:
 1  0 -1  1  1
 5  2  1 -1 -3
 1  3  1 -1  3
 2  2  2  2  3
 3 -3  1  3 -1
 2 -1  2 -2  1

K:
 1  0 -2
 2  1 -2
-3 -2  3

LOSS:
1596

dY_dX:
   14  -18   -4   36  -48
   32   -4   -4   24  -52
  -32  112  -18 -228  136
   -6   -8  -52    4   58
   -2 -220  -12  294 -118
   -6  116   62 -136   24

dY_dK:
   94   92 -226
  280   20 -180
  -74 -112  420

doleron@delegion:~/book-workspace/pbp-deep-learning-in-modern-cpp/gradient_descent_example/build$ ▮
```

Figure 9.16: Using autograd on a convolution

Automatic differentiation is a surprisingly neat and powerful technology. With Eigen, one can use AD in their projects without installing any proprietary or third-party dependence.

Conclusion

This chapter showed how to implement gradient descent, the base algorithm to train deep learning models. We revisited gradients, learning how to use automatic differentiation to obtain partial derivatives automatically. We also discussed how to obtain the gradient of convolutions and how to calculate the gradient with respect to the kernel and the input.

In the next chapter, we will extend the gradient descent algorithm discussed here to implement backpropagation, the algorithm used to train networks with an arbitrary number of layers.

Exercises

1. Consider the following Gaussian blur kernel:

1	2	1
2	4	2
1	2	1

Figure 9.17: Gaussian blur kernel

What is the visual result of applying this kernel to an image? Replace the Sobel kernel in the practical example with this Gaussian Kernel and evaluate the results.

2. Consider again the example of calculating the kernel of convolutions using the images and Sobel filter. Change the example to use Eigen::AutoDiff.

3. Include a condition in gradient descent to stop the algorithm when the gradient is smaller than a defined threshold of 1e-7.

References

[1] Tamoghna & Shravan, Practical Mathematics for AI and Deep Learning, BPB, 2022.

[2] Duda at all, Pattern Classification, Wiley, 2000.

[3] Pavithra Solai, Convolutions and Backpropagations, available at **https://pavisj. medium.com/convolutions-and-backpropagations-46026a8f5d2c**

[4] Backwards Pass for Convolution Layer, CS 4803 / 7643 Deep Learning, Georgia Institute of Technology, available at **https://sites.cc.gatech.edu/classes/AY2021/cs7643_ spring/assets/L11_CNNs.pdf**

[5] Rukayat Sadiq, CNN BackPropagation, 2021, Carnegie Mellon University, available at **https://deeplearning.cs.cmu.edu/F21/document/recitation/Recitation5/CNN_Backprop_ Recitation_5_F21.pdf**

[6] Patrick Peltzer, Johannes Lotz, Uwe Naumann, Eigen-AD: Algorithmic Differentiation of the Eigen Library, avaialble at **https://arxiv.org/abs/1911.12604**

Join our book's Discord space

Join the book's Discord Workspace for Latest updates, Offers, Tech happenings around the world, New Release and Sessions with the Authors:

https://discord.bpbonline.com

CHAPTER 10

Coding the Backpropagation Algorithm

Introduction

This chapter introduces backpropagation, the primary algorithm for training deep neural networks. Aiming for a streamlined and type-agnostic implementation, this chapter describes the algorithm using a mix of matrix expressions, structures, and calculus notation. After discussing the theoretical algorithm mechanics, we will move on to its implementation, starting with an unoptimized version that can accurately fit the model parameters from the data. Then, we will discuss the concerns and decisions to improve the algorithm's time and space utilization to achieve world-class performance.

Structure

This is the chapter roadmap:

- Understanding backpropagation
- Understanding how to train models with many layers
- Backpropagation pseudocode
- Implementing the first version of backpropagation
- Improving the backpropagation processing performance

Objectives

This chapter teaches you how to code algorithms to train real-world models with several layers using backpropagation. You will understand the main bottlenecks that can lead the algorithm to converge slowly, knowing how to implement workarounds to achieve high-performance execution. This chapter also teaches you how to perform tensor computations on multiple cores or using the GPU.

Understanding backpropagation

Eigen Tensor API, other libraries, and deep learning frameworks can automatically compute the gradient of complex expressions using **auto differentiation** [1]. It turns out that defining and implementing gradients is not always straightforward. As a result, most of the bugs in deep learning code reside in the computation of gradients. Therefore, auto differentiation, or autodiff, is really worthwhile since it reduces the cost of developing and maintaining code. Then, why should we learn backpropagation?

Andrej Karpathy, a prominent computer scientist who worked as director of artificial intelligence at Tesla and professor at Stanford, wrote an article titled, *Yes you should understand backprop* [2]. In this text, *Karpathy* argues that deep learning developers must learn backpropagation in detail.

According to *Karpathy*, backpropagation is a **leaky abstraction**, which means that practical problems like **vanishing gradients**, **dying ReLUs**, and **exploding gradients** eventually require that the developer knows the underlying computational details to fix them.

This book assumes that you should be free to implement your own algorithms whenever you want it. To achieve this, you need to understand how backpropagation works.

Understanding how to train models with many layers

The backpropagation algorithm consists of computing the gradients of each trainable model parameter. This computation can be summarized in the calculation of three gradients:

- The model output cost gradient
- The gradient with respect to activations and
- The gradient with respect to the layer's input

To make things less abstract, let us consider the following four-layer network as an example:

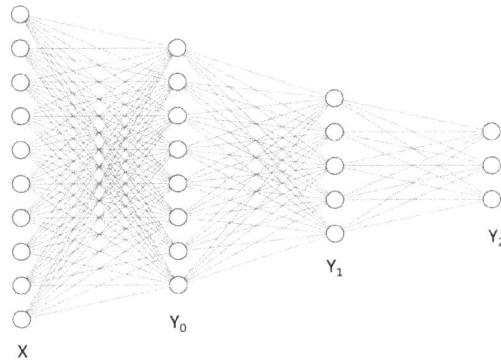

Figure 10.1: 4-layer network

Assuming each layer has its respective activation function **Act(Z)**, we can describe this network by splitting the steps as follows:

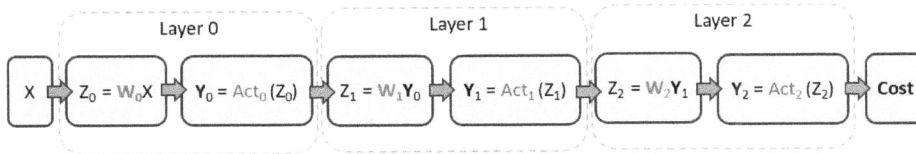

Figure 10.2: Forward propagation computation

This graph describes the computation flow to evaluate the forward pass. Similarly, we can describe the flow of gradients during the backward computation, as shown:

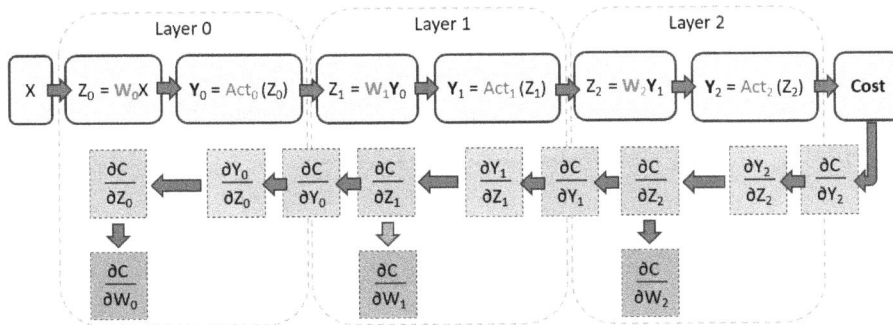

Figure 10.3: Computing the gradients in backward propagation

Note: As we explained in *Chapter 9, Coding the Gradient Descent Algorithm*, $\frac{\partial C}{\partial Y}$ denotes a gradient. It is important to observe that this notation does not correspond to a division of ∂C by ∂Y. Indeed, $\frac{\partial C}{\partial Y}$ means the partial derivative of function C with respect to variable Y.

The objective of every network training is to compute the gradients with respect to the weights. In the case of our particular network, these gradients are $\frac{\partial C}{\partial W_0}$, $\frac{\partial C}{\partial W_1}$, and $\frac{\partial C}{\partial W_2}$, as shown:

$$\frac{\partial C}{\partial W_0} \qquad \frac{\partial C}{\partial W_1} \qquad \frac{\partial C}{\partial W_2}$$

Figure 10.4: The weight gradients

Once $\frac{\partial C}{\partial W_0}$, $\frac{\partial C}{\partial W_1}$ and $\frac{\partial C}{\partial W_2}$ are found, the next step is to update the weights using the update rule:

$$W_0 = W_0 - \eta \frac{\partial C}{\partial W_0}$$

$$W_1 = W_1 - \eta \frac{\partial C}{\partial W_1}$$

$$W_2 = W_2 - \eta \frac{\partial C}{\partial W_2}$$

Thus, our job basically consists of computing the weight gradients $\frac{\partial C}{\partial W}$. Let us see how to get them then.

Computing the weight gradients

Checking *Figure 10.3* again, we can realize that the computation of gradients in each layer follows a pattern:

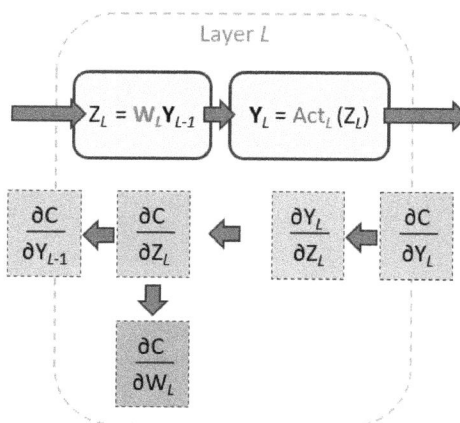

Figure 10.5: Layer gradients computation

The gradients $\frac{\partial C}{\partial Y}$ are called **error propagation**. In the case of the last layer, $\frac{\partial C}{\partial Y}$ is obtained directly from the cost function derivative:

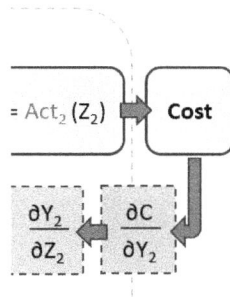

Figure 10.6: *Cost gradient*

For the other layers to the back of the network, there are two other gradients playing the same role:

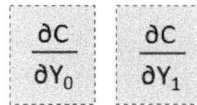

Figure 10.7: *Error propagation*

Considering that L refers to Layer L, these gradients can be computed using the chain rule as usual:

$$\frac{\partial C}{\partial Y_{L-1}} = \frac{\partial C}{\partial Z_L} \times \frac{\partial Z_L}{\partial Y_{L-1}}$$

$$= \frac{\partial C}{\partial Z_L} \times W_L$$

Thus, to find $\frac{\partial C}{\partial Y_{L-1}}$ it is necessary to find $\frac{\partial C}{\partial Z_L}$ first. Using the chain rule, we can deduce the following formula:

$$\frac{\partial C}{\partial Z_L} = \frac{\partial C}{\partial Y_L} \times \frac{\partial Y_L}{\partial Z_L}$$

Where $\frac{\partial Y}{\partial Z}$ is obtained from the particular activation function of layer L. Finally, the gradient $\frac{\partial C}{\partial W_L}$ of layer L is given simply by:

$$\frac{\partial C}{\partial W_L} = \frac{\partial C}{\partial Z_L} \times \frac{\partial Z_L}{\partial W_L}$$

$$= \frac{\partial C}{\partial Z_L} \times Y_{L-1}$$

Note that, in the case of the first layer, $Y_{L-1} = X$, that is, the input values.

Note: Calculating $\frac{\partial C}{\partial Z_L}$ is the critical point in backpropagation.

Checking the previous equations again, it is obvious that once we find $\frac{\partial C}{\partial Z_L}$, we can easily find $\frac{\partial C}{\partial Y_{L-1}}$ and $\frac{\partial C}{\partial W_L}$ too.

Even with years of experience, it is not uncommon to get confused by calculus notation, indexes, and formulas. The following section may shed some light on this by introducing the matrix form notation.

Putting the equations in matrix form

Let us first think of the propagation equations for a single training instance (X, T). By counting the units:

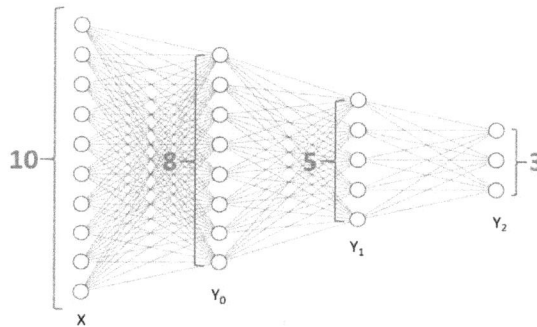

Figure 10.8: Counting units

We can define X as the input vector with size 10:

$$X = [X_0 \quad X_1 \quad X_2 \quad X_3 \quad X_4 \quad X_5 \quad X_6 \quad X_7 \quad X_8 \quad X_9]$$

and T as the expected output vector with size 3:

$$T = [T_0 \quad T_1 \quad T_3]$$

is given by the matrix product of the input X and the weight of the first layer W_0:

$$Z_0 = X \times W_0$$

where size is (10 x 8). As a result, will be a vector with size 8:

$$Z_0 = [Z_{0_0} \quad Z_{0_1} \quad \cdots \quad Z_{0_7}]$$

is the result of applying the activation function to :

$$Y_0 = activation_0(Z_0)$$

This operation results in a vector with the same size:

$$Y_0 = [Y_{0_0} \quad Y_{0_1} \quad \cdots \quad Y_{0_7}]$$

This finishes the forward computation of layer 0. Checking the network, the dimension of layer 1 weights is (8 x 5) and the dimension of the layer 2 weights is (5 x 3). Thus, we can obtain Z_1, Z_2, Y_1, and Y_2 using the same procedure:

$$Z_1 = Y_0 \times W_1 = [Z_{1_0} \quad Z_{1_2} \quad Z_{1_3} \quad Z_{1_4} \quad Z_{1_5}]$$

$$Z_2 = Y_1 \times W_2 = [Z_{2_0} \quad Z_{2_1} \quad Z_{2_2}]$$

$$Y_1 = activation_1(Z_1) = [Y_{1_0} \quad Y_{1_2} \quad Y_{1_3} \quad Y_{1_4} \quad Y_{1_5}]$$

$$Y_2 = activation_2(Z_2) = [Y_{2_0} \quad Y_{2_1} \quad Y_{2_2}]$$

The network output is the output of the last layer, that is, . We can then calculate the cost using the cost function:

$$Cost = C(Y_2, T)$$

where $C(Y_2, T)$ is a cost function such as cross-entropy loss or MSE.

Note that $C(Y_2, T)$ is not a tensor but a scalar value.

Computing the gradients

Once we have obtained the output cost $C(Y_2, T)$, we can calculate the first gradient $\frac{\partial C}{\partial Y_2}$ using the derivative of the cost function in use. The actual value of this gradient will depend on the specific cost function and the values of Y_2 And T. Since it is given in terms of the coefficients of Y_2, this gradient is a vector of size 3:

$$\frac{\partial C}{\partial Y_2} = \begin{bmatrix} \frac{\partial C}{\partial Y_{2_0}} & \frac{\partial C}{\partial Y_{2_1}} & \frac{\partial C}{\partial Y_{2_2}} \end{bmatrix}$$

Now, let us take the Jacobian of the activation function with respect to Z_2. Note that this Jacobian is a square matrix:

$$\frac{\partial Y_2}{\partial Z_2} = \begin{bmatrix} \frac{\partial Y_2}{\partial Z_{2_{0,0}}} & \frac{\partial Y_2}{\partial Z_{2_{0,1}}} & \frac{\partial Y_2}{\partial Z_{2_{0,2}}} \\ \frac{\partial Y_2}{\partial Z_{2_{1,0}}} & \frac{\partial Y_2}{\partial Z_{2_{1,1}}} & \frac{\partial Y_2}{\partial Z_{2_{1,2}}} \\ \frac{\partial Y_2}{\partial Z_{2_{2,0}}} & \frac{\partial Y_2}{\partial Z_{2_{2,1}}} & \frac{\partial Y_2}{\partial Z_{2_{2,2}}} \end{bmatrix}$$

Once we have the gradients $\frac{\partial C}{\partial Y_2}$ and $\frac{\partial Y_2}{\partial Z_2}$, we can calculate the gradient $\frac{\partial C}{\partial Z_2}$:

$$\frac{\partial C}{\partial Z_2} = \frac{\partial C}{\partial Y_2} \times \frac{\partial Y_2}{\partial Z_2}$$

Since Z_2 has size 3, $\frac{\partial C}{\partial Z_2}$ is a vector of size 3 either:

$$\frac{\partial C}{\partial Z_2} = \begin{bmatrix} \frac{\partial C}{\partial Z_{2_0}} & \frac{\partial C}{\partial Z_{2_1}} & \frac{\partial C}{\partial Z_{2_2}} \end{bmatrix}$$

Finally, we can use $\frac{\partial C}{\partial Z_2}$ to calculate two important gradients. The first one is the proper weight update $\frac{\partial C}{\partial W_2}$:

$$\frac{\partial C}{\partial W_2} = Y_1^T \times \frac{\partial C}{\partial Z_2} = \begin{bmatrix} Y_{1_0} \\ Y_{1_1} \\ Y_{1_2} \\ Y_{1_3} \\ Y_{1_4} \end{bmatrix} \times \begin{bmatrix} \frac{\partial C}{\partial Z_{2_0}} & \frac{\partial C}{\partial Z_{2_1}} & \frac{\partial C}{\partial Z_{2_2}} \end{bmatrix} = \begin{bmatrix} \frac{\partial C}{\partial W_{2_{0,0}}} & \frac{\partial C}{\partial W_{2_{0,1}}} & \frac{\partial C}{\partial W_{2_{0,2}}} \\ \frac{\partial C}{\partial W_{2_{1,0}}} & \frac{\partial C}{\partial W_{2_{1,1}}} & \frac{\partial C}{\partial W_{2_{1,2}}} \\ \frac{\partial C}{\partial W_{2_{2,0}}} & \frac{\partial C}{\partial W_{2_{2,1}}} & \frac{\partial C}{\partial W_{2_{2,2}}} \\ \frac{\partial C}{\partial W_{2_{3,0}}} & \frac{\partial C}{\partial W_{2_{3,1}}} & \frac{\partial C}{\partial W_{2_{3,2}}} \\ \frac{\partial C}{\partial W_{2_{4,0}}} & \frac{\partial C}{\partial W_{2_{4,1}}} & \frac{\partial C}{\partial W_{2_{4,2}}} \end{bmatrix}$$

The second one is the error propagation $\frac{\partial C}{\partial Y_1}$:

$$\frac{\partial C}{\partial Y_1} = \frac{\partial C}{\partial Z_2} \times W_2^T = \begin{bmatrix} \frac{\partial C}{\partial Z_{2_0}} & \frac{\partial C}{\partial Z_{2_1}} & \frac{\partial C}{\partial Z_{2_2}} \end{bmatrix} \times \begin{bmatrix} W_{2_{0,0}} & W_{2_{0,1}} & W_{2_{0,2}} & W_{2_{0,3}} & W_{2_{0,4}} \\ W_{2_{1,0}} & W_{2_{1,1}} & W_{2_{1,2}} & W_{2_{1,3}} & W_{2_{1,4}} \\ W_{2_{2,0}} & W_{2_{2,1}} & W_{2_{2,2}} & W_{2_{2,3}} & W_{2_{2,4}} \end{bmatrix}$$

This operation results in a vector of size 5:

$$\frac{\partial C}{\partial Y_1} = \begin{bmatrix} \frac{\partial C}{\partial Y_{1_0}} & \frac{\partial C}{\partial Y_{1_1}} & \frac{\partial C}{\partial Y_{1_2}} & \frac{\partial C}{\partial Y_{1_3}} & \frac{\partial C}{\partial Y_{1_4}} \end{bmatrix}$$

This finalizes the gradient computation of layer 2. Once we finished this calculation, we can feed $\frac{\partial C}{\partial Y_1}$ into the next layer to keep calculating the next gradients $\frac{\partial C}{\partial W_1}$ and $\frac{\partial C}{\partial Y_0}$ in the same way we did here for the layer 2. Finally, using to calculate the last gradient.

Vectorizing backpropagation

When training networks, instead of using a single training instance, we prefer to use large batches containing hundreds or thousands of registers. As discussed in the book's first chapter, we use vectorization to implement this, computing several instances at once to reduce the overall execution time.

At first glance, vectorizing backpropagation seems to be pretty streamlined. Let us start by defining the input X and target T as matrices with sizes (n x 10) and (n x 3), respectively:

$$X = \begin{bmatrix} X_{0,0} & X_{0,1} & X_{0,2} & X_{0,3} & X_{0,4} & X_{0,5} & X_{0,6} & X_{0,7} & X_{0,8} & X_{0,9} \\ X_{1,0} & X_{1,1} & X_{1,2} & X_{1,3} & X_{1,4} & X_{1,5} & X_{1,6} & X_{1,7} & X_{1,8} & X_{1,9} \\ \vdots & \vdots & \vdots & \vdots & \vdots & \vdots & \vdots & \vdots & \vdots & \vdots \\ X_{n-1,0} & X_{n-1,1} & X_{n-1,2} & X_{n-1,3} & X_{n-1,4} & X_{n-1,5} & X_{n-1,6} & X_{n-1,7} & X_{n-1,8} & X_{n-1,9} \end{bmatrix}$$

$$T = \begin{bmatrix} T_{0,0} & T_{0,1} & T_{0,2} \\ T_{1,0} & T_{1,1} & T_{1,2} \\ \vdots & \vdots & \vdots \\ T_{n-1,0} & T_{n-1,1} & T_{n-1,2} \end{bmatrix}$$

Here, n is called **batch size**. Now, each X row contains the data of a single input. Each row in T contains the target for the respective row in X. Thus, the pair (X, T) holds all the data of the n instances.

Vectorizing the forward propagation

Vectorizing the forward propagation pass is straightforward. It turns out that the forward pass consists basically of two operations, the matrix product, and the activation function calculation:

$$Z = X \times W$$

$$Y = activation(Z)$$

Eigen matrix product is highly vectorized. Note that the output of the matrix product results in a matrix containing the same sequence of outputs. For example, calculating the two following products:

$$[x_0 \quad y_0 \quad z_0] \times \begin{bmatrix} a & b & c \\ d & e & f \\ g & h & i \end{bmatrix} = [ax_0 + dy_0 + gz_0 \quad bx_0 + ey_0 + hz_0 \quad cx_0 + fy_0 + iz_0]$$

$$[x_1 \quad y_1 \quad z_1] \times \begin{bmatrix} a & b & c \\ d & e & f \\ g & h & i \end{bmatrix} = [ax_1 + dy_1 + gz_1 \quad bx_1 + ey_1 + hz_1 \quad cx_1 + fy_1 + iz_1]$$

is equivalent to perform only one product:

$$\begin{bmatrix} x_0 & y_0 & z_0 \\ x_1 & y_1 & z_1 \end{bmatrix} \times \begin{bmatrix} a & b & c \\ d & e & f \\ g & h & i \end{bmatrix} = \begin{bmatrix} ax_0 + dy_0 + gz_0 & bx_0 + ey_0 + hz_0 & cx_0 + fy_0 + iz_0 \\ ax_1 + dy_1 + gz_1 & bx_1 + ey_1 + hz_1 & cx_1 + fy_1 + iz_1 \end{bmatrix}$$

Since the matrix product is highly optimized in vectorization, performing only one operation with n stacked inputs into a single matrix is faster than running n times for a single input.

Regarding the activation function vectorization, since the activation function formula is not previously fixed, we cannot guarantee that every activation function will be vectorizable. However, the most popular activations, such as sigmoid, ReLU, and softmax, are all vectorizable.

Vectorizing the backward step

Most of the operations in the backward pass are also vectorizable. For example, the weight gradient calculation is a regular matrix product which is also vectorizable even if $\frac{\partial C}{\partial Z_i}$ and ${Y_{i-1}}^T$ are both matrices:

$$\frac{\partial C}{\partial W_i} = {Y_{i-1}}^T \times \frac{\partial C}{\partial Z_i}$$

This is the case with most of the operations in the backward pass. However, there is a critical point where we find a different schema: the calculation of $\frac{\partial C}{\partial Z}$. Let us remember the formula to get $\frac{\partial C}{\partial Z}$ for a single instance in Z:

$$\frac{\partial C}{\partial Z} = \frac{\partial C}{\partial Y} \times \frac{\partial Y}{\partial Z}$$

It turns out that by batching multiple instances in a single matrix Z_2 makes $\frac{\partial Y}{\partial Z}$ no longer a plain (two-dimensional) matrix, but a 3-rank tensor:

$$Z_2 = \begin{bmatrix} Z2_{0,0} & Z2_{0,1} & Z2_{0,i} \\ Z2_{1,0} & Z2_{1,1} & Z2_{1,i} \\ \vdots & \vdots & \vdots \\ Z2_{n-1,0} & Z2_{n-1,1} & Z2_{n-1,i} \end{bmatrix}$$

$$\left(\frac{\partial Y_2}{\partial Z_2}\right)_i = \left(\begin{bmatrix} \frac{\partial Y_2}{\partial Z2_{0,0}} & \frac{\partial Y_2}{\partial Z2_{0,1}} & \frac{\partial Y_2}{\partial Z2_{0,2}} \\ \frac{\partial Y_2}{\partial Z2_{1,0}} & \frac{\partial Y_2}{\partial Z2_{1,1}} & \frac{\partial Y_2}{\partial Z2_{1,2}} \\ \frac{\partial Y_2}{\partial Z2_{2,0}} & \frac{\partial Y_2}{\partial Z2_{2,1}} & \frac{\partial Y_2}{\partial Z2_{2,2}} \end{bmatrix} \right)$$

Now, we have a squared Jacobian $\left(\frac{\partial Y_2}{\partial Z_2}\right)_i$ for each vector $Z2_i$ from Z_2 :

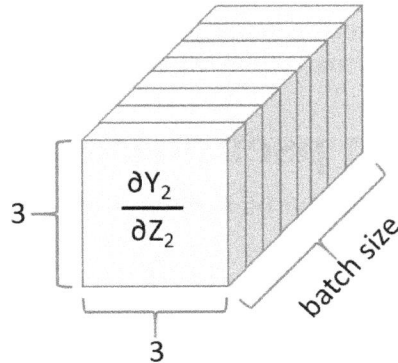

Figure 10.9: 3-rank gradient

As a result, the calculation of gradient $\frac{\partial C}{\partial Z}$ is no longer a regular matrix product:

$$\frac{\partial C}{\partial Z} = \frac{\partial C}{\partial Y} \otimes \frac{\partial Y}{\partial Z}$$

This operation consists in performing the matrix product of each i-th element $\frac{\partial C}{\partial Y_i}$ with the respective i-th squared Jacobian $\frac{\partial Y}{\partial Z_i}$, where i represents an element of the batch. We name this operation **Batched Matrix Multiplication (BMM)**, as illustrated in the following figure:

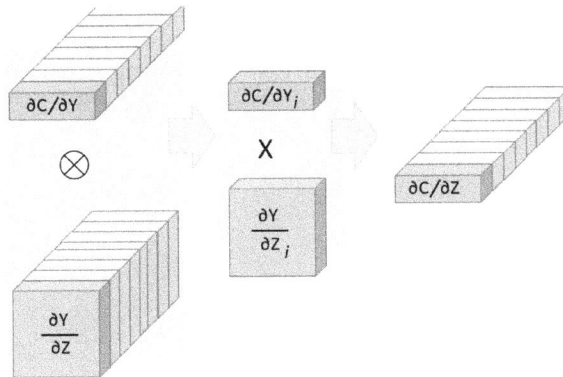

Figure 10.10: Computing using Batched Matrix Multiplication

Considering that the size of $\frac{\partial C}{\partial Y}$ is (n x 1 x S) and $\frac{\partial Y}{\partial Z}$ has size (n x S x S), the resulting size of $\frac{\partial C}{\partial Z}$ is (n x 1 x S). Note that, after this operation, we can reshape $\frac{\partial C}{\partial Z}$ to fit a 2-rank tensor with size (n x S).

BMM is critical for backpropagation because it uses a massive volume of data and processing time, introducing severe scalability issues. Later in this chapter, we will discuss some strategies to approach this matter, aiming to reduce the total cost of computing $\frac{\partial c}{\partial z}$.

Backpropagation pseudo-code

Now we know how to derivate the backpropagation formulas, we can describe the algorithm by its pseudo-code:

```
BACKPROPAGATION(X, T, η, MAX_EPOCHS, LAYERS, Cost_fn):
DO:
    epoch = 0
    WHILE epoch < MAX_EPOCHS:
    DO:
        Y = FORWARD(X, LAYERS)
        Grads = BACKWARD(T, Y, LAYERS, Cost_fn)
        UPDATE(LAYERS, Grads, η)
        epoch++
    END
END
```

If we compare this description with the description of gradient descent in *Chapter 9, Coding the Gradient Descent Algorithm*, we may realize that the two algorithms are, in essence, the same procedure. The key difference between the two algorithms is the presence of layers in backpropagation. Such as gradient descent, backpropagation consists of 3 sub-procedures: **FORWARD**, **BACKWARD**, and **UPDATE**. Let us start by describing the **FORWARD** procedure:

```
FORWARD(X, LAYERS):
DO:
    input = X
    FOR EACH layer L IN LAYERS:
    DO:
        Z = input x L.weigths
        Y = L.activation(Z)
        input = Y
    END
    return input
END
```

The **BACKWARD** can be described as follows:

```
BACKWARD(T, Y, LAYERS, Cost_fn):
DO:
```

```
    Grads = []
    dC_dY = Cost_fn.derivative(T, Y)
    FOR EACH layer L IN reverse(LAYERS):
    DO:
        dY_dZ = L.activation.derivative()
        dC_dZ = dC_dY  dY_dZ
        dC_dW = dC_dZᵀ x L.input
        Grads.add(dW)
        dC_dY = dC_dZ x L.weightsᵀ
    END
    return reverse(Grads)
END
```

Finally, the **UPDATE** procedure:

```
UPDATE(LAYERS, Grads, η):
DO:
    input = X
    FOR i = 0 TO length(LAYERS) - 1:
    DO:
        L = LAYERS[i]
        Grad = Grads[i]
        L.weights = L.weights - η x Grad
    END
END
```

This last line:

```
L.weights = L.weights - η x Grad
```

is known as **update rule**. In the forthcoming chapters, we will learn that we can optimize the algorithm convergence by changing the way how weights are updated in the update rule.

In fact, backpropagation is not a complex algorithm. We loop over the layers during the forward pass to generate an output. Then, in the backward pass, we loop again throughout the layers (but in reverse order) to calculate the gradients of each layer. Once we have evaluated the gradients, we update the layers following the update rule. We repeat these steps by the total number of epochs or by using another **stop condition**.

If the network has only one layer, backpropagation is exactly the same algorithm as gradient descent. Indeed, very often, people refer to backpropagation only to the way the chain rule is applied to calculate gradients.

Now that we understand how backpropagation works, it is time to move on to the algorithm implementation. It is covered in the following section.

Implementing the first version of backpropagation

Let us start coding our first version of backpropagation. At this point, we are only concerned with learning how to correctly execute the forward and backward pass, paying particular attention to how to calculate the gradients accurately.

In this example, we are going to implement the training of a simple network consisting of only four layers: the input layer, the first hidden layer, the second hidden layer, and the output layer. Refer to the following figure:

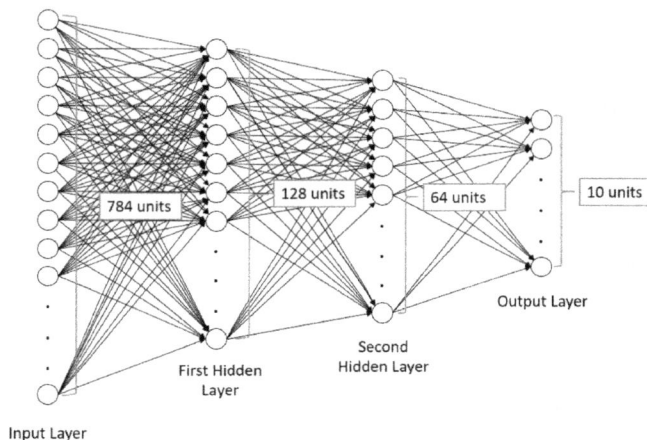

Figure 10.11: *Four-layer network used in the example*

Besides being simple, this network has everything we need to illustrate how backpropagation works. In this example, we assume that the hidden layers are dense layers using ReLU, and the output layer uses softmax activation.

The training loop

The training loop is a straight transcription of the pseudo-code just introduced in the previous section:

```
1. template <typename T>
2. T loop(const Tensor<T, 2> &TRUE, const Tensor<T, 2> &X,
3.        Tensor<T, 2> &W0, Tensor<T, 2> &W1, Tensor<T, 2> &W2,
4.        const T learning_rate)
5. {
6.
7.     // forward pass
```

```
8.      auto [Z0, Z1, Z2, Y0, Y1, Y2] = forward(X, W0, W1, W2);
9.
10.     // Output cost
11.     CategoricalCrossEntropy cost_fn;
12.     T LOSS = cost_fn.evaluate(TRUE, Y2);
13.
14.     // backward pass
15.     auto [grad0, grad1, grad2] = back-
    ward(TRUE, X, Z0, Z1, Z2, Y0, Y1, Y2, W0, W1, W2);
16.
17.     // update pass
18.     update(W0, W1, W2, grad0, grad1, grad2, learning_rate);
19.
20.     return LOSS;
21. }
```

Note: For the sake of simplicity, this implementation uses functions, passing the state variables as parameters. In a more reusable scenario, though, we should use classes to hold the data and behavior.

Let us look at the implementation of forward, backward, and update steps.

The forward pass

The forward step is as simple as should be:

```
1. template <typename T>
2. auto forward(const Tensor<T, 2> &X, const Tensor<T, 2> &W0,
    const Tensor<T, 2> &W1, const Tensor<T, 2> &W2)
3. {
4.     const array<IndexPair<T>, 1> contract_
    dims = {IndexPair<T>(1, 0)};
5.
6.     // First Hidden Layer
7.     ReLU relu;
8.     Tensor<T, 2> Z0 = X.contract(W0, contract_dims);
9.     Tensor<T, 2> Y0 = relu.evaluate(Z0);
10.
11.     // Second Hidden Layer
12.     Tensor<T, 2> Z1 = Y0.contract(W1, contract_dims);
13.     Tensor<T, 2> Y1 = relu.evaluate(Z1);
```

```
14.
15.     // Output Layer
16.     Softmax softmax;
17.     Tensor<T, 2> Z2 = Y1.contract(W2, contract_dims);
18.     auto Y2 = softmax.evaluate(Z2);
19.
20.     return std::make_tuple(Z0, Z1, Z2, Y0, Y1, Y2);
21. }
```

As usual, we are using template functions. Thus, we can reuse our code with different data types, such as double or float.

Note that we are returning the activations **Z** and each layer's output **Y**. They will be used later to calculate the gradients during the backward pass, as explained ahead.

The backward pass

While **forward** flows from the input up to the output layer, **backward** starts by calculating the output loss gradient and then propagates the error throughout each layer in the reverse order. The objective is to find the gradients of each weight **W0**, **W1**, and **W2** with respect to the output cost. The following figure illustrates this calculation:

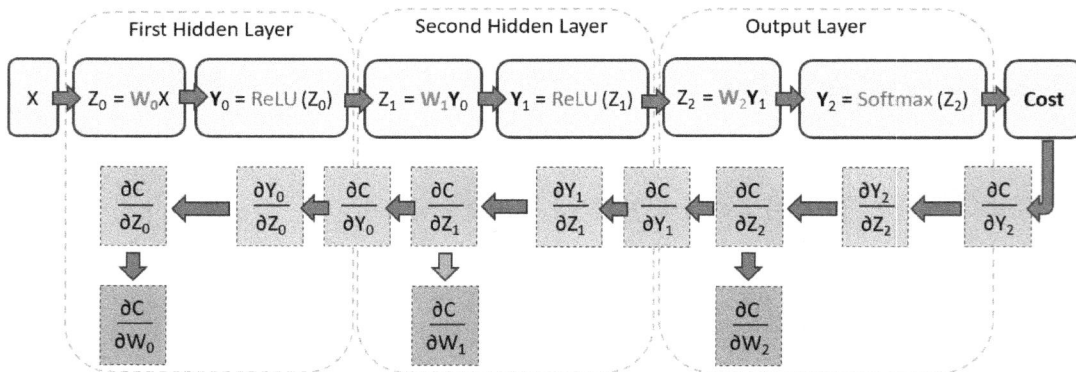

Figure 10.12: *The flow of gradients computation during backward pass*

Each layer's gradients can be calculated using the following function:

```
1. template <typename T, typename Activation>
2. auto gradient(const Tensor<T, 2> &dC_dY, const Tensor<T, 2> &input,
3.                const Tensor<T, 2> &Z, const Tensor<T, 2> &Y, const Tensor<T, 2> &W,
4.                const Activation &activation, const bool propagate = true)
```

```
5.  {
6.      const int batch_size = input.dimension(0);
7.      // calculating dY_dZ
8.      Tensor<float, 3> dY_dZ = activation.jacobian(Z);
9.
10.     // reshaping dC_dY to 3D to meet BMM
11.     const array<Index, 3> dC_dY_3D_dim = {batch_size, 1, Y.
    dimension(1)};
12.     Tensor<float, 3> dC_dY_3D = dC_dY.reshape(dC_dY_3D_dim);
13.
14.     // calculating dC_dZ using BMM
15.     Tensor<float, 3> dC_dZ = batched_matrix_multiplication(dC_
    dY_3D, dY_dZ);
16.
17.     // calculating dC_dW
18.     const array<IndexPair<T>, 1> product_
    dims_0_0 = {IndexPair<T>(0, 0)};
19.     const array<Index, 2> dC_dW_dim = {W.dimension(0), W.
    dimension(1)};
20.     Tensor<float, 2> dC_dW = input.contract(dC_dZ, product_dims_0_0).
    reshape(dC_dW_dim);
21.     Tensor<float, 2> grad = dC_dW / dC_dW.constant(batch_size);
22.
23.     Tensor<float, 2> downstream;
24.     if (propagate) { //false only for the first hidden layer
25.         // calculating the error propagation dC_
    dY for the previous layer
26.         const array<Index, 2> error_propagation_dim = {batch_
    size, input.dimension(1)};
27.         const array<IndexPair<T>, 1> product_dims_2_1 = {Index-
    Pair<T>(2, 1)};
28.         downstream = dC_dZ.contract(W, product_dims_2_1).
    reshape(error_propagation_dim);
29.     }
30.
31.     return std::make_tuple(grad, downstream);
32. }
```

Following the reverse flow, we can implement backward as shown below:

```
1.  template <typename T>
2.  auto backward(const Tensor<T, 2> &TRUE, const Tensor<T, 2> &X,
3.                  const Tensor<T, 2> &Z0, const Tensor<T, 2> &Z1, cons
    t Tensor<T, 2> &Z2,
4.                  const Tensor<T, 2> &Y0, const Tensor<T, 2> &Y1, cons
    t Tensor<T, 2> &Y2,
5.                  const Tensor<T, 2> &W0, const Tensor<T, 2> &W1, cons
    t Tensor<T, 2> &W2)
6.  {
7.
8.      const int batch_size = TRUE.dimension(0);
9.
10.     // First step, calculating the output loss gradient dC_dY2
11.
12.     CategoricalCrossEntropy cost_fn;
13.     auto dC_dY2 = cost_fn.derivative(TRUE, Y2);
14.
15.     // second step: calculating weight gradients
16.
17.     Softmax softmax;
18.     ReLU relu;
19.
20.     auto [grad2, dC_dY1] = gradient(dC_dY2, Y1, Z2, Y2, W2, softmax);
21.
22.     auto [grad1, dC_dY0] = gradient(dC_dY1, Y0, Z1, Y1, W1, relu);
23.
24.     auto [grad0, _]       = gradient(dC_
    dY0, X,  Z0, Y0, W0, relu, false);
25.
26.     return std::make_tuple(grad0, grad1, grad2);
27. }
```

It is easy to see that the backward pass is the more complex step in backpropagation. This complexity also contributes to major memory and processing costs. In the next section, we will learn how to approach these issues. But first, we need to understand how this raw version works.

In a nutshell, this backward example consists of using the cost function to calculate **dC_dY2** and then using **dC_dY2** to calculate the weight **W2** gradient **dC_dW2** and the error propagation gradient **dC_dY1** to find **dC_dW1**. The process repeats to calculate **dC_dW0**.

Note that the function **gradient()** uses **dC_dY** and **dY_dZ** to find **dC_dZ** using the function **batched_matrix_multiplication()**.

Note: The dC_dZ calculation is actually the critical step of backpropagation in terms of processing and memory.

There are several ways to implement **batched_matrix_multiplication**. In this example, we use this straight version:

```
1.  template <typename T>
2.  const Tensor<T, 3> batched_matrix_
      multiplication(const Tensor<T, 3>& A, const Tensor<T, 3>& B)
3.  {
4.      const int batch_size = A.dimension(0);
5.      const int dim1 = A.dimension(1);
6.      const int dim2 = B.dimension(2);
7.      Tensor<T, 3> output(batch_size, dim1, dim2);
8.      const array<IndexPair<T>, 1> dims = {IndexPair<T>(1, 0)};
9.      for (int i = 0; i < batch_size; ++i) {
10.         auto B_chip = B.template chip<0>(i);
11.         output.template chip<0>(i) = A.template chip<0>(i).
      contract(B_chip, dims);
12.     }
13.     return output;
14. }
```

Once **dC_dZ** was found, **gradient()** uses it to calculate the weight gradient **dC_dW** and the error propagation. Finally, **backward()** returns the three gradients **[grad0, grad1, grad2]** which will be used to update the weights.

The update step

Once the gradients were obtained, the algorithm can update the weight as follows:

```
1.  template <typename T>
2.  void update(Tensor<T, 2> &W0, Tensor<T, 2> &W1, Tensor<T, 2> &W2,
3.              Tensor<T, 2> &grad0, Tensor<T, 2> &grad1, Ten-
      sor<T, 2> &grad2,
4.              const T learning_rate)
5.  {
6.      W0 = W0 - grad0 * grad0.constant(learning_rate);
7.      W1 = W1 - grad1 * grad1.constant(learning_rate);
8.      W2 = W2 - grad2 * grad2.constant(learning_rate);
9.  }
```

In *Chapter 13, Implementing Optimizers*, we will discuss how to modify the update step to include **optimizers** such as **RMSprop** and **Adam**. Such optimizers improve the algorithm search, resulting in more accurate models.

The **forward**, **backward**, and **update** steps are executed continuously inside the **training loop** until some stop condition fires. Let us see this in practice in the next section.

Running our first implementation on the MNIST dataset

As discussed in *Chapter 3, Testing Deep Learning Code*, it is hard to determine when an algorithm implementation is correct. To provide some guidance on this, training the model using a known benchmark is always recommended. In our case, we will check our implementation using MNIST, a popular database containing handwritten digits.

The MNIST dataset

The MNIST dataset consists of 60,000 tiny images of handwritten digits. All the digits are stored as *28x28* grayscale images in a single file called **train-images.idx3-ubyte**. Each image has a respective label, an integer digit from zero to nine representing the number written in the image. The labels are stored in a file called **train-labels.idx1-ubyte**.

You can find a code that loads MNIST and displays its images on the book repository on GitHub. Refer to *Figure 10.11* and *Figure 10.12* for reference:

```
1.  int main(int, char **)
2.  {
3.      try
4.      {
5.          std::cout << "Loading data...\n";
6.
7.          auto [training_images, training_labels, test_images, test_
    labels] = load_mnist("data/mnist");
8.
9.          navigate(training_images, training_labels);
10.
11.         std::cout << "exiting...\n";
12.     }
13.     catch (std::exception const &e)
14.     {
15.         std::cerr << "Exception: " << e.what() << std::endl;
16.         return -1;
```

```
17.     }
18.
19.     return 0;
20. }
```

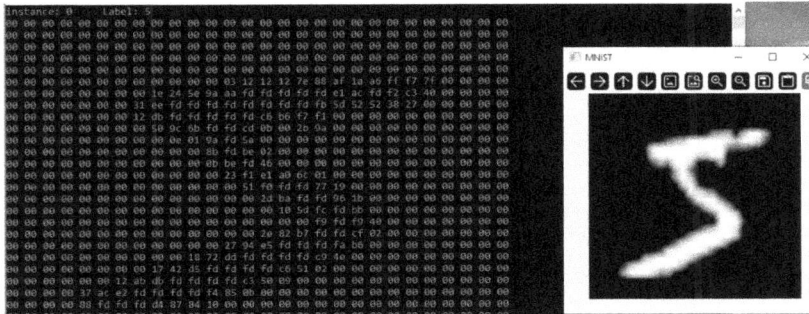

Figure 10.13: Navigating over the MNIST dataset. Instance 0.

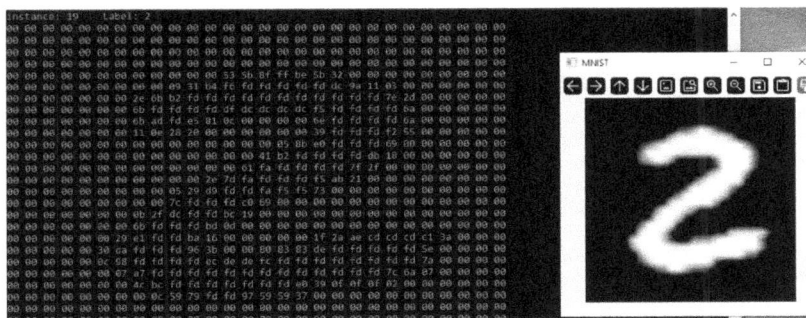

Figure 10.14: Navigating over the MNIST dataset

We will use the following function:

```
1. auto [training_images, training_labels, test_images, test_
   labels] = load_mnist("data/mnist");
```

to load the MNIST dataset again when we train our model in the following section.

Train a model with MNIST

Now that we know how to load MNIST, let us use it to train a model:

```
1. int main(int, char **)
2. {
3.     srand(seed);
4.
5.     auto [training_images, training_labels, test_images, test_
```

```
       labels] = load_mnist("../../data/mnist");
6.     std::cout << "Data loaded!\n";
7.     std::cout << "training_images: " << training_images.
       dimensions() << "\n\n";
8.     std::cout << "training_labels: " << training_labels.
       dimensions() << "\n\n";
9.
10.    const int input_size = training_images.dimension(1);
11.    const int output_size = training_labels.dimension(1);
12.
13.    const int hidden_units_0 = 128;
14.    const int hidden_units_1 = 64;
15.
16.    Tensor<float, 2> W0 = glorot_uniform_initializer(input_
       size, hidden_units_0);
17.    Tensor<float, 2> W1 = glorot_uniform_initializer(hidden_
       units_0, hidden_units_1);
18.    Tensor<float, 2> W2 = glorot_uniform_initializer(hidden_
       units_1, output_size);
19.
20.    const int MAX_EPOCHS = 20;
21.    const float learning_rate = 0.1f;
22.
23.    int epoch = 0;
24.
25.    while (epoch++ < MAX_EPOCHS)
26.    {
27.
28.        auto begin = high_resolution_clock::now();
29.
30.        float training_loss = loop(training_labels, training_
       images, W0, W1, W2, learning_rate);
31.
32.        auto end = high_resolution_clock::now();
33.        auto duration = duration_cast<milliseconds>(end - begin);
34.
35.        auto training_pred = predict(training_labels, training_
       images, W0, W1, W2);
```

```
36.          float training_acc = accuracy(training_labels, training_pred);
37.
38.          std::cout << "epoch:\t" << epoch
39.                         << "\ttook:\t" << duration.count() << " mills\t"
40.                         << "\ttraining_loss:\t" << training_loss
41.                         << "\ttraining_acc:\t" << training_acc
42.                         << "\n";
43.
44.      }
45.      return 0;
46. }
```

This code is very similar to the one introduced in *Chapter 9, Coding the Gradient Descent Algorithm*. The most important difference here is that we are training a model with 4 layers (the input layer, two hidden layers, and the output layer) instead of a two-layer model.

Note: It is suggested to the reader to pack the functions in one or more Layer classes (Input, Dense, etc.). In fact, this is how we will introduce the algorithms in the forthcoming chapters.

The training loops **MAX_EPOCHS** times, calculating the training loss and accuracy for each epoch.

Note: Accuracy and other evaluation metrics are covered in Chapter 11, Implementing Cross-validation, mini batching, and model performance metrics.

Executing this code results in an output similar to this one:

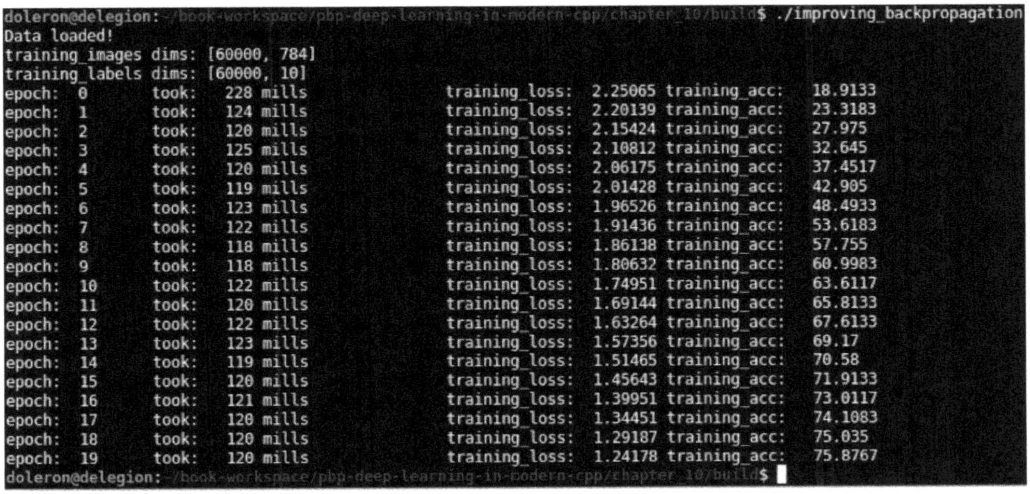

Figure 10.15: Training our first implementation with the MNIST dataset

This output shows that the cost decreases consistently after each epoch, an indication of algorithm correctness. Note that the weights are initialized using **glorot uniform initialization**:

```
1.  auto glorot_uniform_initializer = [](int rows, int cols) {
2.    float range = sqrt(6.f / (rows + cols));
3.      std::uniform_real_distribution<float> uniform_distro(-range, range);
4.    Tensor<float, 2> result(rows, cols);
5.      result = result.unaryExpr([&uniform_distro](float)
6.            { return uniform_distro(rng); });
7.    return result;
8.  };
```

Thus, every execution produces a different (but statistically similar) output. For evaluation, we can compare the previous output with the performance achieved by training an equivalent network using **Google TensorFlow**:

```
1.  import tensorflow as tf
2.  import keras
3.  from keras import layers
4.
5.  inputs = keras.Input(shape=(784,), name="digits")
6.  x = layers.Dense(128, activation="relu", use_bias=False)(inputs)
7.  x = layers.Dense(64, activation="relu", use_bias=False)(x)
8.  outputs = layers.Dense(10, activation="softmax", use_
    bias=False, name="predictions")(x)
9.
10. model = keras.Model(inputs=inputs, outputs=outputs)
11.
12. (x_train, y_train), (x_test, y_test) = keras.datasets.mnist.load_
    data()
13. x_train = x_train.reshape(60000, 784).astype("float32") / 255
14. y_train = tf.one_hot(y_train, 10)
15.
16. model.compile(optimizer=keras.optimizers.SGD(learning_
    rate=0.1, momentum=0.0),
17.     loss=keras.losses.CategoricalCrossentropy(), metrics=[keras.
    metrics.CategoricalAccuracy()])
18.
19. print("Fitting model on training data")
20. model.fit( x_train, y_train, batch_size=60000, epochs=20)
```

Running this TensorFlow code results in:

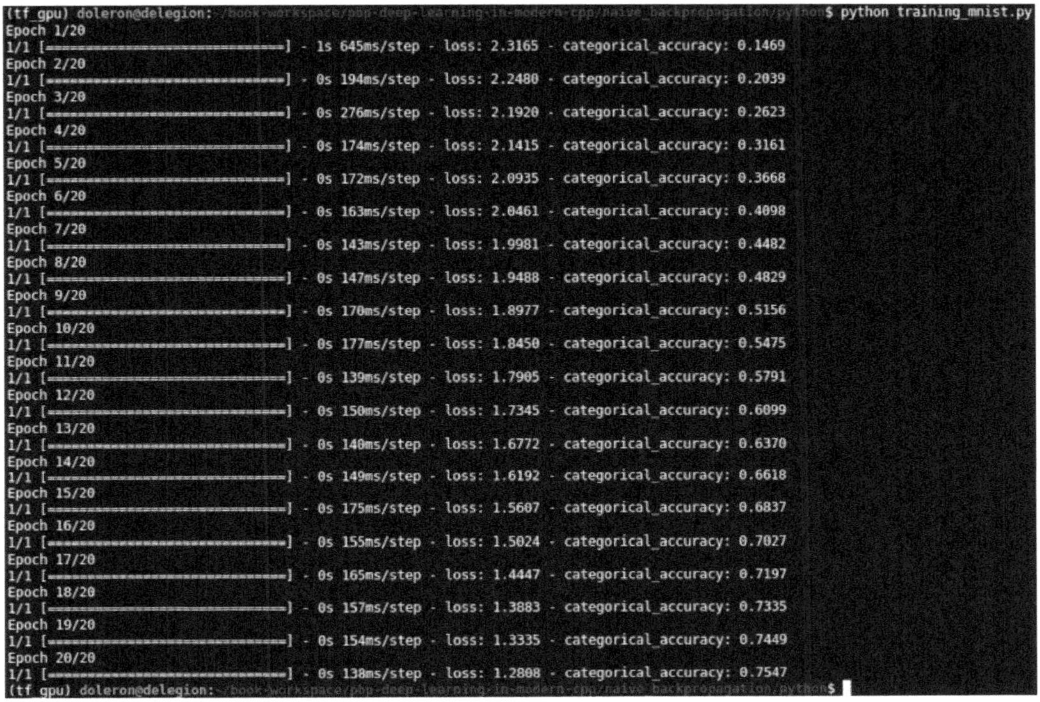

Figure 10.16: Training an equivalent model using Google TensorFlow

If we run our C++ code and the TensorFlow code a sufficient number of times, we will eventually find that the final loss and accuracy of both implementations are statistically equivalent.

However, our C++ implementation time cost was dauntingly long, making the model converge too slowly. Why?

Indeed, the achieved processing time taken by our first C++ code was expected to be high because we did not concern ourselves with any optimization. The following section will explore alternatives to make this training run much faster.

Improving the backpropagation processing performance

Although our backpropagation implementation succeeded in fitting the model to the data in MNIST, the time spent by each training epoch was too high. A comparison against the training of an equivalent network using Google TensorFlow on the same machine achieved about 90 ms per epoch, 100 times faster than our implementation.

Analyzing our implementation, we realize that the main bottleneck resides in how we compute the gradients. In particular, the batched matrix multiplication consumes most of the processing time. Thus, the batched matrix multiplication will be our first aspect to improve.

Furthermore, one can find that our code is wasting valuable opportunities to gain processing time and memory. These opportunities will also be addressed in the next section.

Tackling the batched matrix multiplication

As discussed earlier in this chapter, the batched matrix multiplication plays a key role in the overall algorithm processing time. Thus, one approach to drastically reduce the algorithm time is simply avoiding the batched matrix multiplication. There are two scenarios where avoiding the batched matrix multiplication is possible:

- When the activation function is coefficient-wise, its Jacobian matrix is diagonal. We can use this information to reduce the amount of computation to calculate the gradient $\frac{\partial C}{\partial z}$.
- Even if the activation function is not coefficient-wise, **some combinations of cost functions provide fast calculations of** $\frac{\partial C}{\partial z}$.

Luckily, the two scenarios above are very common. We will cover them next.

Avoiding the batched matrix multiplication for coefficient-wise activation functions

The first and most straightforward way to avoid the batched matrix multiplication is when the activation function is coefficient-wise, such as sigmoid and ReLU. Consider the representation of a generic activation function as shown:

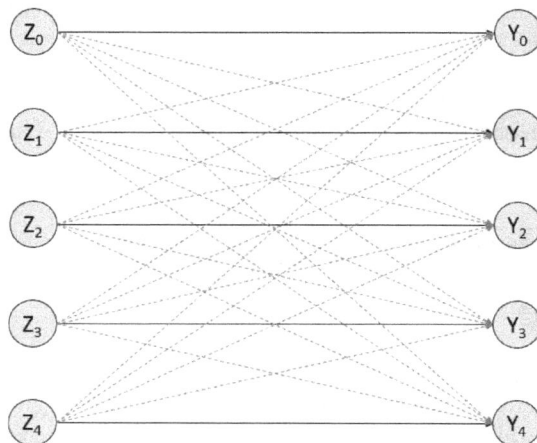

Figure 10.17: Computation flow in a single layer

The dashed red arrows represent the contribution of each Z_j coefficient to the coefficients Y_i for $i \neq j$. The black solid arrows represent the direct dependence of Y_i and Z_i. It is easy to see that, due to the combinatorics of Z and Y, there are more red dashed arrows than solid black ones. As a result, the gradient $\dfrac{\partial Y}{\partial Z}$ is a matrix like this:

$$
\frac{\partial y}{\partial Z} =
\begin{bmatrix}
\dfrac{\partial Y_0}{\partial Z_0} & \dfrac{\partial Y_0}{\partial Z_1} & \dfrac{\partial Y_0}{\partial Z_2} & \dfrac{\partial Y_0}{\partial Z_3} & \dfrac{\partial Y_0}{\partial Z_4} \\
\dfrac{\partial Y_1}{\partial Z_0} & \dfrac{\partial Y_1}{\partial Z_1} & \dfrac{\partial Y_1}{\partial Z_2} & \dfrac{\partial Y_1}{\partial Z_3} & \dfrac{\partial Y_1}{\partial Z_4} \\
\dfrac{\partial Y_2}{\partial Z_0} & \dfrac{\partial Y_2}{\partial Z_1} & \dfrac{\partial Y_2}{\partial Z_2} & \dfrac{\partial Y_2}{\partial Z_3} & \dfrac{\partial Y_2}{\partial Z_4} \\
\dfrac{\partial Y_3}{\partial Z_0} & \dfrac{\partial Y_3}{\partial Z_1} & \dfrac{\partial Y_3}{\partial Z_2} & \dfrac{\partial Y_3}{\partial Z_3} & \dfrac{\partial Y_3}{\partial Z_4} \\
\dfrac{\partial Y_4}{\partial Z_0} & \dfrac{\partial Y_4}{\partial Z_1} & \dfrac{\partial Y_4}{\partial Z_2} & \dfrac{\partial Y_4}{\partial Z_3} & \dfrac{\partial Y_4}{\partial Z_4}
\end{bmatrix}
$$

Luckily, this is the case with a few activation functions, such as softmax. Let us remember the softmax definition formula:

$$
Y_i = S(Z)_i = \frac{e^{Z_i}}{\sum_{j=1}^{K} e^{Z_j}}
$$

Due to the summation in the denominator, each output Y_i depends on every coefficient in Z. Thus, the Jacobian of a softmax layer having five units is given by:

$$
\frac{\partial Y}{\partial Z} = \frac{\partial S(Z)}{\partial Z} =
\begin{bmatrix}
S_0(1-S_0) & -S_1 S_0 & -S_2 S_0 & -S_3 S_0 & -S_4 S_0 \\
-S_0 S_1 & S_1(1-S_1) & -S_2 S_1 & -S_3 S_1 & -S_4 S_1 \\
-S_0 S_2 & -S_1 S_2 & S_2(1-S_2) & -S_3 S_2 & -S_4 S_2 \\
-S_0 S_3 & -S_1 S_3 & -S_2 S_3 & S_3(1-S_3) & -S_4 S_3 \\
-S_0 S_4 & -S_1 S_4 & -S_2 S_4 & -S_3 S_4 & S_4(1-S_4)
\end{bmatrix}
$$

Where S_i means $S(Z)_i$.

Different from softmax, in general, activation functions are coefficient-wise functions. For example, consider the formula of ReLU:

$$
Y_i = ReLU(Z)_i = \max(Z_i, 0)
$$

Since the value of Y_i depends only on the respective coefficient Z_i, every partial derivative $\dfrac{\partial Y_i}{\partial Z_j}$ is zero if $i \neq j$. Thus, the Jacobian of a ReLU activation with five units can be represented by:

$$\frac{\partial Y}{\partial Z} = \frac{\partial ReLU(Z)}{\partial Z} = \begin{bmatrix} \frac{\partial Y_0}{\partial Z_0} & 0 & 0 & 0 & 0 \\ 0 & \frac{\partial Y_1}{\partial Z_1} & 0 & 0 & 0 \\ 0 & 0 & \frac{\partial Y_2}{\partial Z_2} & 0 & 0 \\ 0 & 0 & 0 & \frac{\partial Y_3}{\partial Z_3} & 0 \\ 0 & 0 & 0 & 0 & \frac{\partial Y_4}{\partial Z_4} \end{bmatrix}$$

This Jacobian is an example of a **diagonal matrix**, a special case of a **sparse matrix**.

Note: In a sparse matrix, only a few elements have a non-zero value.

Of course, plenty of zeroes off-diagonal may lead to a waste of memory and processing time, resulting in an opportunity for improvements. For example, if we try to compute the gradient $\frac{\partial C}{\partial Z}$:

$$\frac{\partial C}{\partial Z} = \frac{\partial C}{\partial Y} \times \frac{\partial Y}{\partial Z} = \begin{bmatrix} \frac{\partial C}{\partial Y_0} & \frac{\partial C}{\partial Y_1} & \frac{\partial C}{\partial Y_2} & \frac{\partial C}{\partial Y_3} & \frac{\partial C}{\partial Y_4} \end{bmatrix} \begin{bmatrix} \frac{\partial Y_0}{\partial Z_0} & 0 & 0 & 0 & 0 \\ 0 & \frac{\partial Y_1}{\partial Z_1} & 0 & 0 & 0 \\ 0 & 0 & \frac{\partial Y_2}{\partial Z_2} & 0 & 0 \\ 0 & 0 & 0 & \frac{\partial Y_3}{\partial Z_3} & 0 \\ 0 & 0 & 0 & 0 & \frac{\partial Y_4}{\partial Z_4} \end{bmatrix}$$

We end up with the following formula for $\frac{\partial C}{\partial Z}$:

$$\frac{\partial C}{\partial Z} = \begin{bmatrix} \frac{\partial C}{\partial Y_0} & \frac{\partial C}{\partial Y_1} & \frac{\partial C}{\partial Y_2} & \frac{\partial C}{\partial Y_3} & \frac{\partial C}{\partial Y_4} \end{bmatrix} \odot \begin{bmatrix} \frac{\partial Y_0}{\partial Z_0} & \frac{\partial Y_1}{\partial Z_1} & \frac{\partial Y_2}{\partial Z_2} & \frac{\partial Y_3}{\partial Z_3} & \frac{\partial Y_4}{\partial Z_4} \end{bmatrix}$$

where the operation represents the **coefficient-wise product**. Since the cost of coefficient-wise product is linear and matrix product has cost $O(M^3)$, computing batches of $\frac{\partial C}{\partial Y}$ and $\frac{\partial Y}{\partial Z}$ using the previous formula is considerably faster than computing the raw batched matrix multiplication.

To summarize:

- **The advantage of this approach** is that this reduces the $O(N * M^3)$ cost of using the bathed matrix multiplication to only $O(N * M)$.

- **The disadvantage** is that this approach does not work for a non-coefficient-wise activation function (such as softmax).

In general, inner layers use coefficient-wise activations such as ReLU or sigmoid. Applying this optimization radically improves the computation of these layers, resulting in a huge gain in performance.

Avoiding the batched matrix multiplication when using cross-entropy loss and softmax

Since the Softmax Jacobian is not diagonal, the previous approach to convert the batched matrix multiplication to a simple coefficient-wise product will not work. However, if the loss cost function is the cross-entropy loss, we can replace the batched matrix multiplication with a linear computation. Understanding how we can do it is straightforward. Consider again the Softmax Jacobian $\frac{\partial Y}{\partial Z}$:

$$\frac{\partial S(Z)}{\partial Z} = \frac{\partial Y}{\partial Z} = \begin{bmatrix} Y_0(1-Y_0) & -Y_1Y_0 & -Y_2Y_0 & -Y_3S_0 & -Y_4Y_0 \\ -Y_0Y_1 & Y_1(1-Y_1) & -Y_2Y_1 & -Y_3S_1 & -Y_4Y_1 \\ -Y_0Y_2 & -Y_1Y_2 & Y_2(1-Y_2) & -Y_3S_2 & -Y_4Y_2 \\ -Y_0Y_3 & -Y_1Y_3 & -Y_2Y_3 & Y_3(1-Y_3) & -Y_4Y_3 \\ -Y_0Y_4 & -Y_1Y_4 & -Y_2Y_4 & -Y_3Y_4 & Y_4(1-Y_4) \end{bmatrix}$$

Now, let us remind the cross-entropy derivative with respect to the output $\frac{\partial C}{\partial Y}$:

$$\frac{\partial C}{\partial Y} = \frac{T}{Y}$$

Using the fact that in softmax $Y_0 + Y_1 + Y_2 + Y_3 + Y_4 = 1$, we can realize that the gradient $\frac{\partial C}{\partial Z}$ can be obtained by simply:

$$\frac{\partial C}{\partial Z} = \frac{T}{Y} \times \frac{\partial Y}{\partial Z} = Y - T$$

Again, we reduced the cost of computing the full batch matrix multiplication by a simple linear operation, providing a considerable gain in space and time.

To summarize:

- **The advantage of this approach** is that this reduces the batched matrix multiplication cost of $O(N * M^3)$ to only $O(N * M)$.

- **The disadvantage** is that this approach works only when using softmax in the last layer in combination with the cross-entropy cost function.

In practice, this disadvantage is not critical because cross-entropy cost and softmax are practically the standards of every classifier nowadays. Note that binary cross-entropy is a particular case of cross-entropy loss. Thus, this approach will also work when the network has only two outputs.

Parallel batched matrix multiplication

Suppose you cannot avoid the batched matrix multiplication using one of the above alternatives. In that case, there is only one thing to do: run the batched matrix multiplication. If this is your case, consider performing the task using C++ parallel built-ins or Boost

Thread Pool API. For example, take the following implementation of a single-thread serial batched matrix multiplication:

```
1.  Eigen::Tensor<float, 2> serial_batched_matrix_multiplication(-
    const Eigen::Tensor<float, 2> &A, const Eigen::Tensor<float, 3> &B)
2.  {
3.      const int batch_size = A.dimension(0);
4.      const int input_size = B.dimension(1);
5.      // assert input_size == A.dimension(1) !!!
6.      const int output_size = B.dimension(2);
7.      Eigen::Tensor<float, 2> result(batch_size, output_size);
8.
9.      const Eigen::array<Eigen::Index, 2> B_i_dim = {input_
    size, output_size};
10.     const Eigen::array<Eigen::IndexPair<int>, 1> contract_
    dims = {Eigen::IndexPair<int>(1, 0)};
11.
12.     const Eigen::array<Eigen::Index, 2> A_extent = {1, input_size};
13.     const Eigen::array<Eigen::Index, 3> B_extent = {1, input_
    size, output_size};
14.
15.     const auto mulmat_slice = [&](int index) {
16.         Eigen::array<Eigen::Index, 2> A_offset = {index, 0};
17.         Eigen::array<Eigen::Index, 2> B_offset = {index, 0, 0};
18.
19.         auto A_i = A.slice(A_offset, A_extent);
20.         auto B_i = B.slice(B_offset, B_extent).reshape(B_i_dim);
21.         auto R_i = A_i.contract(B_i, contract_dims);
22.
23.         result.slice(offset, output_extent) = R_i;
24.     };
25.
26.     std::vector<int> batch(batch_size);
27.     std::iota(batch.begin(), batch.end(), 0);
28.     std::for_each(batch.begin(), batch.end(), mulmat_slice);
29.
30.     return result;
31. }
```

This operation is highly costly since it performs **batch_size** calls of a **tensor contraction**. If we have no other way to avoid this operation, we can try to reduce the overall time by running it in parallel. A simple way to do that is running the **for_each** loop using C++ built-in parallelism:

```
1. std::for_each(std::execution::par, batch.begin(), batch.
   end(), mulmat_slice);
```

This time, we called **for_each,** passing a new argument **std::execution::par**. Setting **std::execution::par** makes the **for_each** run in parallel, using one of the available multithread backends (usually TBB [3] or OpenMP [4]) under the wood. A drawback of using **std::execution::par** is that we have no control over how many threads the job can use. An alternative to this issue is using Boost Thread Pool [5] instead:

```
1.  #include <boost/asio/thread_pool.hpp>
2.  #include <boost/asio/post.hpp>
3.
4.  const int threads = 4;
5.  boost::asio::thread_pool pool(threads);
6.  for (int i = 0; i < batch_size; ++i)
7.  {
8.      boost::asio::post(pool, std::bind(mulmat_slice, i));
9.  }
10. pool.join();
```

The boost thread pool will run **mulmat_slice** in parallel, just like running **for_each** with **std::execution::par**. However, at that time, we have some control over the maximum number of threads coming to play:

```
1.  const int threads = std::thread::hardware_concurrency();
2.  boost::asio::thread_pool pool(threads);
```

These two lines set the available number of threads to the real number of available processor cores. Although this does not determine the actual number of threads, it provides some control.

Eigen also has an embedded multithread mechanism based on the ThreadPool device, which is another alternative to performing the **batched_matrix_multiplication** in parallel. This technique is explained in the next section.

Note: When using parallel programming, make sure that your final implementation is lock-free or has no unprotected data dependence. If the code is not lock-free, you need to protect the shareable data using locks like std::lock_guard<std::mutex>.

Only use batched matrix multiplication as a last resource, if none of the previous alternatives is available. Tackling batched matrix multiplication is critical for backpropagation. However, there are other significant concerns for achieving a high-performance execution.

They are covered in the following section.

General Tensor programming optimization guidelines

This section discusses some guidelines for implementing Tensor code in an optimized way.

Using built-in Eigen parallel computing

Backpropagation is mostly a sequential algorithm. In forward propagation, we must calculate the output of the current layer before computing the state of the next layer. In the backward propagation, we must compute each gradient from the last layer until the first, one by one.

Thus, it is difficult to think of using parallel computation when running backpropagation. However, this algorithm often performs massive computations on huge amounts of data. The Eigen API has a built-in mechanism to run those intense computations in parallel: the **Eigen ThreadPool API**. Consider the following example:

```
1.  #include <unsupported/Eigen/CXX11/Tensor>
2.
3.  Eigen::Tensor<float, 2> A(1024, 1024);
4.  Eigen::Tensor<float, 2> B(1024, 1024);
5.
6.  Eigen::array<Eigen::IndexPair<int>, 1> op_
        dims = {Eigen::IndexPair<int>(1, 0)};
7.  Eigen::Tensor<float, 2> C = A.contract(B, op_dims);
```

This code simply performs a contraction between two big tensors using a single processor. We can change this behavior using a simple syntax:

```
1.  #define EIGEN_USE_THREADS
2.  #include <Eigen/ThreadPool>
3.
4.  #include <unsupported/Eigen/CXX11/Tensor>
5.
6.  Eigen::Tensor<float, 2> A(1024, 1024);
7.  Eigen::Tensor<float, 2> B(1024, 1024);
8.
9.  const int threads = 4;
10. Eigen::ThreadPool tp(threads);
11. Eigen::ThreadPoolDevice thread_pool_device(&tp, threads);
```

```
12.
13. Eigen::array<Eigen::IndexPair<int>, 1> op_
    dims = {Eigen::IndexPair<int>(1, 0)};
14. Eigen::Tensor<float, 2> C(1024, 1024);
15. C.device(thread_pool_device) = A.contract(B, op_dims);
```

This time, the contraction was performed using four threads caught from an Eigen thread pool. Depending on hardware availability, executing this operation across four processors results in approximately four times faster execution.

Note: It is necessary to define `EIGEN_USE_THREADS` to use the Eigen `ThreadPool` header.

A genuine use of **ThreadPool** devices is **batched_matrix_multiplication**. The previous definition can be modified as follows:

```
1.  template <typename Device>
2.  const Eigen::Tensor<float, 3> batched_matrix_multiplication(-
    const Device &device, const Eigen::Tensor<float, 3>& A,
    const Eigen::Tensor<float, 3>& B) const
3.  {
4.      typedef Eigen::Tensor<float, 3>::DimensionPair DimPair;
5.      Eigen::array<DimPair, 1> dims{DimPair(1, 0)};
6.      const int batch_size = A.dimension(0);
7.      const int dim1 = A.dimension(1);
8.      const int dim2 = B.dimension(2);
9.      Eigen::Tensor<float, 3> output(batch_size, dim1, dim2);
10.     for (int i = 0; i < batch_size; ++i) {
11.         output.chip<0>(i).device(device) = A.chip<0>(i).contract(B.
    chip<0>(i), dims);
12.     }
13.     return output;
14. }
```

Now, we can call **batched_matrix_multiplication** in the following way:

```
1.  const int threads = 4;
2.  Eigen::ThreadPool tp(threads);
3.  Eigen::ThreadPoolDevice thread_pool_device(&tp, threads);
4.
5.  auto Z = batched_matrix_multiplication(thread_pool_device, X, Y);
```

Where **X** and **Y** are both rank-3 tensors.

Processing massive computations using multiple cores is often faster than a single processor. However, another parallel computation alternative called GPU programming has gained more evidence in the last ten years. The usage of GPUs in the context of deep learning is explained in the next section.

Running on GPU

Originally, **graphic processing units (GPUs)** were designed to improve the performance of games and video/photography editing software. However, for a long time, the machine learning community considered the use of these boards to reduce training time.

In 2012, *Krizhevsky, Sutskever,* and *Hinton* [6] developed the AlexNet network, winning the 2012 *ILSVRC—ImageNet Large Scale Visual Recognition Challenge.* One of the most significant achievements of this work was the use of GPUs to train AlexNet, allowing the training of networks with a large number of parameters. Since then, GPUs gained popularity to train deep learning models.

Today, implementing deep learning code to run on GPU is not exactly trivial but considerably easier than in 2012. Let us introduce some features of Eigen Tensor API to run performance-critical functions on NVIDIA devices using CUDA.

Note: CUDA is a proprietary NVIDIA technology that allows implementing code to run on a family of NVIDIA graphic cards.

Check out the following example of running a contraction on a GPU using Eigen and CUDA:

```
1.  Tensor<float, 2> run_gpu_
    contraction(const Tensor<float, 2> &A, const Tensor<float, 2> &B)
2.  {
3.      const int M = A.dimension(0);
4.      const int K = A.dimension(1); // for production, assert K == B.
    dimension(0)
5.      const int N = B.dimension(1);
6.
7.      // allocating data on GPU
8.
9.      std::size_t A_bytes = M * K * sizeof(float);
10.     std::size_t B_bytes = K * N * sizeof(float);
11.
12.     float *A_data;
13.     float *B_data;
14.
15.     gpuMalloc((void **)(&A_data), A_bytes);
16.     gpuMalloc((void **)(&B_data), B_bytes);
17.
```

```
18.      gpuMemcpy(A_data, A.data(), A_bytes, gpuMemcpyHostToDevice);
19.      gpuMemcpy(B_data, B.data(), B_bytes, gpuMemcpyHostToDevice);
20.
21.      auto M_array = Eigen::array<int, 2>{M, K};
22.      auto K_array = Eigen::array<int, 2>{K, N};
23.      Eigen::TensorMap<Eigen::Tensor<float, 2>> A_on_GPU(A_data, M_
     array);
24.      Eigen::TensorMap<Eigen::Tensor<float, 2>> B_on_GPU(B_data, K_
     array);
25.
26.      std::size_t result_bytes = M * N * sizeof(float);
27.      float *result_data;
28.      gpuMalloc((void **)(&result_data), result_bytes);
29.      auto n_array = Eigen::array<int, 2>{M, N};
30.      Eigen::TensorMap<Eigen::Tensor<float, 2>> gpu_result(result_
     data, n_array);
31.
32.      // running contraction on GPU
33.      Eigen::GpuStreamDevice stream;
34.      Eigen::GpuDevice gpu_device(&stream);
35.      Eigen::array<Eigen::IndexPair<int>, 1> dims = {Eigen::Index-
     Pair<int>(1, 0)};
36.      gpu_result.device(gpu_device) = A_on_GPU.contract(B_on_
     GPU, dims);
37.
38.      // copying the result data to CPU
39.      Tensor<float, 2> result(M, N);
40.      gpuMemcpy(result.data(), result_data, result_
     bytes, gpuMemcpyDeviceToHost);
41.
42.      // freed GPU memory
43.      gpuFree((void *)A_data);
44.      gpuFree((void *)B_data);
45.      gpuFree((void *)result_data);
46.
47.      return result;
48. }
```

Roughly speaking, running on GPU is somehow similar to running in parallel using **Eigen::ThreadPoolDevice**. Using CUDA, we need to use **Eigen::GpuDevice** instead:

```
1. Eigen::GpuStreamDevice stream;
2.     Eigen::GpuDevice gpu_device(&stream);
3.     Eigen::array<Eigen::IndexPair<int>, 1> dims = {Eigen::Index-
   Pair<int>(1, 0)};
4.     gpu_result.device(gpu_device) = A_on_GPU.contract(B_on_
   GPU, dims);
```

The noticeable difference is that using the **Eigen::GpuDevice**, we need also to allocate (and unallocated) the GPU memory.

If you have a NVIDIA GPU with CUDA card on your machine, you can try to run this procedure using the following code:

```
1. Tensor<float, 2> run_cpu_
   contraction(const Tensor<float, 2> &A, const Tensor<float, 2> &B)
2. {
3.     Eigen::array<Eigen::IndexPair<int>, 1> dims = {Eigen::Index-
   Pair<int>(1, 0)};
4.     Tensor<float, 2> expected = A.contract(B, dims);
5.     return expected;
6. }
7.
8. int main()
9. {
10.     srand((unsigned int) time(0));
11.
12.     printCudaVersion();
13.
14.     const int S = 256;
15.
16.     Tensor<float, 2> A(S, S);
17.     Tensor<float, 2> B(S, S);
18.     A.setRandom();
19.     B.setRandom();
20.
21.     auto expected = run_cpu_contraction(A, B);
22.
23.     auto tensor = run_gpu_contraction(A, B);
24.
25.     Tensor<float, 2> diff = (expected - tensor).abs();
26.
```

```
27.     Tensor<float, 0> max_diff = diff.maximum();
28.     Tensor<float, 0> mean_diff = diff.mean();
29.
30.     std::cout << "\nmax_diff is « << max_diff << "\n\n";
31.     std::cout << "mean_diff is « << mean_diff << "\n\n";
32.
33.     auto start_cpu = high_resolution_clock::now();
34.
35.     for (int i = 0; i < 100; ++i) {
36.         run_cpu_contraction(A, B);
37.     }
38.
39.     auto stop_cpu = high_resolution_clock::now();
40.
41.     auto duration_cpu = duration_cast<milliseconds>(stop_cpu - start_cpu);
42.
43.     std::cout << "Tensor size is (" << S << "x" << S << ")\n\n";
44.     std::cout << "Running on CPU took " << duration_cpu.
    count() << " milliseconds.\n";
45.
46.     auto start_cuda = high_resolution_clock::now();
47.
48.     for (int i = 0; i < 100; ++i) {
49.         run_gpu_contraction(A, B);
50.     }
51.
52.     auto stop_cuda = high_resolution_clock::now();
53.
54.     auto duration_cuda = duration_cast<milliseconds>(stop_
    cuda - start_cuda);
55.
56.     std::cout << "Running on GPU took " << duration_cuda.
    count() << " milliseconds.\n";
57.
58.     return 0;
59. }
```

First, let us build this code:

Figure 10.18: Building the CUDA example

Once running, the program outputs something like:

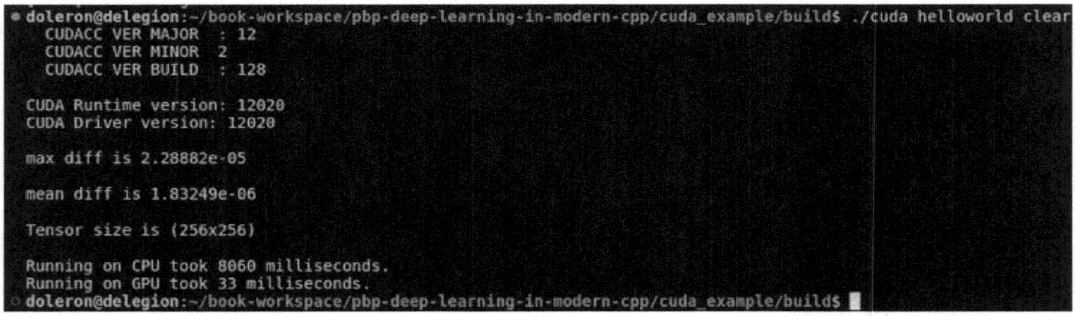

Figure 10.19: Running the CUDA example with tensors 256x256

This result illustrates the considerable gain of running the contraction on GPU. In my case, using an RTX 3050 GPU resulted in an execution that was about 250x faster.

Intense computation on a GPU is much faster than running on CPUs. Notably, the overhead of exchanging data between the CPU and the GPU also implies a time cost. For example, rerunning the last example but using smaller tensors of size (8x8) results in the following output:

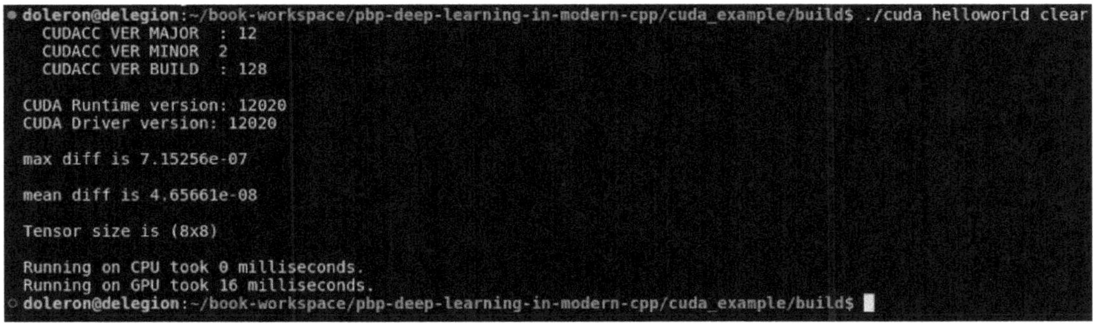

Figure 10.20: Running the CUDA example with tensors 8x8

Note that, using small 8x8 tensors, the GPU total time was greater than the CPU time. In summary, the final performance depends on the data bus throughput, the GPU speed, the size of the data used to compute the operation, and the available memory of the GPU.

Note: In real-world projects, due to the incredible gain of time, we perform the computation on GPUs mostly.

Reducing the memory footprint

Memory copy is a usual concern in C++ development. When training deep learning models, we combine massive data and high-processing algorithms running over computational graphs. The process of computing the data in a layer and then passing all this data to the next layer looks intuitive but usually slows down the overall performance.

To achieve state-of-art performance, we have to follow some guidelines:

- **Delay the computation as much as possible**: Eigen has a lazy evaluation mechanism that evaluates the computation only when the operation is assigned to a real tensor. For example, the following code is not optimal:

```
1. // bad approach
2. Eigen::Tensor<float, 2> C = A.contract(B, dims);
3. Eigen::Tensor<float, 2> D = C + another_tensor;
```

Indeed, the expression resulting from **A.contract(B, dims)** is not a tensor but a lazy tensor operation that knows how to compute the contraction between the tensors **A** and **B**. If we assign it to an actual tensor (by defining **C** as **Eigen::Tensor<float, 2>**), the operation will be unnecessarily evaluated earlier than necessary. A better alternative is to define **C** as an **auto** variable, as follows:

```
1. // optimal approach
2. auto C = A.contract(B, dims);
3. Eigen::Tensor<float, 2> D = C + another_tensor;
```

In this last code, **C** stores not a tensor but a contraction lazy operation. **C** will be evaluated only when summed up with **another_tensor**. Following this approach allows Eigen to compute **C** and **C + another_tensor** optimally.

- **Only compute the data once**: This looks obvious, but sometimes, due to the previously explained lazy evaluation mechanism in Eigen, it may not be easy to know when the data was or was not yet evaluated. Double-check the code to avoid any unnecessary re-computation.

- **Instead of moving the data, pass a pointer**: Moving a high volume of data consumes processing time, auxiliary memory, and registers. When performing high-demanding computing, avoid moving data the much as possible. One way to achieve this is by keeping the data in a safe storage and passing a pointer (or reference) to consumers.

- **Allocate the data only once**: Allocating data consumes important system resources. If you have a huge tensor that is reallocated several times inside, for example, a loop, move it to the next higher scope, pre-allocating it only once.

Programming high-performing tensor code sometimes becomes a cat-and-rat game involving different strategies and approaches. Remember to put the test cases ready before implementing any optimization to make sure that the improvement, in fact, did not break anything.

Putting improvements to work together

Let us write a new version of backpropagation using some of the recommended improvements.

Avoiding batched matrix multiplication

As mentioned, computing the full BMM is expensive and avoidable when training a model with softmax and cross-entropy loss. To avoid BMM, we need only to change the **gradient()** function as follows:

```
1. template <typename Device, typename T>
2. auto gradient(Device &device, const Eigen::Tensor<T, 2> &dC_dZ,
3.                              const Eigen::Tensor<T, 2> &in-
   put, const Eigen::Tensor<T, 2> &W,
4.                              bool propagate = true)
5. {
6.     const int batch_size = input.dimension(0);
7.
8.     // calculating grad
9.     const Eigen::array<Eigen::IndexPair<T>, 1> product_
```

```
        dims_0_0 = {Eigen::IndexPair<T>(0, 0)};
10.     Eigen::Tensor<T, 2> dC_dW(W.dimension(0), W.dimension(1));
11.     dC_dW.device(device) = input.contract(dC_dZ, product_dims_0_0);
12.     Eigen::Tensor<T, 2> grad = dC_dW / dC_dW.constant(batch_size);
13.
14.     // calculating the error propagation dC_dY for the previous layer
15.     const Eigen::array<Eigen::IndexPair<T>, 1> product_
    dims_1_1 = {Eigen::IndexPair<T>(1, 1)};
16.     Eigen::Tensor<T, 2> downstream;
17.     if (propagate) {
18.         downstream = Eigen::Tensor<T, 2>(dC_dZ.dimension(0), W.
    dimension(0));
19.         downstream.device(device) = dC_dZ.contract(W, product_
    dims_1_1);
20.     }
21.
22.     return std::make_tuple(grad, downstream);
23. }
```

Note that we no longer call **batched_matrix_multiplication()**. The gradients are calculated, avoiding this costly operation. Also, note that **gradient()** now has a parameter **dC_dZ** instead of **dC_dY**. Thus, **dC_dZ** is calculated by **backward()**, as shown below:

```
1. template <typename Device, typename T>
2. auto backward(Device &device, const Tensor<T, 2> &TRUE,
3.     const Tensor<T, 2> &X,
4.     const Tensor<T, 2> &Z0, const Tensor<T, 2> &Z1, const Tensor<T,
    2> &Z2,
5.     const Tensor<T, 2> &Y0, const Tensor<T, 2> &Y1, const Tensor<T,
    2> &Y2,
6.     const Tensor<T, 2> &W0, const Tensor<T, 2> &W1, const Tensor<T,
    2> &W2)
7. {
8.
9.     const int batch_size = TRUE.dimension(0);
10.
11.     // First step, calculating the output loss gradient dC_dZ2
12.     Tensor<T, 2> dC_dZ2 = Y2 - TRUE;
13.     // second step: calculating weight gradients
14.     ReLU relu;
15.     auto [grad2, dC_dY1] = gradient(device, dC_dZ2, Y1, W2);
```

```
16.
17.    auto dY_dZ1 = relu.derivative(device, Y1);
18.    Eigen::Tensor<float, 2> dC_dZ1(dY_dZ1.dimension(0), dY_dZ1.
       dimension(1));
19.    dC_dZ1.device(device) = dC_dY1 * dY_dZ1;
20.
21.    auto [grad1, dC_dY0] = gradient(device, dC_dZ1, Y0, W1);
22.
23.    auto dY_dZ0 = relu.derivative(device, Y0);
24.    Eigen::Tensor<float, 2> dC_dZ0(dY_dZ0.dimension(0), dY_dZ0.
       dimension(1));
25.    dC_dZ0.device(device) = dC_dY0 * dY_dZ0;
26.
27.    auto [grad0, _]      = gradient(device, dC_dZ0, X,  W0, false);
28.
29.    return std::make_tuple(grad0, grad1, grad2);
30. }
```

dC_dZ2 is obtained using the softmax-cross entropy trick:

```
1. // First step, calculating the output loss gradient dC_dZ2
2. Tensor<T, 2> dC_dZ2 = Y2 - TRUE;
3. // second step: calculating weight gradients
4. ReLU relu;
5. auto [grad2, dC_dY1] = gradient(device, dC_dZ2, Y1, W2);
```

Similarly, **dC_dZ1** and **dC_dZ0** are computed using the coefficient-wise property of activations:

```
1. auto dY_dZ1 = relu.derivative(device, Y1);
2. Eigen::Tensor<float, 2> dC_dZ1(dY_dZ1.dimension(0), dY_dZ1.
   dimension(1));
3. dC_dZ1.device(device) = dC_dY1 * dY_dZ1;
4.
5. auto [grad1, dC_dY0] = gradient(device, dC_dZ1, Y0, W1);
6.
7. auto dY_dZ0 = relu.derivative(device, Y0);
8. Eigen::Tensor<float, 2> dC_dZ0(dY_dZ0.dimension(0), dY_dZ0.
   dimension(1));
9. dC_dZ0.device(device) = dC_dY0 * dY_dZ0;
10.
11. auto [grad0, _]       = gradient(device, dC_dZ0, X,  W0, false);
```

Note: These two strategies were discussed in one of the previous sections of this chapter, focusing on avoiding batched matrix multiplication.

Rechecking the code is also noteworthy for the use of custom devices to perform the costly computations. For example, in the **forward()** computation:

1. `ReLU relu;`
2. `static Eigen::Tensor<T, 2> Z0(batch_size, W0.dimension(1));`
3. `Z0.device(device) = X.contract(W0, contract_dims);`
4. `Eigen::Tensor<T, 2> Y0 = relu.evaluate(device, Z0);`

This code is intended to use high-performance devices such as CUDA devices or multithread pool devices to calculate the product. In our example, we are using a thread pool:

1. `const int threads = std::thread::hardware_concurrency();`
2. `Eigen::ThreadPool tp(threads);`
3. `Eigen::ThreadPoolDevice device(&tp, threads);`

These two improvements, namely avoiding the batched matrix multiplication and using parallel computing, radically speed up the algorithm throughput. Check the following output:

```
doleron@delegion:~/book-workspace/pbp-deep-learning-in-modern-cpp/chapter_10/build$ ./improving_backpropagation
Data loaded!
training_images dims: [60000, 784]
training_labels dims: [60000, 10]
epoch:  0      took:    195 mills        training_loss:  2.25839 training_acc:    15.2267
epoch:  1      took:    98 mills         training_loss:  2.21076 training_acc:    21.5383
epoch:  2      took:    98 mills         training_loss:  2.16619 training_acc:    27.8083
epoch:  3      took:    97 mills         training_loss:  2.12203 training_acc:    33.3117
epoch:  4      took:    96 mills         training_loss:  2.07668 training_acc:    37.8717
epoch:  5      took:    96 mills         training_loss:  2.02934 training_acc:    42.0967
epoch:  6      took:    98 mills         training_loss:  1.97966 training_acc:    45.985
epoch:  7      took:    99 mills         training_loss:  1.92735 training_acc:    49.795
epoch:  8      took:    97 mills         training_loss:  1.87248 training_acc:    53.1683
epoch:  9      took:    98 mills         training_loss:  1.81522 training_acc:    56.3367
epoch:  10     took:    97 mills         training_loss:  1.75577 training_acc:    59.2617
epoch:  11     took:    97 mills         training_loss:  1.69445 training_acc:    62.0883
epoch:  12     took:    98 mills         training_loss:  1.63169 training_acc:    64.7483
epoch:  13     took:    98 mills         training_loss:  1.56816 training_acc:    67.1183
epoch:  14     took:    99 mills         training_loss:  1.50458 training_acc:    69.1267
epoch:  15     took:    97 mills         training_loss:  1.44194 training_acc:    70.8217
epoch:  16     took:    97 mills         training_loss:  1.38109 training_acc:    72.2517
epoch:  17     took:    98 mills         training_loss:  1.32276 training_acc:    73.475
epoch:  18     took:    100 mills        training_loss:  1.26734 training_acc:    74.515
epoch:  19     took:    98 mills         training_loss:  1.215   training_acc:    75.39
doleron@delegion:~/book-workspace/pbp-deep-learning-in-modern-cpp/chapter_10/build$
```

Figure 10.21: Running the improved version of backpropagation

As expected, the final result is incredibly faster than the previous naïve version without any performance dropping in terms of accuracy.

Now the question is: can we do better? This training can be improved in several ways. For example, we can implement momentum or add bias, which may provide a lower final loss and higher accuracy. The use of optimizers such as Adam and RMSprop can definitely leverage the model performance.

One of the most important things to think of right now is how these results are sufficiently good for estimating the model performance on new data: How does this model perform on data not used in its training? The actual model utility and the model selection techniques will be covered in the forthcoming chapters.

Conclusion

In this chapter, we learned how to implement the backpropagation algorithm by extending gradient descent to deal with the case when the model has multiple layers.

We learned that calculating some gradients, particularly the activation function error-propagation, drastically reduces the algorithm efficiency by introducing a costly operation called batched matrix multiplication. We also learned that, in most cases, we can overcome this issue, achieving a faster execution. Finally, we applied these ideas to train a model using the MNIST dataset.

This was our first step in training deep models. In the next chapter, we will learn how the training is affected by two critical issues: overfitting and underfitting.

Exercises

1. Modify the example of training MNIST to use a deeper network having at least six inner layers. How does including more layers affect the final model performance in terms of time, loss, and accuracy?

2. Again, using the example introduced in this chapter, replace the ReLU activation function with the sigmoid activation function in the first two hidden layers and also in the output layer. What is the practical consequence of making this change?

References

[1] Paul Vicol, autograd tutorial, 2017. Available at **https://www.cs.toronto.edu/~rgrosse/courses/csc321_2017/tutorials/tut4.pdf**

[2] Andrej Karpathy, Yes you should understand backprop, 2016. Available at **https://karpathy.medium.com/yes-you-should-understand-backprop-e2f06eab496b**

[3] Threading Building Blocks, available at **https://www.intel.com/content/www/us/en/developer/tools/oneapi/onetbb.html**

[4] OpenMP, available at **https://www.openmp.org/**

[5] Boost Thread Pool, available at **https://www.boost.org/doc/libs/1_77_0/doc/html/boost_asio/reference/thread_pool.html**

[6] Krizhevsky, Sutskever, and Hinton - ImageNet Classification with Deep Convolutional Neural Networks.

CHAPTER 11
Underfitting, Overfitting, and Regularization

Introduction

This chapter introduces regularization, a fundamental subject in deep learning concerned with finding models that generalize well, that is, models able to represent the data's regularities, even of data not used in their training. In this chapter, we discuss why only using minimization of the cost function is insufficient to achieve practical, useful models. Throughout five reproducible experiments, we learn the two most important modeling problems, underfitting and overfitting, focusing on how to identify and mitigate them.

Structure

This is the chapter roadmap:

- Experiments in this chapter
- Understanding model selection
- Experiment 1: Fitting polynomials from data
- Understanding underfitting
- Understanding overfitting
- Understanding regularization
- Experiment 2: An overfitted model

- Experiment 3: Penalization as regularization
- Experiment 4: Data augmentation
- DropOut
- Experiment 5: DropOut example

Objectives

After reading this chapter, you will know how to identify good and bad models by comparing their performance on training and validation data. This will help you to identify whether your model is suitable or not for selection and what to do if your model is not working as expected. After reading this chapter, you will also know how to implement the most important regularization techniques used in deep learning.

Experiments in this chapter

This chapter includes five experiments:

ID	Description
Exp-11.1	Fitting polynomials from data
Exp-11.2	An overfitted model
Exp-11.3	Penalization as regularization
Exp-11.4	Data augmentation
Exp-11.5	Dropout example

Table 11.1: Chapter experiment list

Understanding model selection

So far, in this book, we have learned how to train models using the strategy of cost function minimization. Since then, our single selection criteria has been pretty straightforward: finding the model that achieves the minimum cost given the training set. Thus, if we have two different models and need to choose one, we select the model with the lowest training loss.

As we will see soon, using only the criteria of cost minimization to select a model very often results in poor models that only memorize the training data, a phenomenon known as **overfitting**.

Experiment 1: Fitting polynomials from data

This experiment introduces a classic example [1] consisting of fitting different degree polynomials to data. This simple but powerful example illustrates how the model's size affects the actual model utility, providing valuable insights into deciding what can be a *good* or a *bad* model in terms of the model's **capacity** to capture the **regularities** in the data. Let us take a brief refresher on what polynomials are.

Polynomials

Consider the following equation:

$$y(x) = a_n x^n + a_{n-1} x^{n-1} + \cdots + a_1 x^1 + a_0$$

This equation represents a polynomial function. A polynomial is a function defined by sums of terms in the form ax^p where is a real number called **coefficient**, and p is a non-negative integer ($p \geq 0$) called **exponent**. Check the following examples:

$$y = 2x^3 - 2x + 3$$
$$y = -10x^5 + x$$
$$y = 4x + 1$$
$$y = x^4 + 1.5x^3 + 0.1x^2 - x + 2$$

In a polynomial, the maximum exponent gains a special name. It is called the **polynomial degree**. Thus, the first example is a 3-degree polynomial (because 3 is the maximum exponent of x). The second is a 5-degree polynomial, the third has degree 1, and the last one has degree 4.

Fitting polynomials from data

Fitting a polynomial from data means finding the polynomial's coefficients given a set of pairs $(x, y(x))$. Note that an n-degree polynomial $y(x) = a_n x^n + a_{n-1} x^{n-1} + \cdots + a_1 x^1 + a_0$ has $n+1$ coefficients $a_n, a_{n-1}, \ldots, a_1, a_0$. Due to the simplicity of polynomials, instead of using an iterative algorithm (like backpropagation), we can find the coefficients more straightforwardly by solving the following linear system:

$$
\begin{bmatrix} y_0 \\ y_1 \\ y_2 \\ \vdots \\ y_{m-1} \end{bmatrix} =
\begin{bmatrix}
1 & x_0 & x_0^2 & \cdots & x_0^n \\
1 & x_1 & x_1^2 & \cdots & x_1^n \\
1 & x_2 & x_2^2 & \cdots & x_2^n \\
\vdots & \vdots & \vdots & \vdots & \vdots \\
1 & x_{m-1} & x_{m-1}^2 & \cdots & x_{m-1}^n
\end{bmatrix}
\begin{bmatrix} a_0 \\ a_1 \\ a_2 \\ \vdots \\ a_n \end{bmatrix}
$$

Since we have m pairs $(x, y(x))$ we can use **matrix decomposition** to solve this system. Luckily, Eigen has a set of built-in linear solvers [3], such as **householderQr** to solve systems like this, as demonstrated:

```
1. Eigen::VectorXd fit_
   polynom(Eigen::VectorXd& X, Eigen::VectorXd& Y, int degree) {
2.     Eigen::MatrixXd terms = Eigen::MatrixXd::Ones(X.
   size(), degree + 1);
3.     for (int i = 1; i <= degree; ++i)
4.         terms.col(i) = terms.col(i - 1).cwiseProduct(X);
5.     }
6.     auto solver = terms.householderQr();
7.     auto coeffs = solver.solve(Y);
8.     return coeffs;
9. }
```

We can fit polynomials with different degrees to our data using this simple function. Now, let us define the data for our experiment.

Setting up the experiment data

In this example, we will use the following **synthetical data**:

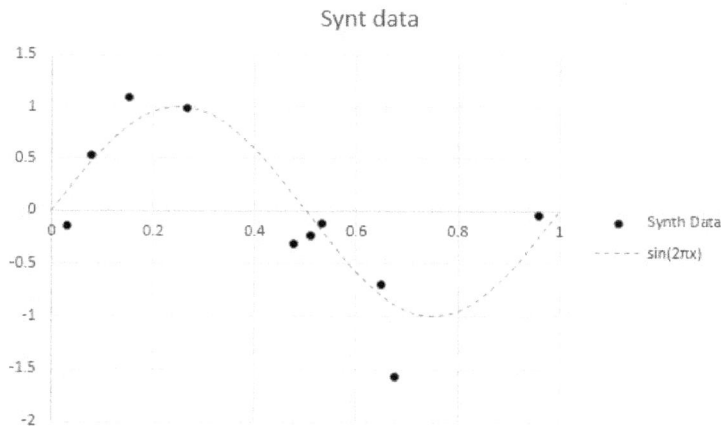

Figure 11.1: *The synthetic dataset used in the experiment*

This data is generated over the interval x = [0, 1] using the formula $y(x) = sin(2\pi x) + N(0, 0.3)$, where N is the **normal distribution**. In this case, N works like a **Gaussian error**. In C++, this synthetical data can be generated in the following way:

```
1. #include <random>
2.
3. auto generate_synthetic_data = [&](int size = 10, double noise_
   dev = 0.3) {
4.     std::random_device rd {};
```

```
5.      long seed = 900027959;
6.      std::mt19937 rng(seed);
7.      srand((unsigned int) seed);
8.      std::cout << "seed: " << seed << "\n\n";
9.
10.     std::uniform_real_distribution<double> uniform_distro(0, range);
11.     Eigen::VectorXd X = Eigen::VectorXd::Zero(size).unaryExpr([&]
   (double){return uniform_distro(rng);});
12.     std::sort(std::begin(X), std::end(X));
13.
14.     Eigen::VectorXd G = X.unaryExpr([&](double x){return sin(2.*M_
   PI*x);});
15.
16.     std::normal_distribution<double> normal_distro(0, noise_dev);
17.     Eigen::VectorXd NOISE = Eigen::VectorXd::Zero(size).
   unaryExpr([&](double){return normal_distro(rng);});
18.
19.     Eigen::VectorXd TRUE = G + NOISE;
20.
21.     return std::make_pair(X, TRUE);
22. };
```

Note that, because we declared **int size = 10,** by default we are generating exactly 10 pairs. Once we have the data at hand, let us use it to fit different polynomials:

```
1.  int main(int, char**)
2.  {
3.      double range = 1.;
4.      const auto [X, TRUE] = generate_synthetic_data();
5.      std::vector<int> poly_degrees{1, 2, 3, 4, 5, 6, 7, 8, 9};
6.      Eigen::MatrixXd results = Eigen::MatrixXd::Zero(11, poly_
   degrees.size());
7.      Eigen::VectorXd input = Eigen::VectorXd::LinSpaced(results.
   rows(), 0., range);
8.
9.      for (unsigned i = 0; i < poly_degrees.size(); ++i)
10.     {
11.         int degree = poly_degrees[i];
12.         auto params = fit_polynom(X, TRUE, degree);
13.         auto Y = eval(params, input);
```

```
14.            results.col(i) = Y;
15.       }
16.
17.       Eigen::IOFormat formatter(4, 0, "\t", "\n", "", "");
18.       for (int degree : poly_degrees) std::cout << "degree " << degree << "\t";
19.       std::cout << "\n" << results.format(formatter) << "\n\n";
20.
21.       return 0;
22. }
```

This code uses the generated synthetic data from a sine function to fit nine different polynomials with degree 1, 2, 3, ..., 9. By running it, we get the following output:

poly degree 1	poly degree 2	poly degree 3	poly degree 4	poly degree 5	poly degree 6	poly degree 7	poly degree 8	poly degree 9
0.5984	0.8086	-0.5117	-0.568	-1.074	0.02559	-0.9056	-0.8131	-0.4727
0.4481	0.5239	0.6706	0.6893	0.8649	0.7104	0.7487	0.7531	0.7735
0.2977	0.2724	1.103	1.126	1.083	1.35	1.219	1.212	1.177
0.1473	0.05401	0.9784	0.978	0.7301	0.5522	0.7347	0.7441	0.7809
-0.003007	-0.1312	0.4874	0.4665	0.2947	-0.2762	-0.1533	-0.115	-0.06207
-0.1534	-0.2832	-0.1779	-0.1995	-0.1545	-0.2289	-0.2662	-0.2659	-0.2696
-0.3037	-0.402	-0.8258	-0.8248	-0.7188	-0.2064	-0.03105	-0.03185	-0.01374
-0.4541	-0.4877	-1.264	-1.227	-1.423	-2.226	-2.691	-2.745	-2.702
-0.6044	-0.5402	-1.302	-1.238	-1.971	-6.742	-10.94	-11.79	-10.02
-0.7548	-0.5595	-0.7473	-0.7012	-1.493	-7.964	-15.4	-17.43	-11.14
-0.9051	-0.5457	0.592	0.5252	1.693	12.81	28.52	33.81	12.28

Figure 11.2: The predictions of polynomial approximations

Each column represents the inference of the respective polynomial over the input data. The question is: Which polynomial is the *best*? That is, which polynomial best fits the training data?

Answering these questions by only observing the tabular data is not easy. There is a better alternative, as shown in the next section.

Selecting the best model

There are two good alternatives to evaluate models: plotting results (also known as **data visualization**) and comparing their **performance metrics**. To illustrate these two approaches, let us visualize each model performance and its respective **mean squared error** (MSE):

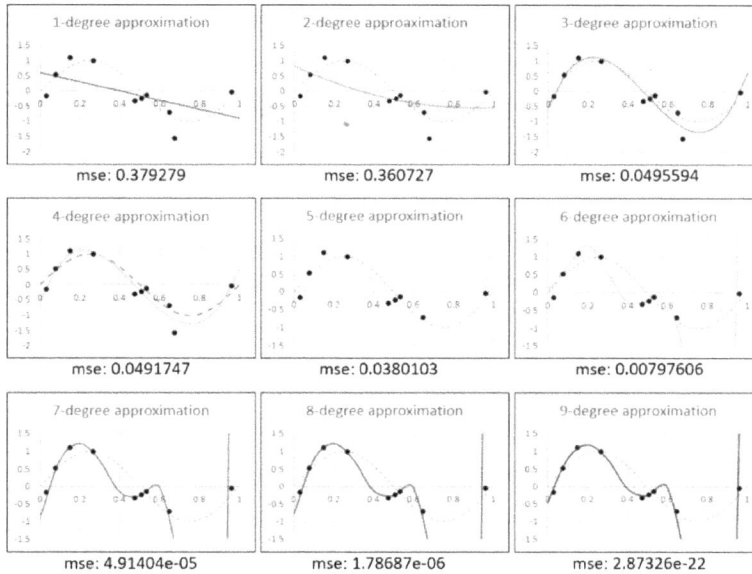

Figure 11.3: Comparing the polynomial approximations

Each chart shows a dashed curve representing the original sine function, the dots representing the training data, and the model curve, represented by a colored solid curve. Now, let us evaluate the results.

Underfitting

Checking the two first models, namely 1 and 2-degree polynomials, we realize that they poorly fit the training data, achieving a considerable high MSE value:

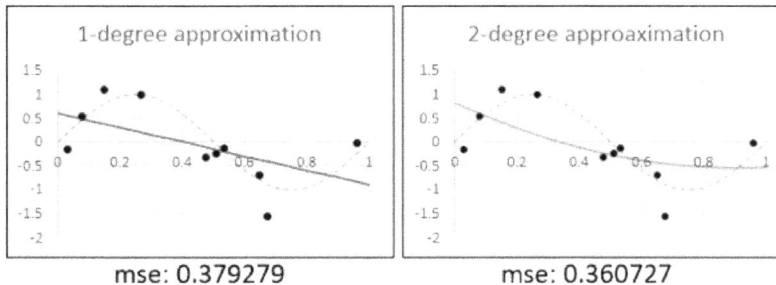

Figure 11.4: Evaluating 1-degree and 2-degree polynomial fitting

These two polynomials do not even roughly represent the original sine curve. It is usually said that these two models **underfitted** the training data, being unable to provide any good approximation even to the data in which they were trained.

Note: In underfitting, the model is unable to provide good predictions even on the training data.

In a real-world project, we would discard models like this. Underfitted models are useless and help only as a reference for other models.

Overfitting

On the other side, there are the higher-order polynomials such as 7, 8, and 9-degree polynomials, as shown:

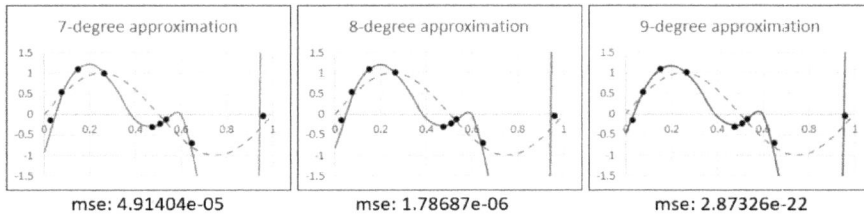

Figure 11.5: *Evaluating high-order polynomial fitting*

These models provide very low MSE values, achieving almost a perfect fit to the training data. Indeed, the 9-degree polynomial is able to pass over each one point of the training instances.

The pitfall here is, by considering only the cost function minimization, the 9-degree model is the perfect fit. However, in fact, this model is one of the worst ones.

Since we know the original sine function (the function used to generate the synthetic training data), we can easily identify that the higher-degree polynomials fail to represent the original data distribution, wildly oscillating around the original generative curve. This is called **overfitting**. Refer to the following figure:

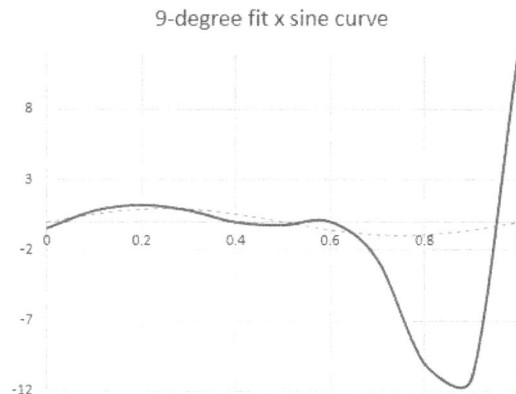

Figure 11.6: *Comparing 9-degree polynomial fitting to the original sine curve*

Note: In overfitting, although the model achieves a high performance on the training data, it is unable to well represent the regularities in the data.

As a result, overfitted models perform very poorly on data not used in its training. We can easily check this issue by applying the same models to new data. For example, let us generate another set of dots using the same sin function and Gaussian noise, and check how well the high-order polynomials approximate them:

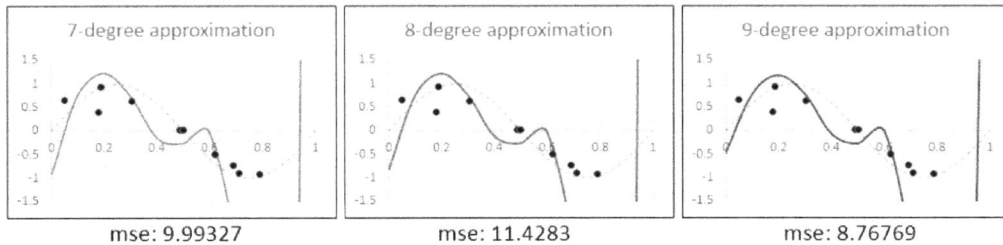

Figure 11.7: *Comparing the high-order polynomial fitting to new data*

Both plots and respective MSE values show that the 7,8,9-degree polynomials miserably fail to represent new data. Indeed, comparing the high-degree models to data not used in their training, one can observe that they do not even barely approximate the new instances. As a result, the MSE values computed using the new data are very high.

This last result shows that, although the high-degree models achieved a very good performance on the training data, they are actually useless for predicting unseen data.

Note: We say that an overfitted model does not GENERALIZE WELL.

Intentionally, we began our analysis at the extremes, that is, at the lowest-degree and highest-degree polynomials. Now, let us check the models in the middle.

Selecting good models

Observing the plot of polynomials, we can find that the 3 and 4-degree polynomials achieved a small MSE value on the training data and fairly approximate the original sine function, as shown:

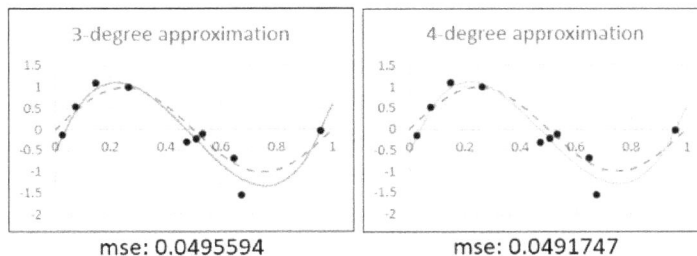

Figure 11.8: *Evaluating 3 and 4-degree polynomial fitting*

Indeed, they look promising. However, how do they perform on new data? Let us take a look:

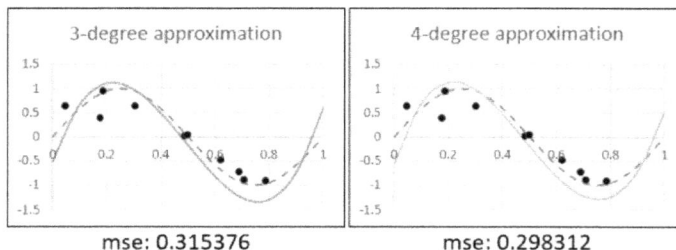

Figure 11.9: Comparing 3 and 4-degree polynomial fitting to new data

Although there is a performance drop, they still work roughly well on new data, that is, data not used to train them. In a real-world scenario, we should pick one of these two models (or both) in the model selection step.

Note: This example illustrates that the number of parameters in a model is a crucial factor in determining model quality.

If we use models with too many parameters, it is likely that the model will overfit the training data. Since an overfitted model only performs well on the training data, it is useless for further usage.

Note: An overfitted model is useless.

On the other side, a model with too few parameters is prone to underfit the training data, being unable to achieve minimally good performance even on the training data.

Note: An underfitted model is also useless.

Finding suitable model sizes is one of the most critical steps when developing machine learning models. Let us know other relevant aspects to identify and avoid overfitting and underfitting.

Understanding underfitting

In underfitting, the training error is high. It means that something earlier in the modeling is not working. The common causes of underfitting are:

- **Data quality issues**: High noise in the data, conflicts, missing variables, outliers, and other data-centric issues affect the model's capacity to capture the underlying pattern. Even if the data encodes a recognizable pattern, issues like **unbalanced classes** can make the training challenging, leading the model to underfit one or more classes. **Feature engineering** and **data preparation** may help. However, in some cases, you eventually need to acquire more data or rethink the system.

- **Hyperparameter tunning**: The most common example of underfitting due to a bad hyperparameter choice is a small learning rate. If the learning rate is too small, the algorithm requires too many epochs to reach the minimum point, often stopping before finding a good approximation or being stuck in a local minimum. Another common issue is a bad parameter initialization, which makes the algorithm start too far from a suitable minimum. Indeed, all hyperparameter choices can contribute to underfitting.

- **Low-capacity models**: As pointed out in the last example, a model with insufficient parameters cannot adequately represent the data regularities. Although the solution may be simple (increasing the number of parameters), this very often can be hard to achieve in real settings due to the practical limitations of the underlying hardware.

- **Implementation mistakes**: Algorithm developers are always prone to failure, eventually inlining bugs as simple or complex as combining different dimensions in a contraction. Due to the usual high volume of operations and the intrinsic randomness, it is usually hard to detect and fix bugs in deep learning code. Consider reading *Chapter 3, Testing Deep Learning Code,* again to understand how to reduce the chance of a bug affecting your model results.

- **Training methodological mistake**: The training routine can also contribute to underfitting. For example, forgetting to shuffle the data can include some ordering bias, affecting the training schemas. The next chapter covers the training routine and sheds light on keeping your training free of methodological mistakes.

The more common modeling challenge is to avoid underfitting. Once the model achieves decent performance on the training data, we have to fight overfitting, as discussed below.

Understanding overfitting

An overfitted model will perform very well on the training data but poorly on unseen data. Thus, it is impossible to detect overfitting by only looking at the training performance. The only way to make sure whether the model is overfitting or not is to use another dataset not used to train the model. This dataset is often called **validation data**.

The model performance on the validation data is an estimate of the model performance on new data, also called **generalization power** or **generalization performance**.

Note: Evaluating the model using a different dataset is essential since this provides a good estimate of the real model performance in production.

Of course, the estimate is as good as the validation data well represents the future data distribution.

Note: Using data from the validation dataset to train the model is one of the most elementary methodological mistakes ever.

Validating the model works to detect overfitting. What can we do to reduce the chance of a model overfitting the data? The most common sources of overfitting are listed as follows:

- **Few data registers**: The most common source of overfitting is scarce data to train. If the model has only a few instances to train, it would be hard to decide if it sees a pattern or only a particular instance. Fixing this issue is simple: more data. In practice, getting new data involves cost or is impractical if the phenomenon is intrinsically rare. In cases like that, **data augmentation** can be helpful.

- **High dimensional data**: The higher dimensional the data, the more data you need for the training. High-dimensional data inserts several challenges in the modeling, an issue commonly known as the **curse of dimensionality**. Again, more data can help the model to avoid overfitting, but not only. You must check the features, reducing the data space if possible. The simplest check is the attribute variation. A feature that does not vary (for example, a region of an image that is always of the same color) is useless. Techniques like **Principal Component Analysis (PCA)** or Auto-encoders can automatically provide reduced versions of the data. These compressed versions are usually called **embeddings**.

- **Models with too many parameters**: In the polynomial regression example, we learned that polynomials with too many degrees are prone to overfitting. It also happens with neural networks with too many layers or unnecessarily huge weight matrices. If your model is overfitting, reducing the model size is one of the first things to do.

- **Training the model for too long**: A good metaphor for training models is cooking. If you roast a cake for too long, you will likely mess up the whole thing, ending up with a useless burned mass at your hands and wasting time and ingredients. It is more or less the same with training a model. Fitting a model for too many epochs can result in a model that overfits the data. Later in this chapter, we will learn an **early stopping** technique to help us avoid scenarios like this.

- **Overly hyperparameters tune**: In addition to the total number of epochs, other hyperparameters can also contribute to getting an overfitted model. In general, bigger batch sizes reduce the chance of overfitting.

The central concern in avoiding overfitting is reducing the generalization error. The set of different approaches addressing this issue is called **regularization**, as covered in the following section.

Understanding regularization

The algorithms covered in this book, mostly deep learning algorithms, are very powerful to fit models to the training data. However, when developing new models, the main concern is not fitting but generalization. In other words, the real challenge in developing good models is finding models that perform well on future, unseen data.

Note: This capacity to perform well on previously unknown data is where the real utility of a model resides.

Achieving good generalization is not easy. In the polynomial fitting experiment, we know a priori the generative function formula . In real-world problems, we do not have this critical information at hand. Indeed, there are two key questions here:

- How can we determine whether a model is or is not overfitting?
- Once we know the model is overfitted, what can we do to fix it?

The answer for the first question is simple: we hold out a small subset of the data to check the model's performance on it. This subset of the data, usually called **validation dataset**, cannot be used in any way to train the model. A model that performs well on the training data but poorly on the validation data has a strong indication of overfitting and, in general, would be discarded. If all of our models are overfitting, we need to find a way to avoid it. Regularization has a wide set of approaches to help us to avoid overfitted models. According to the Deep Learning Book [2]:

Regularization is any modification we make to a learning algorithm that is intended to reduce its generalization error but not its training error.

We can summarize regularization approaches in four categories:

- **Changing the cost function to penalize bad models**: This is the case of L1 and L2 regularization, where the weights themselves are directly included in the cost function evaluation.

- **Changing the data**: Adding more data usually is the best fix for overfitted models. However, very often getting more data is not easy or even available. As discussed later on in this chapter, using data augmentation can be helpful. Other data quality issues can also be addressed, such as outliner removal.

- **Changing the network topology**: This approach usually disconnects some weights or neurons during the training. The most popular example is DropOut.

- **Changing the training schema**: This is a miscellaneous of approaches. For example, we can use Early Stopping to terminate the training when the model starts to overfitting the data. We can also train the model using batches, which objectively reduces overfitting.

We will discuss these approaches in the forthcoming sections where overfitting and several regularization approaches are illustrated by practical experiments.

Experiment 2: An overfitted model

The first experiment used polynomials to illustrate the relationship between the model size and its performance. This experiment uses an actual neural network to illustrate how overfitting occurs with these models.

Defining the model

The following figure represents the model used in this experiment:

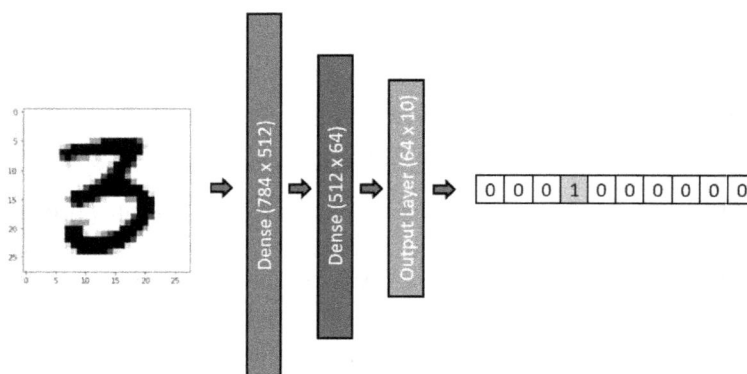

Figure 11.10: *Model used in this experiment*

This simple model consists of only three dense layers:

- The input layer has 784 input neurons and 512 output neurons.
- The hidden layer, having 512 input neurons and 64 output neurons.
- The output layer, a softmax layer with 64 input neurons and 10 output neurons.

We are planning to train this network with MNIST. Thus, we must match the number of input neurons with the size of MNIST records (*28x28 = 784*) and the network output with the number of classes in MNIST (ten classes to represent the numbers from 0 to 9).

The following class implements this model:

```
1.  template <typename Device>
2.  class Model {
3.
4.  public:
5.
6.      Model(Device &device, const int hidden_layer_size) {
7.
8.          Tensor_2D W1(28*28, hidden_layer_size);
9.          glorot_uniform_initializer(rng, W1);
10.         dense_1 = new DenseLayer(device, W1, new ReLU<2>());
11.
12.         Tensor_2D W2(hidden_layer_size, 64);
13.         glorot_uniform_initializer(rng, W2);
```

```
14.         dense_2 = new DenseLayer(device, W2, new ReLU<2>());
15.
16.         Tensor_2D WC(64, 10);
17.         glorot_uniform_initializer(rng, WC);
18.         output_layer = new SoftmaxCrossEntropyLayer(device, WC);
19.     }
20.
21.     //...
22.
23. private:
24.     DenseLayer<Device> *dense_1;
25.     DenseLayer<Device> *dense_2;
26.     SoftmaxCrossEntropyLayer<Device> *output_layer;
27. };
```

Implementing the model as a class is quite convenient. We can define the model behavior by implementing the following three methods:

```
1.  void forward(const Tensor_2D &input) {
2.      dense_1->forward(input);
3.      dense_2->forward(dense_1->get_output());
4.      output_layer->forward(dense_2->get_output());
5.  }
6.
7.  void backward(const Tensor_2D &upstream) {
8.      output_layer->backward(upstream, true);
9.      dense_2->backward(output_layer->get_downstream(), true);
10.     dense_1->backward(dense_2->get_downstream(), false);
11. }
12.
13. void update(const float learning_rate, int epoch) {
14.     dense_1->update(learning_rate, epoch);
15.     dense_2->update(learning_rate, epoch);
16.     output_layer->update(learning_rate, epoch);
17. }
```

Training this model involves looping over the dataset and invoking **forward()**, **backward()**, and **update()**. This is implemented in the following code:

```
1.   template <typename MODEL>
2.   void training(MODEL &model, const Tensor_2D &training_
     images, const Tensor_2D &training_labels,
3.                const Tensor_2D &validation_
     images, const Tensor_2D &validation_labels,
4.                const int MAX_EPOCHS, float learning_rate) {
5.
6.       CategoricalCrossEntropy cost_fn;
7.
8.       int epoch = 0;
9.       while (epoch < MAX_EPOCHS)
10.      {
11.
12.          auto begin = high_resolution_clock::now();
13.
14.          model.forward(training_images);
15.          model.backward(training_labels);
16.          model.update(learning_rate, epoch);
17.
18.          auto end = high_resolution_clock::now();
19.          auto duration = duration_cast<milliseconds>(end - begin);
20.
21.          auto training_pred = model.predict(training_images);
22.          float training_loss = cost_fn.evaluate(training_
     labels, training_pred);
23.          float training_acc = accuracy(training_labels, training_
     pred);
24.
25.          auto validation_pred = model.predict(validation_images);
26.          float validation_acc = accuracy(validation_
     labels, validation_pred);
27.          float validation_loss = cost_fn.evaluate(validation_
     labels, validation_pred);
28.
29.          std::cout
30.                  << "epoch:\t" << epoch << "\t"
31.                  << "took:\t" << duration.count() << " mills\t"
32.                  << "\ttraining_loss:\t" << training_loss
```

```
33.                       << "\ttraining_acc:\t" << training_acc
34.                       << "\tvalidation_loss:\t" << validation_loss
35.                       << "\tvalidation_acc:\t" << validation_acc
36.                       << "\n";
37.
38.            epoch++;
39.
40.      }
41.
42. }
```

The critical part of this code is the invocation of the model inside the loop:

```
1.  while (epoch < MAX_EPOCHS)
2.  {
3.
4.        model.forward(training_images);
5.        model.backward(training_labels);
6.        model.update(learning_rate, epoch);
7.
8.        //...
9.  }
```

As you know, we are using backpropagation here. Thus, for each epoch, we are performing the forward, backward, and update steps.

The model is set. Let us check the data to use in the training.

Loading the data

The idea behind this experiment is to illustrate an overfitted model. Thus, we will train the model using only a very small subset of MNIST. Check below how we are loading the data:

```
1.  std::tuple<Tensor_2D, Tensor_2D, Tensor_2D, Tensor_2D>
2.  load_data(long int training_instances, long int validation_
    instances) {
3.        auto [training_images, training_labels, validation_
    images, validation_labels] = load_mnist("data/mnist", rng);
4.
5.        // getting slice of data
6.        Eigen::array<Eigen::Index, 2> zero_offset = {0, 0};
7.        Eigen::array<Eigen::Index, 2> training_x_extents = {training_
```

```
   instances, 784};
8.    Eigen::array<Eigen::Index, 2> training_y_extents = {training_
   instances, 10};
9.    Eigen::array<Eigen::Index, 2> validation_x_
   extents = {validation_instances, 784};
10.    Eigen::array<Eigen::Index, 2> validation_y_
   extents = {validation_instances, 10};
11.
12.    Eigen::Tensor<float, 2> training_x_ds = training_images.
   slice(zero_offset, training_x_extents);
13.    Eigen::Tensor<float, 2> training_y_ds = training_labels.
   slice(zero_offset, training_y_extents);
14.
15.    Eigen::Tensor<float, 2> validation_x_ds = validation_images.
   slice(zero_offset, validation_x_extents);
16.    Eigen::Tensor<float, 2> validation_y_ds = validation_labels.
   slice(zero_offset, validation_y_extents);
17.
18.    auto result = std::make_tuple(training_x_ds, training_y_
   ds, validation_x_ds, validation_y_ds);
19.
20.    return result;
21. }
```

We call this function as follows:

```
1. auto [training_images, training_labels, validation_
   images, validation_labels] = load_data(100, 2000);
```

As one can see, we are loading only 100 training instances and 2,000 validation instances. Will the model able to learn from only 100 images? The answer is in the next step.

Training the model

We can execute the training by using the following program:

```
1. int main(int, char **)
2. {
3.
4. auto [training_images, training_labels, validation_
   images, validation_labels] = load_data(100, 2000);
5.    std::cout << "Data loaded!\n";
6.
```

```
7.     std::cout << "training_images dims: " << training_images.
   dimensions() << "\n";
8.     std::cout << "training_labels dims: " << training_labels.
   dimensions() << "\n";
9.     std::cout << "validation_images dims: " << validation_images.
   dimensions() << "\n";
10.    std::cout << "validation_labels dims: " << validation_labels.
   dimensions() << "\n";
11.
12.    const int MAX_EPOCHS = 500;
13.    const float learning_rate = 0.01f;
14.
15.    const int threads = std::thread::hardware_concurrency();
16.    Eigen::ThreadPool tp(threads);
17.    Eigen::ThreadPoolDevice device(&tp, threads);
18.
19.    Model model(device, 512);
20.    training(model, training_images, training_labels, validation_
   images, validation_labels, MAX_EPOCHS, learning_rate);
21.
22.    return 0;
23. }
```

Running this code and plotting the output results in the following chart:

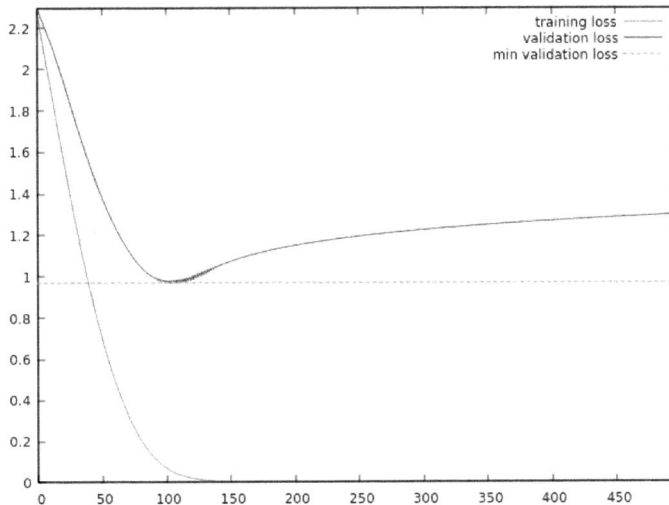

Figure 11.11: *Training and validation loss of an overfitted model*

The first thing to note here is that the **training loss** is lower than the **validation loss**. This is **NOT** a problem. Since we are fitting the model using the training data, it is reasonable that the loss calculated over the training dataset be lower than the loss obtained over the validation dataset.

The real problem here is that the validation loss is very high if compared to the training loss. Another very important issue here is that the validation loss starts to continuously increase at some point after epoch 100. This means that the model is losing its ability to make good predictions after that point. The longer the training, the worse the end result.

Since the validation cost is a fair estimate of the model generalization performance, this behavior indicates that the model will not perform well when predicting using new data.

We can check the training and validation accuracy:

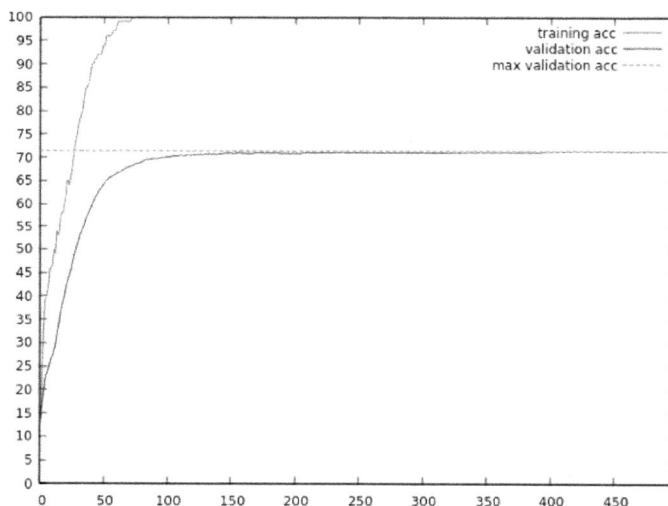

Figure 11.12: Training and validation accuracy of an overfitted model

The training accuracy goes to 100%, while the validation accuracy is stuck at some point below 72%. The model is likely to be memorizing the training dataset, suggesting overfitting.

As we expected, training using only 100 images resulted in an overfitted model. An overfitted model is useless because it will probably perform badly if deployed in production. In the following sections, we will introduce the common approaches to avoid overfitting.

Reducing the model size

When we have an overfitted model at hand, the first thing to try is reducing the model's size. Let us check how the model performs using only two layers and only 32 units in the hidden layer:

```
1. Model model(device, 32);
2. training(model, training_images, training_labels, validation_
   images, validation_labels, MAX_EPOCHS, learning_rate);
```

As discussed in the first part of this chapter, the bigger the model, the more prone to overfitting. Running the code again with this smaller model results in the following performance:

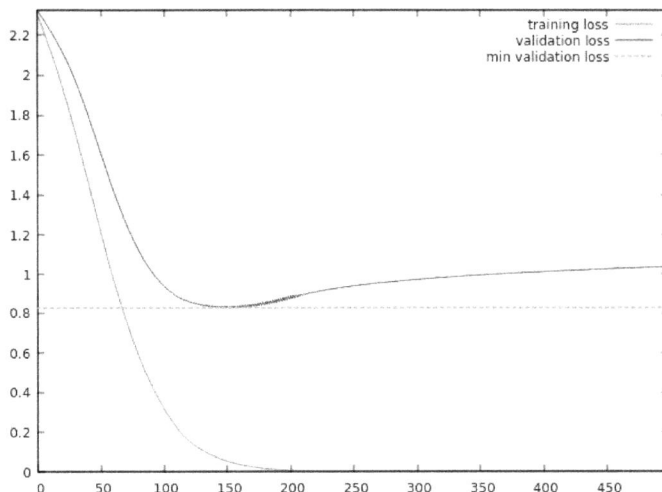

Figure 11.13: The training and validation loss using only 32 hidden neurons

The first thing to note here is that the achieved validation loss is lower than the validation loss using the previous large model. The model is also overfitting, but it starts only after epoch 150. As a result, the model achieved a higher accuracy, as shown:

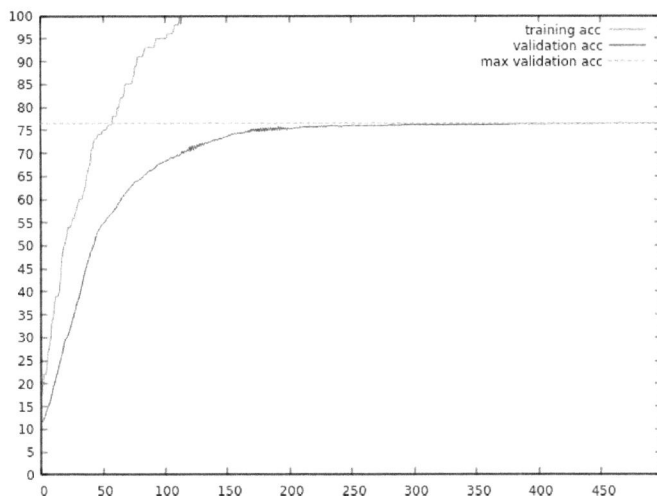

Figure 11.14: The training and validation accuracy using only 32 hidden neurons

Improving the model performance by adjusting the model size actually works. However, knowing the right size of a complex real-world deep model having several layers and parameters is not easy or practical. We will explore other approaches in the forthcoming experiments which provide similar results.

Early stopping

One simple way to prevent the performance drop due to training the model too long is **early stopping**. With early stopping, we can terminate the training if the performance is no longer increasing. Early stopping can be implemented in a straightforward manner:

```cpp
1.    float min_validation_loss = std::numeric_limits<float>::max();
2.    int early_stop_count = 0;
3.    const int patience = 5; // setting max tolerance
4.
5.    int epoch = 0;
6.    while (epoch++ < MAX_EPOCHS && early_stop_count < patience)
7.    {
8.
9.        // running the training loop here
10.       // ...
11.
12.       auto validation_pred = model.predict(validation_images);
13.       float validation_loss = cost_fn.evaluate(validation_labels,
          validation_pred);
14.
15.       if (validation_loss < min_validation_loss) {
16.           min_validation_loss = validation_loss;
17.           early_stop_count = 0;
18.       } else {
19.           early_stop_count++;
20.       }
21.   }
```

Running this code results in the following performance:

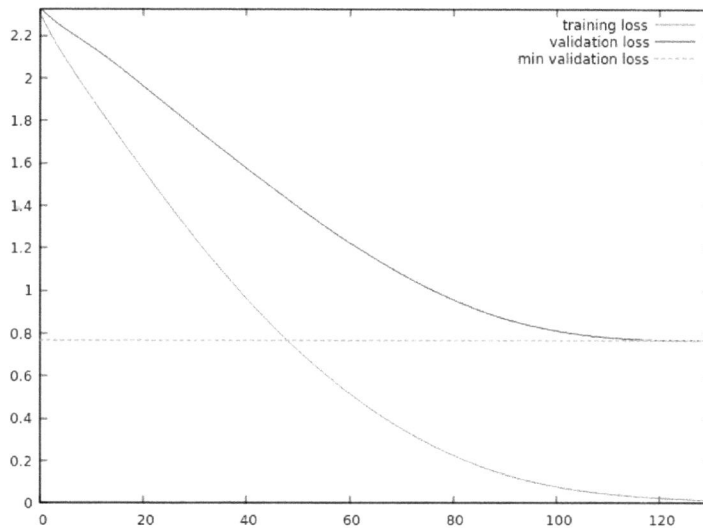

Figure 11.15: *Using early stopping*

In practice, early stopping is always used.

Experiment 3: Penalization as regularization

Penalization is a very popular regularization technique that uses the concept of penalizing models with too many non-zero parameters. Thus, the gradient descent can use the penalization signal to automatically decide where to go over the cost surface.

There are two common penalty-based regularizations: L1 and L2. Both of them work in a similar way by adding a term to the cost function value (the penalization). L2 uses the sum of the quadratic norm of each weight:

$$L2\ Regularization\ Cost = Cost + \lambda \sum_{i} W_i^2$$

L1 uses the sum of absolute coefficients:

$$L1\ Regularization = Cost + \lambda \sum_{i} |W_i|$$

Note: We can control how these regularizations affect the training by the use of the hyperparameter λ.

Using the calculus rules discussed so far in this book, we can find that the weight update using L2 regularization can be rewritten [5] as follows:

$$w = w \left(1 - \frac{\eta\lambda}{m}\right) - \eta\nabla w$$

Where η is the learning rate, λ is the regularization hyperparameter, is the number of training instances and is the gradient of weight .

We can implement **L1** and **L2** regularization by changing the **update()** method in the Dense Layer class. Consider the default implementation:

```
1.  void update(const TYPE learning_rate, int epoch) {
2.
3.      auto weight_update = weight_grad * weight_grad.constant(-
    learning_rate);
4.
5.      this->weight = this->weight + weight_update;
6.
7.  }
```

We can change this method to include the **L2** regularization as follows:

```
1.  void update(const TYPE learning_rate, int epoch) {
2.
3.      Tensor_2D weight_update =  weight_grad * weight_grad.constant(-
    learning_rate);
4.
5.      if (L2_weight_decay_lambda > 0) {
6.          const int batch_size = this->output.dimension(0);
7.          TYPE weight_decay = (learning_rate * L2_weight_decay_
    lambda / batch_size);
8.          Tensor_2D decay = weight.constant(weight_decay) * this-
    >weight;
9.          weight_update = weight_update - decay;
10.     }
11.     this->weight = this->weight + weight_update;
12.
13. }
```

Now, we can set **L2_weight_decay_lam**bda as follows:

```
1.  Model(Device &device, const int hidden_layer_size) {
2.      //...
3.      dense_1->set_L2_weight_decay_lambda(10);
4.      dense_2->set_L2_weight_decay_lambda(10);
5.      output_layer->set_L2_weight_decay_lambda(10);
6.  }
```

After this change, running the training again results in:

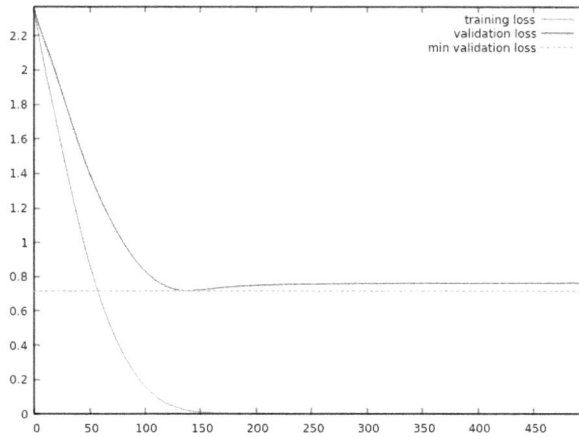

Figure 11.16: *Using L2 regularization*

In the same way, we can proceed with L1 regularization [6]:

```
1.  void update(const TYPE learning_rate, int epoch) {
2.
3.      Tensor_2D weight_update = this->weight_grad * this->weight_grad.
    constant(-learning_rate);
4.
5.      if (this->L1_weight_decay_lambda > 0) {
6.          const int batch_size = this->output.dimension(0);
7.          TYPE weight_decay = (learning_rate * this->L1_weight_decay_
    lambda / batch_size);
8.          auto signal_decay = this->weight.unaryExpr([](TYPE val)
    {return book::utils::signal(val);});
9.          Tensor_2D decay = signal_decay * this->weight.
    constant(weight_decay) * this->weight;
10.         weight_update = weight_update - decay;
11.     }
12.
13.     this->weight = this->weight + weight_update;
14.
15.     if (this->use_bias) {
16.         auto bias_update = this->bias_grad * this->bias_grad.
    constant(-learning_rate);
17.         this->bias = this->bias + bias_update;
18.     }
19. }
```

Similarly setting **L1_weight_decay_lambda** results in:

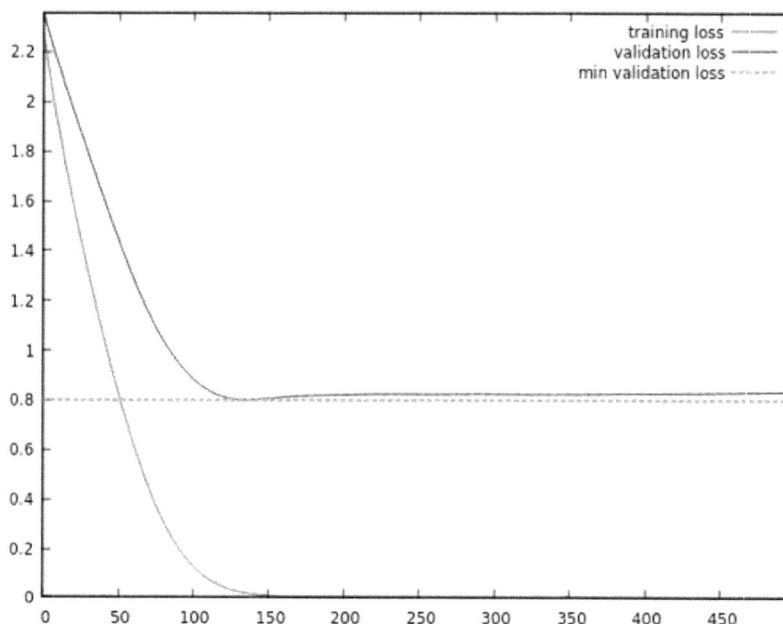

Figure 11.17: *Using L1 regularization*

Note: There is no problem in using both L1 and L2 regularization together.

L1 and L2 regularization work as forcing the weights to be close to zero. Because of this, they are also called **weight decay**.

Experiment 4: Data augmentation

In real-world projects, scarce data is one of the most common sources of overfitting. In practical terms, this is a real problem since data, high-quality data is very often costly or unavailable. For scenarios like this, even the previous regularization approaches may fail.

Note: Scarce data is the most common cause of overfitting.

Data augmentation is an alternative to scenarios where only a few registers are accessible. In data augmentation, we artificially increase the training data by including new copies. These new copies are soft or hard modified clones of the original instances drawn from the training dataset.

Aiming to simulate a scenario of overfitting, in this experiment we are using only a small subset of the MNIST dataset. The experiment consists then of using data augmentation to train a model and check the results.

Data augmentation in MNIST

For image datasets, we have a wide set of transformations to use in data augmentation such as: translations, rotations, color space transformations, blurring, flips, crops, stretching, changing brightness, sharping, and so on.

MNIST is an image dataset consisting of tiny 28x28 grayscale pixel images of handwritten numbers. For this experiment, we generate augmented copies by applying small rotations on the source images. Check some of the following examples:

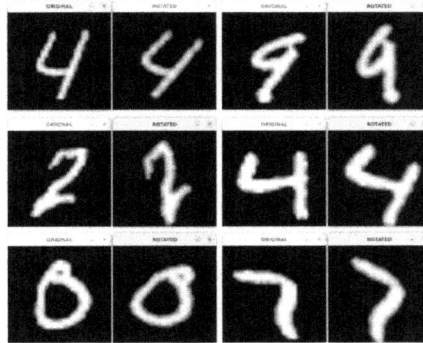

Figure 11.18: Applying random rotations on MNIST

We can rotate the images in MNIST using OpenCV:

```
1. Tensor_1D rotate(Tensor_1D &instance, float angle) {
2.
3.     auto data = instance.data();
4.     cv::Mat1f src(28, 28, data);
5.     cv::Mat1f rotated;
6.
7.     cv::Mat rotation_mat = cv::getRotationMatrix2D(cv::Point2f(src.cols / 2, src.rows / 2), angle, 1.0);
8.     cv::warpAffine(src, rotated, rotation_mat, cv::Size(src.cols, src.rows));
9.
10.    float * float_data = (float*) rotated.data;
11.
12.    Tensor_1D result = Eigen::TensorMap<Tensor_1D>(float_data, instance.dimension(0));
13.
14.    return result;
15. }
```

Note: Rotating images and other useful transformations are covered in more detail in Chapter 14, Introducing Computer Vision Models.

We can generate a dataset with rotated augmented instances using the following function:

```
1.  std::tuple<Tensor_2D, Tensor_2D>
2.  augment_dataset(Tensor_2D &src_images, Tensor_2D &src_
    labels, int number_augmented_instances) {
3.
4.      const int N = src_images.dimension(0);
5.      const int M = N + number_augmented_instances;
6.
7.      Tensor_2D result_images(M, src_images.dimension(1));
8.      Tensor_2D result_labels(M, src_labels.dimension(1));
9.
10.     DimArray<2> zero_offset = {0, 0};
11.     DimArray<2> images_src_extents = {N, src_images.dimension(1)};
12.     DimArray<2> labels_src_extents = {N, src_labels.dimension(1)};
13.
14.     // copying the original data
15.     result_images.slice(zero_offset, images_src_extents) = src_
    images;
16.     result_labels.slice(zero_offset, labels_src_extents) = src_
    labels;
17.
18.     // adding the augmented instances
19.     std::uniform_int_distribution<> index_picker(0, N);
20.     std::uniform_real_distribution<float> angle_picker(-30, 30);
21.
22.     for (int i = N; i < M; ++i) {
23.         int src_index = index_picker(rd);
24.         Eigen::Tensor<float, 1> instance = src_images.chip<0>(src_
    index);
25.         Eigen::Tensor<float, 1> label = src_labels.chip<0>(src_
    index);
26.
27.         float angle = angle_picker(rd);
28.         result_images.chip<0>(i) = rotate(instance, angle);
29.         result_labels.chip<0>(i) = label;
```

```
30.    }
31.
32.    auto result = std::make_tuple(result_images, result_labels);
33.    return result;
34. }
35.
36. int main(int, char **)
37. {
38.    // original images
39.    auto [training_images_original, training_labels_
    original, validation_images, validation_labels] = load_
    data(100, 2000);
40.
41.    // dataset containing original data + augmented instances
42.    auto [training_images, training_labels] = augment_
    dataset(training_images_original, training_labels_original, 100);
43.    ...
44. }
```

In this code, each new copy is **sampled with replacement** and then rotated by a random angle in the range [-30°, 30°].

Training the model with the augmented data results in the following performance:

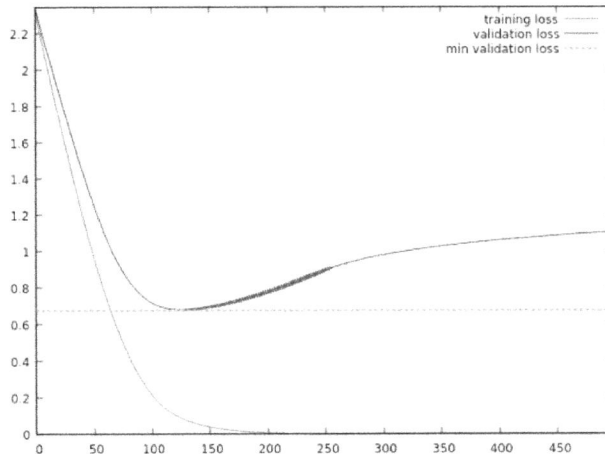

Figure 11.19: Training using augmented data

In this experiment, we are actually increasing the number of training instances using augmented instances. Observe that the augmented instances were created at runtime. This approach is known as **online data augmentation**. In **offline data augmentation**, the augmented instances are generated and then saved on disc for further usage. The pros and cons of the two approaches as well as other important aspects in data augmentation will be covered later on this book.

DropOut

DropOut [7] is the most well-succeeded topological approach for regularizing deep learning models based on the idea of disconnecting one or more model units.

In simple words, during the training, one or more neurons (the units) are disconnected from the network for a short period, like a single epoch. The disconnected neurons are sampled using a binominal distribution. In dropout, the probability of disconnecting a neuron is a number p, such as $0 < p < 1$. Thus, each neuron will be **NOT** disconnected with a probability of $1 - p$. The number $1 - p$ is called **keep probability**. In each step, the disconnected neurons are connected again, being available to be disconnected or keep in the next run.

There are many reasons why this mechanism reduces overfitting. The most commonly accepted is that dropout injects noise into the training, reducing the chances of the model memorizing the training dataset.

Implementing DropOut

In terms of implementation, there are two working scenarios for dropout: training and prediction.

During the training, we do not exactly disconnect a unit. Instead, we generate a mask M of zeroes and ones in which zero means a disconnected unit and one a connected neuron. This mask is used in both forward and backward passes. We can formulate this, as follows:

$$Out_i = M_i \times Y_i$$

Where,

$$P(M_i = 0) = p$$

Thus, each unit i has a probability p to be disconnected and $(1 - p)$ to be kept. The value of p need not be the same for every layer. For output layers, in general, $p = 0$, *which* means that the dropout mechanism does not act in the output layer. For hidden layers, like any other hyperparameters, p must be defined experimentally. Usual values of p are 0.1, 0.2, 0.3, 0.5, and 0.8.

After the model has been trained, it is ready to make predictions. When the model is making predictions, we need to consider the dropping of the units in the training phase. To get into an account, the dropout's original paper suggests scaling the output by the value of $(1 - p)$:

$$Out_i = (1 - p) \times Y_i$$

This is not the most common way dropout is implemented, though. Usually, people implement dropouts using an approach called **inverted dropout** [8]. In inverted dropout, the neuron output is scaled only during the training phase:

$$Out_i = \frac{1}{(1 - p)} \times M_i \times Y_i$$

Thus, during the prediction step, no change in the network is required. That is, we need not change the network to take p or $(1 - p)$ in consideration to make predictions. This way, using inverted dropout, is how we will illustrate dropout in the next section.

Experiment 5: DropOut example

Let us implement a dropout layer as follows:

```
1. template <typename Device, int _RANK, typename GEN>
2. class DropoutLayer : public Layer<Device, _RANK, _RANK>
3. {
4. public:
5.     DropoutLayer(Device &device, TYPE drop_
   prob, GEN & gen) : Layer<Device, _RANK, _RANK>(device, "book.layers.
   dropout"), drop_prob(drop_prob), gen(gen) {}
6.
7.     virtual ~DropoutLayer() {}
8.
9.     virtual Tensor<_RANK> predict(const Tensor<_
   RANK> &input) const {
10.         return input;
11.     }
12.
13.     // forward() and backward() defined here...
14.
15. private:
16.     Eigen::Tensor<bool, _RANK> mask;
17.     TYPE drop_prob;
18.     GEN gen;
19. };
```

In **forward()**, we set a mask using **dropout_mask()** to compute the layer output:

```
1. virtual void forward(const Tensor<_RANK> &input) {
2.
3.     if (this->mask.size() != input.size()) {
4.         this->mask = Eigen::Tensor<bool, _RANK>(input.dimensions());
```

```
5.        }
6.        if (this->output.size() != input.size()) {
7.            this->output = Tensor<_RANK>(input.dimensions());
8.        }
9.        dropout_mask(this->gen, this->mask, this->drop_prob);
10.       auto zero = this->output.constant(0);
11.       TYPE keep = TYPE(1.) - this->drop_prob;
12.       auto scale = this->output.constant(TYPE(1.) / keep);
13.       this->output.device(this->device) = this->mask.
      select(input, zero) * scale;
14. }
```

Note that we store mask for further usage in **backward()**. The function **dropout_mask()** is defined as follows:

```
1.  template<typename Generator, int _RANK>
2.  void dropout_mask(Generator& gen, Eigen::Tensor<bool, _
    RANK> &tensor, TYPE drop_prob)
3.  {
4.
5.      std::uniform_real_distribution<TYPE> uniform_distro(0., 1.);
6.      tensor = tensor.unaryExpr([&uniform_distro, &gen, &drop_prob]
    (TYPE) {
7.                              TYPE val = uniform_distro(gen);
8.                              return val >= drop_prob;
9.                          });
10.
11. }
```

This function samples the mask using a uniform distribution.

The dropout layer has no internal trainable parameter. Thus, we can define **backward()** only to propagate the gradient backward to the previous layer:

```
1.  virtual void backward(const Tensor<_
    RANK> &upstream, bool propagate) {
2.      if (propagate) {
3.          if (this->downstream.size() != this->mask.size()) {
4.              this->downstream = Tensor<_RANK>(this->mask.
    dimensions());
5.          }
6.          auto zero = upstream.constant(0);
7.          TYPE keep = TYPE(1.) - this->drop_prob;
```

```
8.             auto scale = upstream.constant(TYPE(1.) / keep);
9.             this->downstream.device(this->device) = this->mask.
   select(upstream, zero) * scale;
10.     }
11. }
```

backward() sets the downstream gradient by scaling upstream using the following formula:

$$downstream_i = \frac{1}{(1 - p)} \times M_i \times upstream_i$$

which can be derived using the chain rule. Once the **DropoutLayer** has been defined, we can use it to set our model:

```
1. template <typename Device>
2. class Model {
3.
4. public:
5.
6.     Model(Device &device, const int hidden_layer_size) {
7.
8.         Tensor_2D W1(28*28, hidden_layer_size);
9.         glorot_uniform_initializer(rng, W1);
10.        this-
   >dense_1 = new DenseLayer(device, W1, new ReLU<Device, 2>(device));
11.
12.        this-
   >dropout_1 = new DropoutLayer<Device, 2, GEN>(device, 0.2, rng);
13.
14.        Tensor_2D W2(hidden_layer_size, 64);
15.        glorot_uniform_initializer(rng, W2);
16.        this-
   >dense_2 = new DenseLayer(device, W2, new ReLU<Device, 2>(device));
17.
18.        this-
   >dropout_2 = new DropoutLayer<Device, 2, GEN>(device, 0.5, rng);
19.
20.        Tensor_2D WC(64, 10);
21.        glorot_uniform_initializer(rng, WC);
22.        this->output_layer = new SoftmaxCrossEntropyLayer(device, WC);
23.     }
24.
```

```
25.    //...
26.
27. private:
28.     DenseLayer<Device> *dense_1;
29.     DropoutLayer<Device, 2, GEN> *dropout_1;
30.     DenseLayer<Device> *dense_2;
31.     DropoutLayer<Device, 2, GEN> *dropout_2;
32.     SoftmaxCrossEntropyLayer<Device> *output_layer;
33. };
```

The difference between this model and the models used in the previous experiments is the inclusion of the two dropout layers:

```
1. DropoutLayer<Device, 2, GEN> *dropout_1;
2. DropoutLayer<Device, 2, GEN> *dropout_2;
```

They are initialized as follows:

```
1. this->dropout_1 = new DropoutLayer<Device, 2, GEN>(device, 0.2, rng);
2. this->dropout_2 = new DropoutLayer<Device, 2, GEN>(device, 0.5, rng);
```

Note that we are setting a different drop probability for each layer. We can represent this model as follows:

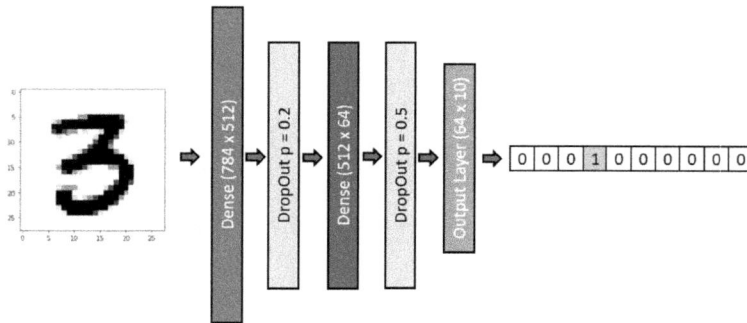

Figure 11.20: *Model using DropOut*

We must redefine the model's methods **forward()** and **backward()** to take the dropout layers into account:

```
1. void forward(const Tensor_2D &input) {
2.     this->dense_1->forward(input);
3.     this->dropout_1->forward(this->dense_1->get_output());
4.     this->dense_2->forward(this->dropout_1->get_output());
5.     this->dropout_2->forward(this->dense_2->get_output());
6.     this->output_layer->forward(this->dropout_2->get_output());
7. }
```

```
8.
9. void backward(const Tensor_2D &upstream) {
10.     this->output_layer->backward(upstream, true);
11.     this->dropout_2->backward(output_layer->get_downstream(), true);
12.     this->dense_2->backward(dropout_2->get_downstream(), true);
13.     this->dropout_1->backward(dense_2->get_downstream(), true);
14.     this->dense_1->backward(this->dropout_1->get_
    downstream(), false);
15. }
```

Since we are implementing dropout using inverted dropout, no change is required in **predict()**:

```
1. Tensor_2D predict(const Tensor_2D &input) {
2.     auto y0 = this->dense_1->predict(input);
3.     auto y1 = this->dense_2->predict(y0);
4.     auto result = this->output_layer->predict(y1);
5.     return std::move(result);
6. }
```

Since the dropout layer have no trainable parameter, we need not call them during the update step:

```
1. void update(const float learning_rate, int epoch) {
2.     this->dense_1->update(learning_rate, epoch);
3.     this->dense_2->update(learning_rate, epoch);
4.     this->output_layer->update(learning_rate, epoch);
5. }
```

The result of these modifications are as follows:

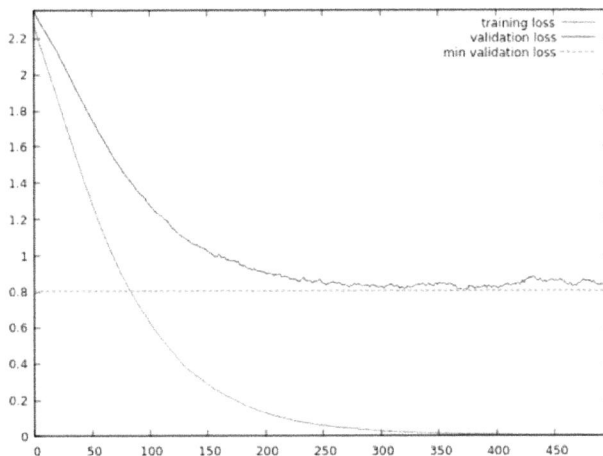

Figure 11.21: *Training and validation loss using dropout*

Including the dropout layers, the model achieved a better response to overfitting. We can note that dropouts introduce a noisy behavior to the training. This can also be observed in the accuracies:

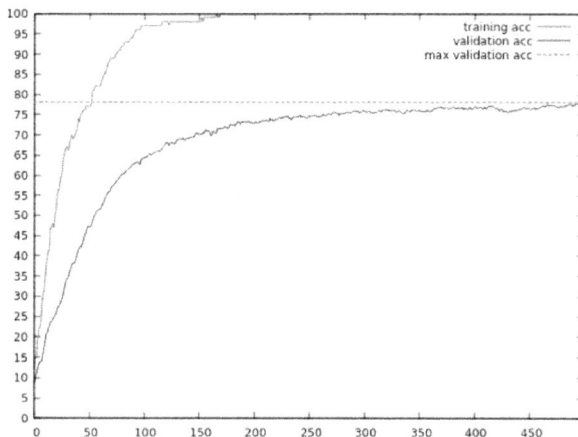

Figure 11.22: *Training and validation accuracy using dropout*

In real world deep learning projects, dropout is often used to regularize the training of models using wild datasets. We can obviously use dropout in conjunction with other regularization techniques discussed in this chapter. In fact, when developing real-world models, we often combine more than one regularization approach, aiming to obtain a final model that does not overfit.

Conclusion

In this chapter, we learned some of the most important regularization techniques, such as L1 and L2 regularization, early stopping, data augmentation, and dropout, using different practical experiments. We also learned that the model size is a key factor in terms of model capacity and generalization performance.

The most important thing to learn here, however, is the importance of properly evaluating the model performance using a validation dataset. We discussed that evaluating the model performance only on training data is a huge methodological mistake.

Optimization and regularization are the two central concerns in ML. In the next chapter, we will talk about the implementation of training pipelines and model evaluation metrics to provide more control of our models.

Exercises

1. Reproduce the experiment of polynomial fitting. Increase the number of training instances and evaluate again the performance of each polynomial model. Explain your findings.

2. Consider again the example of training MNIST using only a small subset of training instances. What happens if the training dataset is unbalanced? For example, if 50% of the training data consists of only one specific label, what problem can we expect?

3. Repeat the model training in experiment 2. This time, use the full dataset (60k) to train and 10k validation instances to validate the model. What can we do to make the model overfit if we use the whole dataset?

References

[1] Bishop, Pattern Recognition and Machine Learning, Springer, 2006.

[2] Goodfellow, Bengio and Courville, Deep Learning, MIT Press, 2016.

[3] Linear algebra and decompositions, **https://eigen.tuxfamily.org/dox/group__ TutorialLinearAlgebra.html**

[4] Yann LeCun, MNIST handwritten digit database, **https://yann.lecun.com/exdb/mnist/**

[5] James D. McCaffrey, L2 Regularization and Back-Propagation, **https://jamesmccaffrey. wordpress.com/2017/02/19/l2-regularization-and-back-propagation/**

[6] James D. McCaffrey, Implementing Neural Network L1 Regularization, **https:// jamesmccaffrey.wordpress.com/2017/06/27/implementing-neural-network-l1-regularization/**

[7] Nitish Srivastava et al, Dropout: A Simple Way to Prevent Neural Networks from Overfitting, **https://www.cs.toronto.edu/~rsalakhu/papers/srivastava14a.pdf**

[8] James D. McCaffrey, Neural Network Dropout and Inverted Dropout, **https:// jamesmccaffrey.wordpress.com/2019/05/07/neural-network-dropout-and-inverted-dropout/**

Join our book's Discord space

Join the book's Discord Workspace for Latest updates, Offers, Tech happenings around the world, New Release and Sessions with the Authors:

https://discord.bpbonline.com

CHAPTER 12
Implementing Cross-validation, Mini Batching, and Model Performance Metrics

Introduction

In the previous chapter, we introduced hold-out, a technique to check if the training process overfits the model. Although generally useful, hold-out consumes valuable data that cannot be used to train the model. This issue can be significant in scenarios where data is scarce. To tackle this scenario, we introduce another validation technique called **cross-validation**. We will also introduce the most common **performance metrics** in deep learning projects, focusing on their applicability for each case. Finally, the chapter discusses an essential training schema called **mini batching**, using stochastic gradient descent as a use case.

Structure

This is the chapter roadmap:

- Experiments in this chapter
- Assessing the model performance
- Common performance evaluation metrics
- Experiment 1: Implementing confusion matrix and derivated indicators
- Other types of metrics

- Understanding cross-validation
- Experiment 2: Implementing stratified k-fold cross-validation
- Training using mini-batches
- Experiment 3: Training a model using mini-batching
- Experiment 4: Implementing stochastic gradient descent

Objectives

By reading this chapter, you will know how to reliably assess the model performance using the right metrics for each case. You will also know different training schemas to better combine with the task and data at hand. Finally, you will know how to use mini-batching to train your models, an essential training schema that allows you to obtain better predictions using most of your computational resources.

Experiments in this chapter

This chapter includes four experiments:

ID	Description
Exp-12.1	Implementing confusion matrix and derivated indicators
Exp-12.2	Implementing stratified k-fold cross-validation
Exp-12.3	Training a model using mini-batching
Exp-12.4	Implementing stochastic gradient descent

Table 12.1: Chapter experiment list

Assessing the model performance

A model metric is a function that assigns one or more values given a model and a dataset. At first glance, a metric is quite similar to a cost function. In fact, a cost function also provides a value given a model and a dataset. However, unlike a cost function, a metric need not be differentiable.

The most intuitive example of a metric is **success rate**, very often called **accuracy**:

$$Accuracy(model, data) = \frac{\# \ correct \ predictions}{\# \ correct \ predictions + \# \ incorrect \ predictions}$$

Suppose we evaluate the model accuracy using a validation dataset, finding 90% of correct predictions. As discussed in the previous chapter, this validation performance is the generalization estimate of the true model performance on future data. How close this estimate is to the true success rate depends on the quality and size of our validation set.

Assuming that each prediction is an independent event, we can take the classifier outcomes as a **Bernoulli process** and evaluate a **confidence interval** for the achieved performance [1]. This procedure provides a confidence range for the true success rate. For example, using a confidence of 80% and 100 validation instances, the true success rate lies somewhere between 84.4% and 95.6%. If the validation dataset is bigger, for example, 1000 instances, we can find a narrower confidence interval of [88.2% – 91.8%]. The smaller the confidence interval, the better.

Saying that the outcomes follow a Bernoulli process means that the predictions obey a **binominal distribution**. We can use this to consider some scenarios. For example, estimating a success rate $p = 90\%$ and using the binomial formula [2]:

$$P(x; p) = \binom{n}{x} p^x (1 - p)^{(n-x)}$$

We can find that the classifier has a 32.3% chance of misclassifying at least three instances out of 20 predictions, a surprisingly high failure probability considering the 90% success rate.

Note: A detailed discussion of using binominal distribution to represent a model's outcomes is beyond this book's scope.

Although an important indicator, evaluating the model's performance by taking only the success rate is not always recommended. This matter is explained in the next section.

Flaw of using only accuracy to select models

At first glance, given two models, deciding on the one with the higher accuracy seems reasonable. However, this is not always true. Considering only accuracy to select a model is very dangerous due to a common data issue called **unbalanced classes** [3]. It turns out that some datasets have very skewed proportions of classes. That is, the number of instances of one class is very different than the number of instances of another class.

For example, consider a dataset with one thousand registers where only 50 instances are labeled as class A and 950 instances are labeled as class B. A bad classifier that always predicts class B has 95% accuracy on this dataset. Despite the high accuracy, this classifier is totally useless, fully underfitting the registers of class A. Refer to the following figure:

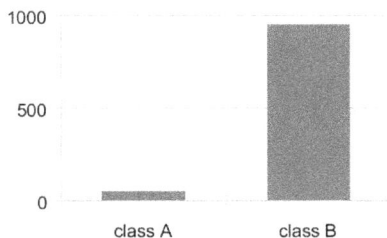

Figure 12.1: A strongly unbalanced dataset

Unbalanced datasets are very common in real projects. Fraud data is usually a classic example of this kind of data issue. Tasks involving outlier detection or rare natural phenomena are common sources of datasets where only a few registers represent one or more classes. Using only accuracy in this type of dataset will eventually provide an unreal high performance for an actually bad model.

In cases like this, using confusion matrices (and the metrics derived from them) is more recommended.

Common performance evaluation metrics

Counting successes and failures per class provides control of how the model actually performs on a given dataset regardless of whether it is unbalanced. This concept is behind the confusion matrix [1], as explained in this section.

The confusion matrix

Consider a binary classifier that assigns the labels A or B to each input instance X. If we know T, the true label of X, after predicting X, there are only four possibilities:

- T is A, and the classifier correctly predicted A. This is called **TRUE POSITIVE**

- T is not A, and the classifier correctly did not predict A. This is called **TRUE NEGATIVE**

- T is not A, but the classifier mistakenly predicted A. This is called **FALSE POSITIVE.**

- T is A, but the classifier mistakenly did not predict A. This is called **FALSE NEGATIVE**

Given a dataset, we can calculate TP as the count of all true positive predictions, TN as the count of all true negative predictions, FP as the count of all false positives, and FN as the count of all false negatives. Finally, we can arrange TP, TN, FP, and FN in a table like this:

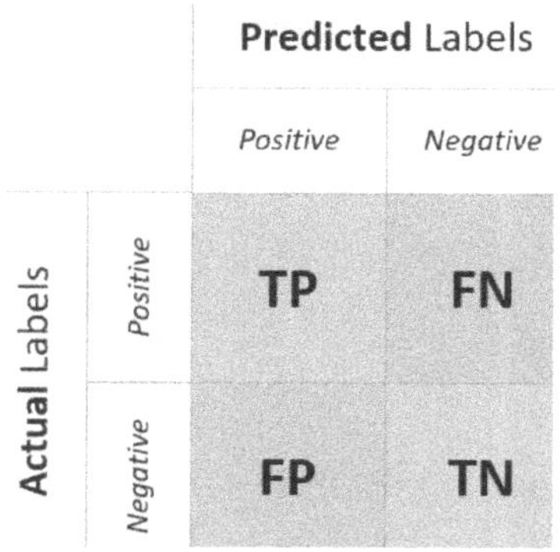

Figure 12.2: Confusion Matrix Layout

This table above is called a confusion matrix. Confusion matrices provide valuable indicators representing the classifier performance: **precision**, **recall**, **accuracy**, **true negative rate**, **F1-score**, and many others.

Precision and recall

Precision is defined as follows:

$$Precision = \frac{TP}{TP + FP}$$

Precision is a 0-100% indicator that provides the proportion of correctly identified true instances in the set of all positive predictions. In the worst scenario, TP and precision are zero. On the other end, there are no false positive predictions. FP is zero and precision is 100%.

Precision does not take false negatives in the count. Thus, a bad system with a high number of false negative predictions can still achieve good precision. Because of this, we also consider recall evaluating the models:

$$Recall = \frac{TP}{TP + FN}$$

Note that false negatives are positive instances not correctly predicted. Thus, recall indicates the true positive predictions proportion in the set of all positive instances.

Accuracy

The success rate, also known as accuracy, can be obtained by the sum of the confusion matrix diagonal divided by the total sum:

$$Accuracy = \frac{TP + TN}{TP + TN + FP + FN}$$

Accuracy has its limitations, as covered in the previous section. However, in combination with precision and recall, it provides a relevant indication of the model's performance.

F1-score

It is challenging to compare the performance of different models using more than one indicator. What should we do if one model has better precision but a bad recall? Thinking on this, we use combined metrics such as F1-score, which is computed using both precision and recall:

$$F_1 = \frac{2 \times precision \times recall}{precision + recall} = \frac{2 \times TP}{2 \times TP + FP + FN}$$

By plotting the F1-score, we get a smooth surface:

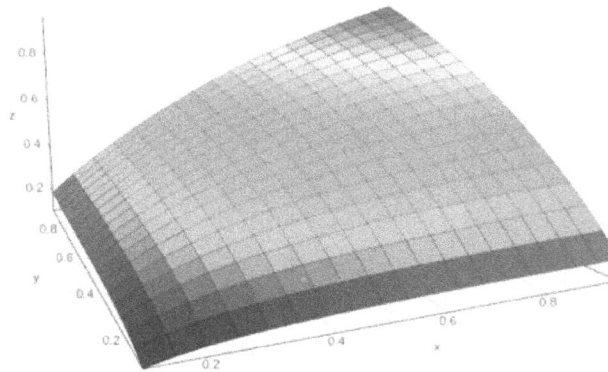

Figure 12.3: F1-score surface

The absence of saddle regions and sharp changes suggests that the F1-score is a good candidate for automatic **hyperparameter optimization**. In hyperparameter optimization, an algorithm generates different sets of hyperparameters, choosing the best one by using a fitness function to compare their performance. A popular approach to achieve this is using **genetic algorithms** to generate candidates and the F1-score as the fitness function.

Genetic algorithms [4] is another bio-inspired category of algorithms used in machine learning, usually applied to optimization problems. Covering them in detail is beyond the scope of this book.

Note: The reader can check the book Learning Genetic Algorithms with Python, Ivan Gridin, BPB, 2021, to learn more about how to use genetic algorithms to solve problems.

Experiment 1: Implementing confusion matrix and derivated indicators

Implementing a confusion matrix for binary classification problems can be trivial. However, calculating these matrices for multiclass problems may introduce some performance challenges. In this experiment, we will implement the confusion matrix and its derived metrics using Eigen.

Multiclass tasks

In addition to binary classification problems, confusion matrices can be applied to **multiclass tasks**. In a multiclass task, there are more than two classes, and each instance is assigned to only one label. A good example of a multiclass dataset is MNIST, in which there are ten classes, and each image is assigned to only one of them.

In a regular scenario, the ground truth data and the predicted consist of two lists containing one-hot encoded arrays. Consider the following example where TRUE represents the ground truth label data, and PRED represents the output predictions of an unknown classifier:

```
1.  int main(int, char **)
2.  {
3.
4.      Eigen::Tensor<float, 2> TRUE(20, 3);
5.      TRUE.
    setValues({{0, 1, 0}, {1, 0, 0}, {0, 0, 1}, {0, 1, 0}, {0, 1, 0},
6.                      {0, 1, 0}, {1, 0, 0}, {0, 1, 0}, {0, 1, 0}, {1,
    0, 0},
7.                      {0, 1, 0}, {0, 1, 0}, {1, 0, 0}, {0, 0, 1}, {0,
    0, 1},
8.
    {0, 1, 0}, {1, 0, 0}, {0, 1, 0}, {1, 0, 0}, {0, 0, 1}});
9.
10.     Eigen::Tensor<float, 2> PRED(20, 3);
11.     PRED.
    setValues({{1, 0, 0}, {1, 0, 0}, {0, 0, 1}, {1, 0, 0}, {0, 1, 0},
12.
    {0, 0, 1}, {0, 1, 0}, {0, 1, 0}, {0, 1, 0}, {1, 0, 0},
13.                      {0, 1, 0}, {1, 0, 0}, {1, 0, 0}, {0, 1, 0}, {0,
    0, 1},
14.
    {0, 1, 0}, {0, 1, 0}, {0, 1, 0}, {0, 0, 1}, {1, 0, 0}});
15.
16.     auto confusion_matrix = calc_confusion_matrix(TRUE, PRED);
17.
18.     std::cout << confusion_matrix << "\n";
19.
20.     return 0;
21. }
```

If the classifier perfectly predicts the data, PRED is equal to TRUE. However, some mispredictions result in divergences between the two arrays. The confusion matrix provides an easy way to measure these divergences.

Using Eigen, we can calculate this confusion matrix using the following function:

```
1.  Eigen::Tensor<int, 2> calc_confusion_
    matrix(const Tensor_2D &TRUE, const Tensor_2D &PRED)
2.  {
3.      if (TRUE.dimension(0) != PRED.dimension(0) || TRUE.
    dimension(1) != PRED.dimension(1))
4.      {
5.          throw std::invalid_
    argument("The dimensions of parameters do not match");
6.      }
7.      if (TRUE.dimension(1) < 2)
8.      {
9.          throw std::invalid_argument("The number of class-
    es need to be greater or equals to 2");
10.     }
11.
12.     const int num_registers = TRUE.dimension(0);
13.     const int num_classes = TRUE.dimension(1);
14.     Eigen::Tensor<int, 2> result(num_classes, num_classes);
15.     result.setZero();
16.
17.     const Eigen::array<Eigen::IndexPair<int>, 1> contract_
    dims = {Eigen::IndexPair<int>(1, 0)};
18.     DimArray<1> max_dim({1});
19.     DimArray<1> sum_dim({0});
20.     DimArray<2> bcast_dim = {1, num_classes};
21.     const Eigen::array<int, 2> reshape_dim = {num_registers, 1};
22.
23.     auto PRED_one_hot = book::utils::one_hot<TYPE>(PRED);
24.
25.     for (size_t clazz = 0; clazz < num_classes; ++clazz)
26.     {
27.
28.         Tensor_2D mold(num_classes, num_classes);
29.         mold.setZero();
30.         mold(clazz, clazz) = 1;
31.
32.         auto matches = TRUE.contract(mold, contract_dims).
    maximum(max_dim).reshape(reshape_dim).broadcast(bcast_dim);
```

```
33.
34.             auto prod = (PRED_one_hot * matches).cast<int>();
35.             auto conters = prod.sum(sum_dim);
36.
37.             result.chip<0>(clazz) = conters;
38.      }
39.
40.      return result;
41. }
```

The line:

```
1. auto mask = TRUE.contract(mold, contract_dims).maximum(max_dim).
   reshape(reshape_dim).broadcast(bcast_dim);
```

Generates a mask like that:

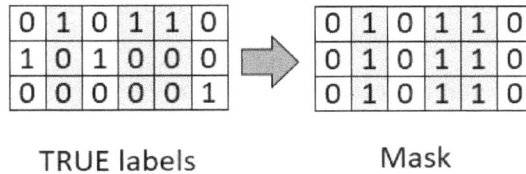

Figure 12.4: *A mask to calculate the confusion matrix*

In this mask, the columns with registers of class-0 are filled with 1's. The other columns are all zero. This mask is used by the next two lines to find the counters for class-0 (*Figure 12.5*):

```
1. auto prod = PRED * mask;
2. auto conters = prod.sum(sum_dim).cast<int>();
```

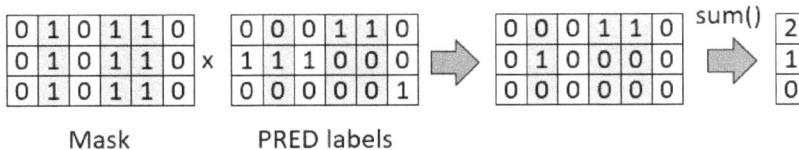

Figure 12.5: *Computing counters of class-0*

The program repeats these steps for class-1 and class-2, then outputs the resulting confusion matrix:

Figure 12.6: *Confusion matrix obtained by our program*

Let us put these values in a convenient layout:

		Predicted Labels		
		Class 0	Class 1	Class 2
Actual Labels	Class 0	3	2	1
	Class 1	3	6	1
	Class 2	1	1	2

Figure 12.7: Example of a confusion matrix for a 3-class dataset

Using the preceding figure, it is easy to figure out some counters. The values in the diagonal are correct predictions. That is, the classifier correctly predicted 3 instances of class-0, 6 instances of class-1, and only 2 instances of class-2.

The values below the diagonal are called false negatives, representing misclassifications. The matrix shows that 3 instances classified as class-0 are, actually, class-1. One instance was classified as class-1, but, indeed, it is class-2.

The values above the diagonal are also counters of wrong classifications. They represent false positives. For example, 2 instances were classified as class-1 although they are, in fact, class-0 instances.

Once we have the confusion matrix, we can evaluate the derived metrics such as precision, recall, accuracy, and F1-score, as shown:

```
1. float precision(const size_t class_
   index, const Eigen::Tensor<int, 2> & confusion_matrix) {
2.     auto column = confusion_matrix.chip<1>(class_index);
3.     float total = ((Eigen::Tensor<int, 0>)(column.sum()))(0);
4.     float tp = confusion_matrix(class_index, class_index);
5.     float result = tp / total;
6.     return result;
7. }
8.
9. float recall(const size_t class_
   index, const Eigen::Tensor<int, 2> & confusion_matrix) {
10.    auto row = confusion_matrix.chip<0>(class_index);
11.    float total = ((Eigen::Tensor<int, 0>)(row.sum()))(0);
12.    float tp = confusion_matrix(class_index, class_index);
```

```
13.    float result = tp / total;
14.    return result;
15. }
16.
17. float accuracy(const Eigen::Tensor<int, 2> & confusion_matrix) {
18.    Eigen::Tensor<int, 0> trace = confusion_matrix.trace();
19.    float diagonal = trace(0);
20.    float total = ((Eigen::Tensor<int, 0>)(confusion_matrix.sum()))(0);
21.    float result = diagonal / total;
22.    return result;
23. }
24.
25. float f1_score(const size_t class_
    index, const Eigen::Tensor<int, 2> & confusion_matrix) {
26.    float _precision = precision(class_index, confusion_matrix);
27.    float _recall = recall(class_index, confusion_matrix);
28.    float result = 2*_precision*_recall/ (_precision + _recall);
29.    return result;
30. }
```

Now, we can invoke these functions as follows:

```
1. std::cout << "\nprecision class 0: « << precision(0, confusion_
   matrix) << "\n";
2. std::cout << "precision class 1: " << precision(1, confusion_
   matrix) << "\n";
3. std::cout << "precision class 2: " << precision(2, confusion_
   matrix) << "\n\n";
4.
5. std::cout << "recall class 0: " << recall(0, confusion_
   matrix) << "\n";
6. std::cout << "recall class 1: " << recall(1, confusion_
   matrix) << "\n";
7. std::cout << "recall class 2: " << recall(2, confusion_
   matrix) << "\n\n";
8.
9. std::cout << "f1_score class 0: " << f1_score(0, confusion_
   matrix) << "\n";
10. std::cout << "f1_score class 1: " << f1_score(1, confusion_
    matrix) << "\n";
```

```
11. std::cout << "f1_score class 2: " << f1_score(2, confusion_
    matrix) << "\n\n";

12.

13. std::cout << "accuracy: " << accuracy(confusion_matrix) << "\n";
```

As a result, the program generates the following output:

Figure 12.8: Obtaining derived metrics from a confusion matrix

Hard-max and one-hot encoding

In the previous example, the PRED tensor consists of 0's and 1's:

```
1. Tensor_2D PRED(20, 3);
2. PRED.setValues({{1, 0, 0}, {1, 0, 0}, {0, 0, 1}, {1, 0, 0},
   {0, 1, 0}, {0, 0, 1}, {0, 1, 0}, {0, 1, 0}, {0, 1, 0}, {1, 0, 0},
3.                 {0, 1, 0}, {1, 0, 0}, {1, 0, 0}, {0, 1, 0},
   {0, 0, 1}, {0, 1, 0}, {0, 1, 0}, {0, 1, 0}, {0, 0, 1}, {1, 0, 0}});
```

In practice, usually PRED is filled with scores, such as logits from a softmax output layer:

```
1. PRED.setValues({{0.44, 0.37, 0.18}, {0.61, 0.29, 0.09},
   {0.01, 0.06, 0.92}, {0.67, 0.19, 0.13154},
2. {0.11, 0.83, 0.05}, {0.2, 0.30, 0.48}, {0.04, 0.60, 0.34},
   {0.19, 0.77, 0.027},
3.                 {0.43, 0.54, 0.02}, {0.61, 0.12, 0.25},
   {0.45, 0.47, 0.06}, {0.99, 0.0, 0.01},
4.                 {0.47, 0.44, 0.07}, {0.11, 0.75, 0.13},
   {0.09, 0.28, 0.62}, {0.31, 0.36, 0.32},
5.                 {0.39, 0.56, 0.04}, {0.22, 0.53, 0.24},
   {0.13, 0.08, 0.77}, {0.92, 0.08, 0.0}});
```

For situations like this, there is a popular operation called **hard max**. Basically, hard max converts the provided tensor using one-hot encoding:

```
one_hot({0.44, 0.37, 0.18}) = {1, 0, 0}
```

Once PRED is one-hot encoded, we can compute the confusion matrix as described earlier.

Other types of metrics

We can use many other metrics in addition to those derived from the confusion matrix, as discussed in this section.

Using cost functions as a performance metric

Cost functions are functions designed to drive the training search over the parameter space. However, there is no problem in using a cost function to measure the model performance.

Furthermore, there is no problem at all in training the model using one type of cost function but evaluating the model performance using a different cost function. Indeed, combining different cost functions to train and evaluate a model is quite common.

Why use a different cost function as a metric? In general, metrics are intended to provide human-readable results. Rarely, the best cost function to train a model is also the best one to be recognized by human inference. That is the reason why we often use **mse()** or **rmse()** as the performance evaluation metric even though the cost function to actually fit the model is a different function.

Application specific metrics

Some tasks are better evaluated using specific metrics. Application-specific metrics are useful only for a specific and well-defined task. A good example is **Bilingual Evaluation Understudy** (**BLEU**), a metric for evaluating the quality of machine-translated texts. Of course, using an application-specific metric to evaluate the performance of a different task can be useless.

In the forthcoming chapters, we will learn how to use a specific metric to measure the quality of object localization systems called **Intersection over Union** (**IoU**). Refer to the following figure:

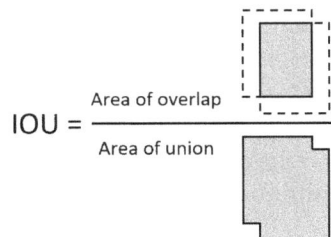

$$IOU = \frac{\text{Area of overlap}}{\text{Area of union}}$$

Figure 12.9: *IoU metric for object localization systems*

We will cover the IoU metric in detail in *Chapter 17, Developing an Object Localization System.*

Understanding cross-validation

Data is abundant, but quality data, labeled data, is usually scarce. Consider that you are developing a model to make predictions of a rare astrophysics phenomenon. All the available data is a few dozen observations made by human civilization over two thousand years. Needless to say, you cannot obtain new real data to increase your dataset in a short time.

If you are planning to use hold-out to validate your model, there is no way other than to retain a significant part of the registers (20% or 30%) to verify whether the model is overfitting. As you know, this data cannot be used to train your model. Now, you are in a trade-off: if you use few registers to train, you will likely end up with an overfitted model. On the other hand, if you use the full dataset to train, you cannot check if the model is overfitting or not.

The solution is to use other alternatives to hold out. In fact, we can use different validation schemas for scenarios like this, such as the cross-validation schemas introduced in this section.

Stratification

Regardless of whether you have small or huge data, stratification [1] is always worth it. Consider again the case where the dataset is divided into 950 instances of class B and 50 instances of class A. Now, imagine that we will use a regular holdout training schema where twenty percent of instances are assigned to the validation set, and the remaining data is assigned to the training data. Now, imagine that, for the sake of randomization, all 50 instances of class A end in the validation dataset. It is hard to think that the model will be able to learn how to recognize instances of class A if there is no one register of this class in the training dataset.

In stratification, both the training and validation datasets have the same proportion of each class. Thus, in the scenario where 50 of the 1000 registers are class A, approximately 10 will be included in the validation set, and the 40 remaining will be included in the training set. Thus, using stratification provides some guarantee that each class is similarly represented in either training or validation datasets.

k-fold cross-validation

Although useful, stratification is only part of the solution to the problem of uneven class representation. In k-fold cross-validation all the data is used to train, and all the data is used to validate the model.

As the name suggests, in k-fold cross-validation, the data is divided into approximately equal k subsets called folds. Then, we train the model k times. In each training course, one-fold is used to validate, and the remainder is used to train the model. This schema is represented in the following figure:

Figure 12.10: An example of a 5-fold cross-validation

The example above divides the data into five folds. As a result, we will train the model five times, or rounds. In each round, four folds are used to compose a single training dataset and one-fold is used only for validation. In the end, we have five sets of metrics. We average them to obtain the overall model performance.

The usual values of k are 5, 10, and 20. The advantage of this approach is that every fold is used to train and validate but in different turns. The disadvantage is the cost to train the model by k times, which can be time expensive. Since cross-validation is recommended to scenarios with few data, this disadvantage is not actually a problem.

Of course, it makes sense to train the models using stratified k-fold cross-validation. In stratified k-fold cross-validation, every fold has about the same proportion of instances for each class. This is how the example in the next section is implemented.

Experiment 2: Implementing stratified k-fold cross-validation

Dividing the data into k subsets is not a difficult task at all. However, guarantee that each subset has roughly the same proportion of each class introduces some challenges. The canonical way to implement stratification is using priority-oriented tree data structures known as **heaps**. To be more precise, the example in this section uses min-heaps and hash maps [5] to provide a final time cost of $O(N \log(K))$, where N is the number of instances and K is the number of folds.

Min-heaps [6] are trees where each node has a key that is greater than or equal to the key of its parent. Check the following representation of a min-heap:

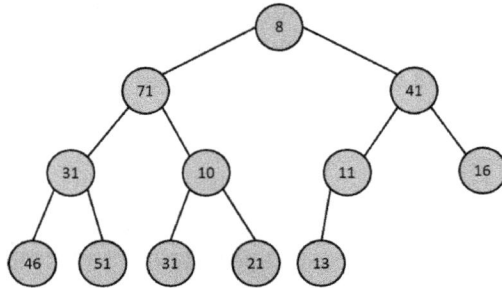

Figure 12.11: *Example of min-heap*

In our algorithm, the key of each node is a fold, and we use a heap like this for each class. The node at the top holds the fold with the smallest number of instances for that class.

Check the pseudo-code of our stratification algorithm below:

```
stratify(registers, K, M):
begin
    // K is the number of folds
    // M is the number of classes
    // initialize K folds
    folds: vector(K)
    // initialize M min-heaps, one for each class
    heaps: map
    for each clazz in M:
        heaps[clazz] = min-heap(clazz)
    // loop over each instance to assign it to the right fold
    for each instance in registers:
        clazz = find_instance_clazz(instance)
        min-heap = heaps[clazz]
        fold = min-heap.top()
        fold.add_instance(instance)
        min-heap.update_order()
    return folds
end
```

The relevant time computational cost of this algorithm resides in the loop:

```
    for each instance in registers:
        //...
```

Indeed, we cannot do any better than $O(N)$ time here. Almost all the operations inside the loop have $O(1)$ time cost. The exception is **update_order()**, which has a cost of $O(log(K))$.

Thus, the overall time cost is $O(N\ log(K))$. The significative space cost consists of data within the folds, counting $O(N)$ memory plus $O(K)$ to store the folds themselves and $O(M\ K)$ to store M min-heaps with size **K**. Note that, in general, **K** and **N** are small values.

Coding the stratification algorithm

Once we modeled our algorithm, let us start defining a **Fold** class:

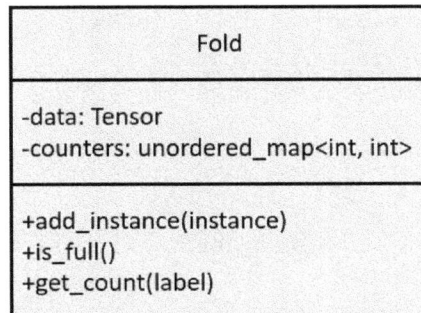

Fold
-data: Tensor -counters: unordered_map<int, int>
+add_instance(instance) +is_full() +get_count(label)

Figure 12.12: *UML representation of our Fold class*

The benefit of using **Unified Modeling Language** (**UML**) [7] diagrams is to communicate the more important aspects of a software component easily. In the case of the **Fold** class, we can note that each fold object stores the respective data and an unordered map to represent the respective counters of each class. This map is useful to avoid re-scanning the whole data every time we need to select a fold.

Note: We use an `std::unordered_map` **here because the order of counters does not matter. Thus, an unordered map is faster and more suitable to this function than a** `std::map`.

Other details can be observed in the following **Fold** implementation:

```
1. class Fold {
2.
3. public:
4.     Fold(long int instance_size, long int num_
   classes, size_t capacity) : num_classes(num_
   classes), capacity(capacity), instance_count(0) {
5.         this->data = Eigen::Tensor<float, 2>(capacity, instance_
   size);
6.         this->data.setZero();
7.     }
8.
9.     void add_instance(const Eigen::Tensor<float, 1> &instance) {
```

```
10.          if (!this->is_full()) {
11.              // storing the instance
12.              data.chip<0>(instance_count) = instance;
13.
14.              // increment counters
15.              auto label_index = find_class_index(instance, this->num_
     classes);
16.              ++this->counters[label_index];
17.              ++this->instance_count;
18.          }
19.      }
20.
21.      bool is_full() const {
22.          return this->instance_count >= this->capacity;
23.      }
24.
25.      const int get_count(int label) const {
26.          int result = 0;
27.          if (this->counters.find(label) != this->counters.end()) {
28.              result = this->counters.at(label);
29.          }
30.          return result;
31.      }
32.
33. private:
34.      long int capacity;
35.      long int num_classes;
36.      Eigen::Tensor<float, 2> data;
37.      size_t instance_count;
38.      std::unordered_map<int, int> counters;
39. };
```

We can store our folds in a container:

```
1. std::vector<Fold> folds;
2. folds.reserve(num_folds);
3.
4. for (size_t i = 0; i < num_folds; ++i) {
5.     Fold fold(instance_size, num_classes, capacity);
6.     folds.emplace_back(fold);
7. }
```

Checking the **add_instance()** method, you may have noted the invocation of **find_class_index**:

```
1. Eigen::Index find_class_
   index(const Eigen::Tensor<float, 1> &instance, long int num_
   classes) {
2.     long int instance_size = instance.size();
3.     Eigen::array<Eigen::Index, 1> offset = {instance_size - num_
   classes};
4.     Eigen::array<Eigen::Index, 1> extents = {num_classes};
5.     auto label_vec = instance.slice(offset, extents);
6.     Eigen::Tensor<Eigen::Index, 0> label_index = label_vec.
   argmax(0);
7.     auto result = label_index(0);
8.     return result;
9. }
```

This function uses the Tensor **argmax()** reducer to find the label index.

> **Note: argmax() is a undocumented Eigen Tensor reducer used to find the index of coefficient with maximum value for a given axis (in our application, we use axis 0). Note that argmax() is different of the maximum() reducer which provides the maximum value itself.**

Now, we can define our min-heap as follows:

```
1. #include <queue>
2. using min_heap = std::priority_queue<Fold *, std::vector<-
   Fold *>, std::function<bool(Fold *, Fold *)>>;
```

In C++, we implement min-heaps using the STL class **std::priority_queue** [8]. In min-heaps, the object with minimum value is always available by the **top()** method. Thus, we can quickly find the fold with the smallest number of instances, at constant time.

We can initialize the heaps and store them in a map as follows:

```
1. std::unordered_map<int, min_heap> heaps;
2.
3. for (size_t I = 0; i < num_classes; ++i) {
4.
5.     auto compare = [i](const Fold *a, const Fold *b) {
6.         int count_a = a->get_count(i);
7.         int count_b = b->get_count(i);
8.         bool result = count_a > count_b;
9.         return result;
```

```
10.    };
11.
12.    auto heap = min_heap(compare);
13.    for (auto &fold : folds) {
14.        heap.push(&fold);
15.    }
16.
17.    heaps[i] = heap;
18. }
```

We have one heap to each class. This way, we can find the fold with the minimum number of each specific label.

Finally, we can insert each instance in the respective **Fold**:

```
1. size_t row = 0;
2. while (row < num_registers) {
3.
4.     auto instance = data.chip<0>(row);
5.     auto label = find_class_index(instance, num_classes);
6.     auto &heap = heaps.at(label);
7.
8.     Fold *fold = heap.top();
9.     heap.pop();
10.
11.    if (!fold->is_full()) {
12.        fold->add_instance(instance);
13.        ++row;
14.        heap.push(fold);
15.    }
16. }
```

The common idiom to update priority queues in C++ is to remove the top (using **pop()**) and insert it again (using **push()**). This forces the heap to reorder itself so that the smallest element moves to the top of the heap.

Now, we can print the distributions of labels in each fold to check if our algorithm actually works:

```
1. int total_registers = 0;
2. for (size_t fold_index = 0; fold_index < num_folds; ++fold_index) {
3.
4.     Fold &fold = folds.at(fold_index);
```

```
5.      std::cout << "Fold #" << fold_index << ":\nLabels:\t";
6.      for (size_t clazz = 0; clazz < num_classes; ++clazz) {
7.          std::cout << clazz << "\t";
8.      }
9.      std::cout << "\n#regs:\t";
10.     for (size_t clazz = 0; clazz < num_classes; ++clazz) {
11.         int count = fold.get_count(clazz);
12.         total_registers += count;
13.         std::cout << count << "\t";
14.     }
15.     std::cout << "\n\n";
16. }
```

Let us check out our algorithm in practice. In the example below, we use a small subset of MNIST with only 200 registers, dividing them into five folds:

```
1.  auto data = load_mnist_chunck("../../data/mnist", 200, true, seed);
2.  std::cout << "Data loaded!\n";
3.  std::cout << "data dimensions: " << data.dimensions() << "\n";
4.
5.  const long int num_registers = data.dimension(0);
6.  const long int instance_size = data.dimension(1);
7.  const long int num_classes = 10;
8.  const size_t num_folds = 5;
```

This program generates the following output:

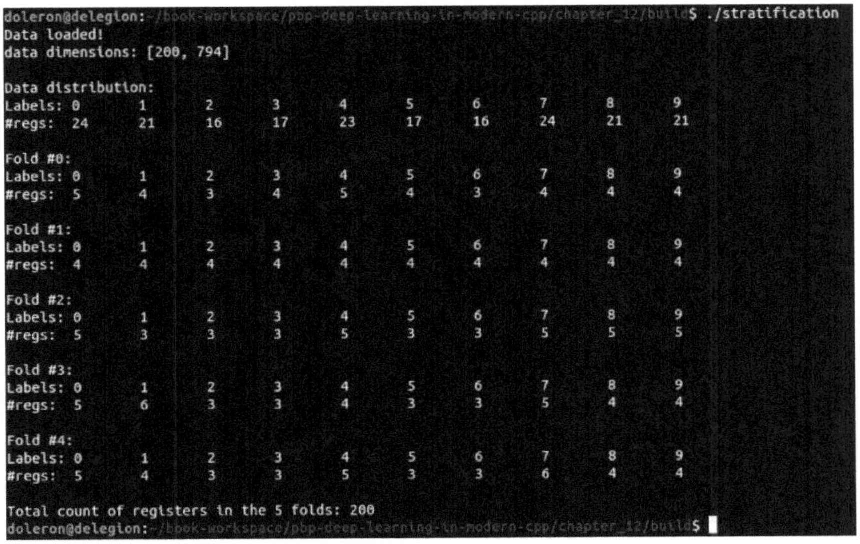

Figure 12.13: Using stratified 5-fold cross validation

In this example, there are only 17 instances of a handwritten number 3. These 17 images were allocated in the 5 folds in the following way: (4, 4, 3, 3, 3). Note that each fold has no more than 40 registers.

> **Note: To learn more about heaps, min-heaps, hashtables, and algorithm complexity we recommend the book Advanced Data Structures and Algorithms, Abirami and Priya, BPB, 2023.**

The smaller the data, the bigger the problems. K-fold cross-validation provides good results when a small dataset comes into play. Of course, the definition of what is a small dataset depends on the underlying hardware to train and the target task to perform.

> **Note: As a rule of thumb, if the number of registers is less than 30 times the number of features, it is time to think of how to deal with a small dataset.**

Cross-validation, data augmentation, and the regularization techniques introduced in the last chapter are important things to talk about in a project with small datasets.

Once the validation schema is set, we can train our model. The next section introduces minibatch, a very common approach to training models by partitioning the dataset into small chunks called minibatches.

Training using mini-batches

Let us revisit the gradient descent pseudocode:

```
Gradient-Descent (W, X, T, η, C, EPOCHS) :
BEGIN:
    for each epoch in EPOCHS:
        Y = forward(X)
        ∇W = backward(Y, T, C)
        W = W - η ∇W
END
```

So far, we have trained our models using the full training dataset at once to obtain Y. In other words, all the training data is used together to calculate the cost and the gradients. This approach works well. However, this is not the best alternative for all scenarios. One notorious scenario where this approach does not work is when we have a huge dataset that does not fit in the computer memory. For scenarios like that, we can use a technique called **minibatching**.

The idea behind using mini batching is to divide the training data into smaller packages called batches (or mini-batches). Thus, in each epoch, the cost of each batch is calculated, resulting in one weight update for each batch. Check out the following modified gradient descent pseudo-code:

```
Minibatch-Gradient-Descent (W, X, T, η, C, EPOCHS, mini-batch-size) :
BEGIN:
    for each epoch in EPOCHS:
        minibatches = divide-in-batches(X, T)
        for each batch in minibatches:
            Y = forward(batch.X)
            ∇W = backward(Y, batch.T, C)
            W = W - η ∇W
END
```

As a result, for each epoch the algorithm performs **size(X)/mini-batch-size** updates. The size of the mini batch does not always perfectly divide the dataset size. In cases like this, there are three alternatives:

- The last batch is smaller than **mini-batch-size**

- Discarding the last batch.

- Filling the missing registers in the last batch with data from other batches.

To reduce any unexpected bias, the mini batches are randomly **sampled without replacement**. This means that, for each epoch, the sequence of each mini batch is different.

The mini-batch size is usually found experimentally, like any other hyperparameter. Aiming to reduce the overall spent time, sometimes people set the batch size using a multiple of the underlying hardware's vectorization units, such as 16, 32, 256, 1024, 2048, etc. Another common approach is to set the mini-batch size focusing only on the model training performance. Indeed, the mini-batch size has an important relationship with the algorithm convergence time, as illustrated in the next experiment.

Experiment 3: Training a model using mini batching

This experiment covers the training of a model using mini batches. The experiment consists of training the same model with different mini-batch sizes, aiming to get insight into how this hyperparameter affects the training performance.

The first step is to define the model. Let us implement a simple 3-layer model as follows:

```
1. template <typename Device>
2. class Model {
3.
4. public:
5.
6.     Model(Device &device) {
```

```
7.
8.          Tensor_2D W1(28*28, 128);
9.          glorot_uniform_initializer(rng, W1);
10.         this-
    >dense_1 = new DenseLayer(device, W1, new ReLU<Device, 2>(device));
11.
12.         Tensor_2D W2(128, 64);
13.         glorot_uniform_initializer(rng, W2);
14.         this-
    >dense_2 = new DenseLayer(device, W2, new ReLU<Device, 2>(device));
15.
16.         Tensor_2D WC(64, 10);
17.         glorot_uniform_initializer(rng, WC);
18.         this->output_layer = new SoftmaxCrossEntropyLayer(devi
    ce, WC);
19.    }
20.
21.    //...
22.
23. private:
24.    DenseLayer<Device> *dense_1;
25.    DenseLayer<Device> *dense_2;
26.    SoftmaxCrossEntropyLayer<Device> *output_layer;
27. };
```

This simple model consists of two dense layers using ReLU followed by one softmax layer as output layer. The following figure represent this network:

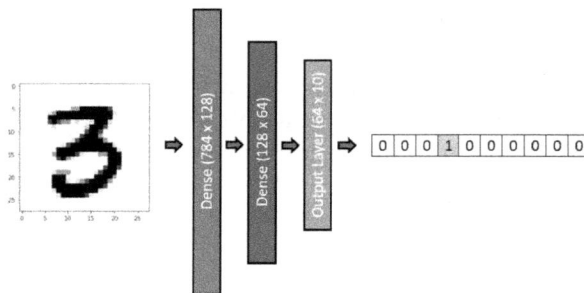

Figure 12.14: *Model used in this experiment*

The training consists of feeding the model with *28x28* images from the MNIST dataset and compare the network output with the ground-truth output.

There are three important methods in this model class we must discuss here:

```
1.  void forward(const Tensor_2D &input) {
2.      this->dense_1->forward(input);
3.      this->dense_2->forward(this->dense_1->get_output());
4.      this->output_layer->forward(this->dense_2->get_output());
5.  }
6.
7.  void backward(const Tensor_2D &upstream) {
8.      this->output_layer->backward(upstream, true);
9.      this->dense_2->backward(output_layer->get_downstream(), true);
10.     this->dense_1->backward(this->dense_2->get_downstream(), false);
11. }
12.
13. void update(const float learning_rate, int epoch) {
14.     this->dense_1->update(learning_rate, epoch);
15.     this->dense_2->update(learning_rate, epoch);
16.     this->output_layer->update(learning_rate, epoch);
17. }
```

The training algorithm invokes these three methods to perform the forward computation to obtain the network output, the backward computation of gradients, and finally, to update the model.

As explained in *Chapter 10, Coding the Backpropagation Algorithm*, the training uses the difference between the network output and the ground-truth to calculate gradients. These gradients are used to update the weights within the layers. This procedure is implemented in the following code:

```
1.  template <typename MODEL, typename GEN>
2.  void training(MODEL &model, GEN rng, const Tensor_2D &training_
    images, const Tensor_2D &training_
    labels, const Tensor_2D &validation_
    images, const Tensor_2D &validation_labels,
    const int minibatch_size, bool verbose = false) {
3.
4.      CategoricalCrossEntropy cost_fn;
5.
6.      const int MAX_EPOCHS = 20;
7.      const float learning_rate = 0.1f;
8.
9.      int epoch = 0;
```

```
10.    while (epoch < MAX_EPOCHS) {
11.
12.        auto begin = high_resolution_clock::now();
13.
14.        Batches batches(rng, minibatch_size, &training_
   images, &training_labels);
15.
16.        Batch<2, 2> * batch = batches.next();
17.
18.        while (batch) {
19.
20.            model.forward(batch->X);
21.            model.backward(batch->T);
22.            model.update(learning_rate, epoch);
23.
24.            batch = batches.next();
25.        }
26.
27.        auto end = high_resolution_clock::now();
28.        auto duration = duration_cast<milliseconds>(end - begin);
29.
30.        auto training_pred = model.predict(training_images);
31.        float training_loss = cost_fn.evaluate(training_
   labels, training_pred);
32.        float training_acc = accuracy(training_labels, training_
   pred);
33.
34.        auto validation_pred = model.predict(validation_images);
35.        float validation_acc = accuracy(validation_
   labels, validation_pred);
36.        float validation_loss = cost_fn.evaluate(validation_
   labels, validation_pred);
37.
38.        if (verbose) {
39.            std::cout
40.                << "epoch:\t" << epoch << "\t"
41.                << "took:\t" << duration.count() << " mills\t"
42.                << "\ttraining_loss:\t" << training_loss
43.                << "\ttraining_acc:\t" << training_acc
44.                << "\tvalidation_loss:\t" << validation_loss
```

```
45.                        << "\tvalidation_acc:\t" << validation_acc
46.                        << "\n";
47.            }
48.
49.         epoch++;
50.
51.    }
52.
53. }
```

The critical point in this code is how the dataset is sliced into mini batches to feed the training:

```
1. Batches batches(rng, minibatch_size, &training_images, &training_
   labels);
2.
3. Batch<2, 2> * batch = batches.next();
4.
5. while (batch) {
6.
7.     model.forward(batch->X);
8.     model.backward(batch->T);
9.     model.update(learning_rate, epoch);
10.
11.    batch = batches.next();
12. }
```

Thus, for each epoch, the training loops for a number of steps, given by:

$$steps = \text{ceil}\left(\frac{number\ of\ training\ instances}{size\ of\ minibatch}\right)$$

We can invoke the model training as shown in the following program:

```
1. int main(int, char **)
2. {
3.
4.     const auto [training_images, training_labels, validation_
   images, validation_labels] = load_mnist("data/mnist");
5.     std::cout << "Data loaded!\n";
6.     std::cout << "training_images: " << training_images.
   dimensions() << "\n";
7.     std::cout << "training_labels: " << training_labels.
   dimensions() << "\n";
```

```
8.      std::cout << "validation_images: " << validation_images.
    dimensions() << "\n";
9.      std::cout << "validation_labels: " << validation_labels.
    dimensions() << "\n\n";
10.
11.     const int threads = std::thread::hardware_concurrency();
12.     Eigen::ThreadPool tp(threads);
13.     Eigen::ThreadPoolDevice device(&tp, threads);
14.
15.     std::cout << std::setprecision(4);
16.
17.     Model model(device);
18.     int minibatch_size = 500;
19.     training(model, rng, training_images, training_
    labels, validation_images, validation_labels, minibatch_size, true);
20.
21.     return 0;
22. }
```

Running this program results in an output similar to the following:

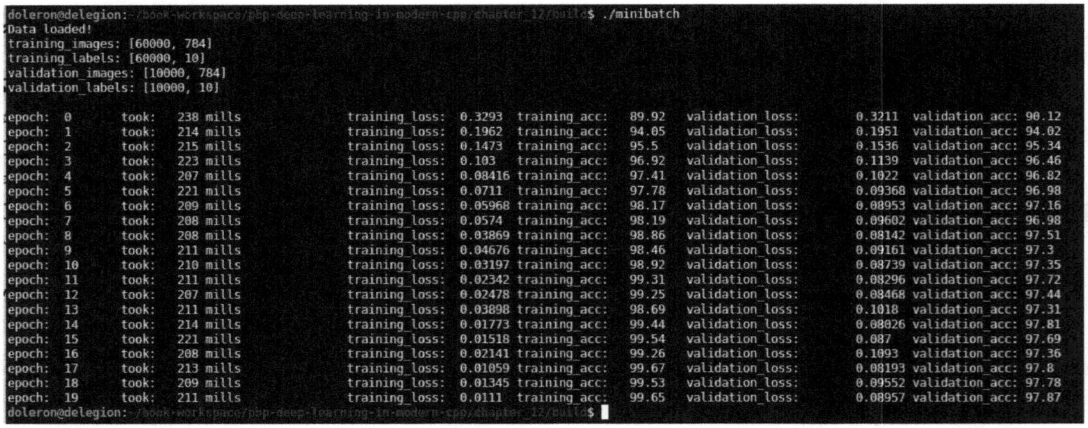

Figure 12.15: Training MNIST using mini-batch size 128

Note: Due to random factors such as the initialization of weights, for each execution this program provides a different result.

In this example, during one epoch the training loops by **60,000/500 = 120** steps, one step to each mini batch. As a result, the training performs 120 weight updates in each epoch. This explains (in part) why the model achieves rough 93% of validation performance only in the first epoch!

We can compare several different mini-batch configurations to understand how the choice of mini-batch affects the final model performance:

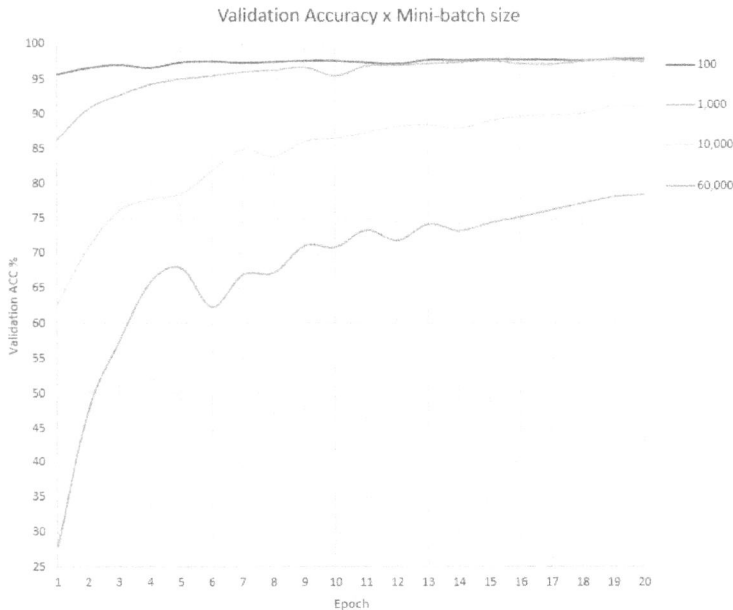

Figure 12.16: Training using different mini-batching sizes

It is obvious the significant performance gain when using small batches. In general, using small batches is beneficial even though there are a few drawbacks. Let us start listing the advantages:

- **Memory size**: Using the full dataset at once to train the model requires putting all the data in memory. For some datasets, this is not possible. For example, the ImageNet training dataset has 138 GB of images. Loading all this data in memory is not feasible for regular machines. By using mini batches, only a small part of the whole data (the batch) needs to be loaded into memory at each step.

- **Regularization**: Using small batches includes a random signal that reduces the change of overfitting. In other words, training models with small batches make them less prone to overfitting.

- **Local minima**: Training using the full dataset very often causes the model stuck in a local minimum. The model cannot escape of this situation which is often a poor solution. The use of minibatches injects noise that allows the algorithm to escape from those suboptimal local solutions.

- **Fast convergence**: Since in mini-batching the model is updated several times in each epoch, the convergence is faster if compared to the full-batch mode where only one update is performed in the final of the epoch.

Using small batches also has its drawbacks. The most known are:

- **Overall time cost**: Depending on the underlying IO system and multithread processor units, training using minibatches very often increases the overall training time. Since less data is processed together, less vectorization comes to play, resulting in a longer training time. Fragmenting the memory in small chunks and the batch allocation mechanism can also impact the total time cost.

- **Smaller learning rates**: Using small batches requires using smaller learning rates. The noise of using small batches makes the training more sensitive to the changes of large steps. As a result, using a large learning rate sometimes causes the model to not converge. Thus, a smaller learning rate must be used.

Due to the large size of current real-world datasets and the mentioned benefits, training using minibatches is the ordinary setup for practical projects.

Of course, we can consider using 1 as a mini batch size. This configuration is known as stochastic gradient descent, and it is explained in the next section.

Experiment 4: Implementing stochastic gradient descent

Stochastic gradient descent [9] (**SGD**) is the name given to the execution of gradient descent using mini batches having only one instance. Running gradient descent in this way injects the most noise possible in the training, usually resulting in a beneficial influence in terms of regularization and model performance. On the other side, running one single instance per step does not use vectorization at the most, sometimes resulting in a slow execution.

Although we can use the previous section code to run a mini batch with size 1, this is not recommended because of the overhead of generating batches with size 1. Instead, we should adapt our code as follows:

```
1.  template <typename MODEL>
2.  void training(MODEL &model, const Eigen::Tensor<float, 2> &training_
    images, const Eigen::Tensor<float, 2> &training_labels,
3.              const Eigen::Tensor<float, 2> &validation_
    images, const Eigen::Tensor<float, 2> &validation_
    labels, bool verbose = false) {
4.
5.      CategoricalCrossEntropy cost_fn;
6.
7.      const int MAX_EPOCHS = 20;
8.      const float learning_rate = 0.01f;
9.
10.     const int input_size = training_images.dimension(1);
```

```
11.      const int output_size = training_labels.dimension(1);
12.      const int num_registers = training_labels.dimension(0);
13.
14.      Eigen::array<Eigen::Index, 2> x_extent = {1, input_size};
15.      Eigen::array<Eigen::Index, 2> t_extent = {1, output_size};
16.
17.      int epoch = 0;
18.      while (epoch < MAX_EPOCHS)
19.      {
20.
21.          std::vector<int> indexes(num_registers);
22.          std::iota(indexes.begin(), indexes.end(), 0);
23.          std::shuffle(indexes.begin(), indexes.end(), rd);
24.
25.          auto begin = high_resolution_clock::now();
26.          for (int index : indexes) {
27.              Eigen::array<Eigen::Index, 2> offset = {index, 0};
28.              const Eigen::Tensor<float, 2> X = training_images.
    slice(offset, x_extent);
29.              const Eigen::Tensor<float, 2> T = training_labels.
    slice(offset, t_extent);
30.
31.              model.forward(X);
32.              model.backward(T);
33.              model.update(learning_rate, epoch);
34.          }
35.
36.          auto end = high_resolution_clock::now();
37.          auto duration = duration_cast<milliseconds>(end - begin);
38.
39.          auto training_pred = model.predict(training_images);
40.          float training_acc = accuracy(training_labels, training_pred);
41.          float training_loss = cost_fn.evaluate(training_
    labels, training_pred);
42.
43.          auto validation_pred = model.predict(validation_images);
44.          float validation_acc = accuracy(validation_
    labels, validation_pred);
45.          float validation_loss = cost_fn.evaluate(validation_
    labels, validation_pred);
```

```
46.
47.        if (verbose) {
48.            std::cout
49.                << "epoch:\t" << epoch << "\t"
50.                << "took:\t" << duration.count() << " mills\t"
51.                << "\ttraining_loss:\t" << training_loss
52.                << "\ttraining_acc:\t" << training_acc
53.                << "\tvalidation_loss:\t" << validation_loss
54.                << "\tvalidation_acc:\t" << validation_acc
55.                << "\n";
56.        }
57.
58.        epoch++;
59.
60.    }
61.
62. }
```

This program results in the following output:

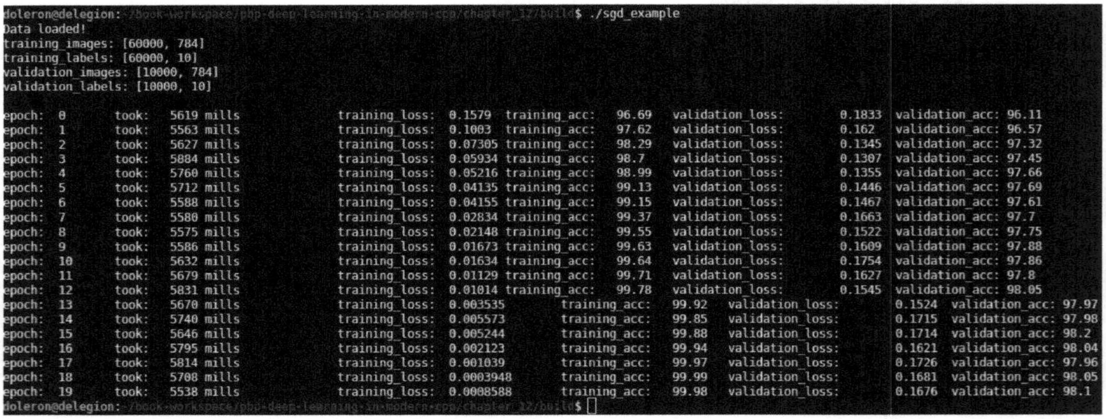

Figure 12.17: Training using SGD

The key point in this implementation is how we are taking single instances from the dataset:

```
1. std::vector<int> indexes(num_registers);
2. std::iota(indexes.begin(), indexes.end(), 0);
3. std::shuffle(indexes.begin(), indexes.end(), rd);
4.
5. auto begin = high_resolution_clock::now();
```

```
6. for (int index : indexes) {
7.     Eigen::array<Eigen::Index, 2> offset = {index, 0};
8.     const Eigen::Tensor<float, 2> X = training_images.
   slice(offset, x_extent);
9.     const Eigen::Tensor<float, 2> T = training_labels.
   slice(offset, t_extent);
10.
11.    model.forward(X);
12.    model.backward(T);
13.    model.update(learning_rate, epoch);
14. }
```

For each epoch, we shuffle the dataset. Of course, because of the performance requirements, we cannot actually shuffle the dataset itself. Instead, we use a vector to store indexes and use these indexes to access each instance. The vector of indexes is then shuffled in each epoch.

As we said when we defined SGD, the algorithm loops over each instance. The overhead causes the training to take longer, achieving thorough six seconds for each epoch.

Terminology of SGD

There is some abuse of terminology in the deep learning community around SGD. Some frameworks, for example, use the term SGD to denote any mode of gradient descent.

The following terminology is more recommended and commonly used, however:

- **Batch gradient descent**: Refer to the execution of gradient descent using the full dataset at once.

- **Stochastic gradient descent**: When executing GD using a single instance per step.

- **Minibatch gradient descent**: When GD uses non-unity fractions of the dataset in each iteration.

The experiments and examples in the forthcoming chapters use mini-batch gradient descent.

Conclusion

This chapter introduced three important concepts: cross-validation, model performance metrics, and mini-batch. We learned how to use confusion matrices and derivated metrics to obtain a reliable understanding of the model performance even when the dataset is not well balanced.

We also learned how to train models using small datasets by using stratified k-fold cross-validation. Finally, the chapter discussed the use of mini batching to achieve the most of the model and training performance. The SGD model was introduced, achieving the top performance on MNIST so far in this book.

The next chapter introduces optimizers and variations of the gradient descent algorithm that improve the algorithm search even more, generally providing better results in terms of time to converge and model performance.

Exercises

1. Consider the following metric called **true negative rate**:

$$True\ negative\ rate = \frac{TN}{TN + FP}$$

   Implement this metric using Eigen given a pre-computed confusion matrix.

2. Explain how a true negative rate can be useful to evaluate the model performance.

3. Train a model with the MNIST dataset using SGD. Use one or more regularization techniques introduced in the previous chapter to obtain a final validation accuracy above 98.5%.

References

[1] Witten, Frank, & Hall, Data Mining, Practical Machine Learning Tools and Techniques, 2011, Morgan Kaufmann.

[2] Paul Meyer, Introductory Probability and Statistical Applications, 1965, Addison-Wesley.

[3] Han, Kamber, & Pei, Data Mining, Concepts and Techniques, 2012, Morgan Kaufmann.

[4] Ivan Gridin, Learning Genetic Algorithms with Python, 2021, BPB.

[5] Abirami and Priya, Advanced Data Structures and Algorithms, 2023, BPB.

[6] Paul E. Black, "min-heap property", in Dictionary of Algorithms and Data Structures [online], Paul E. Black, ed. 17 December 2004. (accessed TODAY) Available from: **https://www.nist.gov/dads/HTML/minheapprop.html**

[7] Martin Fowler, UML Distilled, 2004, Addison-Wesley.

[8] std::priority_queue, available at **https://en.cppreference.com/w/cpp/container/priority_queue**

[9] Leon Bottou, Stochastic Gradient Learning in Neural Networks, 1991, available at **https://leon.bottou.org/publications/pdf/nimes-1991.pdf**

CHAPTER 13

Implementing Optimizers

Introduction

This chapter discusses strategies to improve algorithmic search, specifically the three most popular variations of the gradient descent algorithm: Momentum, RMSProp, and Adam. We will see that these variations, popularly called optimizers, allow us to leverage gradient descent's performance, providing the state-of-the-art in terms of convergence time and quality.

Structure

This is the chapter roadmap:

- Experiments in this chapter
- Optimizing the minimization
- Introducing momentum
- Introducing RMSProp
- Introducing Adam
- Experiment: Comparing optimizers

Objectives

After reading this chapter, the reader will know how to implement the most important variations of gradient descent: **Momentum, RMSProp,** and **Adam.** The reader will understand how these algorithms work and how to apply them to train deep learning models.

Experiments in this chapter

This chapter includes only one experiment:

ID	Description
Exp-13.1	Comparing optimizers

Table 13.1: Chapter experiment list

Optimizing the minimization

Consider the following representation of a hypothetical 2D cost surface:

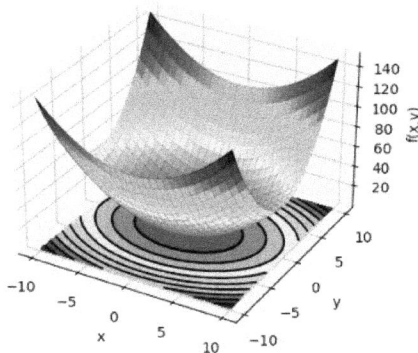

Figure 13.1: Plotting a cost function surface f(x,y)

Now, consider the same surface represented using **level curves** [1]:

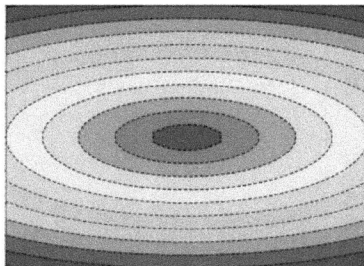

Figure 13.2: Representing the cost surface using contour levels

Very often, due to the particular shape of the cost surface, training a model using gradient descent results in a behavior like this:

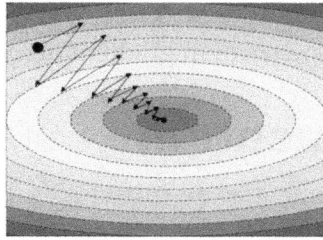

Figure 13.3: Default behavior of updates in gradient descent

The black arrows represent successive weight updates in the algorithm iteration. We can see that they form a zig-zag path by alternating the update direction in each step. Of course, this zig-zag movement is undesirable, eventually increasing the overall convergence time. Can we do better? Yes, we can.

Consider the regular way of how the weight W is updated by the gradient ∇W using the learning rate η in gradient descent:

$$W = W - \eta \nabla W$$

In this chapter, we will explore three techniques that change this rule. Momentum [2] is the first of these three techniques.

Momentum uses the tricky of memorization to change the weight update rule as follows [3]:

$$V = \beta \times V - \eta \nabla W$$

$$W = W + V$$

The expressions above show how to update the weights using momentum by including a memorization element V, which is initially set to zero, and a scalar constant β such as $0 \leq \beta \leq 1$. It turns out that after successive updates of W, V will accumulate a fraction of each update. This fraction is controlled by the hyperparameter β, which is also called momentum.

As a result, using momentum, the training algorithm converges less wildly towards the minimum, as illustrated in the following figure:

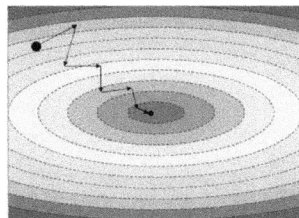

Figure 13.4: Using Momentum to improve the search convergence

Using the metaphor of a physical movement, momentum works similarly to including a kind of mass inertia, reducing the directional changes and speeding up the algorithm convergence.

Let us see how to implement momentum in gradient descent in the following section.

Introducing momentum

Momentum can be easily implemented by including a hook in the **update()** method. Consider our previous version of **update()**:

```
1. void update(const float learning_rate) {
2.     weight = weight - grad * grad.constant(learning_rate);
3. }
```

Now, we can redefine it as follows:

```
1. typedef std::function<Eigen::Tensor<float, 2>(Eigen::Tensor<-
   float, 2>&, float, int)> Optimizer;
2.
3. Optimizer optimizer;
4.
5. void update(const float learning_rate, int epoch) {
6.     auto update = optimizer(grad, learning_rate, epoch);
7.     weight = weight + update;
8. }
```

The object **optimizer** holds any callable object (such as a lambda, a function, or a functor) in which we can pass the gradient, the learning rate, and the current epoch count to obtain the proper weight update. We can define the default update as follows:

```
1. template <int _RANK>
2. class DEFAULT_UPDATE {
3. public:
4.     Eigen::Tensor<float, _RANK> operator()(Eigen::Tensor<float, _
       RANK> &grad, float learning_rate, int epoch) {
5.         Eigen::Tensor<float, _RANK> result = grad * grad.constant(-
           learning_rate);
6.         return result;
7.     }
8.
9. };
```

Set it in the layer initialization:

```
1.  DenseLayer(Device &device, Eigen::Tensor<float, 2> weight, Activa-
    tionFunction<Device, 2> *activation_function) :
2.      Layer<Device, 2, 2>(device, "book.layers.
    dense"), weight(std::move(weight)), activation_function(activation_
    function)
3.  {
4.      grad = weight.constant(0);
5.
6.      optimizer = DEFAULT_UPDATE<2>();
7.  }
```

Note: An object-oriented implementation is not mandatory. We can achieve a similar result by using a pure procedural solution.

Once our hook is set, we can define the **Momentum** functor as follows:

```
1.  template <int _RANK>
2.  class Momentum {
3.
4.  public:
5.      Momentum(float momentum): momentum(momentum) { }
6.      Momentum(): Momentum(0.9) { }
7.
8.      Eigen::Tensor<float, _RANK> operator()(Eigen::Tensor<float, _
    RANK> &grad, float learning_rate, int epoch) {
9.          if (velocity.size() != grad.size()) {
10.             velocity = grad.constant(0);
11.         }
12.         velocity = velocity * grad.constant(momentum) + grad * grad.
    constant(-learning_rate);
13.         return velocity;
14.     }
15.
16. private:
17.     float momentum;
18.     Eigen::Tensor<float, _RANK> velocity;
19. };
```

Finally, we can define a setter to set up the optimizer after constructing a layer:

```
1. DenseLayer<Device> dense(device, initial_
   weight, new ReLU<Device, 2>(device));
2. dense.set_optimizer(Momentum<2>());
```

According to Andrew Ng [4], momentum is always worth it. It means that if we train a model using simple gradient descent, using momentum will always be helpful, resulting in a faster convergence to a minimum.

In recent years, two other different optimization strategies have gained popularity: RMSProp and Adam. Let us start by describing RMSProp in the next section.

Introducing RMSProp

Like Momentum, RMSProp [5] uses the concept of keeping memorization of the previous updates to affect the next updates. However, the way the memorization factor is computed is different.

Consider again the update of weight W given the learning rate η and weight gradient ∇W. In RMSProp, the weight update is obtained [6] by the following expressions:

$$S = \beta \times S + (1 - \beta)\nabla W^2$$

$$W = W - \eta \frac{\nabla W}{\sqrt{S}}$$

We can see the last formula in this way:

$$W = W - \frac{\eta}{\sqrt{S}} \nabla W$$

Or, even:

$$\hat{\eta} = \frac{\eta}{\sqrt{S}}$$

$$W = W - \hat{\eta} \nabla W$$

The last formula is similar to the original update rule formula. The difference is that we are using the learning rate instead of the original learning rate η. This usage of a modified learning rate makes algorithms like RMSProp to be called **adaptive learning rate** algorithms. Adaptive learning rate algorithms are very desirable because the right choice of a constant learning rate is usually a very difficult and time-consuming decision. Thus, using a robust algorithm that can adapt the learning rate during the training is usually a good decision.

Let us see how to implement RMSProp in the next section.

RMSProp implementation

Similarly to Momentum, we can define a **RMSProp** functor as shown below:

```cpp
1.  template <int _RANK>
2.  class RMSProp {
3.
4.  public:
5.
6.      RMSProp(float beta): beta(beta) { }
7.      RMSProp(): RMSProp(0.9) { }
8.
9.      Eigen::Tensor<float, _RANK> operator()(Eigen::Tensor<float, _
    RANK> &grad, float learning_rate, int epoch) {
10.         if (S.size() != grad.size()) {
11.             S = grad.constant(0);
12.         }
13.         S = S * grad.constant(beta) + grad * grad * grad.
    constant(1.f - beta);
14.         Eigen::Tensor<float, _RANK> result = grad * (S + S.
    constant(1e-5)).rsqrt() * grad.constant(-learning_rate);
15.         return std::move(result);
16.     }
17.
18. private:
19.     float beta;
20.     Eigen::Tensor<float, _RANK> S;
21. };
```

`rsqrt()` provides the coefficient-wise reciprocal of the square root:

$$rsqrt(x) = \frac{1}{\sqrt{x}}$$

Note: We added a small positive constant ε = 1e-5 to avoid division by zero.

The deep learning community found that RMSProp is an effective way to train real-world models for a wide range of different applications, rivaled in its importance only by Adam, the optimizer introduced in the next section.

Introducing Adam

Adam [7] was introduced in 2014 and quickly gained the attention of the scientific community and industry due to the impressive results achieved in benchmarks or practical product development. Due to this, people often consider Adam the default training optimizer when using gradient descent, besides RMSProp and stochastic gradient descent, which are still commonly used.

Adam can be seen as a combination of RMSProp and Momentum [8]:

$$V = \beta_1 \times V + (1 - \beta_1) \times \nabla W \text{ (the "momentum" term)}$$

$$S = \beta_2 \times S + (1 - \beta_2) \times \nabla W^2 \text{ (the "RMSProp" term)}$$

$$\hat{V} = \frac{V}{1 - \beta_1^t} \text{ (corrected bias)}$$

$$\hat{S} = \frac{S}{1 - \beta_2^t} \text{ (corrected bias)}$$

$$W = W - \eta \frac{\hat{V}}{\sqrt{\hat{S}}}$$

The variable t represents the t-th epoch counter. β_1 and β_1 are two hyperparameters usually set to 0.9 and 0.999 respectively. The authors of Adam recommend using a learning rate of 0.001.

Adam implementation

We can implement an **Adam** functor in the same way we implemented RMSProp and Momentum:

```
1.  template <int _RANK>
2.  class Adam {
3.
4.  public:
5.
6.      Adam(float beta1, float beta2): beta1(beta1), beta2(beta2) { }
7.      Adam(): Adam(0.9, 0.999) { }
8.
9.      Eigen::Tensor<float, _RANK> operator()(Eigen::Tensor<float, _RANK> &grad, float learning_rate, int epoch) {
10.         if (V.size() != grad.size()) {
11.             V = grad.constant(0);
12.         }
13.         if (S.size() != grad.size()) {
14.             S = grad.constant(0);
```

```
15.          }
16.          if (epoch <= 0) {
17.              epoch = 1; // avoiding nan
18.          }
19.          V = V * grad.constant(beta1) + grad * grad.
   constant(1.f - beta1);
20.          S = S * grad.constant(beta2) + grad * grad * grad.
   constant(1.f - beta2);
21.
22.          auto _V = V * V.constant(1.f/
   (1.f - std::pow(beta1, epoch))); // correct bias in first epochs
23.          auto _S = S * S.constant(1.f/
   (1.f - std::pow(beta2, epoch))); // correct bias in first epochs
24.
25.          Eigen::Tensor<float, _RANK> result = _V * (_S + S.
   constant(1e-5)).rsqrt() * grad.constant(-learning_rate);
26.          return std::move(result);
27.      }
28.
29. private:
30.      float beta1;
31.      float beta2;
32.      Eigen::Tensor<float, _RANK> V;
33.      Eigen::Tensor<float, _RANK> S;
34. };
```

Note: Again, we used a small constant ε=1e-5 to increase the numeric stability.

Adam embodies the best features of other algorithms to provide a fast and high-quality search convergence, making this algorithm a very popular alternative for the training of models in both research and industrial settings.

In the next section, we will compare the performance of gradient descent, momentum, RMSProp, and Adam using MNIST as a benchmark.

Experiment: Comparing optimizers

The choice of the optimizer is one of the most common questions taken when we start off the training of a new model. In this experiment, we will simulate this scenario by comparing different configurations of optimizers, mini-batches, and learning rates using MNIST as a benchmark.

Model architecture

For this experiment, let us assume the following CNN architecture described:

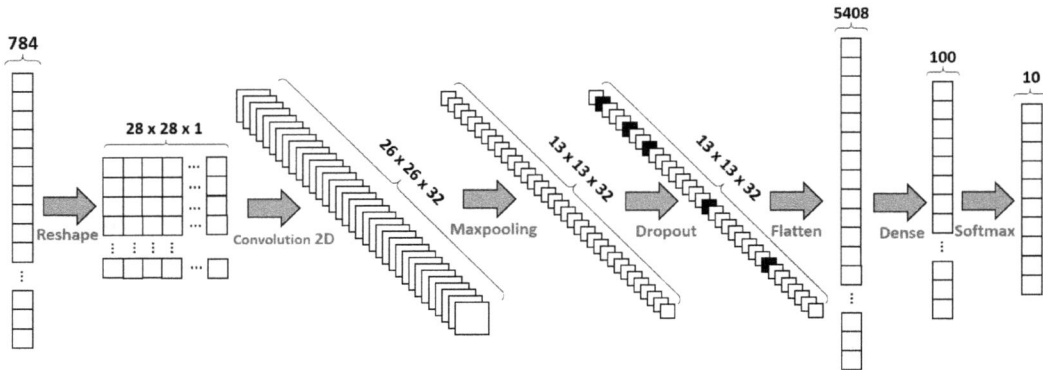

Figure 13.5: Convolutional network for the experiment

This network consists of seven layers, as detailed:

Layer	Input	Output	Number of trainable parameters
Reshape layer	784	28x28x1	0
Convolution 2D	28x28x1	26x26x32	288
Maxpooling 2D	26x26x32	13x13x32	0
Dropout	13x13x32	13x13x32	0
Flatten	13x13x32	5408	0
Dense	5408	128	692,224
Softmax	100	10	1000

Table 13.2: Model architecture

To implement this model, we can define a class **Model**:

```
1. template <typename Device>
2. class Model {
3.
4. public:
5.
6.     //...
7.
```

```
8.  private:
9.      ReshapeLayer<DEVICE, 2, 4> *input_layer;
10.     Conv2DLayer<Device> *conv2d;
11.     MaxPooling<DEVICE> *maxpooling;
12.     DropoutLayer<DEVICE, 4, GEN> *dropout;
13.     FlattenLayer<DEVICE, 4> *flatten;
14.     DenseLayer<Device> *dense;
15.     SoftmaxCrossEntropyLayer<Device> *output_layer;
16.
17. };
```

Its constructor is defined as follows:

```
1.  Model(Device &device) {
2.      const int x_width = 28;
3.      const int x_height = 28;
4.
5.      const int kernel_size = 3;
6.      const int filters = 32;
7.      const int channels = 1;
8.
9.      const int hidden_neurons = 128;
10.     const int num_classes = 10;
11.     const bool use_bias = true;
12.
13.     input_layer = new ReshapeLayer<Device, 2, 4>(device, std::vec-
    tor<Eigen::Index>{x_width, x_height, 1});
14.
15.     Tensor_4D kernels(kernel_size, kernel_size, channels, filters);
16.     glorot_uniform_initializer(rng, kernels);
17.     conv2d = new Conv2DLayer(device, kernels, use_
    bias, new ReLU<Device, 4>(device), std::vector<int>{0, 0, 0, 0});
18.
19.     maxpooling = new MaxPooling(device, 2);
20.
21.     dropout = new DropoutLayer<DEVICE, 4, GEN>(device, 0.2, rng);
22.
23.     const int half_width = (x_width - kernel_size + 1) / 2;
24.     const int half_height = (x_height - kernel_size + 1) / 2;
```

```
25.    const int flatten_size = half_width * half_height * filters;
26.
27.    flatten = new FlattenLayer<DEVICE, 4>(device);
28.
29.    Tensor_2D WD(flatten_size, hidden_neurons);
30.    glorot_uniform_initializer(rng, WD);
31.    dense = new DenseLayer(device, WD, use_
    bias, new ReLU<Device, 2>(device));
32.
33.    Tensor_2D WC(hidden_neurons, num_classes);
34.    glorot_uniform_initializer(rng, WC);
35.    SoftmaxCrossEntropyLayer<Devi
    ce> * softmax = new SoftmaxCrossEntropyLayer(device, WC, use_bias);
36.    output_layer = softmax;
37.
38. }
```

The convolution and dense layers use ReLU as the activation function. The output layer is a special custom dense layer that uses softmax as activation and cross-entropy cost function to calculate the grandient.

Note: In Chapter 10, Coding the Backpropagation Algorithm, we learned that the combination of softmax activation and cross-entropy loss simplifies the computation, reducing the computational time complexity to compute the gradients.

The input layer consists of a conversion function to reshape the linear input provided by the dataset into single-channels 28x28 grids:

```
1. input_layer = new ReshapeLayer<Device, 2, 4>(device, std::vector<Ei-
   gen::Index>{28, 28, 1});
```

We can set the model to use Momentum by setting each trainable layer:

```
1. void set_momentum() {
2.     conv2d->set_kernels_optimizer(Momentum<4>());
3.     dense->set_weight_optimizer(Momentum<2>());
4.     softmax->set_weight_optimizer(Momentum<2>());
5. }
```

Note: There is no problem in setting each layer to use a different type of optimizer even though using the same optimizer type for all trainable layers is more common and also more recommended in general.

Now, we can define **forward()** as a method of the class **Model**:

```
1.  void forward(const Eigen::Tensor<float, 2> &input) {
2.      input_layer->forward(input);
3.      conv2d->forward(input_layer->get_output());
4.      maxpooling->forward(conv2d->get_output());
5.      dropout->forward(maxpooling->get_output());
6.      flatten->forward(dropout->get_output());
7.      dense->forward(flatten->get_output());
8.      output_layer->forward(dense->get_output());
9.  }
```

In the same way, we can define **backward()**:

```
1.  void backward(const Eigen::Tensor<float, 2> &upstream) {
2.      output_layer->backward(upstream, true);
3.      dense->backward(output_layer->get_downstream(), true);
4.      flatten->backward(dense->get_downstream(), true);
5.      dropout->backward(flatten->get_downstream(), true);
6.      maxpooling->backward(dropout->get_downstream(), true);
7.      conv2d->backward(maxpooling->get_downstream(), false);
8.  }
```

Also **update()**:

```
1.  void update(const float learning_rate, int epoch) {
2.      conv2d->update(learning_rate, epoch);
3.      dense->update(learning_rate, epoch);
4.      output_layer->update(learning_rate, epoch);
5.  }
```

Note that only the layers having trainable parameters must invoke update(…).

Now that the model is defined, we can train it using the MNIST dataset. Similarly to the previous examples in this book, we can train this model using a training loop, like in the following training procedure:

```
1.  template <typename Device, typename MODEL>
2.  void training(MODEL &model, const Tensor_2D &training_
    images, const Tensor_2D &training_labels,
3.               const Tensor_2D &validation_
    images, const Tensor_2D &validation_labels, Device &device,
4.               const int MAX_EPOCHS, const int minibatch_
    size, const float learning_rate) {
```

```
5.
6.      CategoricalCrossEntropy cost_fn;
7.
8.    int epoch = 0;
9.    while (epoch < MAX_EPOCHS) {
10.
11.       auto begin = high_resolution_clock::now();
12.
13.       int steps = 0;
14.
15.       Batches batches(rng, minibatch_size, &training_
   images, &training_labels);
16.
17.       Batch<2, 2>* batch = batches.next();
18.
19.       while (batch) {
20.
21.           model.forward(batch->X);
22.           model.backward(batch->T);
23.           model.update(learning_rate, epoch + 1);
24.
25.           batch = batches.next();
26.           steps++;
27.       }
28.
29.       auto end = high_resolution_clock::now();
30.       auto duration = duration_cast<milliseconds>(end - begin);
31.
32.       auto validation_pred = model.predict(validation_images);
33.       float validation_acc = accuracy(validation_
   labels, validation_pred);
34.
35.       float validation_loss = cost_fn.evaluate(validation_
   labels, validation_pred);
36.
37.       std::cout
38.               << "epoch:" << "\t"
39.               << epoch << "\t"
```

```
40.                    << "\tvalidation_loss:" << "\t"
41.                    << validation_loss
42.                    << "\tvalidation_acc:" << "\t"
43.                    << validation_acc
44.                    << "\n";
45.
46.        epoch++;
47.
48.    }
49.
50. }
```

This function divides the training dataset into several mini-batches. For each mini-batch, the program loops over the **forward()**, **backward()**, and **update()** methods:

```
1. while (batch) {
2.
3.     model.forward(batch->X);
4.     model.backward(batch->T);
5.     model.update(learning_rate, epoch + 1);
6.
7.     batch = batches.next();
8.     steps++;
9. }
```

The number of batches generated depends on the size of the mini-batches. In the following example, we are invoking **training()** passing **minibatch_size = 32**:

```
1. int main(int, char **)
2. {
3.     auto [training_images, training_labels, validation_
   images, validation_labels] = load_mnist("data/mnist");
4.     std::cout << "Data loaded!\n";
5.     std::cout << "training_images: " << training_images.
   dimensions() << "\n";
6.     std::cout << "training_labels: " << training_labels.
   dimensions() << "\n";
7.     std::cout << "validation_images: " << validation_images.
   dimensions() << "\n";
8.     std::cout << "validation_labels: " << validation_labels.
   dimensions() << "\n\n";
9.
```

```
10.    const int threads = std::thread::hardware_concurrency();
11.    Eigen::ThreadPool tp(threads);
12.    Eigen::ThreadPoolDevice device(&tp, threads);
13.
14.    std::cout << std::setprecision(4);
15.
16.    const int MAX_EPOCHS = 10;
17.
18.    Model model(device);
19.    model.set_momentum();
20.
21.    training(model, training_images, training_labels, validation_
       images, validation_labels, device, MAX_EPOCHS, 32, 0.001);
22.
23.    return 0;
24. }
```

Running this configuration, we get a result like the following figure:

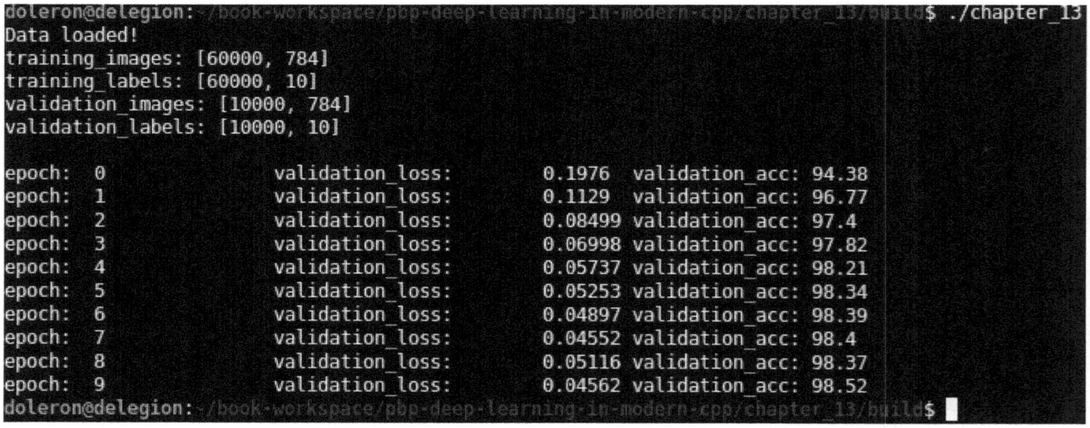

```
doleron@delegion: /book-workspace/pbp-deep-learning-in-modern-cpp/chapter_13/build$ ./chapter_13
Data loaded!
training_images: [60000, 784]
training_labels: [60000, 10]
validation_images: [10000, 784]
validation_labels: [10000, 10]

epoch:   0            validation_loss:        0.1976  validation_acc: 94.38
epoch:   1            validation_loss:        0.1129  validation_acc: 96.77
epoch:   2            validation_loss:        0.08499 validation_acc: 97.4
epoch:   3            validation_loss:        0.06998 validation_acc: 97.82
epoch:   4            validation_loss:        0.05737 validation_acc: 98.21
epoch:   5            validation_loss:        0.05253 validation_acc: 98.34
epoch:   6            validation_loss:        0.04897 validation_acc: 98.39
epoch:   7            validation_loss:        0.04552 validation_acc: 98.4
epoch:   8            validation_loss:        0.05116 validation_acc: 98.37
epoch:   9            validation_loss:        0.04562 validation_acc: 98.52
doleron@delegion: /book-workspace/pbp-deep-learning-in-modern-cpp/chapter_13/build$ ▊
```

Figure 13.6: Training a model with Momentum

Note that in this execution, we are setting the learning rate to 0.001 and using Momentum.

Due to the stochastic nature of weight initialization and random batch scheduling, the results may vary for each run. Thus, to get some confidence about the actual performance, we should run the training several times, summarizing the results as shown in the next section.

Comparing the model performance with different mini-batch configurations

In machine learning, we often say that training deep learning models is more a matter of art than a deterministic science. It turns out that the training of machine learning models requires the tunning of a high number of hyperparameters, some of them correlated, others unrelated.

Thus, knowing how to tune the hyperparameter depends mainly on intuition and experience. This experiment aims to provide some insight into how mini-batch size, learning rate, and the choice of optimizer affect the quality of the training.

Using multiple mini-batch configurations

In this first part of the experiment, we will train the model using a fixed learning rate of 0.001 and different mini-batch sizes: 16, 512, and 4096. For each configuration, we train the model five times and store the average:

```
1.  std::vector<int> batch_sizes {16, 512, 4096};
2.
3.  for (int i = 0; i < 5; ++i) {
4.
5.      std::cout << "\n=== Run #" << i << "\n\n";
6.
7.      for (int minibatch_size : batch_sizes) {
8.
9.          Model model(device);
10.         model.set_momentum();
11.
12.         std::cout << "minibatch_size: " << minibatch_size << "\n";
13.         training(model, training_images, training_
    labels, validation_images, validation_labels, device, MAX_
    EPOCHS, minibatch_size, 0.001);
14.     }
15.
16. }
```

We can repeat this process using RMSProp:

```
1.  for (int minibatch_size : batch_sizes) {
2.
3.      Model model(device);
4.      model.set_rmsprop();
```

```
5.
6.      //...
7. }
```

Alternatively, using Adam:

```
1. for (int minibatch_size : batch_sizes) {
2.
3.       Model model(device);
4.       model.set_adam();
5.
6.       //...
7. }
```

Now, we can compare the performance for each optimizer. The following charts show the results:

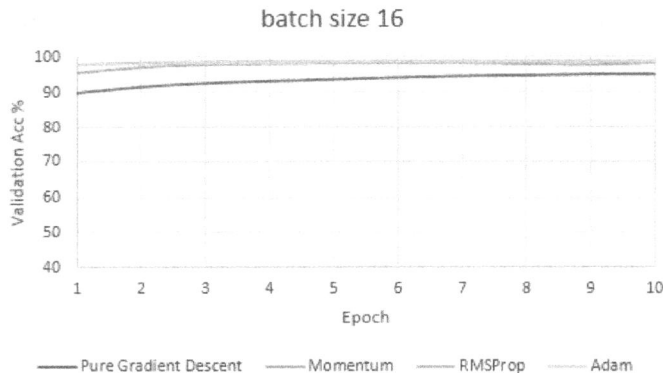

Figure 13.7: *Training models with batch size 16*

The performances of using Adam, RMSProp, or Momentum are rhoughly the same when batch size is 16. Let us check what happens when the mini-batch size is increased to 128:

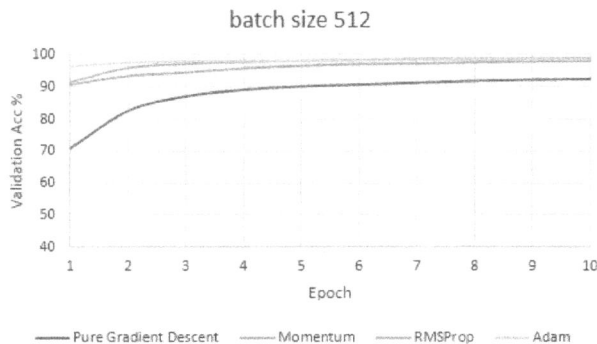

Figure 13.8: *Training models with batch size 512*

With mini-batch 512, the performances are slightly different. Increasing the batch size to 4096 provide more evidence:

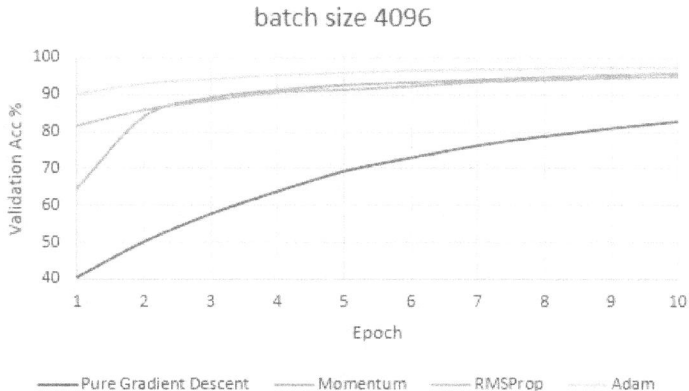

Figure 13.9: *Training models with batch size 4096*

The charts suggest Adam as the best optimizer for different mini-batch configurations, at least considering the validation accuracy. Indeed, the size of the mini-batch affected the other models more significantly in this first part of the experiment.

The next section shows the average performance by training models using a constant mini-batch size and different values of learning rate.

Comparing the model performance with different learning rates

In this part of the experiment, we fix the minibatch size at 32 and train the model using different learning rates: 0.01, 0.001, and 0.0001.

```
1.  std::vector<float> learning_rates {0.01, 0.001, 0.0001};
2.
3.  for (int i = 0; i < 5; ++i) {
4.
5.      std::cout << "\n=== Run #" << i << "\n\n";
6.
7.      for (float learning_rate : learning_rates) {
8.
9.          Model model(device);
10.         model.set_momentum();
11.
12.         std::cout << "learning_rate: " << learning_rate << "\n";
```

```
13.          training(model, training_images, training_
    labels, validation_images, validation_labels, device, MAX_
    EPOCHS, 32, learning_rate);
14.    }
15.
16. }
```

Again, we repeat the process using RMSProp, Adam, and no optimizer. The following charts (*Figure 13.10*, *Figure 13.11* and *Figure 13.12*) show the results:

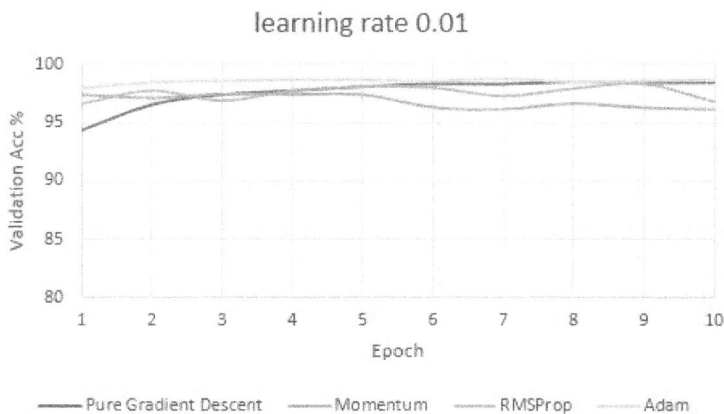

Figure 13.10: *Training models using a learning rate of 0.01*

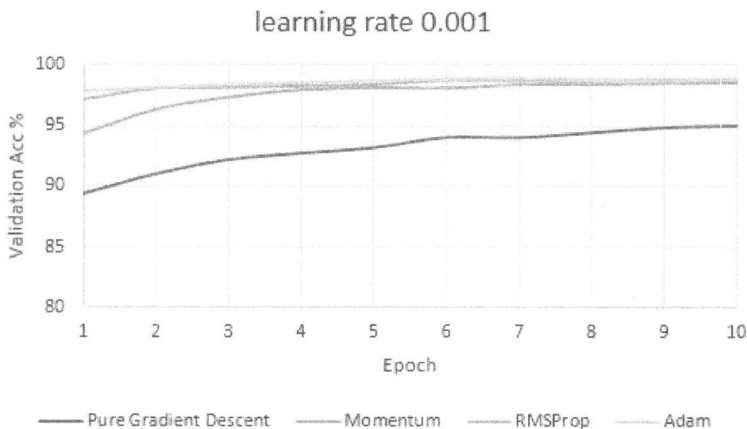

Figure 13.11: *Training models using a learning rate of 0.001*

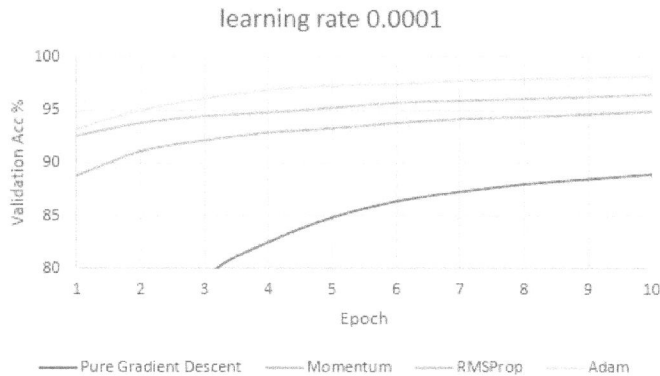

Figure 13.12: *Training models using a learning rate of 0.0001*

Again, Adam dominated the performance even though Momentum and RMSProp were also competitive. In fact, the charts suggest Adam is more robust to changes in learning rate and mini-batch size.

It is noteworthy that, although Adam achieved the best performance in this experiment, we cannot assume that Adam is our only choice as an optimizer. In practice, we must experimentally check different configurations, including mini-batch size, learning rate, regularization, optimizers, and others, to find the setup that provides the best results.

Conclusion

This chapter introduced three important variations of the gradient descent algorithm: Momentum, RMSProp, and Adam. We learned that the standard gradient descent is not optimal in terms of speed convergence. Because of this, we introduced Momentum, which uses inertia to reduce the directional changes of updates, and RMSProp and Adam, which use the approach of adapting the learning rate to improve the algorithm convergence.

This chapter finishes our overview of the main deep learning algorithms and components. The next chapters cover a case study using computer vision and the techniques introduced so far in this book.

Exercises

1. Consider the Nesterov's momentum [9] described by the rule [10] below:

$$V = \beta \times V - \eta \nabla W$$

$$nesterov = \beta \times V - \eta \nabla W$$

$$W = W + nesterov$$

Implement this rule in a NesterovMomentum optimizer and compare the performance with the standard Momentum optimizer using MNIST.

2. The optimizer Adagrad [11] is a predecessor of RMSProp. Consider its rule [3]:

$$S = S + \nabla W^2$$

$$W = W - \eta \frac{\nabla W}{\sqrt{S}}$$

Implement this rule in an Adagrad optimizer and compare the performance with the RMSProp optimizer using MNIST. Can you list some drawbacks of using Adagrad instead of RMSProp?

References

[1] David Jordan, Level curves, MIT 18.02SC Multivariable Calculus, Fall 2010, available at **https://www.youtube.com/watch?v=uaHiAxFESc4&ab_channel=MITOpenCourseWare**

[2] B. T. Polyak. Some methods of speeding up the convergence of iteration methods. USSR Computational Mathematics and Mathematical Physics, 4(5):1–17, 1964.

[3] Ian J. Goodfellow, Yoshua Bengio and Aaron Courville, Deep Learning Book, MIT Press, 2016, *Chapter 8, Optimization for Training Deep Models*.

[4] Andrew Ng, Gradient Descent with Momentum (C2W2L06), available at **https://www.youtube.com/watch?v=k8fTYJPd3_I&ab_channel=DeepLearningAI**

[5] Geoffrey Hinton, Neural Networks for Machine Learning, Coursera, 2012, available at **https://www.cs.toronto.edu/%7Etijmen/csc321/slides/lecture_slides_lec6.pdf**

[6] Andrew Ng, RMSProp (C2W2L07), available at **https://www.youtube.com/watch?v=_e-LFe_igno&ab_channel=DeepLearningAI**

[7] Diederik P. Kingma, Jimmy Ba, Adam: A Method for Stochastic Optimization, 2014.

[8] Andrew Ng, Adam Optimization Algorithm (C2W2L08), available at **https://www.youtube.com/watch?v=JXQT_vxqwIs&ab_channel=DeepLearningAI**

[9] Ilya Sutskever, James Martens, George Dahl, Geoffrey Hinton, On the importance of initialization and momentum in deep learning, 2013.

[10] TensorFlow, tf.keras.optimizers.experimental.SGD, available at **https://www.tensorflow.org/api_docs/python/tf/keras/optimizers/experimental/SGD**

[11] Duchi, J., Hazan, E., & Singer, Y. Adaptive subgradient methods for online learning and stochastic optimization, 2011.

CHAPTER 14

Introducing Computer Vision Models

Introduction

This chapter opens the last part of this book by introducing one of the more important application fields of deep learning: computer vision. We will discuss how computer vision has driven the development of deep learning and how deep learning has changed the computer vision field so drastically. In addition, we will talk about techniques to generate augmented data specifically for the domain of images, such as rotations, color transformations, and so on.

Structure

This is the general roadmap for the chapter:

- Experiments in this chapter
- Computer vision
- Types of computer vision tasks
- Data augmentation
- Experiment: Applying data augmentation to the Dogs x Cats dataset

Objectives

This chapter will show how to start with computer vision models, teaching you how to load, modify, and use image data. After reading this chapter, you will learn how to implement data augmentation in your projects using one or more computer vision transformations.

Experiments in this chapter

This chapter includes only one experiment:

ID	Description
Exp-14.1	Applying data augmentation to the Dogs x Cats dataset

Table 14.1: Chapter experiment list

Computer vision

Computer vision is the field of computer science focused on studying and developing methods to acquire, process, analyze, store, and generate digital media such as images and videos [1][2]. Today, computer vision is popularly known for the achievements of generative AI systems such as DALL-E2 [3]. These systems can automatically produce incredible images from textual natural language input. Refer to the following figure:

Figure 14.1: Images automatically generated by DALL-E2

Although the recent advances in generative AI are really notable, the development of computer vision has been going on for much longer. For example, we can cite the face detection feature in old digital cameras as one important milestone for the computer vision field in people's daily lives.

This book is focused on the use of computer vision to analyze and extract semantic information from images, which is sometimes called discriminant AI. Check the following figure [4]:

Figure 14.2: Using YOLO v5 to detect objects.

In this example, an algorithm called YOLO v5 [5] performs a task known as **object detection**. In object detection, the program finds the type (**label**) and **bounding-box** coordinates of semantic objects in an image. Performing multi-label object detection in real-time is one of the modern applications introduced by the well-succeeded combination of computer vision and deep learning.

Examples of computer vision applications

Before deep learning, several approaches were developed to detect complex structures from images. One popular alternative was **template matching**. Check the following example [6]:

Figure 14.3: Using OpenCV template matching

In this example, an implementation of template matching using OpenCV detects the face in an image. The problem with this approach is that it needs to be more robust to deal with recurring image features such as noise, illumination interference, pose variation, shadows, occlusion, etc. At this point, deep learning comes into play.

Using ML models in computer vision

The idea of using ML models to improve computer vision systems is not new at all. So far, in this book, we used vanilla neural networks to perform handwritten digit recognition using the MNIST dataset. Although conventional multilayer networks can be used to perform this specific task, we cannot think of MNIST as a genuine example of a real-world computer vision problem. We will list some of the aspects that make MNIST diverge from a real-world computer vision task:

- In MNIST, each image is a small *28x28* pixel grid, which is very small in contrast with real-world images with resolutions of *640x480, 1920x768*, or even more.

- In MNIST, each image is grayscale. Real-world images are multi-channel color images with three or more channels, such as RGB, HSV, or CMYK.

- In MNIST, each digit is located in the center of the image. In real-world images, the semantic objects vary in terms of pose and location.

- In MNIST, the objects are 2D handwritten digits. In real images, the objects are usually 3D objects represented in a 2D perspective.

- In MNIST, each label is one of ten possible digits 0-9. Some image datasets have 80, 1000, or even more different labels.

In practice, using old-style neural networks for solving real-life computer vision problems results in slow solutions that do not perform even roughly well. In fact, the first deep-learning models were developed to address these issues. Convolutional neural networks, in particular, were initially developed to perform computer vision tasks [7].

Lessons learned from the old times of computer vision

Before moving to the discussion of modern models, let us talk about the previous steps that drove the decisions for a new technology. In this context, one of the more important lessons from the old times of computer vision was that tasks can be more straightforwardly performed by using **specific application features** (or markers). For example, the following face detector [8] was developed considering the topological markers of a human face, such as eyebrows, nose, eyes, cheeks, etc.

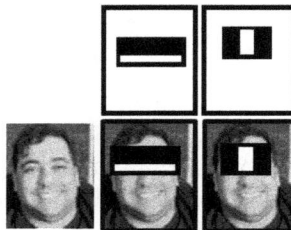

Figure 14.4: *The first and second features selected to detect faces (adapted from the original Viola/Jones paper)*

Note that face detection consists of finding a face in an image. Do not confuse it with face recognition, which is the task of assigning an identifier for a previously detected face.

In the following code, we use only OpenCV built-in functions to detect faces in an image:

```
1.  void detect_face(cv::Mat &image, cv::CascadeClassifier &face_detector)
2.  {
3.      cv::Mat gray;
4.      cv::cvtColor(image, gray, cv::COLOR_BGR2GRAY);
5.      cv::equalizeHist(gray, gray);
6.
7.      std::vector<cv::Rect> faces;
8.      face_detector.detectMultiScale(gray, faces);
9.      cv::Mat dest = image.clone();
10.     for (int i = 0; i < faces.size(); i++) {
11.         cv::Rect &face = faces[i];
12.         cv::rectangle(dest, cv::Point(face.x, face.y), cv::Point(-
    face.x + face.width, face.y + face.height), cv::Sca-
    lar(0, 0, 255), 4);
13.     }
14.     cv::imshow("Face detection", dest);
15.     cv::waitKey();
16. }
```

We can call this function using this program:

```
1.  int main(int, char**) {
2.
3.      std::string haar_cascade_path = "haarcascade_frontalface_alt.
    xml";
4.      cv::CascadeClassifier face_detector;
5.      if(!face_detector.load(haar_cascade_path)) {
6.          throw std::invalid_argument("Haar cascade file not found");
7.      }
8.
9.      std::string image_path = "my_image.jpg";
10.     cv::Mat image = cv::imread(image_path, cv::IMREAD_COLOR);
11.     if(image.empty()) {
12.         throw std::invalid_argument("Image file not found");
13.     }
```

```
14.
15.    detect_face(image, face_detector);
16.
17.    return 0;
18. }
```

Applying this program to a regular image results in the following:

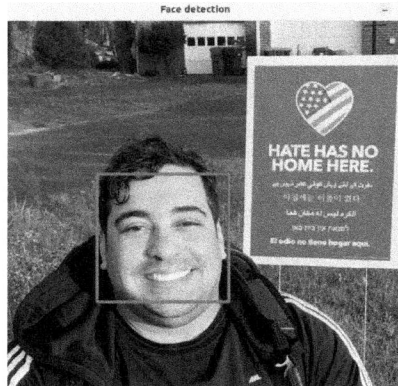

Figure 14.5: *Using Haar Cascade classifiers to detect faces*

This code uses a primitive model schema called **Haar Cascade classifier**. Similarly to deep learning models, Haar Cascade classifiers can be trained using positive and negative examples throughout an iterative training algorithm.

The code using the Haar Cascade classifier is included in the book repository.

The problem with these old classifiers is that they did not generalize well, performing poorly in the presence of variations such as shadows or rotations. For example, if we run again our face detection program using the same image rotated by 90 degrees, we get the following result:

Figure 14.6: *Failing to detect faces in a rotated image using a Haar Cascade classifier.*

This time, the cascade classifier no longer detected any faces in the image. The lesson from this story is that solutions based on old-style Haar Cascade classifiers can perform simple tasks in well-defined configurations using application-specific markers but are unsuitable for performing more complex tasks or tasks with challenging settings.

The absence of robustness to feature variances such as rotation, color, lighting, shadows, and pose drove the research of new models for years, resulting in the emergence of deep learning.

Deep learning changed how we build ML models in computer vision programs. As we will see in the next chapter, using deep learning, we can train deep models with several layers to automatically extract the markers and patterns (such as shapes and textures) directly from data. In particular, the convolution's ability to share weights resulted in the development of modern deep learning models that are robust to rotation or translation variations. Take, for example, the following figure where the faces detection algorithm can detect faces even with different poses and sizes:

Figure 14.7: *Example of massive face detection using deep learning* [9]

Face detection is only one example of a task revolutionized by deep learning. The following section lists other relevant examples of computer vision systems that achieved state-of-art with deep learning.

Types of computer vision tasks

Here we list some of the most common types of computer vision tasks:

- **Classification**: In classification, the model uses an image as input and outputs an index representing one or more categories associated with the image. In the next chapter, we will develop a classifier to determine if an animal in an image is a cat or a dog. In the case of only two possibilities, the classifier is called a binary classifier.

- **Sentimental analysis**: Essentially, sentimental analysis is implemented as a classifier. The model takes an image of a person and assigns one of the labels: happy, neutral, sad, etc.

- **Safety**: A popular use of computer vision models is detecting unsafe behaviors, such as using cell phones on driving or driving drowsy/sleepy.

- **Surveillance**: Access control, intrusion detection, procedural violations, etc.

- **Gesture detection**: Gesture detection is also similar to classification. In gesture detection, the program uses a (time-based) sequence of images to recognize a gesture. For example, a person holding a cell phone is different than a person moving their head to look at the cell phone.

- **3D-reconstruction**: In 3D reconstruction, the program uses a combination of two or more images to estimate the three-dimensional structure of the object. Some deep learning models can build realistic 3D reconstructions using only one image as input.

- **Pose estimation**: In pose estimation, the computer vision program tries to figure out the multi-dof matrix of an object. For example, given an image of a person, the program tries to estimate the direction that the person is looking at.

- **Object localization**: Object localization consists of finding the boundbox coordinates of a single object in an image. In general, the program provides a label in addition to the boundbox coordinates. Thus, object localization can be seen as a combination of a regressor and a classifier.

- **Image segmentation**: In image segmentation, the image is converted into smaller convex or unconvex regions. The regular way to represent these regions is by using masks. For example, given an image with two persons, A and B, you can define a mask to represent the pixels belonging to person A and another mask to represent the pixels belonging to person B.

- **Forensis**: For years, computer vision has been used to estimate how people look with more or less age. This application has been used to help families find lost relatives and police find criminals.

- **Generative imagery**: in recent years, generative AI has revolutionized industries such as entertainment, games, photography, and advertising by providing realistic or surreal images developed by computers.

- **Manufacturing**: The use of computer vision for industrial applications allows human-only tasks to be performed by machines. In particular, systems to detect failures, missing parts, and defects in production lines are part of the so-called Industry 4.0 revolution.

Figure 14.8: *Example of image segmentation*

This list is only a small part of the computer vision applications known so far. In this last part of the book, we will explore some practical examples of computer vision using deep learning.

Data augmentation

Data plays a central role in deep learning. It is impossible to develop deep learning models without data. Luckily, today, data is not so hard to find. There are several publicly available datasets to use as benchmarks or for the development of commercial projects. If the data is not labeled yet, we can use internet services to annotate our datasets manually at a relatively low cost. Even so, sooner or later, you will find a problem where more data is required, but acquiring new instances is not an option. For scenarios like this, we can use data augmentation.

We first introduced data augmentation in *Chapter 11, Underfitting, Overfitting, and Regularization*. In that chapter, we learned how to apply a random rotation to some instances of MNIST to obtain new instances. Rotation is only one of the ways we can use to generate augmented instances. Let us explore other ways in the following experiment.

Experiment: Applying data augmentation to the Dogs x Cats dataset

For this experiment, we will use the Dogs x Cats dataset [10]. As the name suggests, this dataset consists of images of dogs and cats. The following figure shows some examples cat instances from this dataset:

Figure 14.9: Some images of cats from the dataset

Similarly, the following figure shows some instances of dogs:

Figure 14.10: Some images of dogs from the dataset

We will explore this dataset in more detail in the next chapter. So far, we want to learn how to use OpenCV to load and modify these images. In the book repository, you can find the implementation of **load_dogs_x_cats_dataset()** utility function:

```
1. int main(int, char **) {
2.     auto [training_data, validation_data] = load_dogs_x_cats_
   dataset("data/dogs_x_cats/PetImages", rng);
3.     std::cout << "Data loaded!\n";
4.     std::cout << "training: " << training_data.dimensions() << "\n";
5.     std::cout << "validation: " << validation_data.
   dimensions() << "\n";
6.
7.     // ...
8.     return 0;
9. }
```

Once we have loaded the images, we can move forward to learn how to transform them and generate our augmented data.

Resizing the images

Checking the images, you may find that they have variable sizes: *98x162*, *500x375*, etc. Before training a model, we must set them to obtain images with similar resolutions. However, some images are landscape and others are portrait. So, how can we set them to the same resolution? The solution is to center the images in a sort of gray frame, as illustrated:

Figure 14.11: *Arrangement of images with different sizes to fit frames of 244x244 pixels*

After centralizing them, every image has a *244x244* size, even though most of them now have horizontal or vertical gray padding. Note that this modification is applied to all images. The following code implements this transformation:

```
1. cv::Mat dest(cv::Size(IMAGE_SIZE, IMAGE_
   SIZE), CV_8UC3, cv::Scalar(255/2, 255/2, 255/2));
2. cv::Mat image = cv::imread(image_path, cv::IMREAD_COLOR);
3. std::string text = "Unavailable";
4. if (!image.empty()) {
5.
6.     float f;
7.     if (image.cols >= image.rows) {
```

```
8.          f = IMAGE_SIZE / static_cast<float>(image.cols);
9.      } else {
10.         f = IMAGE_SIZE / static_cast<float>(image.rows);
11.     }
12.     cv::Mat resized;
13.     cv::resize(image, resized, cv::Size(), f, f, cv::INTER_LINEAR);
14.
15.     int left = (IMAGE_SIZE - resized.cols) / 2;
16.     int top = (IMAGE_SIZE - resized.rows) / 2;
17.
18.     resized.copyTo(dest(cv::Rect(left, top,resized.cols, resized.
    rows)));
19.
20.     std::string text = "Cat";
21.     if (label.compare("0")) {
22.         text = "Dog";
23.     }
24. }
25. int font = cv::FONT_HERSHEY_DUPLEX; double scale = 1.;
26. int baseline = 0; int thickness = 2;
27. cv::Size text_
    size = cv::getTextSize(text, font, scale, thickness, &baseline);
28. cv::Point text_pos((dest.cols - text_size.width)/2, (dest.
    rows - text_size.height)/2);
29. cv::putText(dest, text, text_
    pos, font, scale, cv::Scalar(0, 255, 0), thickness);
30.
31. cv::imshow(title, dest);
```

This code outputs figures as shown:

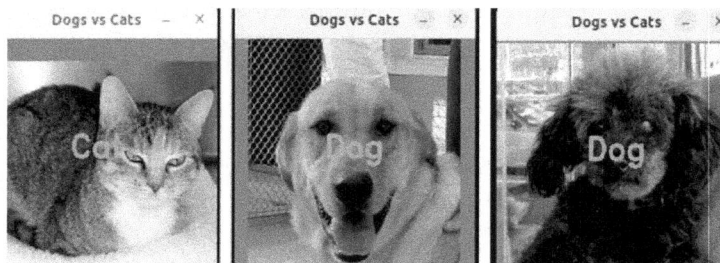

Figure 14.12: *Examples of program output*

Flips and rotations

Flips and rotations are the most common types of augmentation. It is really simple to flip images in OpenCV:

```
1. cv::Mat flip(const cv::Mat &src) {
2.     cv::Mat result = cv::Mat(src.rows, src.cols, CV_8UC3);
3.     cv::flip(src, result, 1);
4.     return result;
5. }
```

Check the following example of this function being applied to an image:

Figure 14.13: Flipping an image horizontally with OpenCV

You can flip an image horizontally, vertically, or both. Check the OpenCV documentation [11] for more information about **cv::flip()**.

Rotating images requires a bit more work:

```
1. cv::Mat rotate(const cv::Mat &src, double angle) {
2.     cv::Mat result = cv::Mat(src.rows, src.cols, CV_8UC3);
3.     cv::Point2f pc(src.cols/2., src.rows/2.);
4.     cv::Mat rotationMatrix = cv::getRotationMatrix2D(pc, angle, 1.0);
5.     cv::warpAffine(src, result, rotationMatrix, src.size());
6.     return result;
7. }
```

We can find an example using this function in the following figure:

Figure 14.14: Rotating an image by 45 degrees around its center

Blurring images

OpenCV has two functions to blur images: the function **cv::blur** and **cv::GaussianBlur**. In the following example, we use **GaussianBlur**:

```
1. cv::Mat blur(const cv::Mat &src) {
2.     cv::Mat result = cv::Mat(src.rows, src.cols, CV_8UC3);
3.     cv::GaussianBlur(src, result, cv::Size(11, 11), 0, 0);
4.     return result;
5. }
```

The following figure shows the result of applying blur to an image:

Figure 14.15: *Using GaussianBlur to an image*

Zoom and translating images

Indeed, applying zoom to an image is to resize the image. To zoom out, the image gets smaller. When zoomed in, the image gets bigger. We must take care to fit the image to the original image resolution:

```
1.  cv::Mat zoom(const cv::Mat &src, double by) {
2.      cv::Mat resized;
3.      cv::resize(src, resized, cv::Size(), by, by);
4.      cv::Mat result(cv::Size(src.rows, src.
    cols), CV_8UC3, cv::Scalar(255/2, 255/2, 255/2));
5.      if (by >= 1) {
6.          int left = (resized.cols - src.cols)/2;
7.          int width = src.cols;
8.          int top = (resized.rows - src.rows)/2;
9.          int height = src.rows;
10.         resized(cv::Rect(left, top, width, height)).copyTo(result);
11.     } else {
12.         int left = (src.cols - resized.cols)/2;
```

```
13.          int width = resized.cols;
14.          int top = (src.rows - resized.rows)/2;
15.          int height = resized.rows;
16.          resized.copyTo(result(cv::Rect(left, top, width, height)));
17.      }
18.      return result;
19. }
```

The following figure illustrates an example of applying zoom to an image:

Figure 14.16: *Zoom out an image by 50%*

In addition to zooming in/out, we can also move the image or, technically speaking, translate the image. OpenCV has a built-in function to translate images called **cv::warpAffine()**. Another solution is cropping the image and placing it in the desired position:

```
1.  cv::Mat translate(const cv::Mat &src, int left, int top) {
2.      cv::Mat result(cv::Size(src.cols, src.
    rows), CV_8UC3, cv::Scalar(255/2, 255/2, 255/2));
3.
4.      int src_left = 0;
5.      int dest_left = left;
6.      if (left < 0) {
7.          src_left = -left;
8.          dest_left = 0;
9.      }
10.     int src_top = 0;
11.     int dest_top = top;
12.     if (top < 0) {
13.         src_top = -top;
14.         dest_top = 0;
15.     }
```

```
16.     int width = src.cols - std::abs(left);
17.     int height = src.rows - std::abs(top);
18.     src(cv::Rect(src_left, src_top, width, height)).
     copyTo(result(cv::Rect(dest_left, dest_top, width, height)));
19.
20.     return result;
21. }
```

The following figure shows an image translated using the previous function:

Figure 14.17: *Translating an image 40 pixels right and 50 pixels down.*

Changing brightness

Illumination is one of the more challenging features to deal with in practical machine vision projects. One valuable trick to improve the generalization performance of these systems, achieving a more robust solution, is using augmented instances modified by increasing or decreasing the brightness.

In OpenCV, we can do it by applying a transformation called **gamma correction**:

```
1. cv::Mat gamma_correction(const cv::Mat &src, float gamma) {
2.     cv::Mat result = cv::Mat(src.rows, src.cols, CV_8UC3);
3.
4.     cv::Mat lookUpTable(1, 256, CV_8U);
5.     uchar* p = lookUpTable.ptr();
6.     for( int i = 0; i < 256; ++i) {
7.         p[i] = cv::saturate_
     cast<uchar>(pow(i / 255.0, gamma) * 255.0);
8.     }
9.
10.     cv::LUT(src, lookUpTable, result);
11.
12.     return result;
13. }
```

The result of applying this function to an image is illustrated as follows:

Figure 14.18: *Applying gamma correction to change the image brightness*

Changing color spaces

Color is a complex and tricky subject in computer vision. The RGB color space is the standard for representing digital images, but this does not make it the best representation for digital media. Usually, RGB is defined in the 0-255 range for each of its 3 pixels. These values are often normalized by dividing each pixel by 255 to end up with values in the range 0-1.

Note: By default, OpenCV represents colored images using BGR, not RGB.

One useful way to generate augmented instances is by changing the image color space. Consider the following function that converts an image from BGR to HSV color space:

```
1.  cv::Mat hsv(const cv::Mat &src) {
2.      cv::Mat result = cv::Mat(src.rows, src.cols, CV_8UC3);
3.      cv::cvtColor(src, result, cv::COLOR_BGR2HSV);
4.      return result;
5.  }
```

Applying this function in an image generates interesting results:

Figure 14.19: *Changing the image color space from BGR to HSV*

This transformation mimics different light conditions, often having a beneficial influence on the model training in terms of regularization.

In practice, the data augmentation code uses some statistical distribution to draw random numbers used to decide which transformation to apply to generate a new augmented instance. The following section discusses some important aspects of how to apply data augmentation in our projects.

Applying data augmentation

The first thing to consider when using data augmentation is **where to apply data augmentation**. The obvious answer to this question is the training data. As we have discussed so far in this book, small data has a big prejudicial impact on the training of models, and more data, even augmented data, can help the training to avoid overfitting and achieve a better generalization performance.

Can we use augmented data in the validation dataset? Yes, we can. Consider the case when we apply translation to move the objects from the center of the images to the peripherical regions. Suppose we only apply this transformation to the training images but not the validation ones. In that case, we cannot say if the model is learning how to process the objects in the borders. In this case, the solution is using augmentation in validation data as well.

At any cost, we **cannot use augmented data from the training dataset in the validation dataset and vice-versa**. To make the generalization estimate reliable, we are not allowed to contaminate the validation dataset with instances from the training dataset in any way, even if they are augmented instances.

Augmented labels

Sometimes, applying augmentation to an instance does not change its label or annotations. For example, flipping an image of a cat is likely to result in an image of a cat as well. However, rotating an image of the number 6 results in a 9. Refer to the following figure:

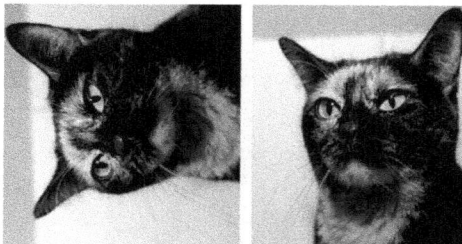

Figure 14.20: On the left is the original image. On the right is the augmented instance obtained by rotation

Suppose the image has positional annotations, like bounding box coordinates. In that case, we must take care to update the annotation to the new coordinates when flipping, rotating, rescaling, or performing any structural transformations in the image space. Refer to the following figure:

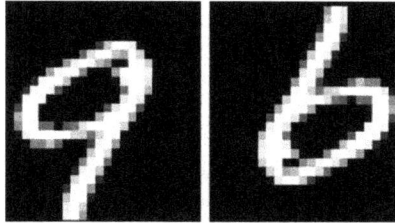

Figure 14.21: An instance of number 9 in MNIST rotated by 180 degrees

Note: The concerns of adjusting the augmented instance labels/annotations are covered in *Chapter 17, Developing an Object Localization System*.

How much data augmentation do we need?

Data cardinality is also a controversial point in statistics, machine learning, and deep learning. In the end, the data availability, the project requirements, the issue of overfitting, and domain expert knowledge should be taken together to define how many augmented instances are needed. Some common scenarios are:

- **Percentage of data**: Define a fixed percentage of data to be augmented, such as 20% or 40%.

- **Fixed multiplier**: For each instance in the original dataset, the system generates a fixed number of augmented instances. For example, for each image, you apply three rotations of 90, 180, and 270 degrees, resulting in three augmented instances for each source instance.

In some implementations, instead of including new instances, the original registers are replaced by augmented instances using some probability distribution. This last approach will be covered in the next chapter.

Offline and online data augmentation

You can load your dataset, randomly apply transformations in the instances, and store the new and original instances all together to create the new augmented dataset. This is called **offline data augmentation**. However, today, it is more and more common to perform **online data augmentation**. In online data augmentation, you generate the augmented instances on the fly during the training loop execution.

There are two main advantages of offline data augmentation:

- It is easy to inspect the augmented data and check for errors or mistakes (like turning a six and getting a nine).

- There is no additional processing overhead during the training to generate the modified instances.

The main drawback of offline data augmentation is the lack of posterior randomization. Since the new augmented data is now static, every training execution uses the same data. The problem is when the data augmentation procedure injects some bias by chance, affecting all the models built onto that data.

In contrast, in online data augmentation, the augmented instances are defined on the fly, that is, during the training. The main drawbacks of online data augmentation are:

- **Computational cost**: The choice of one or more transformations to be used to construct the augmented instance is usually taken by using some random distribution. The random generation is not exactly a cheap process in terms of computational resources, possibly slowing down the overall training speed significantly. In addition, the instance transformation itself can be costly. Together, the cost to perform the randomization and the cost to perform the instance mutation must be considered when planning to use online data augmentation.

- **Leak of observability**: Since the instances are built on the fly, checking if they were correctly constructed is more challenging. Some platforms, such as YOLO v5, store a log of augmented instances just to make sure that the instance and labels were correctly generated.

The advantage of online data augmentation is the gain in generalization due to the absence of static bias. For every run, the training uses a different set of augmented instances, which causes a beneficial decoupling of any specific configuration. We can easily add/remove/change the augmentation procedures without rebuilding all the training data. In addition, less important but also noteworthy, no additional storage is necessary to hold the augmented data.

Nowadays, the use of online data augmentation has become more common. However, some companies still use offline data augmentation in their data pipelines.

Conclusion

This chapter introduced the field of computer vision, focusing on the role of deep learning in performing challenging computer vision tasks such as object detection. We discussed the strategies used in old computer vision before adopting deep learning, such as Haar Cascade classifiers. We discussed that those old algorithms introduced important strategies and approaches to the field of computer vision.

The chapter also covered the use of OpenCV to implement transformations in digital images, focusing on defining data augmentation pipelines.

In the next chapter, we will develop an image classifier using deep learning and the computer vision transformations covered in this chapter.

Exercises

1. Consider the following OpenCV function HoughCircles [12]:

   ```
   1. void cv::HoughCircles(InputArray image, OutputArray cir-
      cles, int method, double dp, double minDist, dou-
      ble param1 = 100, double param2 = 100, int minRadius = 0, int  m
      axRadius = 0)
   ```

   According to the OpenCV documentation, this function finds circles in grayscale images using an algorithm called Hough transform [12]. Using OpenCV, write a program to find circles in an image using the HoughCircles function.

2. Explain in a few lines of text the Hough algorithm used in the previous exercise.

3. Consider the following OpenCV function cornerHarris [13]:

   ```
   1. void cv::cornerHarris (InputArray src, OutputArray dst,
      int blockSize, int ksize, double k, int borderType = BORDER_
      DEFAULT)
   ```

   According to the OpenCV documentation, this function implements the Harris corner detector:

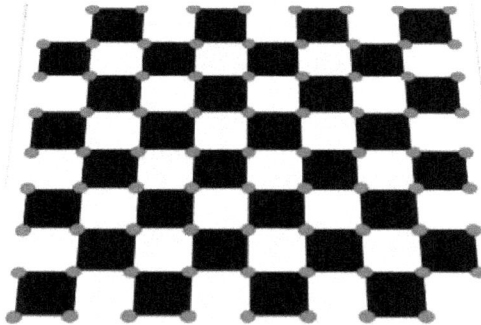

Figure 14.22: *Applying Harris corner detection to perform chessboard recognition*

   Using OpenCV, write a program to find corners in an image using the cornerHarris function.

4. Explain in a few lines of text how the cornerHarris function works.

5. Before deep learning, in 2008, OpenCV was bundled with a set of three face recognition algorithms [14]:

   • Eigenfaces
   • Fisherfaces
   • Local Binary Patterns Histograms

   Explain how these algorithms work, focusing on the limitations of their approaches in comparison to face recognition solutions based on deep learning.

References

[1] Dana H. Ballard; Christopher M. Brown. Computer Vision, Prentice Hall, 1982.

[2] Szeliski., Computer Vision: Algorithms and Applications, 2010.

[3] DALL-E2, OpenAI, available at **https://openai.com/dall-e-2**

[4] Luiz d'Oleron, yolov5-opencv-cpp-python, available at **https://github.com/doleron/yolov5-opencv-cpp-python**

[5] Glenn Jocher, Ultralytics YOLOv5, available at **https://github.com/ultralytics/yolov5**

[6] OpenCV Template Matching, available at **https://docs.opencv.org/3.4/d4/dc6/tutorial_py_template_matching.html**

[7] Le Cun at all, Backpropagation applied to handwritten zip code recognition,1989.

[8] Viola, P; Joes, M. "Rapid object detection using a boosted cascade of simple features", 2001.

[9] Qengineering, YoloV5 face Raspberry Pi 4, available at **https://github.com/Qengineering/YoloV5-face-ncnn-RPi4**

[10] Dogs vs. Cats dataset, available at **https://www.kaggle.com/c/dogs-vs-cats**

[11] OpenCV, Operations on arrays, available at **https://docs.opencv.org/3.4/d2/de8/group__core__array.html**

[12] OpenCV, Hough Circle Transform, available at **https://docs.opencv.org/3.4/d4/d70/tutorial_hough_circle.html**

[13] OpenCV Harris corner detector, available at **https://docs.opencv.org/4.x/d4/d7d/tutorial_harris_detector.html**

[14] OpenCV Face Recognition with OpenCV, available at **https://docs.opencv.org/4.x/da/d60/tutorial_face_main.html**

Join our book's Discord space

Join the book's Discord Workspace for Latest updates, Offers, Tech happenings around the world, New Release and Sessions with the Authors:

https://discord.bpbonline.com

CHAPTER 15
Developing an Image Classifier

Introduction

Classifiers are the most common type of tasks performed by machine learning models, being pivotal in the development of artificial intelligence systems. This chapter shows how to build and train a real image classifier to classify cat and dog images using a convolutional neural network inspired by the VGG16 architecture. The chapter will also discuss the practical, real-world challenges of using massive image datasets to train models. In particular, we will address the issue of handling huge datasets that do not fit the computer's primary memory by introducing an asynchronous mechanism to load and serve data to the training loop in real time.

Structure

The sequence of topics covered in this chapter is as follows:

- Experiments in this chapter
- Introducing image classifiers
- Case study
- Loading mini-batches asynchronously
- Experiment 1: Training a classifier with the Dogs x Cats dataset

- Experiment 2: Using dropout
- Experiment 3: Using data augmentation

Objectives

This chapter illustrates the development of an image classification system using deep learning. After reading this chapter and executing the experiments, the reader will learn the steps and practical challenges of developing a real image classifier using the deep learning components and techniques discussed so far in this book.

Experiments in this chapter

This chapter includes the following three experiments:

ID	Description
Exp-15.1	Training a classifier with the Dogs x Cats dataset
Exp-15.2	Training using dropout
Exp-15.3	Training using data augmentation

Table 15.1: Chapter experiment list

Introducing image classifiers

Image classifiers are a special type of classifier that use digital images as input. Let us understand the key points of these algorithms before moving on to building our first computer vision system.

Introduction to classifiers

In the sense of machine learning, **classifiers** are systems that assign one or more categories to an object given its features [1].

Classification, the act of assigning a category to an object, is a very natural task for us humans. Indeed, we often perform—with very high performance—tasks such as sorting objects without any significant training or effort.

One of the main objectives of artificial intelligence is to develop systems that can perform tasks like this with the same (or better) performance as humans.

It is difficult to determine exactly how and what the human brain does to solve tasks such as classification. One of the first steps toward solving this mystery is defining the environment in which an object is represented. We call this environment **feature space**.

Let us illustrate these concepts with a concrete example. Consider the following plot of our already-known Iris dataset:

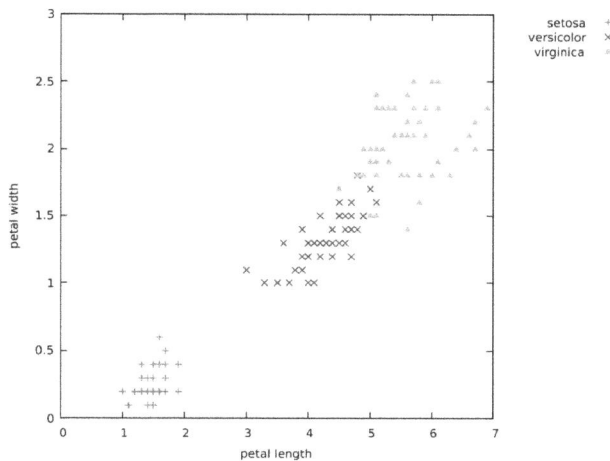

Figure 15.1: *Plotting the Iris dataset*

We first introduced the Iris dataset in *Chapter 7, Defining Activation Functions*. You should remember that this dataset has only 150 registers, whereas each register has four features and one label. The features are:

- Sepal length
- Sepal width
- Petal length
- Petal width

The label is one of the following classes (or categories):

- Setosa
- Versicolour
- Virginica

Note that the previous plot uses only two features: petal length and petal width. Thus, in this reduced example, these two features form the feature space. Consider the same plot again. In this new plot, we include two decision boundaries [2] to divide the feature space into three regions:

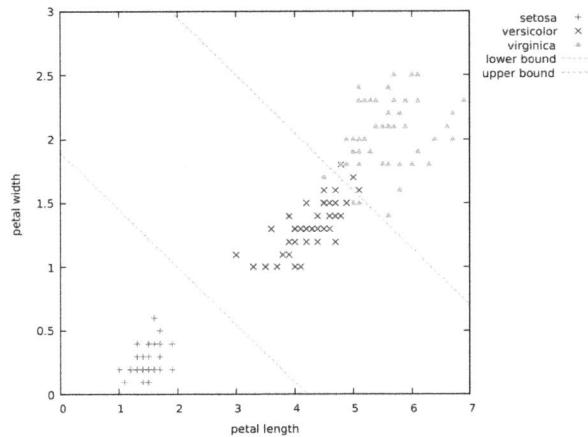

Figure 15.2: *Decision hyperplanes in the three-dimensional feature space*

The motivation for defining these three regions is depicted in the image: we want to separate the elements of each class. Note that these two decision boundaries do not achieve full separation: three instances of class versicolor lay on the region above the upper boundary, and three virginica instances lay on the region below the upper boundary. Also, note that the class setosa is fully separable by the lower decision boundary. Therefore, if we use these two decision boundaries to classify the instances, we will take six mistakes, achieving an accuracy of.

In the jargon of models, decision boundaries are **hypersurfaces** or **decision surfaces** that divide the feature space into two or more subregions. Inside each of such regions, the instances are considered equivalent in terms of their features so that we can assign them to the same category.

The most common type of decision surfaces are hyperplanes. We can think of hyperplanes as linear geometric structures. For example, in the previous 2D example using the Iris dataset, the two decision boundaries are straight lines. In a 3D feature space, the decision surfaces are regular planes lying in the three-dimensional room. Check the following figures (*Figure 15.3* and *Figure 15.4*):

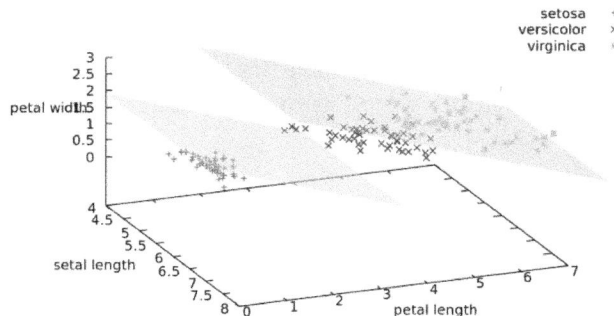

Figure 15.3: *Decision hyperplanes in the three-dimensional feature space*

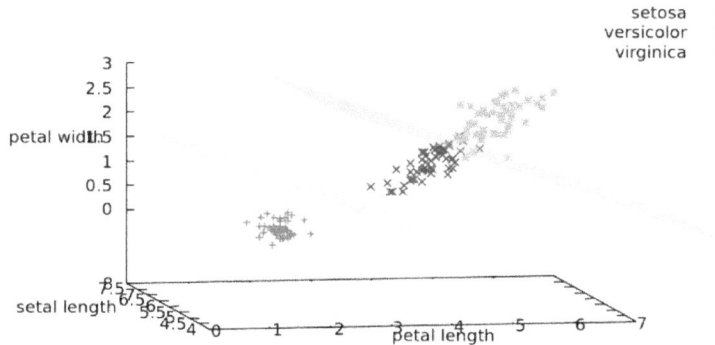

Figure 15.4: *Same chart, a different angle of view*

Note: These two figures above represent the same data and the same hyperplanes. We only showed them using different angles to make it easier to visualize.

Although the planes in the figures look limited (like rectangles), they are actually infinite, dividing the whole space into three separated regions. Each region defines a class so that instances inside the same region have the same label (even though three instances of versicolor and three of virginica violate this rule, causing misclassification).

The Iris dataset is an example where linear decision boundaries provide roughly good separation. The next topic talks about the linearity and non-linearity of systems.

Non-linear systems

Systems where hyperplanes provide good separation have a special name. We call them **linearly separable systems**. Linearly separable systems are great because they are straightforward to represent, model, compute, and fit. Not every system is linearly separable, however. For example, consider the following synthetic circular data:

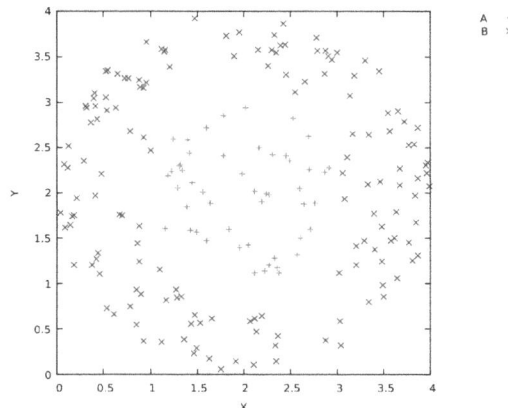

Figure 15.5: *Synthetically generated circular data*

There is no way to use one single hyperplane to separate the A instances from the B instances. For a problem like this, we can use non-linear decision boundaries:

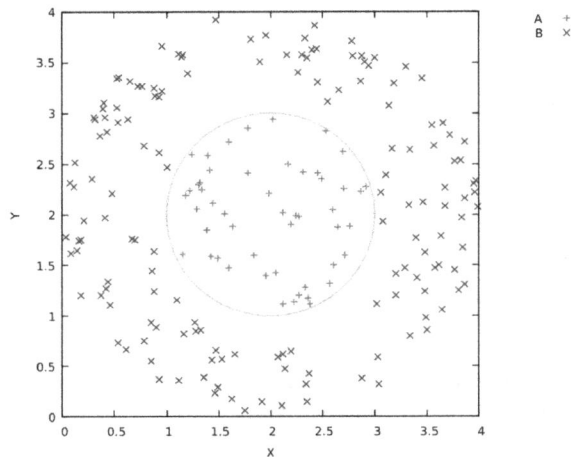

Figure 15.6: *A circular decision boundary*

Now, we can define a classifier using the geometric properties of a circle to detect if an instance belongs to class A or class B. In this particular case, there is another option: we can apply a transformation to polar coordinates:

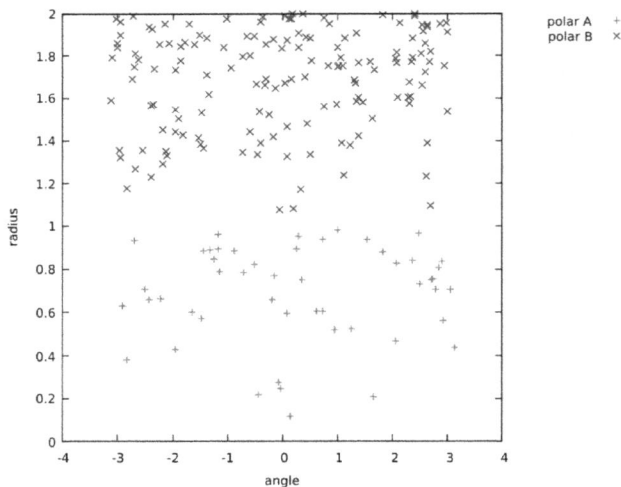

Figure 15.7: *Convert the circular data to polar coordinates*

Now, the problem is obviously linearly separable by the line *radius = 1*.

Although the transformation to polar coordinates worked for this particular case, there is no general procedure to transform a generic non-linear system into a linear one. Indeed, most non-linear data cannot be transformed into linear without losing significant information. In summary, non-linear systems are a reality, and we must find ways to deal with them directly.

The challenges of using non-linear data drove the efforts to develop more powerful models, resulting in the development of technologies such as deep learning.

The universal approximation theorem

Considering these decision boundaries as functions, we need a way to represent and fit them from data, which is exactly what neural networks are designed for. In 1989, a mathematician and professor called George Cybenko found that, under some constraints, any continuous function defined on a compact subset can be approximated by a single-hidden-layer neural network with arbitrary precision [3]. This finding is known as **the universal approximation theorem**. Refer to the following figure:

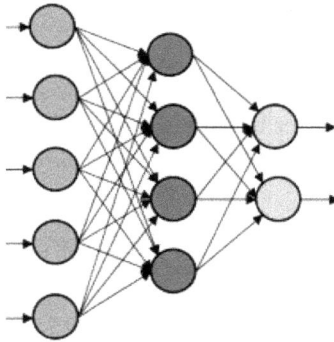

Figure 15.8: An example of a single hidden layer network

Although the theorem does not indicate how to train a network or even how many neurons the layer needs to achieve a given precision, it solidly endorses the use of neural networks to represent decision boundaries in both linear and non-linear systems.

However, if the theorem states that a single hidden-layer network is powerful enough to represent any function, why do we need deep networks with dozens or hundreds of layers?

The answer to this question no longer relies on the theoretical properties of mathematical systems but on a more practical, engineering-oriented matter: feasibility to train. It turns out that when we have a complex problem, such as a compute vision task, dividing the network into more layers makes the training easier (possible). We can use mission-specific types of layers, combining multiple layers that work hierarchically to learn how to detect raw features up to sophisticated semantic objects. Trying to fit a single hidden layer to support all these requirements is not feasible from an engineering point of view.

In the next section, we will introduce the case study of this chapter, where we develop an image classifier to determine if a picture has an image of a cat or a dog.

Case study

In this chapter, we will build an image classifier for the Dogs x Cats dataset using a convolutional neural network similar to the one shown:

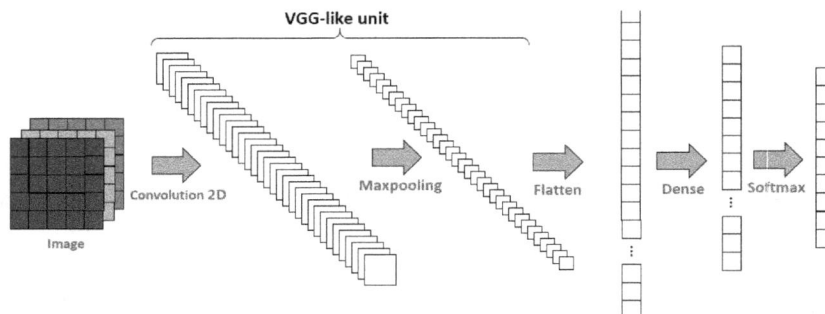

Figure 15.9: Model having one VGG-like unit

This network uses a sort of computation unit inspired by the VGG16 architecture. This unit consists of a convolutional layer followed by a ReLU activation and one max-pooling layer. Like in VGG, the convolution uses *3x3* kernels, and the max-pooling layer uses a resolution of 2 with strides of 2.

We can stack several units in sequence to build deeper networks. For example, consider the following model having two units:

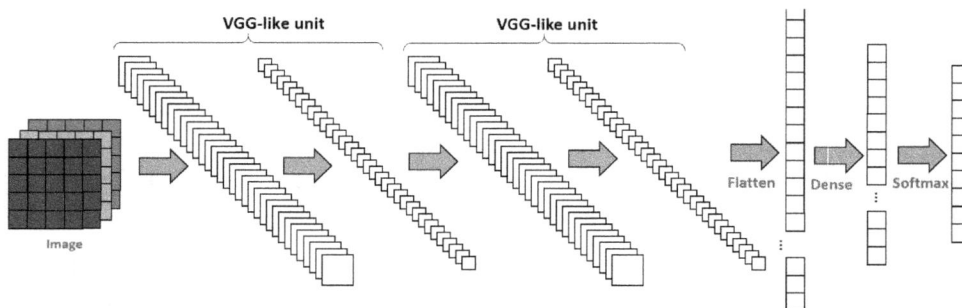

Figure 15.10: A model with two VGG units

Of course, we can stack more units to achieve deeper models. The network's last part is a sequence of a few dense layers, which is commonly called the network's **top**. Later on in this book, we will learn that we can reuse a pre-trained network to perform new tasks simply by replacing its top.

In this case study, we aim to train models like this with three units using the Dogs x Cats dataset to build an image classifier. However, before moving forward to the model's training phase, we must consider some issues and practical challenges of using large image datasets. These aspects are covered in the next section.

Practical challenges of image datasets

So far, in this book, we used only one example of an image dataset to train a model, the MNIST dataset. MNIST is a relatively small dataset, having 60,000 instances where each instance is a *28x28x1* grid, that is, a very tiny *28x28* grayscale pixel image. The compressed dataset bundle takes only 37 MB of storage. However, loading this data into the primary computer memory requires *60,000x28x28x1x4 = 188,160,000* bytes or almost 180 MB. Refer to the following figure:

Figure 15.11: Comparison between an image from Dogs x Cats and an image from MNIST

In the case of the Dogs x Cats dataset, we have about 25,000 3-channel images with variable sizes compressed into an 851.6 MB file. Assuming an average resolution of *150x150*, the total memory required to load the full dataset in the primary computer memory is *25,000x150x150x3x4 = 12,000,000,000* bytes, about 11.2 GB, a prohibitive amount of memory for some users. Even though your computer can support this memory footprint, sooner or later, you will find a dataset that does not fit your computational resources. For example, the ImageNet training bundle file has 138 GB of data.

Indeed, holding the full dataset in memory is a waste of resources. As seen in *Chapter 12, Implementing Cross-validation, Mini Batching, and Model Performance Metrics*, we learned how to use mini-batching to train our models. In mini-batching, only a small slice of the data—the mini-batch—needs to be loaded into memory each time. Thus, instead of loading the full dataset at once in memory, we need only to load the mini-batch and serve it to the training algorithm. This actually reduces the memory footprint, allowing the training of indefinitely large datasets or regular machines.

Of course, using this approach introduces other issues. It turns out that IO operation on discs, even modern solid-state discs, takes much longer time than primary memory read operations. As a result, synchronally loading the minibatches thousands or hundred times each epoch slows down the algorithm speed, which makes this approach useless. The solution here is to use an alternative technique called asynchronous IO, as explained ahead.

The Dogs x Cats data

The Dogs x Cats dataset was part of a challenge on Kaggle [4] to develop an algorithm to distinguish dogs from cats. According to the website, this dataset is a small subset of a much bigger set of animal images created using pictures of lost pets.

The Dogs x Cats dataset used in this experiment has about 25k images, where nearly 50% are images of cats and 50% are images of dogs. Check some of these images in the following figure:

Figure 15.12: Examples of Cat images in the Dogs x Cats dataset

We discussed some features of this dataset in *Chapter 14, Introducing Computer Vision Models*. Unlike MNIST, the data in Dogs x Cats is quite challenging, having wild issues such as broken or blank images, distortions, occlusions, and all sorts of outliers. Check below a small sampling of problematic instances:

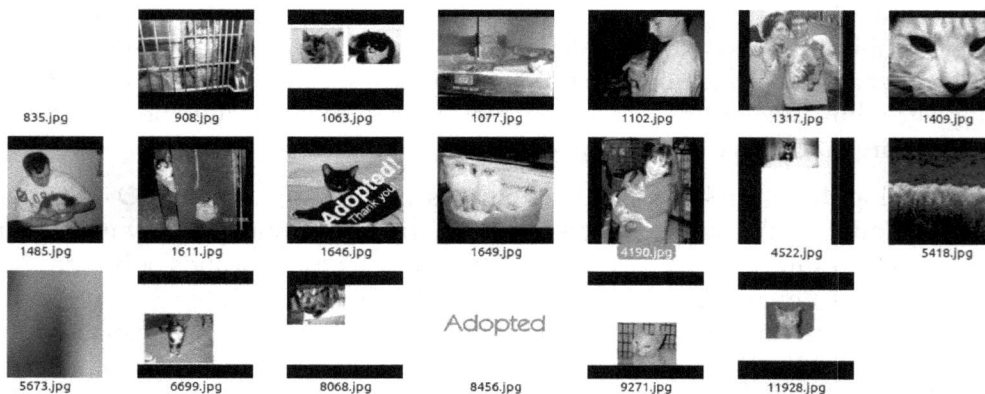

Figure 15.13: Examples of problematic instances in the Dogs x Cats dataset

Note that the first image is only a blank picture. Whereas broken images should be actually removed early, in general, we see the quality issues as an opportunity to check the robustness of the algorithms to deal with outliers and noise properly. Thus, we keep those problematic images in the dataset.

Due to a fixed network top, we need to fix the size of the input images. We will use the standard VGG image size (*224x224*) to train the model in the three experiments later in this chapter.

Note: The bigger the image, the slower the training. Thus, feel free to reduce the image size to 200 or 180.

A common issue in real-world image datasets is that the images often have different resolutions. In addition, some images are portrait-oriented, and others are landscape-oriented. There are two options here: to stretch or centralize. The result of the two approaches can be seen in the following figure:

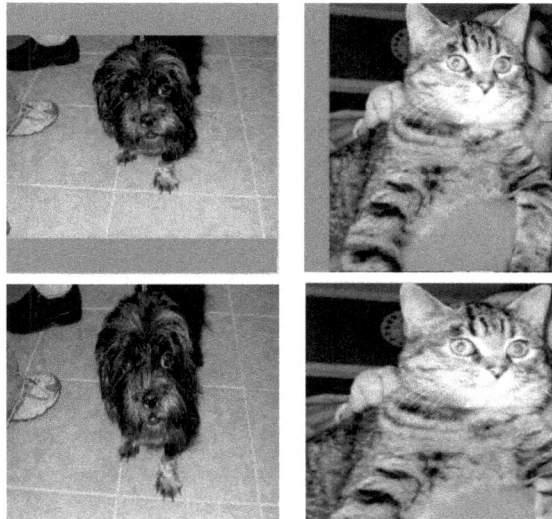

Figure 15.14: *Stretching or centering images to make them squared*

Both stretching and centralizing result in a square image. The difference is the distortion in stretching and the inclusion of blank pads to centralize the image. In OpenCV, making an image square is simple:

```
1. void make_image_square(cv::Mat &src, cv::Mat &dest) {
2.
3.     const int max_size = std::max(src.cols, src.rows);
4.
5.     dest = cv::Mat(cv::Size(max_size, max_
   size), CV_8UC3, cv::Scalar(255/2,255/2,255/2));
6.
7.     int left = (max_size - src.cols) / 2;
```

```
8.        int top = (max_size - src.rows) / 2;
9.
10.       cv::Mat dest_roi = dest(cv::Rect(left, top, src.cols, src.
   rows));
11.       src.copyTo(dest_roi);
12. }
```

Note: During the experiments, we will stretch the images to square them in frames of 224x224 pixels.

Correlated work and benchmarks

The quality issues in this dataset make it a good first example of real-world image data, making Dogs x Cats an active object of study by the deep learning community in recent years. In particular, *Jason Brownlee* trained several convolutional networks using Google TensorFlow with this dataset [5].

Regarding expected results, Kaggle reported an accuracy of 80% as the state-of-the-art [6]. Nevertheless, we consider this an obsolete number. Thus, we prefer to use Jason's scores as a reference. Refer to the following table:

Model	Topology	Validation accuracy
Bare metal	3 VGG-like units	80.184%
Dropout	3 VGG-like units + 3 dropout layers	81.279%
Data augmentation	3 VGG-like units + data augmentation	85.816%

Table 15.2: Jason's scores

In the forthcoming sections, we will train models using the Dogs x Cats dataset, following the same steps as Jason. That is, we will also perform three experiments: training a raw model with the Dogs x Cats dataset, training a model using dropout, and finally, training a model using data augmentation.

There are some points we need to discuss before starting the model training, for instance, the challenges of using a gigabyte-large dataset to train a model on a regular, domestic computer infrastructure.

Loading mini-batches asynchronously

Loading the whole dataset into the computer memory works well only for small datasets. This approach is not an alternative to training a model if the dataset is medium-sized or bigger.

In fact, sometimes people load the full dataset in memory only because loading the data on demand drastically slows down the algorithm training. This approach, however, is suboptimal if we have a large gigabyte-sized dataset and totally unpractical if the dataset is huge (100GB or more).

Consider the following representation of a synchronous execution of the training algorithm:

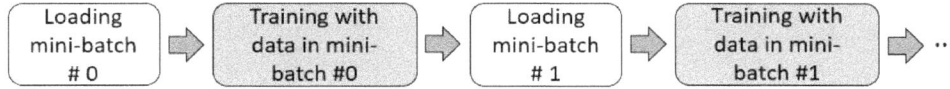

Figure 15.15: A synchronous training execution representation

If the cost to load each mini-batch is not significant, most of the time, the algorithm will be consuming the available processing time to fit the model, which is the ideal scenario. However, loading data from discs is usually very slow compared to CPU or GPU processing speeds. Thus, using this strategy of synchronous IO significantly degrades the algorithm convergence overall time, reducing the training speed even though there is processing unit time available in the system. The solution for this issue is using **asynchronous IO**, as represented:

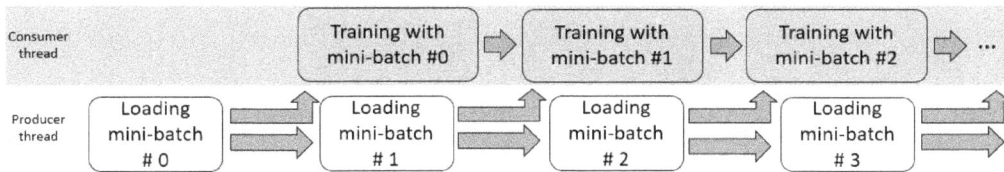

Figure 15.16: A training execution using asynchronous IO

In this new execution, after the first loading, the system will compute the data in the current (previously loaded) mini-batch while loading the next mini-batch in parallel. As a result, after the processing of the current mini-batch, the system can immediately start the processing of the next batch, providing continuous use of the system processing resources and reducing the overall training time.

This approach is useful because it accelerates the algorithm speed without impacting the model quality. In addition, implementing it is not hard at all. The canonical way to implement this mechanism is using an old and effective strategy called **producer-consumer**.

Using producer-consumer to implement asynchronous IO

Producer-consumer was first proposed by the famous Dutch computer scientist *Edsger Dijkstra* [7]. As its name suggests, in producer-consumer, we have two roles: the producer and the consumer. In our application:

- The **producer** loads the mini-batches
- The **consumer** uses the mini-batches to train the model

Since we need the producer and the consumer running in parallel (or concurrently), we will implement this approach using two C++ threads:

- The **consumer** is the default main thread, which consumes the batches to train the model, and
- The **producer** is a daemon thread, which loads the batches.

Consider the following implementation of a parallel batching controller:

```
1.  enum BATCH_STATUS {AVAILABLE, IN_USE, UNAVAILABLE};
2.
3.  template<typename Generator>
4.  class ParallelBatches {
5.
6.  public:
7.      // ...
8.
9.  private:
10.     int batch_size;
11.     const Eigen::Tensor<std::string, 2> *training_data;
12.
13.     int num_registers;
14.     std::vector<int> indexes;
15.     int index_pointer;
16.
17.     int buffer_size;
18.     std::vector<Batch<4,2>> buffer;
19.     std::vector<BATCH_STATUS> buffer_status;
20.     int read_pointer = 0;
21.     int write_pointer = 0;
22.     bool done;
23.
24.     std::mutex _mutex;
25.     std::condition_variable _cond_var;
26.
27. };
```

This class is similar to the batching controller used in *Chapter 12, Implementing Cross-validation, Mini Batching, and Model Performance Metrics. However, it has* some important modifications.

First, we defined a buffer as a vector of batches:

```
1.  std::vector<Batch<4,2>> buffer;
```

This allows not only preloading one batch but several ones. The **buffer_size** attribute defines the number of preloaded batches. To avoid unnecessary memory write operations, we can implement this buffer as a circular buffer [8], which is a coding standard for buffering data streams. Check the following representation:

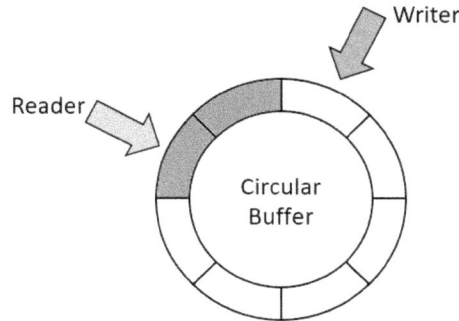

Figure 15.17: *A representation of a circular buffer*

As shown in the figure above, the implementation of circular buffers requires two pointers: the writer pointer and the reader pointer:

```
1.  int read_pointer = 0;
2.  int write_pointer = 0;
```

We cannot read a batch in the buffer if it is not yet properly loaded. In the same way, we cannot override a batch in the buffer that was not read yet. To control the operations of read and write in the buffer, we need a set of flags to keep the state of the batches in the buffer:

```
1.  enum BATCH_STATUS {AVAILABLE, UNAVAILABLE};
2.  std::vector<BATCH_STATUS> buffer_status;
```

Once we set the circular buffer, we can read batches from it:

```
1.  Batch<4,2>* next() {
2.
3.      Batch<4,2>* result = nullptr;
4.
5.      auto begin = high_resolution_clock::now();
6.
```

```
7.      std::unique_lock<std::mutex> lock(_mutex);
8.      _cond_var.wait(lock, [&]{ return (done || (buffer_status[read_
   pointer] == AVAILABLE)); });
9.      auto end = high_resolution_clock::now();
10.     auto duration = duration_cast<milliseconds>(end - begin);
11.     waiting_time += duration.count();
12.
13.     if (buffer_status[read_pointer] == AVAILABLE) {
14.         result = &buffer[read_pointer];
15.         read_pointer = (read_pointer + 1) % buffer_size;
16.     }
17.
18.     lock.unlock();
19.
20.     return result;
21. }
```

The critical point in this method is:

```
1.  std::unique_lock<std::mutex> lock(_mutex);
2.  _cond_var.wait(lock, [&]{ return (done || (buffer_status[read_
    pointer] == AVAILABLE)); });
```

Here, we are using a **std::mutex** and **std::condition_variable** to lock the current thread while the two conditions are both false:

done

buffer_status[read_pointer] == AVAILABLE

If at least one of these conditions is true, the execution continues to the next lines. If **buffer_status[read_pointer] == AVAILABLE** is true, the method increments **read_ pointer**, and returns the pointer to the buffer position. The batch pointer will be served to the training algorithm as usual. After the batch is processed, the algorithm must invoke the **release()** function:

```
1.  void release(Batch<4,2>* batch) {
2.      int index = std::distance(buffer.data(), batch);
3.      buffer_status[index] = UNAVAILABLE;
4.      _cond_var.notify_one();
5.  }
```

To notify the producer that the batch was finally consumed and is no longer available.

Meanwhile, the producer thread is trying to load new batches to fill the buffer:

```
1. std::thread producer([&]() {
2.     while(!done) {
3.         load_batch();
4.     }
5. });
6.
7. producer.detach();
```

Calling **producer.detach()** transforms the thread into a daemon. A daemon thread is not joinable, meaning the thread will silently auto-join when it is done.

load_batch() is defined as follows:

```
1. void load_batch(){
2.     std::unique_lock<std::mutex> lock(_mutex);
3.     _cond_var.wait(lock, [&]{ return (done || (buffer_status[write_
       pointer] == UNAVAILABLE)); });
4.
5.     if (!done) {
6.         load_batch_helper();
7.     }
8.
9.     lock.unlock();
10.     _cond_var.notify_one();
11. }
```

The producer also uses **std::mutex** and **std::condition_variable** to control its execution. It will be locked while the following two conditions are both false:

done

buffer_status[write_pointer] == UNAVAILABLE

Once at least one of these conditions is true, the producer can proceed to the next lines. If **buffer_status[write_pointer] == UNAVAILABLE** is true, then there exists at least one slot to fill:

```
1. void load_batch_helper() {
2.     int index = indexes[index_pointer];
3.     index_pointer++;
4.     int begin = index * batch_size;
5.     int end = std::min(begin + batch_size, num_registers);
6.     int length = end - begin;
7.     Eigen::array<Eigen::Index, 2> offset = {begin, 0};
8.     Eigen::array<Eigen::Index, 2> extent = {length, training_data-
```

```
      >dimension(1)};
9.      Eigen::Tensor<std::string, 2> slice = training_data-
   >slice(offset, extent);
10.     Batch<4,2> & batch = buffer[write_pointer];
11.     fill_batch(slice, batch);
12.     buffer_status[write_pointer] = AVAILABLE;
13.     write_pointer = (write_pointer + 1) % buffer_size;
14.     done = index_pointer >= indexes.size();
15. }
```

The code in **load_batch_helper()** is similar to how we have loaded batches in *Chapter 12*. The main difference here is the use of the circular buffer, which we set as follows:

```
buffer_status[write_pointer] = AVAILABLE
```

This flags the consumer that the slot is finally available to consume, which means that the batch can be used to train the model (or to validate the model).

In the next section, when we execute backpropagation using this batching controller, we will realize that the actual time taken by the training loop to fit the model is much longer than the time spent loading the batches. Thus, loading the batches asynchronously will definitely be worth it, reducing the overall time.

Note that different combinations of IO systems, hard discs, and processing units can achieve different results.

> **Note: The work of ML engineers is mostly finding practical ways to perform high-demanding algorithms in limited real computer architectures.**

The algorithm's final speed results from the combination of the underlying computer infrastructure, the processing load, and how memory is handled to feed the algorithm. A slow execution takes longer to converge. In practice, this eventually results in bad models because waiting the required time for a better convergence is usually prohibited if the training is too slow.

Now that we understand how to use asynchronous IO to feed the training algorithm, we can move to the next section, focusing on the model performance with respect to validation loss and accuracy.

Experiment 1: Training a classifier with the Dogs x Cats dataset

Let us start with a three-unit model following the model architecture described earlier in this chapter. Consider the following model:

```
1.  template <typename DEVICE, typename GEN>
2.  class Model {
3.
4.  public:
5.
6.      Model(DEVICE &device, GEN &rng, int img_size): IMG_SIZE(img_size) {
7.          const int kernel_size = 3;
8.          const int channels = 3;
9.
10.         const int hidden_neurons = 512;
11.         const int num_classes = 2;
12.
13.         Tensor_4D kernels_0(kernel_size, kernel_size, channels, 16);
14.         glorot_uniform_initializer(rng, kernels_0);
15.         conv2d_0 = new Conv2DLayer(device, kernels_0, new ReLU<4>());
16.
17.         maxpooling_0 = new MaxPooling(device, 2);
18.
19.         Tensor_4D mask_0(1, IMG_SIZE/2, IMG_SIZE/2, 16);
20.
21.         Tensor_4D kernels_1(kernel_size, kernel_size, kernels_0.
    dimension(3), 32);
22.         glorot_uniform_initializer(rng, kernels_1);
23.         conv2d_1 = new Conv2DLayer(device, kernels_1, new ReLU<4>())
    ;
24.
25.         maxpooling_1 = new MaxPooling(device, 2);
26.
27.         Tensor_4D mask_1(1, IMG_SIZE/4, IMG_SIZE/4, 32);
28.
29.         Tensor_4D kernels_2(kernel_size, kernel_size, kernels_1.
    dimension(3), 64);
30.         glorot_uniform_initializer(rng, kernels_2);
31.         conv2d_2 = new Conv2DLayer(device, kernels_2, new ReLU<4>());
32.
33.         maxpooling_2 = new MaxPooling(device, 2);
34.
35.         Tensor_4D mask_2(1, IMG_SIZE/8, IMG_SIZE/8, 64);
```

```
36.
37.         flatten = new FlattenLayer<DEVICE, 4>(device);
38.
39.         int reduced_image_size = IMG_SIZE / 8;
40.
41.         const int flatten_size = reduced_image_size * reduced_image_
    size * kernels_2.dimension(3);
42.
43.         Tensor_2D W1(flatten_size, hidden_neurons);
44.         glorot_uniform_initializer(rng, W1);
45.         dense = new DenseLayer(device, W1, new ReLU<2>());
46.
47.         Tensor_2D mask(1, 512);
48.
49.         Tensor_2D W2(hidden_neurons, num_classes);
50.         glorot_uniform_initializer(rng, W2);
51.         output_layer = new SoftmaxCrossEntropyLayer(device, W2);
52.     }
53.
54.     // ...
55.
56. private:
57.     const int IMG_SIZE;
58.     Conv2DLayer<DEVICE> *conv2d_0;
59.     MaxPooling<DEVICE> *maxpooling_0;
60.
61.     Conv2DLayer<DEVICE> *conv2d_1;
62.     MaxPooling<DEVICE> *maxpooling_1;
63.
64.     Conv2DLayer<DEVICE> *conv2d_2;
65.     MaxPooling<DEVICE> *maxpooling_2;
66.
67.     FlattenLayer<DEVICE, 4> *flatten;
68.     DenseLayer<DEVICE> *dense;
69.     DenseLayer<DEVICE> *output_layer;
70.
71. };
```

This model has three units where each unit consists of one conv2D and one maxpooling layer. Note that the layers are configured to use Adam as an optimizer. We can forward a batch of instances on this model as follows:

```
1.  void forward(const Eigen::Tensor<float, 4> &input) {
2.      conv2d_0->forward(input);
3.      maxpooling_0->forward(conv2d_0->get_output());
4.
5.      conv2d_1->forward(maxpooling_0->get_output());
6.      maxpooling_1->forward(conv2d_1->get_output());
7.
8.      conv2d_2->forward(maxpooling_1->get_output());
9.      maxpooling_2->forward(conv2d_2->get_output());
10.
11.     flatten->forward(maxpooling_2->get_output());
12.     dense->forward(flatten->get_output());
13.     output_layer->forward(dense->get_output());
14. }
```

In the same way, we can propagate the gradients backward as follows:

```
1.  void backward(const Eigen::Tensor<float, 2> &upstream) {
2.      output_layer->backward(upstream, true);
3.      dense->backward(output_layer->get_downstream(), true);
4.      flatten->backward(dense->get_downstream(), true);
5.
6.      maxpooling_2->backward(flatten->get_downstream(), true);
7.      conv2d_2->backward(maxpooling_2->get_downstream(), true);
8.
9.      maxpooling_1->backward(conv2d_2->get_downstream(), true);
10.     conv2d_1->backward(maxpooling_1->get_downstream(), true);
11.
12.     maxpooling_0->backward(conv2d_1->get_downstream(), true);
13.     conv2d_0->backward(maxpooling_0->get_downstream(), false);
14. }
```

Finally, update the model:

```
1.  void update(const float learning_rate, int epoch) {
2.      conv2d_0->update(learning_rate, epoch);
3.      conv2d_1->update(learning_rate, epoch);
4.      conv2d_2->update(learning_rate, epoch);
```

```
5.      dense->update(learning_rate, epoch);
6.      output_layer->update(learning_rate, epoch);
7.  }
```

Note: Maxpooling and flatten layers need not call update() since they do not have trainable parameters to fit.

Now, we can train this model as usual, but this time, replace the mini-batching manager with our new parallel batch manager:

```
1.  using DEVICE = Eigen::ThreadPoolDevice;
2.  using GEN = std::mt19937;
3.  using MODEL = Model<DEVICE, GEN>;
4.
5.  std::random_device rd{};
6.  const auto seed = rd();
7.  GEN rng(seed);
8.  std::cout << "Using seed " << seed << "\n";
9.
10. const int threads = std::thread::hardware_concurrency();
11. Eigen::ThreadPool tp(threads);
12. DEVICE device(&tp, threads);
13.
14. const int IMAGE_SIZE = 224;
15.
16. MODEL model(device, rng, IMAGE_SIZE);
17.
18. const int max_epochs = 10;
19. const int minibatch_size = 32;
20. const TYPE learning_rate = 0.001;
21. bool center_images = false;
22. const int batch_buffer_size = 3;
23.
24. std::cout << "Loading the data, please wait!\n";
25. auto [training_data, validation_data] = load_dogs_x_cats_
    dataset("data/dogs_x_cats/PetImages", rng, 0.7);
26. std::cout << "Data loaded!\n";
27.
28. std::cout << "Using image size " << model.get_IMG_
    SIZE() << "x" << model.get_IMG_SIZE() << "\n";
```

```
29.
30. std::cout << "Training for " << max_epochs << " epochs\n";
31.
32. training<DEVICE, GEN, MODEL, BATCH_MANAGER>(model, rng, training_
    data, validation_data, device, max_epochs, minibatch_size, learning_
    rate, center_images, batch_buffer_size);
```

These settings results in a performance like this:

```
doleron@delegion:~/book-workspace/php-deep-learning-in-modern-cpp/chapter_15/build$ ./3conv_net
Using seed 821395054
Loading the data, please wait!
Total of images: 24946
Training size: 17462
Validation size 7484
Data loaded!
Using image size 224x224
Training for 10 epochs
epoch:  0        training_loss:  0.6065  training_acc:   67.28   validation_loss:        0.5376  validation_acc: 71.59
epoch:  1        training_loss:  0.4646  training_acc:   77.78   validation_loss:        0.4555  validation_acc: 78.62
epoch:  2        training_loss:  0.3919  training_acc:   82.23   validation_loss:        0.4419  validation_acc: 79.63
epoch:  3        training_loss:  0.3293  training_acc:   85.94   validation_loss:        0.4316  validation_acc: 80.65
epoch:  4        training_loss:  0.2696  training_acc:   89.07   validation_loss:        0.4245  validation_acc: 81.52
epoch:  5        training_loss:  0.2104  training_acc:   91.78   validation_loss:        0.4533  validation_acc: 81.18
epoch:  6        training_loss:  0.1538  training_acc:   94.63   validation_loss:        0.4835  validation_acc: 81.41
epoch:  7        training_loss:  0.1032  training_acc:   96.79   validation_loss:        0.5408  validation_acc: 81.26
epoch:  8        training_loss:  0.0654  training_acc:   98.32   validation_loss:        0.737   validation_acc: 79.12
epoch:  9        training_loss:  0.04188 training_acc:   99.06   validation_loss:        0.6547  validation_acc: 80.99
success
doleron@delegion:~/book-workspace/php-deep-learning-in-modern-cpp/chapter_15/build$
```

Figure 15.18: The performance of the first model

Our first attempt outperformed the state-of-the-art performance (80%) informed by Kaggle in the 5th epoch with a validation accuracy of 81.52%. This shows how deep learning overtaken the ML scene in the later few years.

Note: The code of this experiment can be found in the book repository.

In general, one run is never enough to find a conclusion. A much better or bad result always can be a result of a chance. We should run the train several times and summarize the results to get some confidence about the results.

In this case study, we repeat the experiment five times and average the losses and accuracies. The following charts show the results:

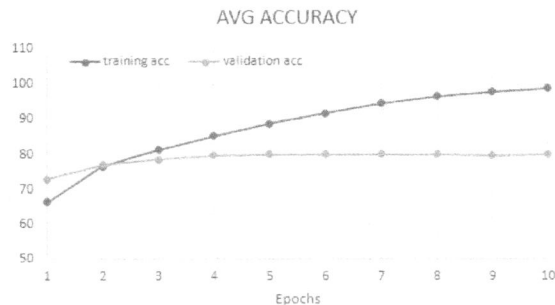

Figure 15.19: The performance in terms of accuracy

Checking the chart, we can find a continuous growth in training accuracy while the validation accuracy stabilizes at nearly 80%. If we check the loss behavior, however, we can find that the training loss continuously decreases while the validation loss increases at epoch five and afterward:

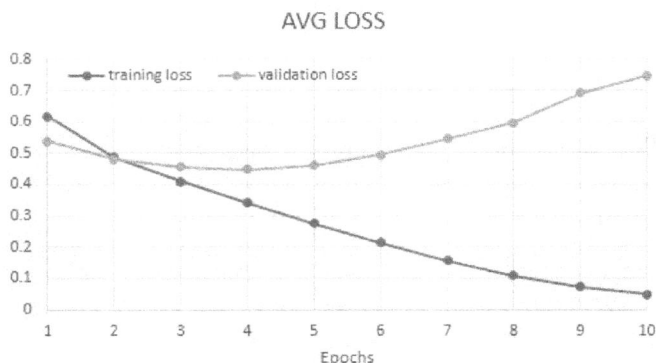

Figure 15.20: *The indication of overfitting after epoch five in the validation loss*

In *Chapter 11, Underfitting, Overfitting, and Regularization,* we learned that the behavior depicted in these plots is a strong indication of overfitting. If we deploy this model in production, it will perform with the validation performance, not with the training performance.

Note: The code in this experiment runs on multiple CPU cores, aiming to be runnable on most readers' machines. Refer to Chapter 10 to learn how to speed up the training process by running the tensor operations using CUDA/GPU.

To face the influence of overfitting, in the next sections, we will test two regularization alternatives: dropout and data augmentation.

Experiment 2: Using dropout

Aiming to avoid overfitting, we can include some dropout layers as follows:

```
1.  template <typename DEVICE, typename GEN>
2.  class Model {
3.
4.  public:
5.
6.      Model(DEVICE &device, GEN &rng, int img_size): IMG_SIZE(img_size) {
7.          const int x_width = IMG_SIZE;
8.          const int x_height = IMG_SIZE;
9.
10.         const int kernel_size = 3;
```

```
11.          const int channels = 3;
12.
13.          const int hidden_neurons = 512;
14.          const int num_classes = 2;
15.
16.          Tensor_4D kernels_0(kernel_size, kernel_size, channels, 16);
17.          glorot_uniform_initializer(rng, kernels_0);
18.          conv2d_0 = new Conv2DLayer(device, kernels_0, new ReLU<4>());
19.          conv2d_0->set_optimizer(Adam<4>());
20.
21.          maxpooling_0 = new MaxPooling(device, 2);
22.
23.          dropout_0 = new DropoutLayer<DEVICE, 4, GEN>(de-
     vice, 0.2, rng);
24.
25.          Tensor_4D kernels_1(kernel_size, kernel_size, kernels_0.
     dimension(3), 32);
26.          glorot_uniform_initializer(rng, kernels_1);
27.          conv2d_1 = new Conv2DLayer(device, kernels_1, new ReLU<4>());
28.          conv2d_1->set_optimizer(Adam<4>());
29.
30.          maxpooling_1 = new MaxPooling(device, 2);
31.
32.          dropout_1 = new DropoutLayer<DEVICE, 4, GEN>
     (device, 0.2, rng);
33.
34.          Tensor_4D kernels_2(kernel_size, kernel_size, kernels_1.
     dimension(3), 64);
35.          glorot_uniform_initializer(rng, kernels_2);
36.          conv2d_2 = new Conv2DLayer(device, kernels_2, new ReLU<4>
     ());
37.          conv2d_2->set_optimizer(Adam<4>());
38.
39.          maxpooling_2 = new MaxPooling(device, 2);
40.
41.          dropout_2 = new DropoutLayer<DEVICE, 4, GEN>
     (device, 0.2, rng);
42.
43.          flatten = new FlattenLayer<DEVICE, 4>(device);
44.
```

```
45.         int reduced_image_size = IMG_SIZE / 8;
46.
47.         const int flatten_size = reduced_image_size * reduced_image_
    size * kernels_2.dimension(3);
48.
49.         Tensor_2D W1(flatten_size, hidden_neurons);
50.         glorot_uniform_initializer(rng, W1);
51.         dense = new DenseLayer(device, W1, new ReLU<2>());
52.         dense->set_optimizer(Adam<2>());
53.
54.         dropout = new DropoutLayer<DEVICE, 2, GEN>
    (device, 0.5, rng);
55.
56.         Tensor_2D W2(hidden_neurons, num_classes);
57.         glorot_uniform_initializer(rng, W2);
58.         output_layer = new SoftmaxCrossEntropyLayer(device, W2);
59.         output_layer->set_optimizer(Adam<2>());
60.     }
61.
62.     // ...
63.
64. private:
65.     const int IMG_SIZE;
66.     Conv2DLayer<DEVICE> *conv2d_0;
67.     MaxPooling<DEVICE> *maxpooling_0;
68.     DropoutLayer<DEVICE, 4, GEN> *dropout_0;
69.
70.     Conv2DLayer<DEVICE> *conv2d_1;
71.     MaxPooling<DEVICE> *maxpooling_1;
72.     DropoutLayer<DEVICE, 4, GEN> *dropout_1;
73.
74.     Conv2DLayer<DEVICE> *conv2d_2;
75.     MaxPooling<DEVICE> *maxpooling_2;
76.     DropoutLayer<DEVICE, 4, GEN> *dropout_2;
77.
78.     FlattenLayer<DEVICE, 4> *flatten;
79.     DenseLayer<DEVICE> *dense;
80.     DropoutLayer<DEVICE, 2, GEN> *dropout;
81.     DenseLayer<DEVICE> *output_layer;
82. };
```

Note that we are including dropout layers after the maxpooling layers, such as:

```
dropout_0 = new DropoutLayer<DEVICE, 4>(device, 0.2);
```

Another 2D dropout layer after the dense layer:

```
dropout = new DropoutLayer<DEVICE, 2>(device, 0.5);
```

We cannot forget to adjust the forward method to include the dropout layers:

```
1.  void forward(const Tensor_4D &input) {
2.      conv2d_0->forward(input);
3.      maxpooling_0->forward(conv2d_0->get_output());
4.      dropout_0->forward(maxpooling_0->get_output());
5.
6.      conv2d_1->forward(dropout_0->get_output());
7.      maxpooling_1->forward(conv2d_1->get_output());
8.      dropout_1->forward(maxpooling_1->get_output());
9.
10.     conv2d_2->forward(dropout_1->get_output());
11.     maxpooling_2->forward(conv2d_2->get_output());
12.     dropout_2->forward(maxpooling_2->get_output());
13.
14.     flatten->forward(dropout_2->get_output());
15.     dense->forward(flatten->get_output());
16.     dropout->forward(dense->get_output());
17.     output_layer->forward(dropout->get_output());
18. }
```

Also, backward:

```
1.  void backward(const Tensor_2D &upstream) {
2.      output_layer->backward(upstream, true);
3.      dropout->backward(output_layer->get_downstream(), true);
4.      dense->backward(dropout->get_downstream(), true);
5.      flatten->backward(dense->get_downstream(), true);
6.
7.      dropout_2->backward(flatten->get_downstream(), true);
8.      maxpooling_2->backward(dropout_2->get_downstream(), true);
9.      conv2d_2->backward(maxpooling_2->get_downstream(), true);
10.
11.     dropout_1->backward(conv2d_2->get_downstream(), true);
12.     maxpooling_1->backward(dropout_1->get_downstream(), true);
```

```
13.    conv2d_1->backward(maxpooling_1->get_downstream(), true);
14.
15.    dropout_0->backward(conv2d_1->get_downstream(), true);
16.    maxpooling_0->backward(dropout_0->get_downstream(), true);
17.    conv2d_0->backward(maxpooling_0->get_downstream(), false);
18. }
```

Note that we should not add dropout to the prediction. Thus, the prediction procedure keeps untouched:

```
1.  Tensor_2D predict(const Tensor_4D &input) {
2.      auto y1 = conv2d_0->predict(input);
3.      auto y2 = maxpooling_0->predict(y1);
4.
5.      auto y3 = conv2d_1->predict(y2);
6.      auto y4 = maxpooling_1->predict(y3);
7.
8.      auto y5 = conv2d_2->predict(y4);
9.      auto y6 = maxpooling_2->predict(y5);
10.
11.     auto y7 = flatten->predict(y6);
12.     auto y8 = dense->predict(y7);
13.     auto result = output_layer->predict(y8);
14.     return std::move(result);
15. }
```

Training the model after including dropout results in something like this:

Figure 15.21: First attempt to avoid overfitting with dropout

This result does not look very promising. The training achieved a smaller performance than the one achieved by the first bare metal model. *What could be happening?*

It seems that the model is still overfitting after epoch 7. The solution is to increase the drop rate of one or more dropout layers. The question is, which ones?

The layers with the largest volume are those where dropout has the most influence. In our model, the biggest layer is the first dense layer at the network top. Changing the drop rate of the dropout layer after this layer will have the greatest impact.

For example, let us change the last dropout layer's rate from 0.5 to 0.8:

```
1. dropout = new DropoutLayer<DEVICE, 2, GEN>(device, 0.8, rng);
```

Running the training again after this change, finally provides better results:

```
doleron@delegion:~/book-workspace/pbp-deep-learning-in-modern-cpp/chapter_15/build$ ./3conv_dropout_net
Using seed 3044487690
Loading the data, please wait!
Total of images: 24946
Training size: 17462
Validation size 7484
Data loaded!
Using image size 224x224
Training for 25 epochs
epoch:  0    training_loss:  0.6878  training_acc:  56.49  validation_loss:  0.5799  validation_acc: 71.37
epoch:  1    training_loss:  0.5577  training_acc:  71.52  validation_loss:  0.5306  validation_acc: 73.62
epoch:  2    training_loss:  0.5111  training_acc:  74.74  validation_loss:  0.5194  validation_acc: 73.98
epoch:  3    training_loss:  0.4776  training_acc:  77.4   validation_loss:  0.4902  validation_acc: 77.11
epoch:  4    training_loss:  0.4521  training_acc:  79.01  validation_loss:  0.4761  validation_acc: 77.81
epoch:  5    training_loss:  0.4305  training_acc:  80.38  validation_loss:  0.4554  validation_acc: 78.9
epoch:  6    training_loss:  0.4112  training_acc:  81.5   validation_loss:  0.4495  validation_acc: 79.4
epoch:  7    training_loss:  0.3922  training_acc:  82.37  validation_loss:  0.4559  validation_acc: 79.18
epoch:  8    training_loss:  0.3735  training_acc:  83.75  validation_loss:  0.4321  validation_acc: 80.46
epoch:  9    training_loss:  0.3567  training_acc:  84.37  validation_loss:  0.429   validation_acc: 80.42
epoch: 10    training_loss:  0.3339  training_acc:  85.11  validation_loss:  0.4313  validation_acc: 80.54
epoch: 11    training_loss:  0.3156  training_acc:  86.23  validation_loss:  0.4373  validation_acc: 80.91
epoch: 12    training_loss:  0.2975  training_acc:  87.61  validation_loss:  0.4596  validation_acc: 79.83
epoch: 13    training_loss:  0.2815  training_acc:  87.98  validation_loss:  0.4319  validation_acc: 81.05
epoch: 14    training_loss:  0.2679  training_acc:  88.86  validation_loss:  0.4207  validation_acc: 81.82
epoch: 15    training_loss:  0.2487  training_acc:  89.81  validation_loss:  0.4223  validation_acc: 81.88
epoch: 16    training_loss:  0.2334  training_acc:  90.44  validation_loss:  0.4349  validation_acc: 81.65
epoch: 17    training_loss:  0.2219  training_acc:  91.02  validation_loss:  0.452   validation_acc: 81.38
epoch: 18    training_loss:  0.2025  training_acc:  91.88  validation_loss:  0.4342  validation_acc: 82.12
epoch: 19    training_loss:  0.1934  training_acc:  92.48  validation_loss:  0.4438  validation_acc: 82.28
epoch: 20    training_loss:  0.1774  training_acc:  93.05  validation_loss:  0.4847  validation_acc: 81.54
epoch: 21    training_loss:  0.1684  training_acc:  93.3   validation_loss:  0.4931  validation_acc: 81.58
epoch: 22    training_loss:  0.1554  training_acc:  94.1   validation_loss:  0.4896  validation_acc: 81.94
epoch: 23    training_loss:  0.1504  training_acc:  94.25  validation_loss:  0.485   validation_acc: 82.36
epoch: 24    training_loss:  0.1395  training_acc:  94.85  validation_loss:  0.5038  validation_acc: 81.81
success
doleron@delegion:~/book-workspace/pbp-deep-learning-in-modern-cpp/chapter_15/build$
```

Figure 15.22: Avoid overfitting with dropout

The first thing to point out here is that models with dropout require more epochs to converge. Thus, we are training the dropout version with 25 epochs instead of 10. Another important point in using dropout is that the training is strongly affected by random noise. As a result, getting a smooth monotonic validation loss curve is not possible. It is also noteworthy that the validation loss shows a tendency of growth in the last epochs, which means that training the model for more time will not be beneficial.

Note that the results may vary since they depend on random factors such as the weights initialization, shuffling of mini-batches, and dropout disconnections.

Now, the system achieved a validation accuracy of 82.36%, an improvement compared to the previous bare metal model. *Can we do better?* We expect to achieve an even better result using data augmentation, in the next section.

Experiment 3: Using data augmentation

The previous chapter introduced several ways of using OpenCV to generate augmented image instances. We discussed the original concept of data augmentation, where the augmented data is actually added to the dataset, increasing the total number of instances available.

This experiment uses a slightly different approach, which has become very popular in recent years. In this alternative way, instead of adding the new generated instances, we replace each instance with a (possibly) augmented copy using a uniform distribution to decide when to apply the transformations:

```
1.  template<typename Generator>
2.  class Data_Augmentation_
    ParallelBatches : public ParallelBatches<Generator> {
3.
4.  public:
5.      Data_Augmentation_ParallelBatches(Generator& gen, int batch_size,
6.          const Eigen::Tensor<std::string, 2> *data, int buffer_
    size, int image_size, bool square_image):
7.          ParallelBatches<Generator>(gen, batch_size, data, buffer_
    size, image_size, square_image) {
8.              distribution = std::uniform_real_
    distribution<float>(0.0f, 1.0f);
9.          }
10.
11.     virtual void processing_image(cv::Mat &src, cv::Mat &dest) {
12.
13.         cv::Mat flipped, rotated;
14.
15.         if (distribution(rng) > 0.5) {
16.             flipped = horizontal_flip(src);
17.         } else {
18.             flipped = src;
19.         }
20.
21.         int angle = static_
```

```
        cast<int>((2.f * distribution(rng) - 1.f) * 15);
22.         int vertical_delta = static_
    cast<int>((2.f * distribution(rng) - 1.f) * src.rows * 0.1);
23.         int horizontal_delta = static_
    cast<int>((2.f * distribution(rng) - 1.f) * src.cols * 0.1);
24.
25.         dest = rotate_and_translate(flipped, angle, horizontal_
    delta, vertical_delta);
26.     }
27.
28. private:
29.     std::uniform_real_distribution<float> distribution;
30. };
```

The class above extends our previous **ParallelBatches** batch manager by overriding the **processing_image** method. We use a **uniform_distribution** to drawn numbers between 0 and 1, flipping the image 50% of time. This distribution is also used to generate random vertical and horizontal translations of maximum 10% and rotations in the [-15°, 15°] interval.

We can check the following examples of augmented images generated by this procedure:

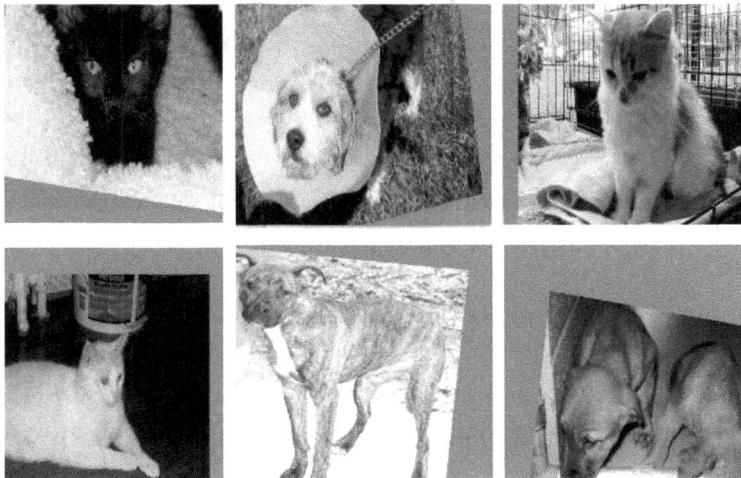

Figure 15.23: Examples of augmented images

Note: Rotating, resizing, translating and other imagespace transformations often cause blank regions. In this study, we are filling these areas with gray pixels.

Now, training the model again using the augmented data results in the following performance:

```
doleron@delegion:~/book-workspace/pbp-deep-learning-in-modern-cpp/chapter_15/build$ ./3conv_data_augmentation
Using seed 1144681502
Loading the data, please wait!
Total of images: 24946
Training size: 17462
Validation size 7484
Data loaded!
Using image size 224x224
Training for 40 epochs
epoch:  0     training_loss: 0.6962  training_acc:   55.86  validation_loss:     0.6463  validation_acc: 64.68
epoch:  1     training_loss: 0.6223  training_acc:   65.8   validation_loss:     0.5771  validation_acc: 69.2
epoch:  2     training_loss: 0.5789  training_acc:   69.87  validation_loss:     0.5402  validation_acc: 72.95
epoch:  3     training_loss: 0.5541  training_acc:   72.1   validation_loss:     0.5437  validation_acc: 73.15
epoch:  4     training_loss: 0.5287  training_acc:   73.88  validation_loss:     0.5027  validation_acc: 75.42
epoch:  5     training_loss: 0.5164  training_acc:   74.69  validation_loss:     0.4906  validation_acc: 75.94
epoch:  6     training_loss: 0.5041  training_acc:   75.46  validation_loss:     0.4721  validation_acc: 77.83
epoch:  7     training_loss: 0.4912  training_acc:   76.62  validation_loss:     0.4599  validation_acc: 79.06
epoch:  8     training_loss: 0.4808  training_acc:   77.07  validation_loss:     0.4491  validation_acc: 79.02
epoch:  9     training_loss: 0.47    training_acc:   77.74  validation_loss:     0.4558  validation_acc: 79.08
epoch:  10    training_loss: 0.4583  training_acc:   78.43  validation_loss:     0.4323  validation_acc: 80.18
epoch:  11    training_loss: 0.45    training_acc:   79.27  validation_loss:     0.427   validation_acc: 80.61
epoch:  12    training_loss: 0.4413  training_acc:   79.83  validation_loss:     0.4174  validation_acc: 80.9
epoch:  13    training_loss: 0.4349  training_acc:   80.1   validation_loss:     0.4103  validation_acc: 81.56
epoch:  14    training_loss: 0.4205  training_acc:   80.99  validation_loss:     0.424   validation_acc: 80.51
epoch:  15    training_loss: 0.4194  training_acc:   80.8   validation_loss:     0.4086  validation_acc: 82.08
epoch:  16    training_loss: 0.4133  training_acc:   81.44  validation_loss:     0.4016  validation_acc: 82.26
epoch:  17    training_loss: 0.4062  training_acc:   81.76  validation_loss:     0.4018  validation_acc: 82.17
epoch:  18    training_loss: 0.4044  training_acc:   81.56  validation_loss:     0.3951  validation_acc: 82.2
epoch:  19    training_loss: 0.394   training_acc:   82.01  validation_loss:     0.4013  validation_acc: 82.21
epoch:  20    training_loss: 0.3898  training_acc:   82.55  validation_loss:     0.3942  validation_acc: 83.11
epoch:  21    training_loss: 0.3841  training_acc:   82.95  validation_loss:     0.3654  validation_acc: 84.03
epoch:  22    training_loss: 0.3774  training_acc:   83.2   validation_loss:     0.3742  validation_acc: 83.72
epoch:  23    training_loss: 0.3747  training_acc:   83.58  validation_loss:     0.4122  validation_acc: 82.54
epoch:  24    training_loss: 0.365   training_acc:   83.85  validation_loss:     0.374   validation_acc: 83.53
epoch:  25    training_loss: 0.3684  training_acc:   83.6   validation_loss:     0.3477  validation_acc: 85.22
epoch:  26    training_loss: 0.3581  training_acc:   84.3   validation_loss:     0.3654  validation_acc: 84.24
epoch:  27    training_loss: 0.3581  training_acc:   84.31  validation_loss:     0.3462  validation_acc: 84.95
epoch:  28    training_loss: 0.3488  training_acc:   84.85  validation_loss:     0.3416  validation_acc: 85.32
epoch:  29    training_loss: 0.3463  training_acc:   84.97  validation_loss:     0.3378  validation_acc: 85.55
epoch:  30    training_loss: 0.3467  training_acc:   84.69  validation_loss:     0.3384  validation_acc: 85.71
epoch:  31    training_loss: 0.3406  training_acc:   85.14  validation_loss:     0.3353  validation_acc: 85.82
epoch:  32    training_loss: 0.3364  training_acc:   85.08  validation_loss:     0.328   validation_acc: 85.87
epoch:  33    training_loss: 0.3302  training_acc:   85.84  validation_loss:     0.3249  validation_acc: 85.95
epoch:  34    training_loss: 0.3327  training_acc:   85.51  validation_loss:     0.3197  validation_acc: 86.07
epoch:  35    training_loss: 0.3312  training_acc:   85.6   validation_loss:     0.3194  validation_acc: 86.46
epoch:  36    training_loss: 0.3191  training_acc:   86.07  validation_loss:     0.3128  validation_acc: 86.49
epoch:  37    training_loss: 0.315   training_acc:   86.55  validation_loss:     0.3321  validation_acc: 85.43
epoch:  38    training_loss: 0.3177  training_acc:   86.3   validation_loss:     0.3051  validation_acc: 87.3
epoch:  39    training_loss: 0.307   training_acc:   87.16  validation_loss:     0.2993  validation_acc: 87.47
success

doleron@delegion:~/book-workspace/pbp-deep-learning-in-modern-cpp/chapter_15/build$
```

***Figure 15.24**: Avoiding overfitting with data augmentation*

The beneficial influence of augmented data is clear here. The model achieved 87.47% of validation accuracy in the last epoch. There are some points to highlight:

- The model in this data augmentation example is similar to the first bare metal model. That is, the only regularization in this case is the one provided by the data augmentation.
- The model was trained by 40 epochs without providing any indication of overfitting. It is pretty much possible that training the model over more epochs would result in an even better performance.
- Training the model using augmented data performed better than using only dropout. This finding should not be taken as a general rule, though.

In terms of comparison, the validation performances in this case study are not significantly different from the ones reported by Jason Brownlee in his work, even though he used slightly different settings and models implemented with Google TensorFlow.

Experiment	Accuracy
Training a classifier with Dogs x Cats dataset	81.52%
Training using dropout	82.36%
Training using data augmentation	87.47%

Table 15.3: *Result of experiments*

For our purposes, the results achieved here are very significant in terms of strengthening our capacity to implement complex computer vision classifiers using C++ and Eigen.

Conclusion

This chapter introduced a practical case study where an image classifier was developed from scratch using C++ and Eigen. The challenges of loading and storing large image datasets in memory were discussed in relative detail, introducing the use of asynchronous IO to preload slices of data aiming to continuously feed the training algorithm. The image classifier was trained using the Dogs x Cats dataset using a network inspired in the VGG 16 architecture.

Though the first attempt achieved the reported state-of-the-art performance, the result was strongly affected by overfitting. Because of this, two regularization techniques, dropout and data augmentation, were used to reduce the impact of overfitting, achieving a final validation accuracy above 87%.

As usual, we would ask if we can do better than this. The answer is yes. However, to achieve higher performance, we need to increase the model capacity and reuse some of the previously trained weights, a technique called **transfer learning**, which will be covered in the next chapter.

Exercises

1. In the case study, we used two regularization approaches: Dropout and data augmentation. Change the example to include L1 or L2 regularization.

2. Repeat the experiment, replacing the Adam optimizer with RMSProp or Momentum.

3. By default, the training uses a circular buffer of size 3:

   ```
   1. void run_experiment(const std::string &datapath, MODEL &model,
         Device &device, ..., const int batch_buffer_size = 3)
   ```

   Analyze the impact on the training speed when changing batch_buffer_size to 1.

References

[1] Duda, Stork, and Hart, Pattern Classification, Wiley, 2000.

[2] Witten, Frank, and Hall, Data Mining, Practical Machine Learning Tools and Techniques, 2011, Morgan Kaufmann.

[3] Cybenko, Approximation by superpositions of a sigmoidal function, 1989.

[4] Dogs vs Cats, available at **https://www.kaggle.com/c/dogs-vs-cats**

[5] Jason Brownlee, How to Classify Photos of Dogs and Cats (with 97% accuracy), available at   **https://machinelearningmastery.com/how-to-develop-a-convolutional-neural-network-to-classify-photos-of-dogs-and-cats/**

[6] Philippe Golle, Machine Learning Attacks Against the Asirra CAPTCHA, 2013.

[7] Edsger Dijkstra; WD123 Cooperating sequential processes, 1965.

[8] Circular Buffers, available at **https://www.kernel.org/doc/Documentation/circular-buffers.txt**

Join our book's Discord space

Join the book's Discord Workspace for Latest updates, Offers, Tech happenings around the world, New Release and Sessions with the Authors:

https://discord.bpbonline.com

CHAPTER 16

Leveraging Training Performance with Transfer Learning

Introduction

Transfer learning is one of the striking advances in deep learning. It consists of reusing a model to build a new model which performs a different task. In practice, it facilitates the development of new models by allowing us to reuse pre-trained models, thus reducing the time and cost of building the model from scratch. This chapter introduces this technique through practical examples.

Structure

The sequence of topics covered in this chapter is:

- Introduction to transfer learning
- Loading and storing models
- Reusing a model trained with the Dogs x Cats dataset
- Using VGG16 and ImageNet

Objectives

This chapter introduces the use of transfer learning to develop new models. By reading this chapter, the reader will learn the details of loading a pre-trained model from the dis, using the model to build a new different model. Using only C++ and Eigen, the reader will learn how to load a VGG16 network pre-trained on the ImageNet dataset, aiming to develop new powerful systems very quickly.

Introduction to transfer learning

It amazes us how some techniques and concepts figured out in deep learning after decades of research are so close to their reciprocal behavior in biological systems. In this chapter, we will discuss another genuine instantiation of this observation.

Consider that, after some training, you learn a new task, such as playing an instrument or speaking another language. The acquisition process of this new competence probably required the learning of very different explicit and implicit abilities, some of them at the muscular level. Then, you start to learn a new correlated task. Even though you do not have the same skill level on this new task, you perceive that the learning process is much easier than the first task.

It happened that, somehow, our brain has the capacity to reuse knowledge from one set of tasks to another to improve our performance on tasks in which we have no experience yet. This process is very similar to the knowledge transmission in machine learning models, as discussed here.

Transfer learning is a modeling technique consisting of reusing a previously trained model to perform a new task [1].

Applications of this technique are diverse. For example, it is possible to reuse a classifier to perform a different task, such as regression or even an unsupervised learning task. In another example, it is possible to reuse a model trained with reinforcement learning to build a new model to transcript sequences of inputs. Since models basically represent probability distributions, there are no restrictions to reuse the knowledge of one model within another one.

Common use of transfer learning in deep learning models

In most cases, the use of transfer learning relies upon one or more of the following scenarios [2]:

- The feature extraction part of a pre-trained network is reused to build a new model. The head of the pre-trained network is replaced by a new head which will be trained from scratch.

- The whole model is then trained using a new dataset. Very often, the pre-trained part of the new model is not retrained. Only the new head is adjusted by the new training. Thus, the pre-trained part is *frozen*, that is, its weights are no longer modified/trained.

- Sometimes, a few layers in the top of the pre-trained part are unfrozen to allow a *fine-tuning* of the high-order feature representations.

Reusing models requires that they be somehow persisted between executions. The following section describes how to store and load models using native C++ 17 functions.

Loading and storing models

When thinking about storing models, there are two main concerns:

- Storing the model architecture
- Storing the model parameters

In this section, we will address only the matter of storing weights and kernels for posterior usage.

Storing the layer's weights

In essence, weights and kernels are grids of float numbers. Thus, storing them relies on the same issues of serializing float numbers using persistent recipients. Indeed, persisting a number in binary format is usually problematic due to the endianness [3] representation, which is not standard for each operating system. A system with big-endian representation will recognize different values if the file was written using little-endian and vice-versa.

> **Note: In computing, endianness refers to the order in which the most significant bytes of a number are stored.**

In addition, the number of bits used to represent floats is not standardized, introducing another source of problems.

A workaround for these issues is to store the numbers as text. Consider the following implementation of the **save_tensor_to_file()** function:

```
1.  using TYPE = float;
2.
3.  template <int _RANK>
4.  void save_tensor_to_file(const Tensor<_
    RANK> &tensor, const std::string& file_path, bool as_row_major) {
5.      std::ofstream file;
6.      file.open(file_path, std::ios::out | std::ios::trunc);
7.      if (!file.is_open()) {throw std::invalid_
    argument("Can't open " + file_path);}
8.
9.      const TYPE * data = tensor.data();
10.     Eigen::Tensor<TYPE, _RANK, Eigen::RowMajor> tensor_rm;
```

```
11.
12.     if (as_row_major) {
13.         Eigen::array<Eigen::Index, _RANK> suffle_dims;
14.         for (int i = 0; i < _RANK; ++i) {
15.             suffle_dims[i] = _RANK - i - 1;
16.         }
17.         tensor_rm = Eigen::TensorLayoutSwapOp<Eigen::Tensor<TYPE, _
    RANK, Eigen::ColMajor>>(tensor).shuffle(suffle_dims);
18.         data = tensor_rm.data();
19.     }
20.
21.     const int size = tensor.size();
22.     for (int i = 0; i < size; ++i) {
23.         file << data[i];
24.         file << "\n";
25.     }
26.     file.close();
27. }
```

Tensors are grid objects, but internally, they are implemented in memory using contiguous linear storage. Since files are also linear streams, our job is basically to stream the tensor storage straight to the file, including newline characters to delimit each number.

One tricky detail is that Eigen uses column-major by default. Thus, storing and loading data using column-major will work for most cases. However, we included an option to output the data as row major. This can be helpful if you think of loading the data using other libraries with row-major storage schema.

Load data now can be performed in a straight-forward manner by the following function:

```
1. template <int _RANK>
2. void load_tensor_from_file(Tensor<_
   RANK> &tensor, const std::string& file_path, bool as_row_
   major = true) {
3.
4.     std::ifstream file;
5.     file.open(file_path);
6.
7.     if (!file) {throw std::invalid_argument("Can't open " + file_
   path);}
8.
9.     std::vector<TYPE> vec;
```

```
10.      vec.reserve(tensor.size());
11.
12.      TYPE val;
13.      for(std::string line; std::getline(file, line); ) {
14.          std::istringstream in(line);
15.          in >> val;
16.          vec.push_back(val);
17.      }
18.
19.      if (vec.size() != tensor.size()) {throw std::invalid_
    argument("Illegal number of lines " + std::to_string(vec.size()));}
20.
21.      auto dimensions = tensor.dimensions();
22.      if (as_row_major) {
23.          Eigen::array<Eigen::Index, _RANK> suffle_dims;
24.          for (int i = 0; i < _RANK; ++i) {
25.              suffle_dims[i] = _RANK - i - 1;
26.          }
27.          auto mapped = Eigen::TensorMap<Eigen::Tensor<TYPE, _
    RANK, Eigen::RowMajor>>(&vec[0], dimensions);
28.          tensor = Eigen::TensorLayoutSwapOp<Eigen::Tensor<TYPE, _
    RANK, Eigen::RowMajor>>(mapped).shuffle(suffle_dims);
29.      } else {
30.          tensor = Eigen::TensorMap<Eigen::Tensor<TYPE, _
    RANK>>(&vec[0], dimensions);
31.      }
32.
33.      file.close();
34. }
```

There is not much to talk about here. We are using **std::istringstream** to read the data in the file as float numbers, converting the stream from row-major to col-major if necessary.

Since training a model takes considerable time, finding a way to store and retrieve its parameters is really useful. In the forthcoming sections, we will see examples of using these procedures.

Reusing the model trained in the Dogs x Cats dataset

In the previous chapter, we developed a model to classify images into two categories: dogs and cats. In this section, we will use this same model to build a classifier to categorize images of flowers in one of the five classes: daisy, dandelion, roses, sunflowers, and tulips. When we say the same model, we are saying the same weights. That is, we will use the same weights that we obtained by training a model using the Dogs x Cats dataset to set up a model to classify flowers from the TF flowers dataset [4]. Refer to the following figure:

Figure 16.1: Some instances of class daisy in TF flowers

Note: You can find instructions for downloading the TF flowers dataset from the TensorFlow website in the book GitHub repository.

At first glance, images of dogs and cats do not share any evident semantic features with flower images. Would it be really useful to reuse those weights, then? We will try to answer this question in this first experiment.

Training a model with the TF flowers dataset

Before reusing the Dogs x Cats model weights, let us see which results come up by training a model from scratch with the TF flowers dataset. For this purpose, we define the following model:

```
1. template <typename DEVICE, typename GEN>
2. class Model {
3.
```

```
4.  public:
5.
6.      Model(DEVICE &device, GEN &rng, int img_size): IMG_SIZE(img_size) {
7.          const int x_width = IMG_SIZE;
8.          const int x_height = IMG_SIZE;
9.
10.         const int kernel_size = 3;
11.         const int channels = 3;
12.
13.         const int hidden_neurons = 128;
14.         const int num_classes = 5;
15.
16.         Tensor_4D kernels_0(kernel_size, kernel_size, channels, 16);
17.         glorot_uniform_initializer(rng, kernels_0);
18.         this->conv2d_0 = new Conv2DLayer
    (device, kernels_0, new ReLU<DEVICE, 4>(device),
     std::vector<int>{1, 1, 1, 1});
19.         this->conv2d_0->set_optimizer(Adam<4>());
20.
21.         this->maxpooling_0 = new MaxPooling(device, 2);
22.
23.         Tensor_4D kernels_1
    (kernel_size, kernel_size, kernels_0.dimension(3), 32);
24.         glorot_uniform_initializer(rng, kernels_1);
25.         this->conv2d_1 = new Conv2DLayer
    (device, kernels_1, new ReLU<DEVICE, 4>(device),
     std::vector<int>{1, 1, 1, 1});
26.         this->conv2d_1->set_optimizer(Adam<4>());
27.
28.         this->maxpooling_1 = new MaxPooling(device, 2);
29.
30.         Tensor_4D kernels_2
    (kernel_size, kernel_size, kernels_1.dimension(3), 64);
31.         glorot_uniform_initializer(rng, kernels_2);
32.         this->conv2d_2 = new Conv2DLayer
    (device, kernels_2, new ReLU<DEVICE, 4>(device),
     std::vector<int>{1, 1, 1, 1});
33.         this->conv2d_2->set_optimizer(Adam<4>());
34.
```

```
35.          this->maxpooling_2 = new MaxPooling(device, 2);
36.
37.          this->flatten = new FlattenLayer<DEVICE, 4>(device);
38.
39.          int reduced_image_size = IMG_SIZE / 8;
40.
41.          const int flatten_size = reduced_image_size *
      reduced_image_size * kernels_2.dimension(3);
42.
43.          Tensor_2D W1(flatten_size, hidden_neurons);
44.          glorot_uniform_initializer(rng, W1);
45.          this->dense = new DenseLayer(device, W1, new ReLU<DEVICE,
      2>(device));
46.          this->dense->set_optimizer(Adam<2>());
47.
48.          Tensor_2D W2(hidden_neurons, num_classes);
49.          glorot_uniform_initializer(rng, W2);
50.          this->output_layer = new SoftmaxCrossEntropyLayer(device, W2);
51.          this->output_layer->set_optimizer(Adam<2>());
52.      }
53.
54. private:
55.      const int IMG_SIZE;
56.      Conv2DLayer<DEVICE> *conv2d_0;
57.      MaxPooling<DEVICE> *maxpooling_0;
58.
59.      Conv2DLayer<DEVICE> *conv2d_1;
60.      MaxPooling<DEVICE> *maxpooling_1;
61.
62.      Conv2DLayer<DEVICE> *conv2d_2;
63.      MaxPooling<DEVICE> *maxpooling_2;
64.
65.      FlattenLayer<DEVICE, 4> *flatten;
66.      DenseLayer<DEVICE> *dense;
67.      DenseLayer<DEVICE> *output_layer;
68.
69. };
```

You may have noted that this model is very similar to the models used in the previous chapter. Indeed, the only differences here are the number of output neurons (five, to match the number of five flower classes) and the use of a smaller dense layer:

```
1. const int hidden_neurons = 128;
2. const int num_classes = 5;
```

Now, training this model again using the same data augmentation procedure that we used in the previous chapter, results in the following output:

```
doleron@delegion:~/book-workspace/pbp-deep-learning-in-modern-cpp/chapter_16/build$ ./net_training_flowers
Loading the data, please wait!
Total of images: 3670
Training size: 2569
Validation size 1101
Data loaded!
Using image size 224x224
Training for 40 epochs
epoch:  0    training_loss:  1.49102     training_acc:  37.56  validation_loss:  1.20787     validation_acc: 47.59
epoch:  1    training_loss:  1.11838     training_acc:  55     validation_loss:  1.15022     validation_acc: 55.22
epoch:  2    training_loss:  1.0594      training_acc:  58.69  validation_loss:  1.04497     validation_acc: 57.22
epoch:  3    training_loss:  1.00697     training_acc:  60.02  validation_loss:  1.0552      validation_acc: 57.85
epoch:  4    training_loss:  0.989784    training_acc:  61.15  validation_loss:  1.02744     validation_acc: 59.49
epoch:  5    training_loss:  0.949768    training_acc:  63.79  validation_loss:  0.981853    validation_acc: 61.03
epoch:  6    training_loss:  0.930133    training_acc:  63.99  validation_loss:  1.01559     validation_acc: 59.85
epoch:  7    training_loss:  0.903329    training_acc:  65     validation_loss:  1.00515     validation_acc: 61.12
epoch:  8    training_loss:  0.893491    training_acc:  66.36  validation_loss:  1.00187     validation_acc: 61.48
epoch:  9    training_loss:  0.878769    training_acc:  66.56  validation_loss:  0.985864    validation_acc: 60.3
epoch:  10   training_loss:  0.85972     training_acc:  67.45  validation_loss:  0.942973    validation_acc: 62.94
epoch:  11   training_loss:  0.858297    training_acc:  67.34  validation_loss:  0.933724    validation_acc: 64.21
epoch:  12   training_loss:  0.840637    training_acc:  67.8   validation_loss:  0.921169    validation_acc: 64.39
epoch:  13   training_loss:  0.824849    training_acc:  68.78  validation_loss:  0.959278    validation_acc: 62.94
epoch:  14   training_loss:  0.83442     training_acc:  69.44  validation_loss:  0.924358    validation_acc: 63.76
epoch:  15   training_loss:  0.80973     training_acc:  69.32  validation_loss:  0.897326    validation_acc: 65.94
epoch:  16   training_loss:  0.792829    training_acc:  69.4   validation_loss:  0.933672    validation_acc: 64.94
epoch:  17   training_loss:  0.791024    training_acc:  69.67  validation_loss:  0.898768    validation_acc: 65.39
epoch:  18   training_loss:  0.776247    training_acc:  70.68  validation_loss:  0.931115    validation_acc: 65.39
epoch:  19   training_loss:  0.776371    training_acc:  71.31  validation_loss:  0.864484    validation_acc: 66.57
epoch:  20   training_loss:  0.755114    training_acc:  71.15  validation_loss:  0.87511     validation_acc: 67.02
epoch:  21   training_loss:  0.74409     training_acc:  72.28  validation_loss:  0.858623    validation_acc: 68.02
epoch:  22   training_loss:  0.748455    training_acc:  72.2   validation_loss:  0.851588    validation_acc: 67.57
epoch:  23   training_loss:  0.715997    training_acc:  72.82  validation_loss:  0.845572    validation_acc: 67.93
epoch:  24   training_loss:  0.71586     training_acc:  72.55  validation_loss:  0.897402    validation_acc: 66.48
epoch:  25   training_loss:  0.703532    training_acc:  73.25  validation_loss:  0.85628     validation_acc: 67.21
epoch:  26   training_loss:  0.716306    training_acc:  73.02  validation_loss:  0.825872    validation_acc: 69.39
epoch:  27   training_loss:  0.698985    training_acc:  73.72  validation_loss:  0.860355    validation_acc: 68.75
epoch:  28   training_loss:  0.681613    training_acc:  73.68  validation_loss:  0.790418    validation_acc: 69.93
epoch:  29   training_loss:  0.681809    training_acc:  73.56  validation_loss:  0.796279    validation_acc: 69.2
epoch:  30   training_loss:  0.663302    training_acc:  75     validation_loss:  0.815839    validation_acc: 68.75
epoch:  31   training_loss:  0.659533    training_acc:  74.58  validation_loss:  0.79131     validation_acc: 69.02
epoch:  32   training_loss:  0.654848    training_acc:  74.65  validation_loss:  0.777423    validation_acc: 70.75
epoch:  33   training_loss:  0.643196    training_acc:  76.48  validation_loss:  0.759561    validation_acc: 71.02
epoch:  34   training_loss:  0.627887    training_acc:  76.25  validation_loss:  0.813625    validation_acc: 70.39
epoch:  35   training_loss:  0.623592    training_acc:  76.52  validation_loss:  0.803537    validation_acc: 70.84
epoch:  36   training_loss:  0.624296    training_acc:  76.95  validation_loss:  0.80591     validation_acc: 70.29
epoch:  37   training_loss:  0.604285    training_acc:  77.07  validation_loss:  0.765255    validation_acc: 70.84
epoch:  38   training_loss:  0.611971    training_acc:  76.33  validation_loss:  0.801373    validation_acc: 69.39
epoch:  39   training_loss:  0.614549    training_acc:  76.76  validation_loss:  0.770191    validation_acc: 71.84
success
doleron@delegion:~/book-workspace/pbp-deep-learning-in-modern-cpp/chapter_16/build$
```

Figure 16.2*: Training a model from scratch with the TF flowers dataset*

Note that because of the randomization of parameters and augmentation, this program outputs a slightly different result for every run.

In this example, training the model from scratch using data augmentation results in a max performance of 71.84% accuracy. We will use this result as the baseline to compare the performance of the next model using transfer learning.

Reusing the weights from the Dogs x Cats model

To reuse the weights from the model trained with the Dogs x Cats model, we need to store the model weights in a persistent storage, like a file. For this purpose, we will include a new method in our model class:

```cpp
1.  void save(const std::string &folder, bool override, bool as_
    rowmajor) const {
2.
3.      bool fail = fs::exists(folder);
4.      if (fail) {
5.          if (override) {
6.              fail = fs::remove_all(folder) == 0;
7.          } else {
8.              std::cerr << folder << " already exists. Use over-
    ride = true to override.\n";
9.          }
10.     }
11.
12.     fail = fail || !fs::create_directory(folder);
13.
14.     if (!fail) {
15.         fs::path dir(folder);
16.
17.         save_tensor_to_file(this->conv2d_0->get_
    kernels(), (dir / fs::path("conv2d_0.txt")).string(), as_rowmajor);
18.         save_tensor_to_file(this->conv2d_1->get_
    kernels(), (dir / fs::path("conv2d_1.txt")).string(), as_rowmajor);
19.         save_tensor_to_file(this->conv2d_2->get_
    kernels(), (dir / fs::path("conv2d_2.txt")).string(), as_rowmajor);
20.         save_tensor_to_file(this->dense->get_
    weight(), (dir / fs::path("dense.txt")).string(), as_rowmajor);
21.         save_tensor_to_file(this->output_layer->get_
    weight(), (dir / fs::path("output_layer.txt")).string(), as_
    rowmajor);
22.     }
23. }
```

Now, we can call this method after each epoch:

```cpp
1.  model.save("models/dogs_cats_augmentation/" + std::to_string(start_
    ts) + "/" + std::to_string(epoch) + "/", true, true);
```

This results in a bunch of text files for each epoch, as shown in the following figure:

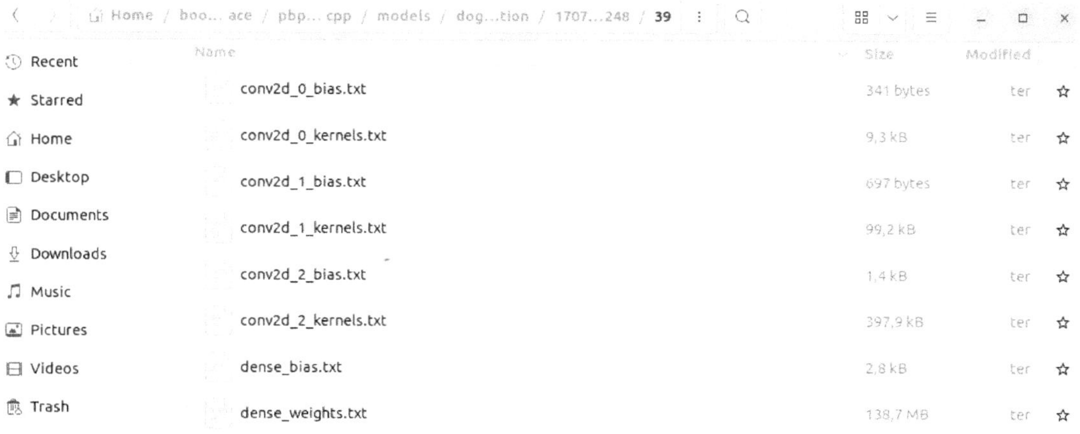

Figure 16.3: Persisted weights from the Dogs x Cats model

Now, we can pre-load these weights when initializing other models. Check the following model:

```
1. template <typename DEVICE, typename GEN>
2. class Model {
3.
4. public:
5.
6.     Model(DEVICE &device, GEN &rng, int img_size): IMG_SIZE(img_size) {
7.         const int x_width = IMG_SIZE;
8.         const int x_height = IMG_SIZE;
9.
10.        const int kernel_size = 3;
11.        const int channels = 3;
12.
13.        const int hidden_neurons = 128;
14.        const int num_classes = NUMBER_CLASSES;
15.
16.        Tensor_4D kernels_0(kernel_size, kernel_size, channels, 16);
17.        load_tensor_from_file(kernels_0, "models/dogs_cats_
    augmentation/runs/87.27/39/conv2d_0.txt");
18.        this->con-
    v2d_0 = new Conv2DLayer(device, kernels_0, new ReLU<DEVICE, 4>(de-
    vice), std::vector<int>{1, 1, 1, 1});
```

```
19.          this->conv2d_0->set_optimizer(Adam<4>());
20.
21.          this->maxpooling_0 = new MaxPooling(device, 2);
22.
23.          Tensor_4D kernels_1(kernel_size, kernel_size, kernels_0.
    dimension(3), 32);
24.          load_tensor_from_file(kernels_1, "models/dogs_cats_
    augmentation/runs/87.27/39/conv2d_1.txt");
25.          this->con-
    v2d_1 = new Conv2DLayer(device, kernels_1, new ReLU<DEVICE, 4>(de-
    vice), std::vector<int>{1, 1, 1, 1});
26.          this->conv2d_1->set_optimizer(Adam<4>());
27.
28.          this->maxpooling_1 = new MaxPooling(device, 2);
29.
30.          Tensor_4D kernels_2(kernel_size, kernel_size, kernels_1.
    dimension(3), 64);
31.          load_tensor_from_file(kernels_2, "models/dogs_cats_
    augmentation/runs/87.27/39/conv2d_2.txt");
32.          this->con-
    v2d_2 = new Conv2DLayer(device, kernels_2, new ReLU<DEVICE, 4>(de-
    vice), std::vector<int>{1, 1, 1, 1});
33.          this->conv2d_2->set_optimizer(Adam<4>());
34.
35.          this->maxpooling_2 = new MaxPooling(device, 2);
36.
37.          this->flatten = new FlattenLayer<DEVICE, 4>(device);
38.
39.          int reduced_image_size = IMG_SIZE / 8;
40.
41.          const int flatten_size = reduced_image_size * reduced_image_
    size * kernels_2.dimension(3);
42.
43.          Tensor_2D W1(flatten_size, hidden_neurons);
44.          glorot_uniform_initializer(rng, W1);
45.          this-
    >dense = new DenseLayer(device, W1, new ReLU<DEVICE, 2>(device));
46.          this->dense->set_optimizer(Adam<2>());
47.
```

```
48.          Tensor_2D W2(hidden_neurons, num_classes);
49.          glorot_uniform_initializer(rng, W2);
50.          this->output_layer = new SoftmaxCrossEntropyLayer(device, W2);
51.          this->output_layer->set_optimizer(Adam<2>());
52.      }
53.
54. private:
55.      const int IMG_SIZE;
56.      Conv2DLayer<DEVICE> *conv2d_0;
57.      MaxPooling<DEVICE> *maxpooling_0;
58.
59.      Conv2DLayer<DEVICE> *conv2d_1;
60.      MaxPooling<DEVICE> *maxpooling_1;
61.
62.      Conv2DLayer<DEVICE> *conv2d_2;
63.      MaxPooling<DEVICE> *maxpooling_2;
64.
65.      FlattenLayer<DEVICE, 4> *flatten;
66.      DenseLayer<DEVICE> *dense;
67.      DenseLayer<DEVICE> *output_layer;
68. };
```

This model is exactly equal to the previous model we used to train with the flowers dataset. The only difference here is the usage of the previously trained models from the Dogs x Cats models:

```
1.  Tensor_4D kernels_0(kernel_size, kernel_size, channels, 16);
2.  load_tensor_from_file(kernels_0, "models/dogs_cats_augmentation/
    runs/87.27/39/conv2d_0.txt");
3.  this->con-
    v2d_0 = new Conv2DLayer(device, kernels_0, new ReLU<DEVICE, 4>(de-
    vice), std::vector<int>{1, 1, 1, 1});
4.
5.  Tensor_4D kernels_1(kernel_size, kernel_size, kernels_0.
    dimension(3), 32);
6.  load_tensor_from_file(kernels_1, "models/dogs_cats_augmentation/
    runs/87.27/39/conv2d_1.txt");
7.  this->con-
    v2d_1 = new Conv2DLayer(device, kernels_1, new ReLU<DEVICE, 4>(de-
    vice), std::vector<int>{1, 1, 1, 1});
```

8.

9. ```
   Tensor_4D kernels_2(kernel_size, kernel_size, kernels_1.
   dimension(3), 64);
   ```

10. ```
    load_tensor_from_file(kernels_2, "models/dogs_cats_augmentation/
    runs/87.27/39/conv2d_2.txt");
    ```

11. ```
    this->con-
    v2d_2 = new Conv2DLayer(device, kernels_2, new ReLU<DEVICE, 4>(de-
    vice), std::vector<int>{1, 1, 1, 1});
    ```

12. ```
    this->conv2d_2->set_optimizer(Adam<4>());
    ```

Note that we are reusing only the convolutional kernels. The dense and output layers of the Dogs x Cats model have different sizes. Thus, we cannot use them to set our model with the Flowers dataset.

Now, we can train the model as usual:

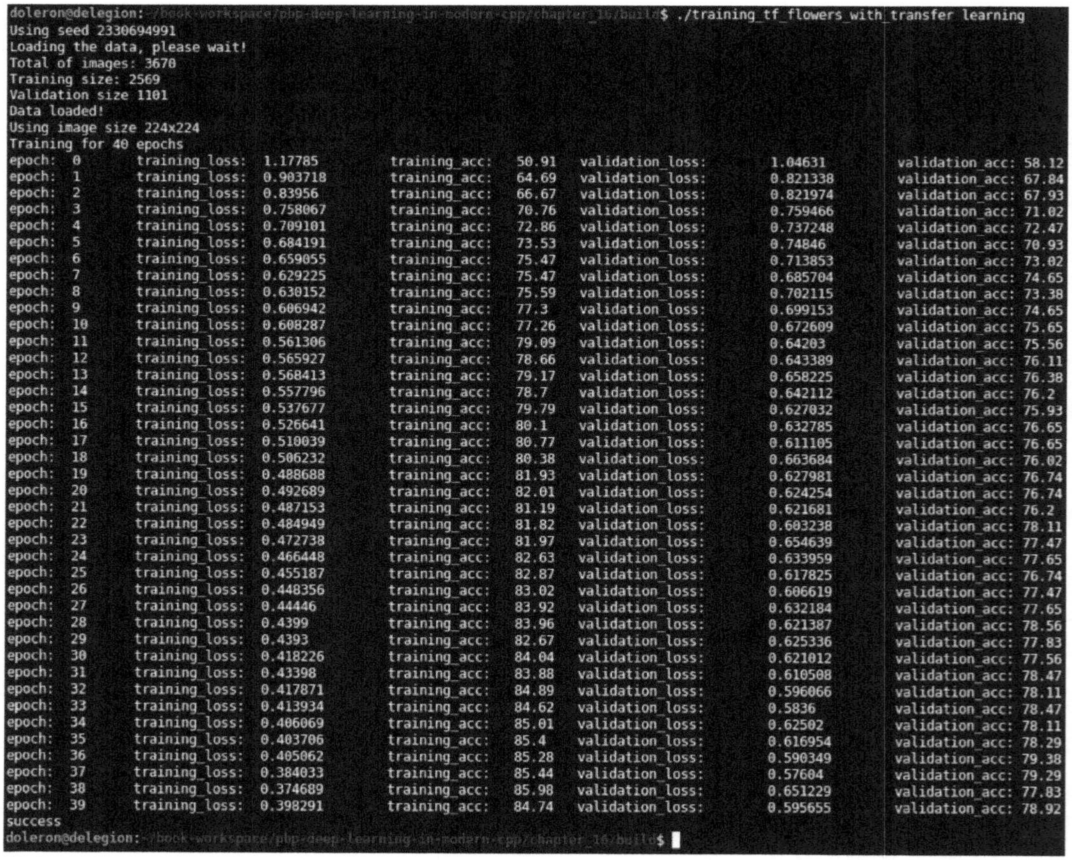

Figure 16.4: Reusing the Dogs x Cats weights to train TF flowers

The result is pretty sound. The model achieved an accuracy of 77.38%, 5.5 percentage points above the previous model on this same dataset.

Now, we can return to the question: *Would it be useful to reuse weights from a model for dogs and cats to classify flowers?* Yes, the result above shows that reusing the weights is worth it. But why? What do dogs, cats, and flowers have in common? Nothing and everything. Although dogs and cats are very different semantic objects if compared to flowers, their images share lots of low-level features, like patterns of segmentation, lighting, shadows, and textures that are basic building blocks of their images, regardless they are dogs, cats, flowers, persons or so on.

We discussed these concerns in *Chapter 9, Coding the Gradient Descent Algorithm*, when we learned that we can use gradient descent to automatically extract filters to detect edges in images. In fact, edges are only one type of feature used by models to extract more complex patterns from images. In particular, due to weight sharing, convolutions are good for capturing these features. That is why those first segments in CNNs consisting only of convolutions and poolings are commonly known as feature extraction.

Using VGG16 and ImageNet

In the previous chapter, we discussed the relevance of VGG networks [5] in developing deep learning models. We have seen that VGG16 is a specific type of convolutional neural network with 16 trainable layers, 13 convolutional layers, and three fully connected layers. Refer to the following figure:

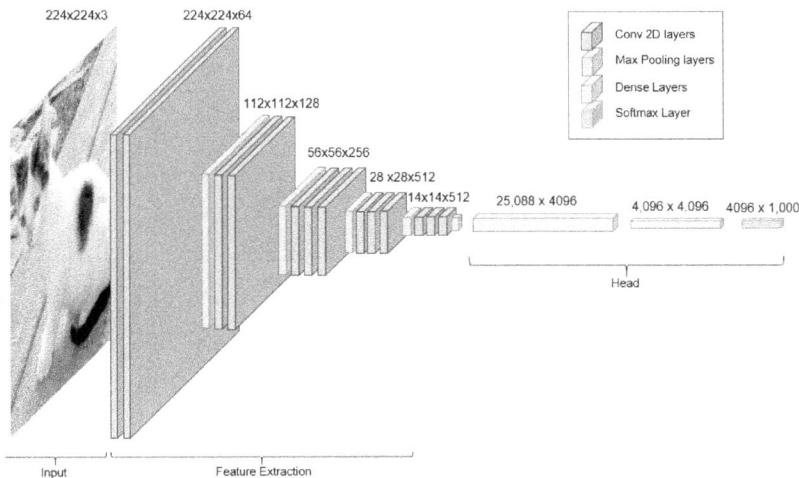

Figure 16.5: The VGG16 schema

Although VGG16 was not the winner of ILSVRC-2014 [6], it achieved one of the top performances of the competition, losing the first position to Google LeNet. Despite this, VGG established the—so far—new convolutional network architecture paradigm by using small kernels and a very deep network. This architecture has been proven effective in a wide range of scenarios and applications.

The following table describes the dimensions of each column in VGG16. Note that the number of parameters does not consider bias.

	Layer	Input	Output	# parameters
1	block 1 conv 1	224x224x3	224x224x64	1,728
2	block 1 conv 2	224x224x64	224x224x64	36,864
	block 1 max pool	224x224x64	112x112x64	0
3	block 2 conv 1	112x112x64	112x112x128	73,728
4	block 2 conv 2	112x112x128	112x112x128	147,456
	block 2 max pool	112x112x128	56x56x128	0
5	block 3 conv 1	56x56x128	56x56x256	294,912
6	block 3 conv 2	56x56x256	56x56x256	589,824
7	block 3 conv 3	56x56x256	56x56x256	589,824
	block 3 max pool	56x56x256	28x28x256	0
8	block 4 conv 1	28x28x256	28x28x512	1,179,648
9	block 4 conv 2	28x28x512	28x28x512	2,359,296
10	block 4 conv 3	28x28x512	28x28x512	2,359,296
	block 4 max pool	28x28x512	14x14x512	0
11	block 5 conv 1	14x14x512	14x14x512	2,359,296
12	block 5 conv 2	14x14x512	14x14x512	2,359,296
13	block 5 conv 3	14x14x512	14x14x512	2,359,296
	block 5 max pool	14x14x512	7x7x512	0
14	dense 1	25,088	4,096	102,760,448
15	dense 2	4,096	4,096	16,777,216
16	softmax	4,096	1,000	4,096,000
Total of parameters (not counting bias):				138,344,128

Table 16.1: *VGG 16 dimensions*

The canonical scenario of using a pre-trained VGG network to develop new models is reusing the first part of the network, the feature extractor, and replacing the head with a sequence of two or three dense, fully connected layers. People often use VGG in this way with pre-trained ImageNet weights to build new models to perform tasks such as classification or regression. This scenario is exemplified in the next section.

Defining a VGG16-based model

The following model implements a VGG16 feature extractor followed by two fully connected layers:

```
1.  template <typename DEVICE, typename GEN>
2.  class Model {
3.
4.  public:
5.      // ...
6.  private:
7.      const int IMG_SIZE;
8.
9.      // VGG16 feature extractor
10.
11.     Conv2DLayer<DEVICE> *block1_conv1;
12.     Conv2DLayer<DEVICE> *block1_conv2;
13.     MaxPooling<DEVICE> *block1_pool;
14.
15.     Conv2DLayer<DEVICE> *block2_conv1;
16.     Conv2DLayer<DEVICE> *block2_conv2;
17.     MaxPooling<DEVICE> *block2_pool;
18.
19.     Conv2DLayer<DEVICE> *block3_conv1;
20.     Conv2DLayer<DEVICE> *block3_conv2;
21.     Conv2DLayer<DEVICE> *block3_conv3;
22.     MaxPooling<DEVICE> *block3_pool;
23.
24.     Conv2DLayer<DEVICE> *block4_conv1;
25.     Conv2DLayer<DEVICE> *block4_conv2;
26.     Conv2DLayer<DEVICE> *block4_conv3;
27.     MaxPooling<DEVICE> *block4_pool;
28.
29.     Conv2DLayer<DEVICE> *block5_conv1;
30.     Conv2DLayer<DEVICE> *block5_conv2;
31.     Conv2DLayer<DEVICE> *block5_conv3;
32.     MaxPooling<DEVICE> *block5_pool;
33.
34.     // network top / head
```

```
35.
36.    FlattenLayer<DEVICE, 4> *flatten;
37.    DenseLayer<DEVICE> *dense;
38.    DenseLayer<DEVICE> *output_layer;
39.
40. };
```

The constructor of this model is defined as follows:

```
1. Model(DEVICE &device, GEN &rng, int img_size): IMG_SIZE(img_size) {
2.     const int kernel_size = 3;
3.     const int hidden_neurons = 128;
4.     const int num_classes = 2;
5.
6.     Tensor_4D blk1_c1_knl(kernel_size, kernel_size, 3, 64);
7.     load_tensor_from_file(blk1_c1_knl, "data/vgg16/imagenet/blk1_c1_
   knl.txt");
8.     this->block1_conv1 = new Conv2DLayer(device, blk1_c1_
   knl, new ReLU<4>());
9.
10.    Tensor_4D blk1_c2_knl(kernel_size, kernel_size, 64, 64);
11.    load_tensor_from_file(blk1_c2_knl, "data/vgg16/imagenet/blk1_c2_
   knl.txt");
12.    this->block1_conv2 = new Conv2DLayer(device, blk1_c2_
   knl, new ReLU<4>());
13.
14.    this->block1_pool = new MaxPooling(device, 2);
15.
16.    Tensor_4D blk2_c1_knl(kernel_size, kernel_size, 64, 128);
17.    load_tensor_from_file(blk2_c1_knl, "data/vgg16/imagenet/blk2_c1_
   knl.txt");
18.    this->block2_conv1 = new Conv2DLayer(device, blk2_c1_
   knl, new ReLU<4>());
19.
20.    Tensor_4D blk2_c2_knl(kernel_size, kernel_size, 128, 128);
21.    load_tensor_from_file(blk2_c2_knl, "data/vgg16/imagenet/blk2_c2_
   knl.txt");
22.    this->block2_conv2 = new Conv2DLayer(device, blk2_c2_
   knl, new ReLU<4>());
23.
```

```
24.     this->block2_pool = new MaxPooling(device, 2);
25.
26.     Tensor_4D blk3_c1_knl(kernel_size, kernel_size, 128, 256);
27.     load_tensor_from_file(blk3_c1_knl, "data/vgg16/imagenet/blk3_c1_
    knl.txt");
28.     this->block3_conv1 = new Conv2DLayer(device, blk3_c1_
    knl, new ReLU<4>());
29.
30.     Tensor_4D blk3_c2_knl(kernel_size, kernel_size, 256, 256);
31.     load_tensor_from_file(blk3_c2_knl, "data/vgg16/imagenet/blk3_c2_
    knl.txt");
32.     this->block3_conv2 = new Conv2DLayer(device, blk3_c2_
    knl, new ReLU<4>());
33.
34.     Tensor_4D blk3_c3_knl(kernel_size, kernel_size, 256, 256);
35.     load_tensor_from_file(blk3_c3_knl, "data/vgg16/imagenet/blk3_c3_
    knl.txt");
36.     this->block3_conv3 = new Conv2DLayer(device, blk3_c3_
    knl, new ReLU<4>());
37.
38.     this->block3_pool = new MaxPooling(device, 2);
39.
40.     Tensor_4D blk4_c1_knl(kernel_size, kernel_size, 256, 512);
41.     load_tensor_from_file(blk4_c1_knl, "data/vgg16/imagenet/blk4_c1_
    knl.txt");
42.     this->block4_conv1 = new Conv2DLayer(device, blk4_c1_
    knl, new ReLU<4>());
43.
44.     Tensor_4D blk4_c2_knl(kernel_size, kernel_size, 512, 512);
45.     load_tensor_from_file(blk4_c2_knl, "data/vgg16/imagenet/blk4_c2_
    knl.txt");
46.     this->block4_conv2 = new Conv2DLayer(device, blk4_c2_
    knl, new ReLU<4>());
47.
48.     Tensor_4D blk4_c3_knl(kernel_size, kernel_size, 512, 512);
49.     load_tensor_from_file(blk4_c3_knl, "data/vgg16/imagenet/blk4_c3_
    knl.txt");
50.     this->block4_conv3 = new Conv2DLayer(device, blk4_c3_
    knl, new ReLU<4>());
```

```
51.
52.      this->block4_pool = new MaxPooling(device, 2);
53.
54.      Tensor_4D blk5_c1_knl(kernel_size, kernel_size, 512, 512);
55.      load_tensor_from_file(blk5_c1_knl, "data/vgg16/imagenet/blk5_c1_
    knl.txt");
56.      this->block5_conv1 = new Conv2DLayer(device, blk5_c1_
    knl, new ReLU<4>());
57.
58.      Tensor_4D blk5_c2_knl(kernel_size, kernel_size, 512, 512);
59.      load_tensor_from_file(blk5_c2_knl, "data/vgg16/imagenet/blk5_c2_
    knl.txt");
60.      this->block5_conv2 = new Conv2DLayer(device, blk5_c2_
    knl, new ReLU<4>());
61.
62.      Tensor_4D blk5_c3_knl(kernel_size, kernel_size, 512, 512);
63.      load_tensor_from_file(blk5_c3_knl, "data/vgg16/imagenet/blk5_c3_
    knl.txt");
64.      this->block5_conv3 = new Conv2DLayer(device, blk5_c3_
    knl, new ReLU<4>());
65.
66.      this->block5_pool = new MaxPooling(device, 2);
67.
68.      this->flatten = new FlattenLayer<DEVICE, 4>(device);
69.
70.      int reduced_image_size = IMG_SIZE / 32;
71.
72.      const int flatten_size = reduced_image_size * reduced_image_size * 512;
73.
74.      Tensor_2D W1(flatten_size, hidden_neurons);
75.      glorot_uniform_initializer(rng, W1);
76.      this->dense = new DenseLayer(device, W1, new ReLU<2>());
77.      this->dense->set_optimizer(Adam<2>());
78.
79.      Tensor_2D W2(hidden_neurons, num_classes);
80.      glorot_uniform_initializer(rng, W2);
81.      this->output_layer = new SoftmaxCrossEntropyLayer(device, W2);
82.      this->output_layer->set_optimizer(Adam<2>());
83. }
```

We are preloading the feature extraction kernels with the weight files stored in the **"data/vgg16/imagenet/"** folder using the **load_tensor_from_file(...)** utility function.

Note: Check out the book repository on GitHub for the instructions to download these files.

The dense layers weights of the network top are randomly initialized as usual using Glorot (or He) uniform initialization. We are not going to train the convolutional layer weights again. Thus, we can define the **forward()** and **backward()** procedures as follows:

```
1.  void forward(const Tensor_4D &input) {
2.
3.      this->block1_conv1->forward(input);
4.      this->block1_conv2->forward(this->block1_conv1->get_output());
5.      this->block1_pool->forward(this->block1_conv2->get_output());
6.
7.      this->block2_conv1->forward(this->block1_pool->get_output());
8.      this->block2_conv2->forward(this->block2_conv1->get_output());
9.      this->block2_pool->forward(this->block2_conv2->get_output());
10.
11.     this->block3_conv1->forward(this->block2_pool->get_output());
12.     this->block3_conv2->forward(this->block3_conv1->get_output());
13.     this->block3_conv3->forward(this->block3_conv2->get_output());
14.     this->block3_pool->forward(this->block3_conv3->get_output());
15.
16.     this->block4_conv1->forward(this->block3_pool->get_output());
17.     this->block4_conv2->forward(this->block4_conv1->get_output());
18.     this->block4_conv3->forward(this->block4_conv2->get_output());
19.     this->block4_pool->forward(this->block4_conv3->get_output());
20.
21.     this->block5_conv1->forward(this->block4_pool->get_output());
22.     this->block5_conv2->forward(this->block5_conv1->get_output());
23.     this->block5_conv3->forward(this->block5_conv2->get_output());
24.     this->block5_pool->forward(this->block5_conv3->get_output());
25.
26.     this->flatten->forward(this->block5_pool->get_output());
27.     this->dense->forward(this->flatten->get_output());
28.     this->output_layer->forward(this->dense->get_output());
29.
30. }
```

```
31.
32. void backward(const Tensor_2D &upstream) {
33.     this->output_layer->backward(upstream, true);
34.     this->dense->backward(this->output_layer->get_
    downstream(), false);
35. }
```

Even though we forward the inputs throughout the whole network as usual, the backpropagation runs only over the last two dense layers, which are the unique model's trainable layers. It turns out that we are not aiming to fit the kernels in the VGG segment of the model, which were previously trained on ImageNet. Thus, any call of **backward()** on these layers would be only a waste of computational resources and time.

Note: The process of training a model without updating one or more trainable parameters is usually called freezing.

Finally, we need to update the model. Since we are freezing the feature extractor part of the model, there is no point in calling **update()** on convolutional layers. Thus, we call **update()** only on the layers in the head of the network:

```
1. void update(const TYPE learning_rate, int epoch) {
2.     this->dense->update(learning_rate, epoch);
3.     this->output_layer->update(learning_rate, epoch);
4. }
```

ImageNet preprocessing

Before we move to train our VGG16-based model using ImageNet pre-trained weights, there is something we must know. ImageNet weights are usually shared with a BGR, zero-centered *distribution*. This means that the weights were trained by images preprocessed as follows:

- BGR channel sequence (instead of the usual RGB sequence)

- Each channel is zero-centered by subtracting the value of each pixel from the mean of pixels in that channel of images in the ImageNet dataset

This makes our preprocessing function as follows:

```
1. void processing_image(cv::Mat &src, cv::Mat &dest) {
2.     cv::Mat converted;
3.     src.convertTo(converted, CV_32F);
4.     dest = converted - cv::Scalar(103.939f, 116.779f, 123.68f);
5. }
```

Where **103.939**, **116.779**, and **123.68** are the ImageNet averages for a BGR channel sequence.

Training the VGG16-based model

Once we have defined the model and how to train it, we can finally move to the network training step. Here, we can use the same dataset, that is, the Dogs x Cats dataset, and the same hyperparameters and setup as in the previous examples:

```cpp
1.  int main(int, char **)
2.  {
3.
4.      using DEVICE = Eigen::ThreadPoolDevice;
5.      using GEN = std::mt19937;
6.      using MODEL = Model<DEVICE, GEN>;
7.
8.      std::random_device rd{};
9.      const auto seed = rd();
10.     GEN rng(seed);
11.     std::cout << "Using seed " << seed << "\n";
12.
13.     const int threads = std::thread::hardware_concurrency();
14.     Eigen::ThreadPool tp(threads);
15.     DEVICE device(&tp, threads);
16.
17.     const int IMAGE_SIZE = 224;
18.
19.     MODEL model(device, rng, IMAGE_SIZE);
20.
21.     run_experiment<DEVICE, GEN, MODEL, Data_Augmentation_
    ParallelBatches<GEN>>(
22.         "data/dogs_x_cats/PetImages",
23.         model, device, rng,
24.         1, // epochs
25.         32, // minibatch_size
26.         0.001, // learning_rate
27.         false // square_images
28.     );
29.
30.     std::cout << "success\n";
31.
32.     return 0;
33. }
```

Indeed, these are almost the same settings. Note that we are setting the number of epochs for only one single epoch.

Building and running this program as usual provides an output like the following:

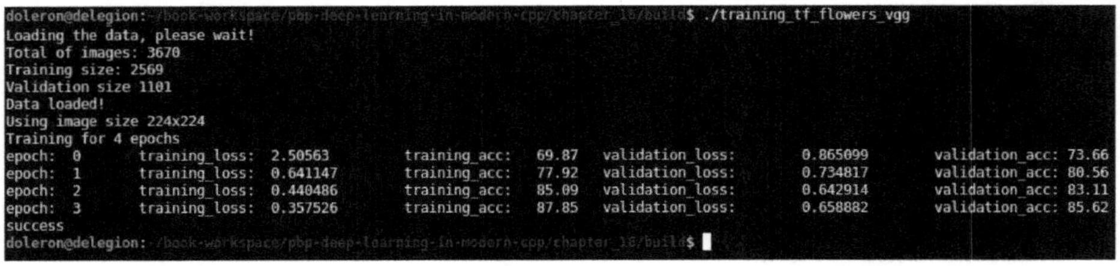

Figure 16.6: *Training the VGG16-based model using the Dogs x Cats*

This result is partly surprising and partly expected. In only one single epoch, the model achieved 97.8% validation accuracy. Knowing the quality issues of the Dogs x Cats dataset, this performance is pretty awesome, surpassing all previous models by far. Only in one epoch. But what happened here? Why did the model achieve such a high performance in only one epoch?

As expected, the pre-trained ImageNet weights provided very high performance, even though they were not trained specifically to distinguish dogs from cats. In combination with the VGG16 architecture, the ImageNet parameters could extract the more essential features from the images, requiring only one training epoch to the network's head to learn how to separate dog images and cat images from those features. In simple words, all the hard work was done during the previous training of VGG16 on the ImageNet dataset.

In summary, once we froze the VGG weights, only one epoch was actually required to fit the two dense layers of the network's head. This is clear evidence of the capacity of transfer learning to reuse pre-trained models to build robust new models that perform a different set of tasks.

Conclusion

This chapter introduced transfer learning, one powerful and useful tool for developing new models by reusing one or more pre-trained models to perform new tasks. As a practical example, we learned how to reuse the binary classifier introduced in the previous chapter to develop a new classifier to classify flowers in one of the five possible categories.

We also learned how to load a pre-trained VGG16 model with the ImageNet dataset to build a new model that exceeds the previous performances of models trained from scratch with the Dogs x Cats dataset. What these experiments show is that transfer learning is an essential tool to develop new powerful models very quickly.

In the next chapter, we will use transfer learning to speed up the development of an object localization system, a model that performs two different tasks: classification of the object type and regression of the object coordinates.

Exercises

1. In this chapter, we showed a function to serialize the contents of tensors using plain text files. This approach avoids portability issues related to the byte representation of float numbers. Nevertheless, persisting float numbers using their text representation introduces other issues. Enumerate these issues and propose solutions if applicable.

2. Modify the load and store functions to also store the tensor dimensions in the file. For this purpose, define a header in the file containing the tensor dimensions information.

3. Train a model with the TF flowers dataset using transfer learning to reuse the VGG 16 network pre-trained with ImageNet weights.

References

[1] Goodfellow, Bengio & Courville, Deep Learning, MIT Press, 2016.

[2] Transfer learning and fine-tuning, available at **https://www.tensorflow.org/tutorials/ images/transfer_learning**

[3] How to write endian-independent code in C, available at **https://developer.ibm.com/ articles/au-endianc/**

[4] tf_flowers, available at **https://www.tensorflow.org/datasets/catalog/tf_flowers**

[5] Very Deep Convolutional Networks for Large-Scale Image Recognition, available at **https://arxiv.org/abs/1409.1556**

[6] Large Scale Visual Recognition Challenge 2014 (ILSVRC2014), available at **https:// www.image-net.org/challenges/LSVRC/2014/results.php**

Join our book's Discord space

Join the book's Discord Workspace for Latest updates, Offers, Tech happenings around the world, New Release and Sessions with the Authors:

https://discord.bpbonline.com

CHAPTER 17
Developing an Object Localization System

Introduction

This chapter introduces the project of an object localization system, a specific type of hybrid deep learning model able to determine an object's class and coordinates in an image. We will discuss the nature of these systems and develop three experiments to learn how to train an object localization system from scratch, beginning with basic regression and then combining the model with a classifier to obtain a hybrid two-head model.

Structure

The sequence of topics covered in this chapter is:

- Experiments in this chapter
- Defining object localization systems
- Experiment 1: Building a regression model
- Experiment 2: Training the object localization model
- Using IoU to compare bounding box predictions
- Experiment 3: Using transfer learning with fine-tuning

Objectives

This chapter illustrates the development of object localization systems by implementing a hybrid model to find and classify objects in images using the techniques and algorithms discussed so far in this book. By reading this chapter, the reader will understand the key challenges of developing a real and complex hybrid computer vision system using only C++ and Eigen. The reader will also learn the standard metrics used to compare systems like that and apply transfer learning to increase the model performance by reusing a pretrained network.

Experiments in this chapter

This chapter includes three experiments:

ID	Description
Exp-17.1	Building a regressor model
Exp-17.2	Training the object localization model
Exp-17.3	Using transfer learning to improve the model performance

Table 17.1: Chapter experiment list

Defining object localization systems

One of the key abilities of biological beings is the ability to recognize an object and its position in the visual field. Reproducing this ability was one of the more active areas of research in deep learning for years, resulting in advances such as object localization systems.

Object localization systems are a particular type of hybrid model that combines two tasks: the localization of the object coordinates and the classification of the object category. Check the following example:

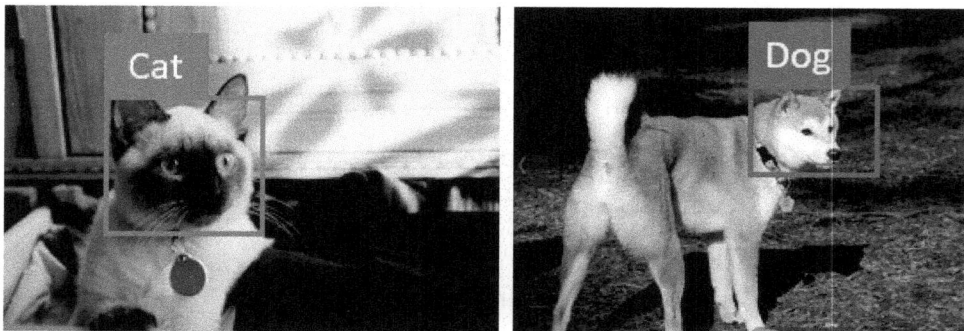

Figure 17.1: Images with bounding box annotation

In the preceding figure, we have the identification of the object coordinates and its class. The coordinates are given as a **bounding box**. A bounding box is a minimal rectangular area delimiting an object. In the examples above, each image has only one object of interest. Of course, very often, a single image depicts several objects. Consider the following example:

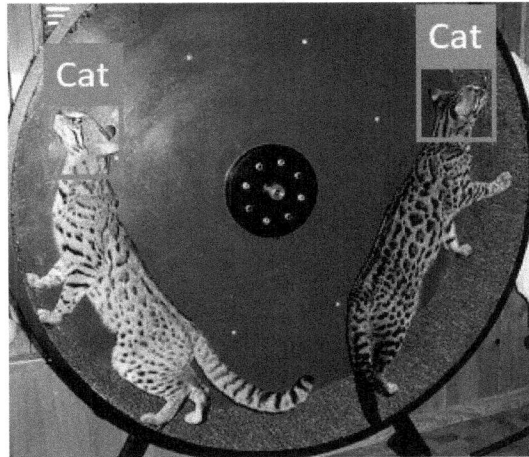

Figure 17.2: Example of image with two semantic objects

An object localization model can deal with only one object in an image. A model that can recognize multiple objects in the same image receives the special name of an **object detector**.

Note: For the sake of simplicity, this chapter focuses only on object localization models.

Bounding boxes are rectangles defined on the 2D image space using four numbers. Unfortunately, there is not a standard here. Some popular configurations are:

- **(x, y, w, h)**: Where (x,y) is the coordinate of the top leftmost corner point, w means the rectangle width, and h is the rectangle height.

- **(x_c, y_c, w_h, h_h)**: Where (x_c, y_c) is the rectangle's center, w_h is the half-width, and h_h is the half-height.

- **(x_1, y_1, x_2, y_2)**: (x_1, y_1) is the top leftmost corner of the image, and (x_2, y_2) is the bottom rightmost corner of the image.

In addition, sometimes these coordinates are given in pixels, but sometimes they are normalized as values between 0 and 1.

Essentially, an object localization model performs two tasks:

- Classification of the object
- Regression of the four bounding box coordinates

Classifiers were covered in detail in this book in both theory and practice. However, we have not talked about regression so far. The next experiment sheds light on this topic.

Experiment 1: Building a regression model

This experiment introduces the training of a model to detect the bounding box of a single object in an image using regression. Before covering model engineering, let us talk about regression.

Whereas a classifier predicts categories, a regression model predicts real numbers. A typical example of a regression model is a system that predicts a house's sales price based on its features, such as area, age, address, shape, utilities, etc. A well-known dataset used as a benchmark for this task is *The Boston Housing Dataset* [1].

This type of problem was intensely studied in the early ages of machine learning when the number of input variables needed to be small. For such small inputs, the results provided by multilayer perceptrons were somehow useful and acceptable.

The task of predicting the bounding box using a digital image as input exceeds the practical limits of multilayer perceptrons, requiring a more advanced model such as our well-known convolutional networks. Consider the following example:

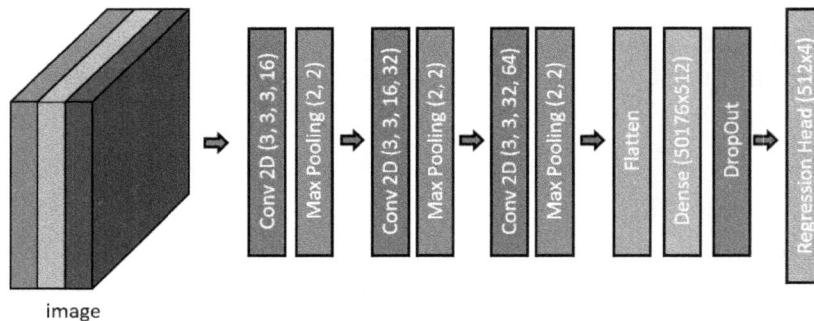

Figure 17.3: The first regression model for bounding box prediction

We will use this model to make the bounding box regression. It can be implemented as follows:

```
1. template <typename DEVICE, typename GEN>
2. class Model {
3.
4. public:
5.
6.     Model(DEVICE &device, GEN &rng, int img_size): IMG_SIZE(img_size) {
7.
8.         const int kernel_size = 3;
```

```
9.          const int channels = 3;
10.
11.         const int hidden_neurons = 512;
12.
13.         Tensor_4D kernels_0(kernel_size, kernel_size, channels, 16);
14.         glorot_uniform_initializer(rng, kernels_0);
15.         conv2d_0 = new Conv2DLayer(device, ker-
    nels_0, new ReLU<4>());
16.
17.         maxpooling_0 = new MaxPooling(device, 2);
18.
19.         Tensor_4D kernels_1(kernel_size, kernel_size, kernels_0.
    dimension(3), 32);
20.         glorot_uniform_initializer(rng, kernels_1);
21.         conv2d_1 = new Conv2DLayer(device, ker-
    nels_1, new ReLU<4>());
22.
23.         maxpooling_1 = new MaxPooling(device, 2);
24.
25.         Tensor_4D kernels_2(kernel_size, kernel_size, kernels_1.
    dimension(3), 64);
26.         glorot_uniform_initializer(rng, kernels_2);
27.         conv2d_2 = new Conv2DLayer(device, ker-
    nels_2, new ReLU<4>());
28.
29.         maxpooling_2 = new MaxPooling(device, 2);
30.
31.         flatten = new FlattenLayer<DEVICE, 4>(device);
32.
33.         int reduced_image_size = IMG_SIZE / 8;
34.
35.         const int flatten_size = reduced_image_size * reduced_image_
    size * kernels_2.dimension(3);
36.
37.         Tensor_2D WD(flatten_size, hidden_neurons);
38.         glorot_uniform_initializer(rng, WD);
39.         dense = new DenseLayer(device, WD, new ReLU<2>());
40.
```

```
41.          dropout = new DropoutLayer<DEVICE, 2, GEN>(de-
    vice, 0.5, rng);
42.
43.          Tensor_2D WR(hidden_neurons, 4);
44.          glorot_uniform_initializer(rng, WR);
45.          regressor_
    head = new DenseLayer(device, WR, new Sigmoid<2>());
46.
47.      }
48.
49. private:
50.
51.      Conv2DLayer<DEVICE> *conv2d_0;
52.      MaxPooling<DEVICE> *maxpooling_0;
53.
54.      Conv2DLayer<DEVICE> *conv2d_1;
55.      MaxPooling<DEVICE> *maxpooling_1;
56.
57.      Conv2DLayer<DEVICE> *conv2d_2;
58.      MaxPooling<DEVICE> *maxpooling_2;
59.
60.      FlattenLayer<DEVICE, 4> *flatten;
61.      DenseLayer<DEVICE> *dense;
62.      DropoutLayer<DEVICE, 2, GEN> *dropout;
63.
64.      DenseLayer<DEVICE> *regressor_head;
65.
66. };
```

Let us dive into the model's details.

The output layer

Unlike a classifier, the regression model does not use a softmax layer as output. Remember that softmax mimics a discrete probabilistic distribution. For example, the outputs of softmax must sum up to 1. Of course, this restriction does not apply to the bounding box coordinates of objects in images. Thus, using coefficient-wise activation functions such as linear, sigmoid, or even ReLU to define the output layer is more convenient:

```
1.  Tensor_2D WR(hidden_neurons, 4);
2.  glorot_uniform_initializer(rng, WR);
3.  regressor_head = new DenseLayer(device, WR, new Sigmoid<2>());
4.  regressor_head->set_optimizer(Adam<2>());
```

The backward pass

Similarly, the cross-entropy loss function is more addressable to classification problems. In general, there is no numeric relationship among the different classes. It turns out that, in regression, the outputs are numerical values, allowing us to use loss functions that take advantage of this numerical relationship.

Due to its simplicity and speed, **mean squared error** (**MSE**) is the more popular loss function for regression problems:

$$mse(TRUE, PRED) = \frac{1}{N} \sum_{i=0}^{N-1} (PRED_i - TRUE_i)^2$$

where *TRUE* is the ground truth, *PRED* is the model prediction, and *N* is the size of *TRUE*.

Note: MSE was introduced in Chapter 6, Learning by Minimizing Cost Functions.

We can use MSE in the backward step of the regression model as follows:

```
1.  void backward(const Tensor_2D &TRUE) {
2.
3.      MSE mse_fn;
4.      auto PRED = regressor_head.get_output();
5.      auto upstream_gradient = mse_fn.derivative(TRUE, PRED);
6.
7.      regressor_head->backward(upstream_gradient, true);
8.
9.      dropout->backward(regressor_head->get_downstream(), true);
10.
11.     dense->backward(dropout->get_downstream(), true);
12.     flatten->backward(dense->get_downstream(), true);
13.
14.     maxpooling_2->backward(flatten->get_downstream(), true);
15.     conv2d_2->backward(maxpooling_2->get_downstream(), true);
16.
17.     maxpooling_1->backward(conv2d_2->get_downstream(), true);
18.     conv2d_1->backward(maxpooling_1->get_downstream(), true);
```

```
19.
20.    maxpooling_0->backward(conv2d_1->get_downstream(), true);
21.    conv2d_0->backward(maxpooling_0->get_downstream(), false);
22.
23. }
```

Loading the bounding box data

The data used to train the model consists of quadruples (Xmin, Ymin, Xmax, Ymax):

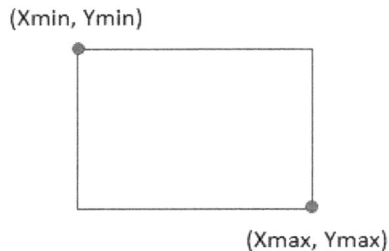

Figure 17.4: *The coordinate system used in this chapter*

The annotation data of each image must be fed to the model using a batch as follows:

```
1.  for (int i = 0; i < batch_size; ++i) {
2.      int instance = instance_indexes[begin + i];
3.
4.      const std::string &path = (*data)(instance, 0);
5.      cv::Mat src = cv::imread(path, cv::IMREAD_COLOR);
6.      if (src.empty()) {
7.          throw std::invalid_argument(path + " is not a valid image.");
8.      }
9.
10.     int width = std::stoi((*data)(instance, 2));
11.     int height = std::stoi((*data)(instance, 3));
12.     int xmin = std::stoi((*data)(instance, 4));
13.     int ymin = std::stoi((*data)(instance, 5));
14.     int xmax = std::stoi((*data)(instance, 6));
15.     int ymax = std::stoi((*data)(instance, 7));
16.
17.     cv::Mat processed_image, squared;
18.
19.     if (center_images) {
```

```
20.         make_image_square(src, squared, xmin, ymin, xmax, ymax);
21.         int max_side = std::max(width, height);
22.         width = max_side;
23.         height = max_side;
24.     } else {
25.         squared = src;
26.     }
27.
28.     processing_image(squared, processed_
    image, xmin, ymin, xmax, ymax);
29.
30.     convert_to_tensor(processed_image, tensor, scale);
31.     batch.X.chip<0>(i) = tensor;
32.
33.     batch.B(i, 0) = std::max(TYPE(0.), static_
    cast<TYPE>(xmin) / width);
34.     batch.B(i, 1) = std::max(TYPE(0.), static_
    cast<TYPE>(ymin) / height);
35.     batch.B(i, 2) = std::min(TYPE(1.), static_
    cast<TYPE>(xmax) / width);
36.     batch.B(i, 3) = std::min(TYPE(1.), static_
    cast<TYPE>(ymax) / height);
37.
38. }
```

Note that, because of data augmentation, we must take care and ensure that Xmin, Ymin, Xmax, and Ymax lay into the interval [0..1].

Everything else in the model is quite similar to the classification models described in the previous chapters.

Training the regression model

Once we finish the model's definition, we can finally move to the model's training. For this purpose, we need a dataset with bounding box annotations. Since none of the previously used datasets have these annotations, we must find a new one for the mission. The Oxford Pets III [2] is one example of a dataset that provides the bounding box annotation data. We will describe this dataset in more detail later on.

Note: Instructions for downloading the Oxford Pets dataset are available on the online book repository.

We can invoke the training of our new model using the following well-known code:

```
1.  int main(int, char **)
2.  {
3.
4.      using DEVICE = Eigen::ThreadPoolDevice;
5.      using GEN = std::mt19937;
6.      using MODEL = Model<DEVICE, GEN>;
7.
8.      std::random_device rd{};
9.      const auto seed = rd();
10.     GEN rng(seed);
11.
12.     const int threads = std::thread::hardware_concurrency();
13.     Eigen::ThreadPool tp(threads);
14.     DEVICE device(&tp, threads);
15.
16.     const int IMAGE_SIZE = 224;
17.
18.     MODEL model(device, rng, IMAGE_SIZE);
19.
20.     run_experiment<DEVICE, GEN, MODEL, Data_Augmentation_
    ParallelBatches<GEN>>(
21.         "../../data/Oxford-IIIT_Pet_Dataset",
22.         model, device, rng,
23.         40, // epochs
24.         16, // minibatch_size
25.         0.001, // learning_rate
26.         false // square_images
27.     );
28.     std::cout << "success\n";
29.     return 0;
30. }
```

This program results in the following output:

Figure 17.5: Training the regression model

Since this is our first attempt to train this model, one may wonder how good these results are. One simple way to check the effectiveness of the training is by using the model to predict some bounding boxes with images drawn from the validation data:

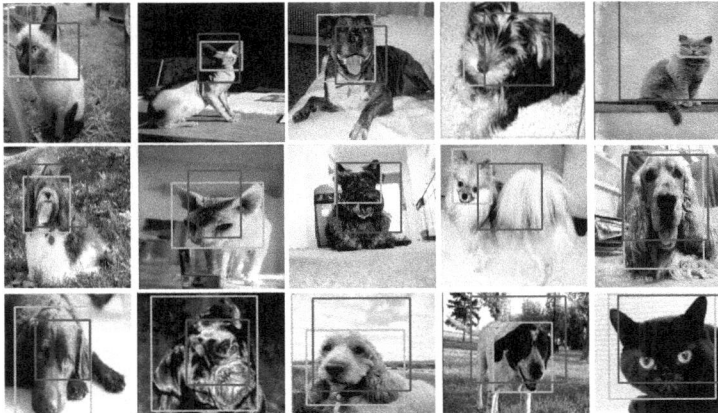

Figure 17.6: Bounding boxes for the first regression model

Note: The green bounding box represents the ground truth. The blue rectangle represents the predicted bounding box.

Notably, the difference between the ground truth and predicted bound boxes suggests some quality metric. This idea will be explored later in one of the forthcoming sections when we introduce the IoU metric.

Now that we know how to train a regression model, it is time to build the object localization model by combining a regressor and a classifier in the same network.

Experiment 2: Training the object localization model

This experiment consists of building an object localization system, a model that simultaneously performs the task of classification and regression.

One brute-force way to combine the two models is to build two independent models and then call them, passing the same input to both. Of course, mounting the object localization in this way is a waste of resources, training time, memory, and duplicate processing. *Can we do better? Of course, we can.*

In a better solution, we combine the two models in only one, as illustrated in the following figure:

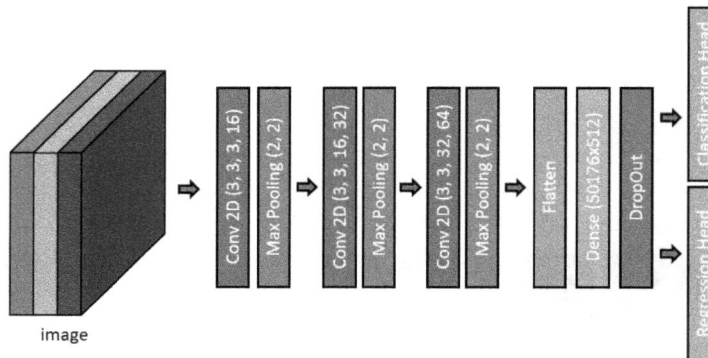

Figure 17.7: A two-head network implementing the object localization system

The previous models introduced in this book were somehow linear, having only one input and one output. The model above, however, has one input but two outputs. *How can we wire up a model like this?* Check the following implementation:

```
1. template <typename DEVICE, typename GEN>
2. class Model {
3.
4. public:
```

```
5.
6.     Model(DEVICE &device, GEN &rng, int img_size): IMG_SIZE(img_
   size) {
7.
8.         const int kernel_size = 3;
9.         const int channels = 3;
10.
11.        const int hidden_neurons = 512;
12.        const int num_classes = NUMBER_CLASSES;
13.
14.        Tensor_4D kernels_0(kernel_size, kernel_size, channels, 16);
15.        glorot_uniform_initializer(rng, kernels_0);
16.        conv2d_0 = new Conv2DLayer(device, ker-
   nels_0, new ReLU<4>());
17.
18.        maxpooling_0 = new MaxPooling(device, 2);
19.
20.        Tensor_4D kernels_1(kernel_size, kernel_size, kernels_0.
   dimension(3), 32);
21.        glorot_uniform_initializer(rng, kernels_1);
22.        conv2d_1 = new Conv2DLayer(device, ker-
   nels_1, new ReLU<4>());
23.
24.        maxpooling_1 = new MaxPooling(device, 2);
25.
26.        Tensor_4D kernels_2(kernel_size, kernel_size, kernels_1.
   dimension(3), 64);
27.        glorot_uniform_initializer(rng, kernels_2);
28.        conv2d_2 = new Conv2DLayer(device, ker-
   nels_2, new ReLU<4>());
29.
30.        maxpooling_2 = new MaxPooling(device, 2);
31.
32.        flatten = new FlattenLayer<DEVICE, 4>(device);
33.
34.        int reduced_image_size = IMG_SIZE / 8;
35.
36.        const int flatten_size = reduced_image_size * reduced_image_
```

```
   size * kernels_2.dimension(3);
37.
38.         Tensor_2D W1(flatten_size, hidden_neurons);
39.         glorot_uniform_initializer(rng, W1);
40.         dense = new DenseLayer(device, W1, new ReLU<2>());
41.         dense->set_optimizer(Adam<2>());
42.
43.         dropout = new DropoutLayer<DEVICE, 2, GEN>(de-
   vice, 0.5, rng);
44.
45.         Tensor_2D WC(hidden_neurons, num_classes);
46.         glorot_uniform_initializer(rng, WC);
47.         classifier_head = new SoftmaxCrossEntropyLayer(device, WC);
48.         classifier_head->set_optimizer(Adam<2>());
49.
50.         Tensor_2D WR(hidden_neurons, 4);
51.         glorot_uniform_initializer(rng, WR);
52.         regressor_
   head = new DenseLayer(device, WR, new Sigmoid<2>());
53.
54.     }
55.
56. private:
57.
58.     Conv2DLayer<DEVICE> *conv2d_0;
59.     MaxPooling<DEVICE> *maxpooling_0;
60.
61.     Conv2DLayer<DEVICE> *conv2d_1;
62.     MaxPooling<DEVICE> *maxpooling_1;
63.
64.     Conv2DLayer<DEVICE> *conv2d_2;
65.     MaxPooling<DEVICE> *maxpooling_2;
66.
67.     FlattenLayer<DEVICE, 4> *flatten;
68.     DenseLayer<DEVICE> *dense;
69.     DropoutLayer<DEVICE, 2, GEN> *dropout;
70.
71.     DenseLayer<DEVICE> *classifier_head;
```

```
72.
73.     DenseLayer<DEVICE> *regressor_head;
74.
75. };
```

This model is what we know as a two-head model. The model has a single sequence of convolutional layers (feature extraction layers) followed by an adaptor layer from which branches two independent heads:

- One softmax layer for classification
- One dense layer for regression

The sequence of the layers is not imposed by the constructor but by the forward and backward procedures. The following code shows how to perform the forward pass with this model:

```
1.  void forward(const Tensor_4D &input) {
2.
3.      conv2d_0->forward(input);
4.      maxpooling_0->forward(conv2d_0->get_output());
5.
6.      conv2d_1->forward(maxpooling_0->get_output());
7.      maxpooling_1->forward(conv2d_1->get_output());
8.
9.      conv2d_2->forward(maxpooling_1->get_output());
10.     maxpooling_2->forward(conv2d_2->get_output());
11.
12.     flatten->forward(maxpooling_2->get_output());
13.     dense->forward(flatten->get_output());
14.     dropout->forward(dense->get_output());
15.
16.     classifier_head->forward(dropout->get_output());
17.
18.     regressor_head->forward(dropout->get_output());
19. }
```

Note that the output of the dropout layer is forwarded to both layers, **classifier_head**, and **regressor_head**, creating two branches in the model:

```
1.  dropout->forward(dense->get_output());
2.
3.  classifier_head->forward(dropout->get_output());
4.
5.  regressor_head->forward(dropout->get_output());
```

This simple solution actually works, propagating the computation from the previous layers to the two model's heads.

Now, we must think of a way to perform the backward computation, combining the gradients from the two individual heads and propagating it throughout the shared trunk. Luckily, the solution is also very simple, as shown below:

```
1.  void backward(const Tensor_2D &classifier_
    TRUE, const Tensor_2D &regressor_TRUE) {
2.
3.      classifier_head->backward(classifier_TRUE, true);
4.
5.      MSE mse_fn;
6.      const Tensor_2D regressor_upstream = mse_
    fn.derivative(regressor_TRUE, regressor_head->get_output());
7.      regressor_head->backward(regressor_upstream, true);
8.
9.      // combined backward
10.
11.     Tensor_2D combined_gradient = classifier_head->get_
    downstream() + regressor_head->get_downstream();
12.
13.     dropout->backward(combined_gradient, true);
14.
15.     dense->backward(dropout->get_downstream(), true);
16.     flatten->backward(dense->get_downstream(), true);
17.
18.     maxpooling_2->backward(flatten->get_downstream(), true);
19.     conv2d_2->backward(maxpooling_2->get_downstream(), true);
20.
21.     maxpooling_1->backward(conv2d_2->get_downstream(), true);
22.     conv2d_1->backward(maxpooling_1->get_downstream(), true);
23.
24.     maxpooling_0->backward(conv2d_1->get_downstream(), true);
25.     conv2d_0->backward(maxpooling_0->get_downstream(), false);
26.
27. }
```

The trick here is straightforward: summing up the two head gradients in the intersection layer. Thus, we add the gradient propagated from the softmax head to the gradient propagated from the regression layer to form a single combined gradient:

```
1.      // combined backward
2.      Tensor_2D combined_gradient = classifier_head->get_
        downstream() + regressor_head->get_downstream();
```

The combined gradient then flows through the main trunk of the network to fit the kernels of the feature extraction convolutional layers. You may be wondering where the sum comes from. It turns out that the total model cost is the sum of the loss computed in both heads. This is due to the chain rule:

The derivative of the sum is the sum of derivatives.

The resulting combined gradient is the sum of the two upstream gradients.

Once the backward pass computes the gradients, we can update the weights as usual:

```
1. void update(const TYPE learning_rate, int epoch) {
2.      conv2d_0->update(learning_rate, epoch);
3.      conv2d_1->update(learning_rate, epoch);
4.      conv2d_2->update(learning_rate, epoch);
5.      dense->update(learning_rate, epoch);
6.
7.      classifier_head->update(learning_rate, epoch);
8.
9.      regressor_head->update(learning_rate, epoch);
10. }
```

Note that some layers, such as dropout and max pooling, do not have trainable parameters to update.

The model is finally defined. Now, we can start the training, as shown in the next section.

Data used in the experiment

In this experiment, we will train the object localization model with the Oxford Pet Dataset, the same dataset we used in the previous experiment. This dataset has more than 7k images of cats and dogs. For each image, there is an XML file with the bounding box annotation, the object class (**dog** or **cat**), and other metadata. Check the following example:

```
1. <annotation>
2.  <folder>OXIIIT</folder>
3.  <filename>staffordshire_bull_terrier_177.jpg</filename>
4.  <source>
5.   <database>OXFORD-IIIT Pet Dataset</database>
6.   <annotation>OXIIIT</annotation>
7.   <image>flickr</image>
```

```
 8.  </source>
 9.  <size>
10.   <width>500</width>
11.   <height>375</height>
12.   <depth>3</depth>
13.  </size>
14.  <segmented>0</segmented>
15.  <object>
16.   <name>dog</name>
17.   <pose>Frontal</pose>
18.   <truncated>0</truncated>
19.   <occluded>0</occluded>
20.   <bndbox>
21.    <xmin>244</xmin>
22.    <ymin>105</ymin>
23.    <xmax>345</xmax>
24.    <ymax>211</ymax>
25.   </bndbox>
26.   <difficult>0</difficult>
27.  </object>
28. </annotation>
```

There is more information in this file than we need, such as pose, difficult, etc.

Note: Using XML to annotate datasets is old and obsolete. Modern datasets use more compact formats.

We can use a utility to load the data, as shown:

```
1. std::cout << "Loading the data, please wait!\n";
2. auto [training_data, validation_data] = load_oxford_pets_
   dataset(datapath, rng, 0.8);
3. std::cout << "Data loaded!\n";
```

Note: You can find the source code of this experiment in the book repository on GitHub.

Once the data is loaded, we can train the model as usual. Again, we will use data augmentation to implement regularization. Although data augmentation is not a new concept at this point in the book, there are some important details we must cite.

Data augmentation and annotations

One point must be highlighted here: augmentations that change spatial features such as translations, rotations, stretching, cropping, zooms, flips, etc., require adjusting the bounding box coordinates, accordingly, as illustrated in the following figure:

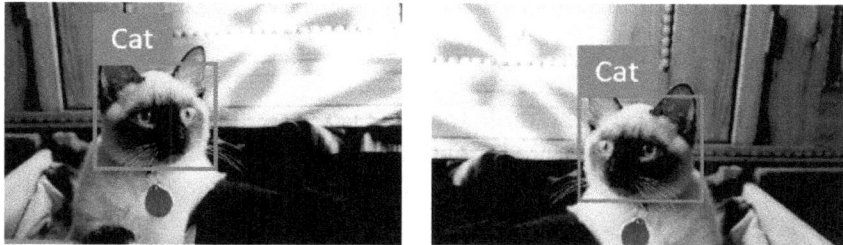

Figure 17.8: Annotations and data augmentation

In this example, the image was horizontally flipped and vertically translated by a small number of pixels. Of course, the bounding box coordinates must be updated to represent these changes.

Redefinition of the bounding box due to translation or even an image resize is not more than a linear algebra exercise. However, rotating the bounding boxes because of data augmentation is not so straightforward.

It turns out that the sides of the rotated bounding box must be parallel to the sides of the augmented image, as illustrated:

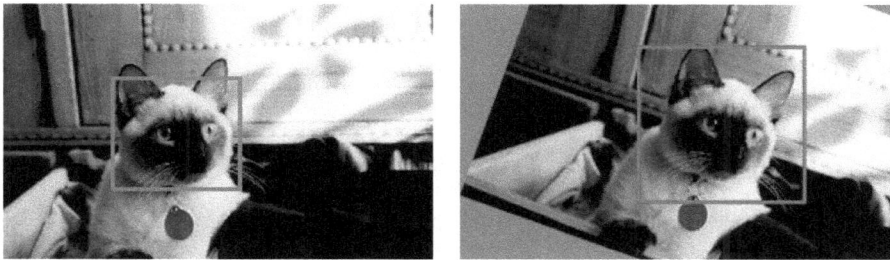

Figure 17.9: Rotating the bounding box

The next topic covers the steps to find a suitable rotation for the bounding box after rotation.

Rotating bounding boxes

The augmented rotated bounding box can be found in two steps. First, we rotate the original bounding box with the same warp transformation used to rotate the original image:

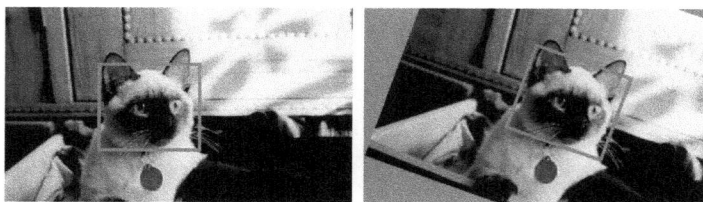

Figure 17.10: Rotating bounding boxes

This rotated bounding box is not suitable for our purposes of training a model because its sides are not parallel to the augmented image sides. It is possible to fix it by replacing the rotated bounding box with a new bound box that holds the rotated one, as illustrated in the following figures:

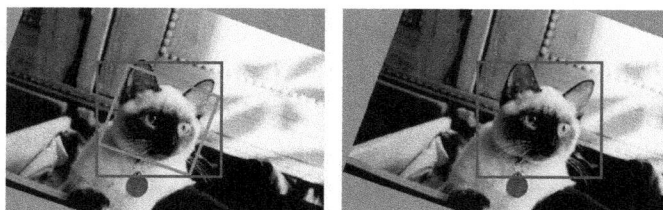

Figure 17.11: Fix bounding box rotation

This last bounding box is the desired augmented bounding box. This operation is implemented in the following function:

```
1.  void processing_image(cv::Mat &src, cv::Mat &dest, int &xmin,
    int &ymin, int &xmax, int &ymax) {
2.
3.      cv::Mat flipped, rotated;
4.
5.      if (distribution(rng) > 0.5) {
6.          flipped = horizontal_flip(src);
7.
8.          int temp = src.cols - xmax;
9.          xmax = src.cols - xmin;
10.         xmin = temp;
11.
12.     } else {
13.         flipped = src;
14.     }
15.
16.     int angle = static_
    cast<int>((2.f * distribution(rng) - 1.f) * 15);
```

```
17.     int vertical_delta = static_
   cast<int>((2.f * distribution(rng) - 1.f) * src.rows * 0.1);
18.     int horizontal_delta = static_
   cast<int>((2.f * distribution(rng) - 1.f) * src.cols * 0.1);
19.
20.     dest = rotate_and_translate(flipped, angle, horizontal_
   delta, vertical_delta);
21.
22.     // updating bounding box
23.
24.     // translating
25.     xmin += horizontal_delta;
26.     xmax += horizontal_delta;
27.
28.     ymin += vertical_delta;
29.     ymax += vertical_delta;
30.
31.     // rotating
32.
33.     if (angle != 0) {
34.
35.         float c_x = src.cols / 2;
36.         float c_y = src.rows / 2;
37.
38.         float angle_rad = M_PI * angle / 180.;
39.
40.         float cos_a = std::cos(angle_rad);
41.         float sin_a = std::sin(angle_rad);
42.
43.         float x1 = c_x + cos_a * (xmin - c_x) - sin_a * (ymin - c_x);
44.         float y1 = c_y + sin_a * (xmin - c_y) + cos_a * (ymin - c_y);
45.
46.         float x2 = c_x + cos_a * (xmax - c_x) - sin_a * (ymin - c_x);
47.         float y2 = c_y + sin_a * (xmax - c_y) + cos_a * (ymin - c_y);
48.
49.         float x3 = c_x + cos_a * (xmax - c_x) - sin_a * (ymax - c_x);
50.         float y3 = c_y + sin_a * (xmax - c_y) + cos_a * (ymax - c_y);
51.
52.         float x4 = c_x + cos_a * (xmin - c_x) - sin_a * (ymax - c_x);
53.         float y4 = c_y + sin_a * (xmin - c_y) + cos_a * (ymax - c_y);
```

```
54.
55.         // obtaining the new bounding box parallel to image sides
56.
57.         xmin = static_cast<int>(std::min(x1, x4));
58.         xmax = static_cast<int>(std::max(x2, x3));
59.         ymin = static_cast<int>(std::min(y1, y2));
60.         ymax = static_cast<int>(std::max(y3, y4));
61.     }
62.
63. }
```

The code is illustrated in the following figure:

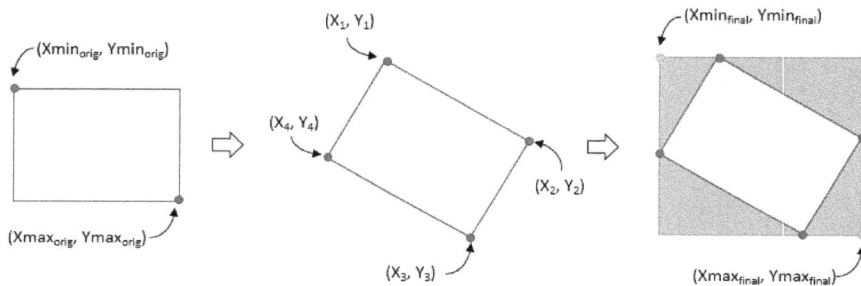

Figure 17.12: Steps to calculate the bounding box after augment rotation

The products of cosines and sines in **processing_image(...)** are a hand-coded implementation of the image rotation performed by the homography in the OpenCV cv::warp(...) function.

Sometimes, data augmentation transformations generate corrupt instances. The following section covers this scenario.

Destructive augmentations

It is noteworthy that some transformations can be destructive. Consider the following example where the pet's head went outside the limits of the image:

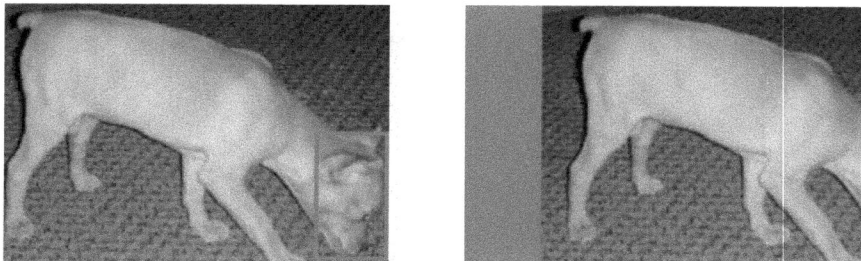

Figure 17.13: Destructive augmentation

Preferably, transformations like this should not be allowed. If they are rare and hard to prevent, one simple solution is to replace the original bounding box with a random small one, as shown:

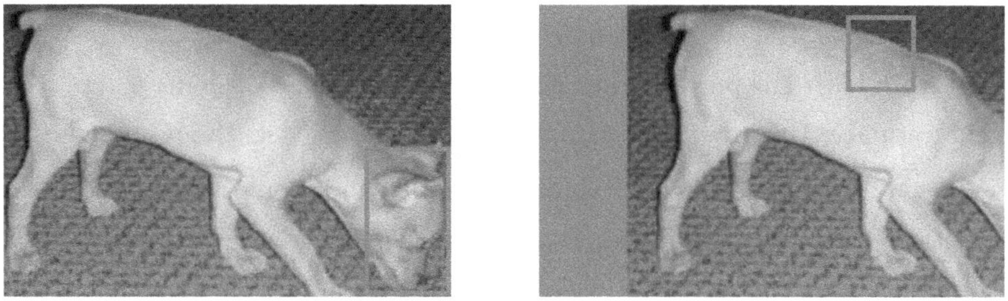

Figure 17.14: Workaround for a destructive augmentation

Once the augmentation procedure is set, we can move to the model training.

Training the hybrid model

Training the model for 40 epochs results in the following output:

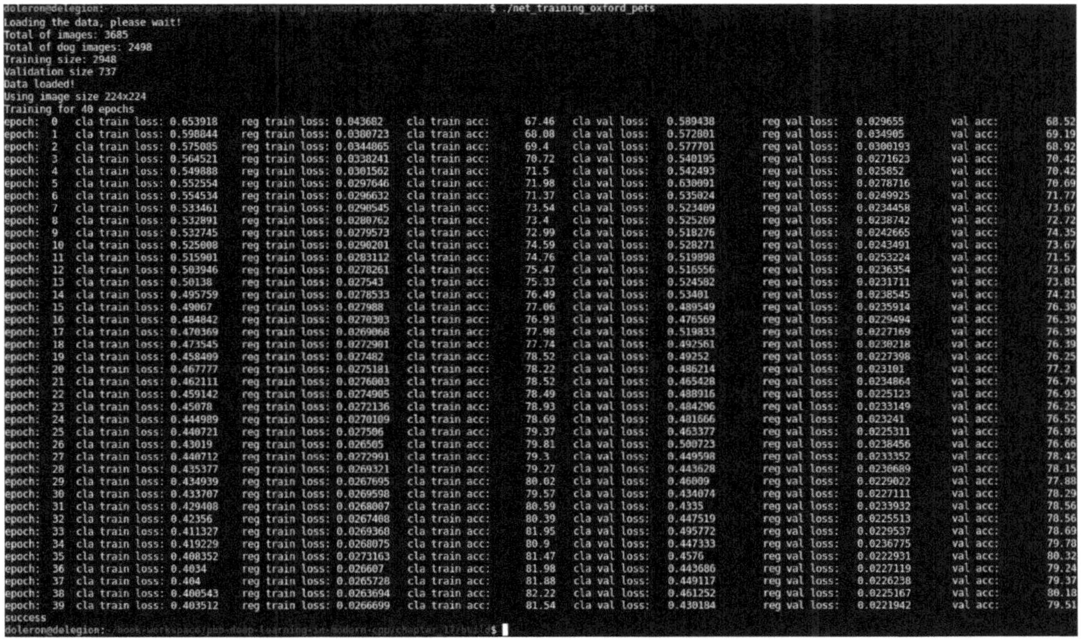

```
doleron@delegion:~/book-workspace/pdp-deep-learning-in-modern-cpp/chapter_17/build$ ./net_training_oxford_pets
Loading the data, please wait!
Total of images: 3685
Total of dog images: 2498
Training size: 2948
Validation size 737
Data loaded!
Using image size 224x224
Training for 40 epochs
epoch:  0   cla train loss: 0.653918   reg train loss: 0.043682    cla train acc:  67.46  cla val loss:  0.589438   reg val loss:  0.029655   val acc:  68.52
epoch:  1   cla train loss: 0.598844   reg train loss: 0.0300723   cla train acc:  68.08  cla val loss:  0.572001   reg val loss:  0.034905   val acc:  69.19
epoch:  2   cla train loss: 0.575085   reg train loss: 0.0344865   cla train acc:  69.4   cla val loss:  0.577701   reg val loss:  0.0300193  val acc:  68.92
epoch:  3   cla train loss: 0.564521   reg train loss: 0.0338241   cla train acc:  70.72  cla val loss:  0.540195   reg val loss:  0.0271623  val acc:  70.42
epoch:  4   cla train loss: 0.549888   reg train loss: 0.0301562   cla train acc:  71.5   cla val loss:  0.542493   reg val loss:  0.025852   val acc:  70.42
epoch:  5   cla train loss: 0.552554   reg train loss: 0.0297646   cla train acc:  71.98  cla val loss:  0.630091   reg val loss:  0.0278716  val acc:  70.69
epoch:  6   cla train loss: 0.554534   reg train loss: 0.0296632   cla train acc:  71.37  cla val loss:  0.535024   reg val loss:  0.0249925  val acc:  71.77
epoch:  7   cla train loss: 0.533461   reg train loss: 0.0290545   cla train acc:  73.54  cla val loss:  0.523409   reg val loss:  0.0234458  val acc:  73.67
epoch:  8   cla train loss: 0.532891   reg train loss: 0.0280762   cla train acc:  73.4   cla val loss:  0.525269   reg val loss:  0.0238742  val acc:  72.72
epoch:  9   cla train loss: 0.532745   reg train loss: 0.0279573   cla train acc:  72.99  cla val loss:  0.518276   reg val loss:  0.0242665  val acc:  74.35
epoch: 10   cla train loss: 0.525008   reg train loss: 0.0290201   cla train acc:  74.59  cla val loss:  0.528271   reg val loss:  0.0243491  val acc:  73.67
epoch: 11   cla train loss: 0.515901   reg train loss: 0.0283112   cla train acc:  74.76  cla val loss:  0.519898   reg val loss:  0.0253224  val acc:  71.5
epoch: 12   cla train loss: 0.503946   reg train loss: 0.0278261   cla train acc:  75.47  cla val loss:  0.516556   reg val loss:  0.0236354  val acc:  73.67
epoch: 13   cla train loss: 0.50138    reg train loss: 0.027543    cla train acc:  75.33  cla val loss:  0.524582   reg val loss:  0.0231711  val acc:  73.81
epoch: 14   cla train loss: 0.495759   reg train loss: 0.0278533   cla train acc:  76.49  cla val loss:  0.53401    reg val loss:  0.0238545  val acc:  74.21
epoch: 15   cla train loss: 0.49067    reg train loss: 0.0279088   cla train acc:  77.06  cla val loss:  0.489549   reg val loss:  0.0235914  val acc:  76.39
epoch: 16   cla train loss: 0.484842   reg train loss: 0.0270303   cla train acc:  76.93  cla val loss:  0.476569   reg val loss:  0.0229494  val acc:  76.39
epoch: 17   cla train loss: 0.470369   reg train loss: 0.0269068   cla train acc:  77.98  cla val loss:  0.519833   reg val loss:  0.0227169  val acc:  76.39
epoch: 18   cla train loss: 0.473545   reg train loss: 0.0272901   cla train acc:  77.74  cla val loss:  0.492561   reg val loss:  0.0230218  val acc:  76.39
epoch: 19   cla train loss: 0.458409   reg train loss: 0.027482    cla train acc:  78.52  cla val loss:  0.49252    reg val loss:  0.0227398  val acc:  76.25
epoch: 20   cla train loss: 0.467777   reg train loss: 0.0275181   cla train acc:  78.22  cla val loss:  0.486214   reg val loss:  0.023101   val acc:  77.2
epoch: 21   cla train loss: 0.462111   reg train loss: 0.0276003   cla train acc:  78.52  cla val loss:  0.465428   reg val loss:  0.0234864  val acc:  76.79
epoch: 22   cla train loss: 0.459142   reg train loss: 0.0274905   cla train acc:  78.49  cla val loss:  0.488916   reg val loss:  0.0225123  val acc:  76.93
epoch: 23   cla train loss: 0.45078    reg train loss: 0.0272136   cla train acc:  78.93  cla val loss:  0.484296   reg val loss:  0.0233149  val acc:  76.25
epoch: 24   cla train loss: 0.444989   reg train loss: 0.0270109   cla train acc:  78.69  cla val loss:  0.481666   reg val loss:  0.023241   val acc:  76.52
epoch: 25   cla train loss: 0.440721   reg train loss: 0.027506    cla train acc:  79.37  cla val loss:  0.463377   reg val loss:  0.0225311  val acc:  76.93
epoch: 26   cla train loss: 0.43019    reg train loss: 0.026505    cla train acc:  79.81  cla val loss:  0.500723   reg val loss:  0.0238456  val acc:  76.66
epoch: 27   cla train loss: 0.440712   reg train loss: 0.0272991   cla train acc:  79.3   cla val loss:  0.449598   reg val loss:  0.0233352  val acc:  78.42
epoch: 28   cla train loss: 0.435377   reg train loss: 0.0269321   cla train acc:  79.27  cla val loss:  0.443628   reg val loss:  0.0230689  val acc:  76.93
epoch: 29   cla train loss: 0.434939   reg train loss: 0.0267695   cla train acc:  80.02  cla val loss:  0.46009    reg val loss:  0.0229022  val acc:  77.88
epoch: 30   cla train loss: 0.433707   reg train loss: 0.0269598   cla train acc:  79.57  cla val loss:  0.434074   reg val loss:  0.0227111  val acc:  78.29
epoch: 31   cla train loss: 0.429408   reg train loss: 0.0268007   cla train acc:  80.59  cla val loss:  0.4335     reg val loss:  0.0233932  val acc:  78.56
epoch: 32   cla train loss: 0.42356    reg train loss: 0.0267408   cla train acc:  80.39  cla val loss:  0.447519   reg val loss:  0.0225513  val acc:  78.56
epoch: 33   cla train loss: 0.411327   reg train loss: 0.0269360   cla train acc:  81.95  cla val loss:  0.495772   reg val loss:  0.0229537  val acc:  78.69
epoch: 34   cla train loss: 0.419229   reg train loss: 0.0268075   cla train acc:  80.9   cla val loss:  0.447333   reg val loss:  0.0236775  val acc:  79.78
epoch: 35   cla train loss: 0.408352   reg train loss: 0.0273163   cla train acc:  81.47  cla val loss:  0.4576     reg val loss:  0.0222931  val acc:  80.32
epoch: 36   cla train loss: 0.4034     reg train loss: 0.026607    cla train acc:  81.98  cla val loss:  0.443686   reg val loss:  0.0227119  val acc:  79.24
epoch: 37   cla train loss: 0.404      reg train loss: 0.0265728   cla train acc:  81.88  cla val loss:  0.449117   reg val loss:  0.0226238  val acc:  79.37
epoch: 38   cla train loss: 0.400543   reg train loss: 0.0263694   cla train acc:  82.22  cla val loss:  0.461252   reg val loss:  0.0225167  val acc:  80.18
epoch: 39   cla train loss: 0.403512   reg train loss: 0.0266699   cla train acc:  81.54  cla val loss:  0.430184   reg val loss:  0.0221942  val acc:  79.51
success
doleron@delegion:~/book-workspace/pdp-deep-learning-in-modern-cpp/chapter_17/build$
```

Figure 17.15: Training the hybrid model

Note: Remember that the result may vary because of the randomization of weight initialization, batching, and data augmentation.

The dual output of this hybrid model doubled the number of indicators. Let us check them now.

First, we have the metrics evaluated on the training dataset:

- **cla train loss**: The classification training loss. The lower, the better.
- **reg train loss**: The regresssion training loss. The lower, the better.
- **cla train acc**: The accuracy calculated on the training set. The higher, the better.

Now, we have the same metrics but evaluated on the validation dataset:

- **cla train loss**: The classification validation loss. The lower, the better.
- **reg train loss**: The regression validation loss. The lower, the better.
- **val acc**: The validation training accuracy. The higher, the better.

The training metrics are not much different from the validation metrics. This is because we are using two regularization techniques here: data augmentation and dropout. Without them, due to the small number of training instances, the fitting process would likely result in an overfitted model.

We can check the validation accuracy, which achieved a maximum value of 80%. We will use this value as a reference for this model.

Let us print some images, their ground truth and predicted bounding boxes:

Figure 17.16: *Ground-truth and the respective predicted bounding boxes*

They look as bad or good as the predictions achieved by the regression-only model. At this moment, we want to quantify how good these bounding box predictions actually are. **Intersection over Union (IoU)** is a metric designed for this mission, as discussed in the next section.

Using IoU to compare bounding box predictions

The prediction of an object localization model outputs two pieces of information: the object class and the object bounding box. While accuracy works very well to demonstrate how well a model performed over a (balanced) dataset, assessing the performance of predicting the bounding boxes is not easy.

With this challenge in mind, the deep learning community developed IoU, a simple metric to calculate the performance of bounding box predictors [3].

The easiest way to explain how IoU works is by the following figure:

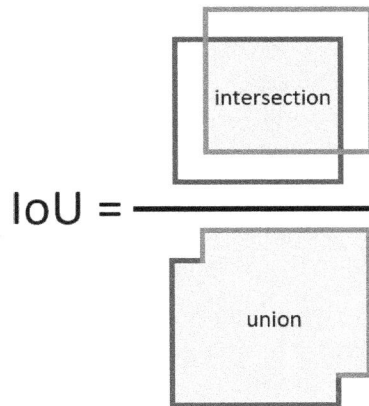

Figure 17.17: Graphical representation of the IoU formula

As its name suggests, IoU is calculated by the reason between the intersection and the union of the predicted and ground-truth bounding boxes. We can use the following function to calculate IoU:

```
1. TYPE intersection_over_
   union(const BoundingBox &A, const BoundingBox &B) {
2.     TYPE result = TYPE(0.);
3.
4.     // calculating the intersection area
5.     TYPE xA = std::max(A.xmin, B.xmin);
6.     TYPE yA = std::max(A.ymin, B.ymin);
7.     TYPE xB = std::min(A.xmax, B.xmax);
8.     TYPE yB = std::min(A.ymax, B.ymax);
9.     TYPE intersection_
   area = std::max(0, xB - xA) * std::max(0, yB - yA);
```

```
10.
11.    // Calculating union
12.    TYPE area_A = (A.xmax - A.xmin) * (A.ymax - A.ymin);
13.    TYPE area_B = (B.xmax - B.xmin) * (B.ymax - B.ymin);
14.    TYPE union_area = area_A + area_B - intersection_area;
15.
16.    if (union_area > TYPE(0.)) {
17.        result = intersection_area / union_area;
18.    }
19.    return result;
20. }
```

We can understand IoU by thinking in the two opposite scenarios:

- If the predicted bounding box and the ground truth bounding box do not overlap at any point, the intersection is zero, and, as a result, IoU is also zero. This is the worst scenario where the prediction completely fails to provide even a rough approximation.

- If the predicted bounding box perfectly fits the ground truth bounding box, the intersection area is equal to the union area. In this case, IoU is one.

Any other intermediary situation where the predicted bounding box partially overlaps the ground truth bounding box provides a value between zero and one. Refer to the following figure:

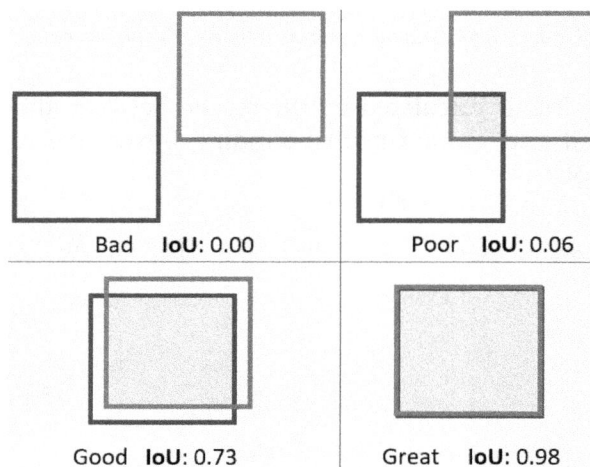

Bad   IoU: 0.00   Poor IoU: 0.06

Good IoU: 0.73   Great IoU: 0.98

Figure 17.18: Obtaining IoU for different configurations

The higher the IoU, the better the prediction. Let us check some predictions and respective IoU using the previous model:

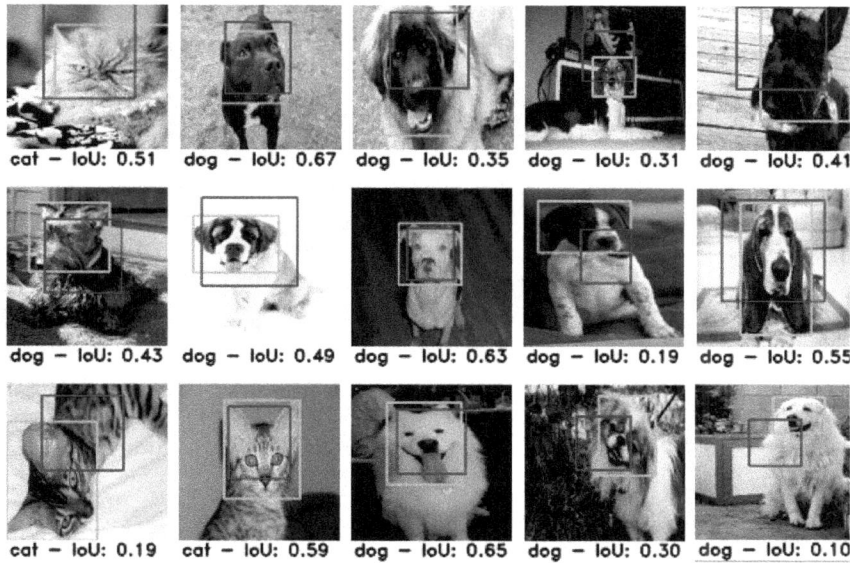

Figure 17.19: *Localizating Pets and computing IoU*

Computing the IoU for each prediction of the last model over the validation dataset and averaging the results provides a mean value of 0.36:

$$IoU_{avg} = \frac{1}{N} \sum_{i}^{N} IoU_i$$

How good is this value? The best way to answer this question is by comparing this result to the IoU achieved by a different model, as demonstrated in the next section.

Experiment 3: Using transfer learning with fine-tuning

We can reuse a pre-trained model to build an object localization system like any other model. In this new experiment, we will reuse a VGG16 network pre-trained on the ImageNet weights to build a new object localization model:

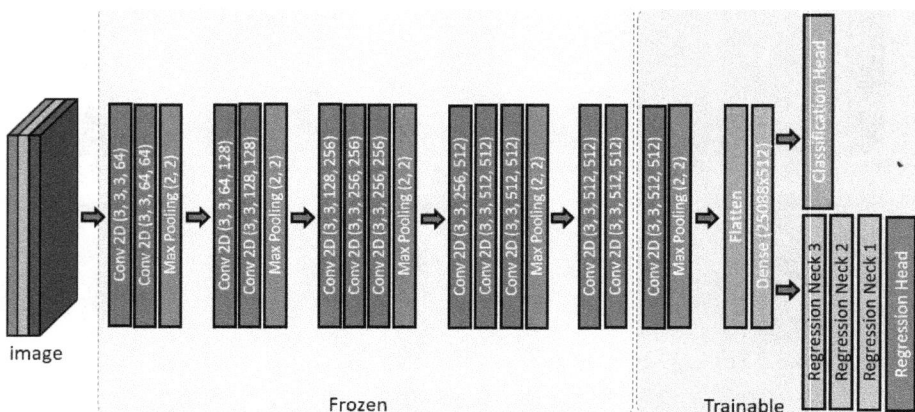

***Figure 17.20**: Reusing VGG 16 and ImageNet to build the object localization model*

This technique is known as transfer learning.

Note: Transfer learning was introduced in the previous chapter.

The image shows that we include 3 more dense layers before the regression head. Note also that we will be unfrozen the last VGG16 convolutional layer, aiming to fine-tune the performance of our new model. Check the following implementation:

```
1.  template <typename DEVICE, typename GEN>
2.  class Model {
3.
4.  public:
5.
6.      Model(DEVICE &device, GEN &rng, int img_size): IMG_SIZE(img_
    size) {
7.          const int kernel_size = 3;
8.          const int channels = 3;
9.
10.         const int hidden_neurons = 512;
11.         const int num_classes = NUMBER_CLASSES;
12.
13.         Tensor_4D block1_conv1_kernel(kernel_size, kernel_
    size, 3, 64);
14.         load_tensor_from_file(block1_conv1_kernel, "data/vgg16/
    imagenet/block1_conv1_kernel.txt");
15.         block1_conv1 = new Conv2DLayer(device, block1_conv1_
    kernel, block1_conv1_bias, new ReLU<4>());
```

```
16.
17.        Tensor_4D block1_conv2_kernel(kernel_size, kernel_
   size, 64, 64);
18.        load_tensor_from_file(block1_conv2_kernel, "data/vgg16/
   imagenet/block1_conv2_kernel.txt");
19.        block1_conv2 = new Conv2DLayer(device, block1_conv2_
   kernel, block1_conv2_bias, new ReLU<4>());
20.
21.        block1_pool = new MaxPooling(device, 2);
22.
23.        Tensor_4D block2_conv1_kernel(kernel_size, kernel_
   size, 64, 128);
24.        load_tensor_from_file(block2_conv1_kernel, "data/vgg16/
   imagenet/block2_conv1_kernel.txt");
25.        block2_conv1 = new Conv2DLayer(device, block2_conv1_
   kernel, block2_conv1_bias, new ReLU<4>());
26.
27.        Tensor_4D block2_conv2_kernel(kernel_size, kernel_
   size, 128, 128);
28.        load_tensor_from_file(block2_conv2_kernel, "data/vgg16/
   imagenet/block2_conv2_kernel.txt");
29.        block2_conv2 = new Conv2DLayer(device, block2_conv2_
   kernel, block2_conv2_bias, new ReLU<4>());
30.
31.        block2_pool = new MaxPooling(device, 2);
32.
33.        // more VGG blocks loading here ...
34.
35.        Tensor_4D block5_conv3_kernel(kernel_size, kernel_
   size, 512, 512);
36.        load_tensor_from_file(block5_conv3_kernel, "data/vgg16/
   imagenet/block5_conv3_kernel.txt");
37.        block5_conv3 = new Conv2DLayer(device, block5_conv3_
   kernel, block5_conv3_bias, new ReLU<4>());
38.
39.        block5_pool = new MaxPooling(device, 2);
40.
41.        flatten = new FlattenLayer<DEVICE, 4>(device);
42.        int reduced_image_size = IMG_SIZE / 32;
```

```
43.          const int flatten_size = reduced_image_size * reduced_image_
    size * 512;
44.
45.          Tensor_2D WD(flatten_size, hidden_neurons);
46.          glorot_uniform_initializer(rng, WD);
47.          dense = new DenseLayer(device, WD, new ReLU<2>());
48.
49.          Tensor_2D WC(hidden_neurons, num_classes);
50.          glorot_uniform_initializer(rng, WC);
51.          classifier_head = new SoftmaxCrossEntropyLayer(device, WC);
52.
53.          Tensor_2D WR_3(hidden_neurons, 128);
54.          glorot_uniform_initializer(rng, WR_3);
55.          regressor_
    neck_3 = new DenseLayer(device, WR_3, new ReLU<2>());
56.
57.          Tensor_2D WR_2(128, 64);
58.          glorot_uniform_initializer(rng, WR_2);
59.          regressor_
    neck_2 = new DenseLayer(device, WR_2, new ReLU<2>());
60.
61.          Tensor_2D WR_1(64, 32);
62.          glorot_uniform_initializer(rng, WR_1);
63.          regressor_
    neck_1 = new DenseLayer(device, WR_1, new ReLU<2>());
64.
65.          Tensor_2D WR(32, 4);
66.          glorot_uniform_initializer(rng, WR);
67.          WR = WR * WR.constant(0.001);
68.          regressor_head = new DenseLayer(de-
    vice, WR, new Sigmoid<DEVICE, 2>(device));
69.
70.          // Fine tuning. Setting up optimizers for the last VGG layer
71.          block5_conv3->set_kernels_optimizer(Adam<4>());
72.      }
73.
74. private:
75.      // VGG16 feature extractor
```

```
76.
77.     Conv2DLayer<DEVICE> *block1_conv1;
78.     Conv2DLayer<DEVICE> *block1_conv2;
79.     MaxPooling<DEVICE> *block1_pool;
80.
81.     Conv2DLayer<DEVICE> *block2_conv1;
82.     Conv2DLayer<DEVICE> *block2_conv2;
83.     MaxPooling<DEVICE> *block2_pool;
84.
85.     Conv2DLayer<DEVICE> *block3_conv1;
86.     Conv2DLayer<DEVICE> *block3_conv2;
87.     Conv2DLayer<DEVICE> *block3_conv3;
88.     MaxPooling<DEVICE> *block3_pool;
89.
90.     Conv2DLayer<DEVICE> *block4_conv1;
91.     Conv2DLayer<DEVICE> *block4_conv2;
92.     Conv2DLayer<DEVICE> *block4_conv3;
93.     MaxPooling<DEVICE> *block4_pool;
94.
95.     Conv2DLayer<DEVICE> *block5_conv1;
96.     Conv2DLayer<DEVICE> *block5_conv2;
97.     Conv2DLayer<DEVICE> *block5_conv3;
98.     MaxPooling<DEVICE> *block5_pool;
99.
100.        FlattenLayer<DEVICE, 4> *flatten;
101.        DenseLayer<DEVICE> *dense;
102.
103.        // heads
104.
105.        DenseLayer<DEVICE> *classifier_head;
106.
107.        DenseLayer<DEVICE> *regressor_head;
108.        DenseLayer<DEVICE> *regressor_neck_1;
109.        DenseLayer<DEVICE> *regressor_neck_2;
110.        DenseLayer<DEVICE> *regressor_neck_3;
111.
112.    };
```

Note: The details behind reusing VGG16 and ImageNet weights were covered in Chapter 16, Leveraging Training Performance with Transfer Learning.

Again, we use **load_tensor_from_file()** to pre-load the ImageNet weights from file during the model instantiation.

In this experiment, we are freezing almost but not all VGG layers, leaving only the last convolutional layer as trainable (note that the maxpooling layer does not have a trainable state). Thus, the **backward()** method is as simply as:

```
1.  void backward(const Tensor_2D &classifier_
    TRUE, const Tensor_2D &regressor_TRUE) {
2.
3.      classifier_head->backward(classifier_TRUE, true);
4.
5.      MSE mse_fn;
6.      const Tensor_2D regressor_upstream = mse_
    fn.derivative(regressor_TRUE, regressor_head->get_output());
7.      regressor_head->backward(regressor_upstream, true);
8.      regressor_neck_1->backward(regressor_head->get_
    downstream(), true);
9.      regressor_neck_2->backward(regressor_neck_1->get_
    downstream(), true);
10.     regressor_neck_3->backward(regressor_neck_2->get_
    downstream(), true);
11.
12.     // combined backward
13.
14.     Tensor_2D combined_gradient = classifier_head->get_
    downstream() + regressor_neck_3->get_downstream();
15.
16.     dense->backward(combined_gradient, true);
17.
18.     // Fine tunning. Backwards the last VGG layer
19.     flatten->backward(dense->get_downstream(), true);
20.     block5_pool->backward(flatten->get_downstream(), true);
21.     block5_conv3->backward(block5_pool->get_downstream(), false);
22.
23. }
```

As explained in the last experiment, we are combining the two branches (the classifier head and the regressor head) to form a unique gradient in the intersection layer.

Due to the frozen layers, the update method actually updates only four layers:

```
1.  void update(const TYPE learning_rate, int epoch) {
2.      dense->update(learning_rate, epoch);
3.
4.      classifier_head->update(learning_rate, epoch);
5.
6.      regressor_head->update(learning_rate, epoch);
7.      regressor_neck_1->update(learning_rate, epoch);
8.      regressor_neck_2->update(learning_rate, epoch);
9.      regressor_neck_3->update(learning_rate, epoch);
10.
11.     block5_conv3->update(learning_rate, epoch);
12. }
```

Training this model with the Oxford Pet Dataset for five epochs results in the following output:

Figure 17.21: *Training a VGG16-based model with fine-tuning and Oxford Pets Database*

The new model's performance is notably superior to the previous model in terms of classification accuracy and regression loss. Let us sample some bounding box predictions on the validation data:

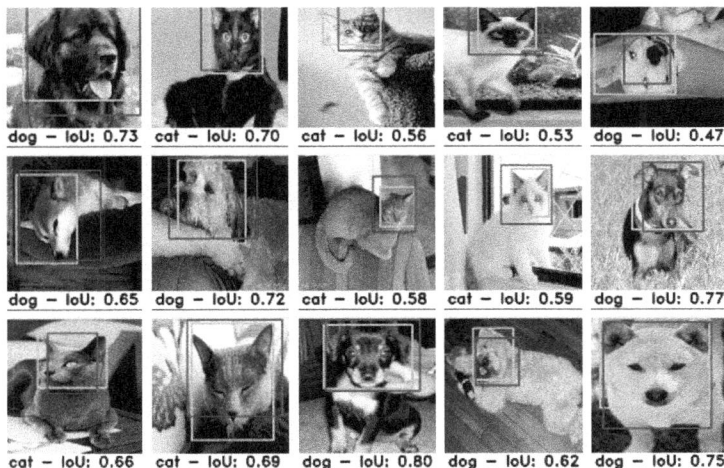

Figure 17.22: *Examples of bounding box detections on validation data*

The achieved validation regression loss (0.00918072) is very close to the training regression loss (0.0109948), indicating no overfitting.

Note: In hybrid models, one branch can overfit, but the other cannot. The same goes for underfitting.

Experiment	IoU	Regression loss	Classification accuracy
Training a regression model	n.a.	0.012	n.a.
Training an object localization model	0.36	0.022	80.18%
Reusing ImageNet weights with VGG16 architecture	0.52	0.009	99.59%

Table 17.2: Result of experiments

What is the meaning of a regularization loss of, for example, 0.01? Since we are using MSE, we can calculate to obtain a rough approximation of the average distance between the predicted and ground-truth bounding box coordinates x1, y1, x2, and y2. Since these values vary in the interval [0..1], it follows that we get a mean error of 10% for each bounding box coordinate. Of course, this is an average. Note that some instances show inaccurate predictions which exceed this percentage:

Figure 17.23: Examples of inaccurate bounding box predictions on validation data

As result, the averaged IoU for this new model was 0.52. Comparing this result with the average IoU obtained using the model trained from scratch suggests again that transfer learning is a powerful and handy technique to build new models.

In this experiment, we used a technique called fine-tuning. In general, training with fine-tuning requires more processing and time to converge. Indeed, using fine-tuning is not always worth it. This is discussed in the next topic.

When to use fine-tuning

In fine-tuning, one or more layers from the pre-trained model are trained during the training loop. That is, in fine-tuning, we unfreeze a few layers from the top of the pre-trained model.

The real gain of fine-tuning the model in the last example was not really significant. Indeed, we only used the technique here to illustrate its usage. In practical settings, fine-tuning is more addressable to scenarios with about the same amount of data to re-train the unfrozen layers.

Note: Fine-tuning is suitable for scenarios with large training datasets.

Note that, in the example, we are reusing a model trained on the ImageNet dataset, a model probably trained using 1.5 million images. However, we are retraining the layer with a very small dataset (~3k images), which has no way to provide the same generalization training experience.

Conclusion

This chapter introduced the project of an object localization system using the Oxford Pet dataset. Using the backpropagation and other techniques discussed in the book, we developed a model that learned how to find both the bounding box and species of pets depicted in the images (dog or cat).

This example shows how to build more complex models with multiple branches to perform different tasks in a single inference, such as classification and regression. We learned how to train hybrid models like this by using different loss functions to better fit to the branch output datatype and task.

Finally, we revisited the subject of transfer learning, improving the model performance and—this time—using fine-tuning to update the last VGG layer.

Exercises

1. Re-run experiment 2, including a 3-layer neck to the regression head, similarly to what we did in experiment 3.

2. Consider the last experiment of training a model reusing a VGG pre-trained network. Compare the results of training the model without fine-tuning the last VGG layer. Explain your findings.

References

[1] The Boston Housing Dataset, available at **https://www.cs.toronto.edu/~delve/data/boston/bostonDetail.html**

[2] The Oxford Pets III, available at **https://www.robots.ox.ac.uk/~vgg/data/pets/**

[3] Rezatofighi, Hamid and Tsoi, Nathan and Gwak, JunYoung and Sadeghian, Amir and Reid, Ian and Savarese, Silvio, Generalized Intersection over Union, IEEE Conference on Computer Vision and Pattern Recognition, 2019.

Join our book's Discord space

Join the book's Discord Workspace for Latest updates, Offers, Tech happenings around the world, New Release and Sessions with the Authors:

https://discord.bpbonline.com

Index

www.ingramcontent.com/pod-product-compliance
Lightning Source LLC
Chambersburg PA
CBHW061740210326
41599CB00034B/6742